W9-ADB-069

Critical Essays on
William Wordsworth

Critical Essays on William Wordsworth

George H. Gilpin

G. K. Hall & Co. • Boston, Massachusetts

Library of Congress Cataloging in Publication Data

Gilpin, George H.
    Critical essays on William Wordsworth/George H. Gilpin.
        p.   cm. — (Critical essays on British literature)
    Includes bibliographical references.
    ISBN 0-8161-8774-6
    1. Wordsworth, William, 1770–1850—Criticism and interpre-
tation.
    I. Title. II. Series.
    PR5888.G48 1990
    821'.7—dc20   89-71694
                                                          CIP

This publication is printed on permanent/durable acid-free paper
MANUFACTURED IN THE UNITED STATES OF AMERICA

First Published 1990.
10 9 8 7 6 5 4 3 2 1

CRITICAL ESSAYS ON BRITISH LITERATURE

The Critical Essays on British Literature series provides a variety of approaches to both the classical writers of Britain and Ireland and the best contemporary authors. The formats of the volumes in the series vary with the thematic designs of individual editors, and with the amount and nature of existing reviews, criticism, and scholarship. In general, the series represents the best in published criticism, augmented, where appropriate, by original essays by recognized authorities. It is hoped that each volume will be unique in developing a new overall perspective on its particular subject.

George Gilpin's introduction traces the history of critical opinion on Wordsworth, while his selection of essays includes several on each of Wordsworth's major works, the *Lyrical Ballads,* the *Intimations* ode, and *The Prelude,* as well as others with diverse perspectives regarding the poet's work and life. Most of the selected criticism is of recent origin. Original essays especially written for this volume include Gilpin's own study of Wordsworth's fascination with gardens and Alan Grob's concluding treatment of Wordsworth's politics.

University of Miami   Zack Bowen, GENERAL EDITOR

For Billie and George Gilpin

The Child is father of the Man;
And I could wish my days to be
Bound each to each by natural piety.
                    —"My heart leaps up"

CONTENTS

WORDSWORTH THE MAN

INTRODUCTION: REPRESENTATIONS OF WORDSWORTH

In spite of shifts in cultural perspective that have recognized William Wordsworth as a radical of the 1790s in style and thought, as an "establishment" poet laureate, as the "Daddy Wordsworth" admired by the Victorians, as the "simple" Anglican poet of nature, as the "problematic" poet of "consciousness," and, recently, as a "Nobodaddy" who was too conservative in the Age of Revolution, the poet's reputation as one of the great masters of English poetry continues. Along with Chaucer, Spenser, Shakespeare, Milton, Pope, Tennyson, and Eliot, Wordsworth is one of those poets whose name still defines an age; as recently as 1988 an extensive exhibition of English literary and visual art from the turn of the nineteenth century was touring the United States under the title, "William Wordsworth and the Age of Romanticism," asserting the centrality of the poet in spite of the undisputed genius of his contemporaries, Coleridge, Byron, Shelley, Keats, and, especially, Blake. The exhibition represents the renewal of Wordsworth's reputation in the twentieth century after the indifference of the Modernists (who favored, if any of the Romantics, the "aesthetic" Keats) and the disfavor of some contemporary scholars who prefer "revolutionary" Blake.

Wordsworth fashioned himself into the emblem of his own age. His poems in *Lyrical Ballads* (1798) and his defense of them in the Preface added to the second edition (1800) proclaimed what should represent English taste and style at the beginning of the nineteenth century and articulated issues by defining the ideal characteristics of the poet and poetry. (That Coleridge contributed to the volume was usually overlooked.) Wordsworth found in the old pastoral themes of the importance of nature and the joys of a simple life a basis for renewal of the human spirit in an age marked by the uncertainty of European war and revolution, both political and social. It was his critique of eighteenth-century assumptions about art and of the neo-classical idea of civilization that set the agenda for literary debate and caused his contemporaries to react: Coleridge, in *Biographia Literaria*, by criticizing Wordsworth's lack of intellectual sophistica-

1

tion—in spite of Coleridge's own role in his friend's philosophical development; Shelley, by expanding Wordsworth's claims in the Preface for the social significance of the poet, in his *Defence of Poetry;* Keats, in his private admiration and poetic indebtedness, especially in his sonnets; even Byron, in his mockery in *Don Juan.* While the "egotism" of Wordsworth's effort drew complaint (from Hazlitt, from Keats), he succeeded in placing himself while young in the active center of European culture; he gained firsthand knowledge of the French Revolution and was exposed to Germany and its idealist philosophy in the company of Coleridge. When older Wordsworth was at the national heart of an imperial nation—spokesman for preserving the beauty of the Lake District, poet laureate during the reign of a beloved queen, and posthumously, author of the monumental *Poem on my own life*, which was autobiography fashioned into an epic for his age.

With the publication of *The Prelude* under Mary Wordsworth's title in a quite allegorical version (compared to the more Miltonic version of 1805) in 1850, the same year as the grand achievement of Tennyson's *In Memoriam A. H. H.* (also a highly personal narrative poem) and in the formative period of the careers of Arnold and Browning, the ghostly presence of Wordsworth haunted the Victorians. In the company of a generation of poets who were trying to assert their own "new" voices, this poet out of the past produced an epic that nevertheless was hailed as an exemplar of Victorian—Anglican—propriety and decorum. Reviewing it for *Fraser's* magazine, an anonymous critic wrote: "The poetry of Mr. Wordsworth has undoubtedly effected a great revolution in public taste, nor has its influence been less observable upon individual character. . . . He broke the spell in which the Circean charms of Moore and the infernal incantation of Byron had bound the public taste and corrupted the national morality; the one by directly ministering to sensuality—the other, by his persevering efforts to efface the divine image from the human mind, and to fill it with the despair engendered in the darkness of his own disconsolable soul."[1]

Later in the century, Leslie Stephen (Virginia Woolf's father) would continue to point to Wordsworth as a poet who expounded the moral philosophy of a believer in an orderly universe and who in his statement of the myth of the "preexistence of the soul" in the *Intimations* ode presented a viable alternative to the Darwinists' vision of chaos and violence:

> Man, it is agreed, is furnished with sentiments which cannot be explained as the result of his individual experience. They may be intelligible, according to the evolutionist, when regarded as embodying the past experience of the race; or, according to Wordsworth,

as implying a certain mysterious faculty imprinted upon the soul. The scientific doctrine, whether sound or not, has modified the whole mode of approaching ethical problems; and Wordsworth, though with a very different purpose, gives a new emphasis to the facts, upon a recognition of which, according to some theorists, must be based the reconciliation of the great rival schools—the intuitionists and the utilitarians.[2]

Matthew Arnold, once he was well established as a literary authority, sought to circumscribe Wordsworth's relevance by framing the Romantic's reputation as that of, in John Dover Wilson's colorful assessment, " 'Venerable Poet' at Rydal . . . the relic of a past age, of the rude uncivilised period before 'Papa' [Arnold's father] went to Rugby to undertake the taming of the Barbarians."[3] In the preface for an edition of Wordsworth's poems that Arnold undertook, he seized control of the canon: first, he dismissed Stephen's claims for a formal philosophy in the long poems, finding *The Excursion* to be "a tissue of elevated but abstract verbiage alien to the very nature of poetry"; then he derided Wordsworth's own system for classifying his poems as "a scheme of mental physiology"; and, finally, he even denigrated Wordsworth's style—"when he seeks to have a style he falls into ponderosity and pomposity." Building on Coleridge's opinion in *Biographia Literaria*, Arnold presents a portrait of an emotional but less sophisticated poet, a pastoral and Pindaric poet: "Wordsworth's poetry is great because of the extraordinary power with which Wordsworth feels the joy offered to us in nature, the joy offered to us in the simple primary affections and duties; and because of the extraordinary power with which, in case after case, he shows us this joy, and renders it so as to make us share it."[4] Of course, Arnold liked the shorter poems—the ballads, odes, and sonnets—of Wordsworth's early career; his preface and selection were to influence generations of critics, until scholars began reassessing the importance of *The Prelude* and *The Excursion* after World War II.

George McLean Harper's revelation in 1916 of Wordsworth's French love affair with Annette Vallon laid to rest the ghost of the Victorian, ethical Wordsworth—"Daddy Wordsworth"[5]—and prepared the way for what M. H. Abrams has termed the "problematic Wordsworth,"[6] a view of the poet first suggested by A. C. Bradley in the Edwardian twilight of 1909, on the brink of the Modernist period. For Bradley, "the road into Wordsworth's mind must be through his strangeness and his paradoxes, and not round them"; he directs our attention to a canon very different from Arnold's selection, to the "dark world" of "poverty, crime, insanity, ruined innocence, torturing hopes doomed to extinction, solitary anguish, even despair" that appeared often in the long narratives of the later career.[7] This was one of the first attempts in the century of Freud to connect

Wordsworth to the previously ignored strain of nineteenth-century nightmare poetry that included Coleridge's supernatural *The Rime of the Ancient Mariner* and *Christabel* as well as Browning's disturbing *'Childe Roland to the Dark Tower Came.'* Conceived at almost the same time as T. S. Eliot's composition of his Modernist city-georgic, *The Love Song of J. Alfred Prufrock* (written 1911), Bradley's insight was to remain a dormant seed of criticism amid the indifference to the Romantics in the period between the world wars as Eliot and Pound—like Arnold during the Victorian period and Wordsworth during his own—sought to educate the public to a taste for their own styles.

Eliot, in his revival of neoclassical criticism, encouraged a taste for the "wit" of the metaphysical poets and the irony of Browning's dramatic monologues and had little regard for the personal emotion of the Romantics; however, in the swing of reputation that authentic genius enjoys, esteem for Wordsworth revived during World War II, as one reaction against Modernism. The war engendered not only the inevitable nationalistic celebration of "green England" with its picturesque hills and countryside, an England of which Wordsworth, to the public mind, was still chief priest, but it inspired efforts to reclaim humanizing and, perhaps, civilizing experiences of powerful feelings—a kind of sentimentalism—as well as confrontations with the patriarchal rationalism that had come to dominate Europe between the wars and had contributed, to the thinking of many, to disaster. Among those at the forefront of the reaction was the poet Robert Graves, according to whom, "poetry which deeply affects readers— pierces them to the heart, sends shivers down their spine, and makes their scalp crawl—cannot be written by Apollo's rhetoricians or scientists."[8] In 1942 the artist John Piper published a study of painters from the turn of the nineteenth century, *English Romantic Artists*, and the same year Geoffrey Grigson dedicated his anthology, *The Romantics*, to Piper. English poets and artists were looking again to the Romantic period for models of taste and style.[9] This "neo-Romantic movement" cleared the way for the exuberant revival of interest in Wordsworth in the academy.

Following the war, the foundations of contemporary Wordsworth scholarship were laid in the preparation of valuable modern tools for research. New editions of the poems by Ernest de Selincourt and Helen Darbishire were published at Oxford in the 1940s and 1950s, paving the way for the Cornell edition of the complete works, edited by Stephen Parrish, still in progress. Especially valuable in overcoming the Arnoldian bias against the longer poems and stimulating research on the Romantic epic by a new generation of scholars was the revised 1959 Oxford edition of *The Prelude*, which presented versions from 1805 and 1850 side by side for easy comparison. Republication of

Prose Works in a new edition has prompted reconsideration of Words-worth's writings about his own work, Robert Burns, the aesthetics of the picturesque and sublime, and his beloved Lake District. Under-standing of Wordsworth's life has been enhanced by revised editions of William and Dorothy Wordsworth's letters and Dorothy Words-worth's journal, by Mary Moorman's two-volume biography, by Mark L. Reed's detailed chronologies to events of Wordsworth's life, and by volumes of the collected works of Coleridge—as well as his invaluable notebooks.

In 1972 M. H. Abrams published a collection of critical essays from the flowering of Wordsworth scholarship in the postwar period. In the introduction he charted "two roads": one in England, where the "simple Wordsworth" of emotion and feeling was newly appre-ciated and where Arnold's view was built upon but revised in light of the wartime experience and in reaction to Modernist values; and the other in America, where A. C. Bradley's "problematic Words-worth" seed sprouted in a fertile soil of fascination with literary psychology and took form in explorations of what Abrams called "consciousness," a term that critics began to think encapsulated what had been most original to human thought of the early nineteenth century. From this point of view, Romanticism and Wordsworth were particularly congenial subjects for some of the most probing minds of the period: critics like Lionel Trilling, Harold Bloom, Geoffrey Hartman, and Abrams himself. Moreover, *The Prelude*, which had been neglected since the Victorian era, gained attention as a pi-oneering effort in the self-expression of "consciousness."

Since Abrams published his collection of essays, examination of Wordsworth and "consciousness" has continued to be an attractive pursuit to scholars. In his collection Abrams published an essay taken from his then newly published book, *Natural Supernaturalism: Tra-dition and Revolution in Romantic Literature* (1971); my collection includes a different piece from that magisterial study, an excerpt from his chapter, "Wordsworth's *Prelude* and the Crisis-Autobiography." A more clinical treatment is Richard Matlak's look at the "psycho-biographical" context of the disturbing Lucy poems. Less formal essays that relate the poet's life to his art are Donald Reiman's judicious description of Wordsworth's "heroism" in struggling to channel the passions of intimate family relationships into his creativity, and Jean H. Hagstrum's not so tame portrait of the obsessed poet whose sexuality lurks in the poetry.

The study of Romantic ideas, though not a new perspective on Wordsworth, has been greatly expanded during the past twenty-five years. Essays collected here dealing with the influence of aesthetic traditions are Carl Woodring's placement of *Lines Composed a Few Miles Above Tintern Abbey* in the context of Wordsworth's understanding of the theory of the sublime; Stephen J. Spector's study of the poet's use of mirror images drawn from the tradition of the picturesque; and my own look at the analogy between Wordsworth's way of seeing Nature and his ideas on landscape and English gardening. Study of Wordsworth's uniquely Romantic employment of rhetorical devices also enhances understanding of the poetry: Susan J. Wolfson examines the poet's reliance on the interrogative mode in the *Lyrical Ballads,* including *Tintern Abbey;* Peter J. Manning explicates *Ode: Intimations of Immortality from Recollections of Early Childhood* by allusion to Virgil's fourth eclogue; and Paul H. Fry studies Wordsworth's adaptation of the genre of the ode to the philosophical needs of the *Intimations* ode.

New, indeed, since Abrams's collection is the emergence of William Blake as a true rival to Wordsworth for the role of Romantic "spirit of the age," not only because of the sheer energy of the explosion of Blake scholarship but also because of controversy about Wordsworth's political commitment. Since the Vietnam and Watergate period of American radicalism in the late 1960s and early 1970s, some readers have not found Wordsworth meaningful because he did not take an energetic enough role in the politics of the Age of Revolution; ironically, it is the battle between the life of action and the life of the mind that Wordsworth dramatizes in Books IX through XI of *The Prelude.* This controversy is the background of the reconsiderations of the poet's political and social ideas in essays reprinted here. Ronald Paulson describes how in *The Prelude* Wordsworth had to come to terms with his own identity as a result of his experience of the French Revolution. Arguing against traditional "literary" readings of the *Intimations* ode, Marjorie Levinson decodes the references in that poem to Wordsworth's experiences in France and to his nostalgia over losing his innocence during the Revolution. Karl Kroeber admits the rivalry with Blake for critical esteem and defends Wordsworth's merit on grounds relevant to the late twentieth-century interest in conserving the natural world: he treats *Home at Grasmere* as the expression of a preservationist's ecological vision. In the afterword to the collection, Alan Grob responds to recent critics who view Wordsworth as reactionary; looking back to Abrams, he argues that out of the poet's turn to "consciousness" evolved the very means by which he could assume the role of an influential exponent of change.

Such arguments touch on a crucial development in scholarship today: the rise of critics who ascribe an "ideology" to an artist or his defenders, or, conversely, argue rigidly from the point of view of a particular ideology rather than give real consideration to the creative work. The ideologies vary and are often identified with the name of a master-critic. These ideological "critics" claim value for their pronouncements from the authority of their theories rather than from their care and honesty in analyzing the accomplishment of genius; the justification given is that since words really have no meaning anymore, only the disciplined exercise of method is relevant. In selecting essays, I have sought to avoid this neoclassical legacy of Modernism, which continues under the auspices of "postmodern" claims for the authority of method; rather, I present a gathering of scholars with diverse approaches who are committed first and foremost to their subject of study, Wordsworth and his poems. Their efforts offer instructive and, I hope, occasionally delightful access to the most frequently read poems. Arranged for the convenience of students, the contents are organized by reference to three major works, *Lyrical Ballads*, the *Intimations* ode, and *The Prelude*. General studies of the poems appear in the section, "Wordsworth the Poet," and essays with a biographical and psychological focus in the section, "Wordsworth the Man." I regret not being able to fit in more of the splendid essays that have been written by dedicated scholars during the past twenty years. Whether the present obsession in the academy with method is revealing any new insights into Wordsworth can be appraised over the next twenty years. In the meantime, the caring reader's curiosity about Wordsworth's creativity, which has tolerated the criticism of Victorian, Modern, and now Contemporary scholars, will no doubt endure.[10]

GEORGE H. GILPIN

University of Miami

Notes

1. *Fraser's* 52 (August 1850): 129.

2. Leslie Stephen, "Wordsworth's Ethics," reprinted in *Hours in the Library* (London: Smith, Elder and Co., 1892), II: 280–81.

3. John Dover Wilson, *Leslie Stephen and Matthew Arnold as Critics of Wordsworth* (Cambridge, England: Cambridge University Press, 1939), 25–26.

4. *Poems of Wordsworth*, ed. Matthew Arnold (London: Macmillan, 1879), xix, xiii, xxii, xxi.

5. Wilson, *Stephen and Arnold as Critics*, 22.

6. "Introduction: Two Roads to Wordsworth," in *Wordsworth: A Collection of Critical Essays*, ed. M. H. Abrams (Englewood Cliffs, N.J.: Prentice-Hall, 1972), 5–10.

7. "Wordsworth," in Abrams, *Wordsworth*, 13, 17.

8. Robert Graves, *On Poetry: Collected Talks and Essays* (New York: Doubleday, 1969), 237.

9. Robert Hewison, *Under Siege: Literary Life in London 1939–1945* (New York: Oxford University Press, 1977), 150; also see *A Paradise Lost: The Neo-Romantic Imagination in Britain 1935–55*, ed. David Mellor (London: Lund Humphries in association with Barbican Art Gallery, 1988).

10. *Bibliográphical Note:* For information about books and articles on English

Romanticism and William Wordsworth published before 1983, the reader is advised to consult *The English Romantic Poets: A Review of Research and Criticism*, 4th ed., ed. Frank Jordan (New York: Modern Language Association of America, 1985), which includes an extensive section on Wordsworth with very helpful commentary by Karl Kroeber. More recent work is listed in the comprehensive *MLA International Bibliography of Books and Articles on the Modern Languages and Literatures* published each year.

LYRICAL BALLADS

The New Sublimity in "Tintern Abbey"

Carl Woodring*

Wordsworth's poems about daisies and cuckoo birds are concerned with the human condition. Both *The Prelude* and *The Excursion* assert, to a degree beyond the assent of Byron and Shelley, the potential and therefore the essential equality of all persons. His conclusion in *The Prelude* that "the inner frame is good" (XII:280) is to be equated with his assertion that, however low of station a person may be, "high service is perform'd within" (XII:226). One of his most famous phrases of concern for our kind occurs in the poem called "Tintern Abbey"—"the still, sad music of humanity." Critics with an ear for English agree that the phrase is justly famous; they quote it as representative of Wordsworth's *ethos;* but they have not made clear how the phrase found its way into "Tintern Abbey." It belongs there, I will suggest, because of a current change, marked by Wordsworth as early as 1798, in attitudes toward the sublime.

The "Lines Composed on Revisiting the Banks of the Wye" begin by confronting a speaker with "a wild secluded scene" of "steep and lofty cliffs," seen again after the passing of five years. When Wordsworth took his vacations from college, and when he composed this poem, rules had been established for the observation of landscape. Books told you where to go, how to stand, how to look, and what to see. William Gilpin had published several editions of accumulated "Observations" and essays on where to stand, how to look, and how to sketch picturesque vistas.[1] For most who wrote concurrently with *Lyrical Ballads*, everything in nature or art was either beautiful or sublime, much as critics who thought they were Freudian used to declare every object in a symbolic poem, a novel by Kafka, or a realistic drama either male or female. Instead of saying male trees

* Reprinted from *The Evidence of the Imagination: Studies of Interactions Between Life and Art in English Romantic Literature*, eds. Donald H. Reiman, Michael C. Jaye, and Betty T. Bennett. © 1978 by New York University. Used by permission of New York University Press.

11

and female hills, writers in the age of sensibility and taste said beautiful trees and sublime hills.[2]

In 1756 Edmund Burke had made "A Philosophical Inquiry into the Origin of Our Ideas of the Sublime and Beautiful." With a rough hand, he separated the beautiful sheep from the sublime goats. Beautiful things are small, smooth, gently curved, and delicate. The colors of a beautiful object are clear and bright. To be sublime, a thing must be vast, "rugged and negligent," massive, angular, dark, gloomy, and obscure.

Burke and other writers on the Longinian sublime were trying to explain why certain things give a kind of pleasure even though in some sense they terrify. A beautiful landscape, said Burke, ought to evoke a pleasure akin to love. A sublime landscape ought to evoke awe, terror, a sense of the awful power of divinity. The sublime smacks into your feelings. Soon came those many novels, dramas, and ballads of terror; in Jane Austen's phrase, horrid novels, horrid ballads, horrid plays; in the denigrating phrase of Coleridge, Lamb, and Keats, "the *material* sublime."

In Burke's account, the characteristics of the object determine the reaction of the observer. By this account, transferred to art, one can paint a beautiful picture only of a pretty object; as if to say, one can ignore Sophocles if one sees enough sadness in life itself. In the counterview that we call Romantic, value lies in an interrelationship with the object, in response to it, in an artist's treatment of it, seldom if ever in the artist alone but not in the object itself.

The materials for history are seldom neatly structured. The paintings most admired in Burke's day, and in Wordsworth's youth, were neither merely beautiful nor purely sublime. The landscapes of Poussin and Claude, and of their imitators, were asymmetrical but balanced. Not determinedly "sublime," they were uniformly ideal. They revealed the beauty of repose, but also the mystery of some power beyond: Poussin sought that power, it may be, through reason, Claude through feeling.

A third category began to be talked about, the picturesque, meaning "like a painting." For most, "picturesque" meant like a painting by Poussin; "sublime" meant like a painting by Salvator Rosa. Late in the century, the picturesque took over the intermediate ground unoccupied by the beautiful or the sublime. The space available seemed to be that of intricate variety. Neither smooth nor grand, but varied and intricate. The emergence of a third category helped change critical and popular views of the other two, especially the sublime. The idea of the picturesque was concerned with the composition of a scene. "Tintern Abbey" curls its way toward the word *sublime* and a redefinition of it, but it seems to open with the picturesque. It lays out a scene, intricately various.

To take it as picturesque, even with the double focus of the five-year interval, would be to leave out not only the poet but nearly everything that has made the poem endure. Philosophers after Locke had gone on to say that objects depend on the observer not only for sound and color, taste and smell, but also for any knowable mass and weight and shape, that the human mind can know only its own perceptions, never the object itself. If a person can know only through individual experience, it follows that the mind itself must play a very large part in any awareness of sublimity. Richard Payne Knight, in *An Analytical Inquiry into the Principles of Taste* (1805), went far beyond John Baillie's point in *An Essay on the Sublime* (1747) that an encounter with the sublime expands the mind; rather, Knight explained, the mind creates its own feelings of sublimity by grasping at the sublime. In grasping at infinity, the mind exalts itself until its own feelings become sublime. "Tintern Abbey" had already gone further, to point toward the mind's part in the continuous creation of a sublime universe. Like other major poems to follow, the lines written on the banks of the Wye concern the uses, including the misuse, of mankind's essential sublimity.

When the poem first appeared, argument over the picturesque was nearing its peak. Soon the picturesque could be anything you liked, provided that you resembled everybody else in liking an asymmetrical arrangement of natural forms. Amidst the plethora of talk and the dearth of sublime new poetry, William Lisle Bowles, Byron's "maudlin prince of mournful sonneteers," seemed important and revolutionary. He attached to the picturesque a variety of tender feelings. Allowing for a few exceptions within Wordsworth's family, probably all the first readers of "Tintern Abbey" had read—and fewer than we might think had forgotten—Bowles's sonnet "At Tynemouth Priory," published in the year of the French Revolution:

> As slow I climb the cliff's ascending side,
> Much musing on the track of terror past,
> When o'er the dark wave rode the howling blast,
> Pleased I look back, and view the tranquil tide
> That laves the pebbled shore: and now the beam
> Of evening smiles on the gray battlement,
> And yon forsaken tower that time has rent;
> The lifted oar far off with transient gleam
> Is touched, and hushed is all the billowy deep!
> Soothed by the scene, thus on tired Nature's breast
> A stillness slowly steals, and kindred rest,
> While sea-sounds lull her, as she sinks to sleep,
> Like melodies that mourn upon the lyre,
> Waked by the breeze, and, as they mourn, expire.

As in the opening stanza of "Resolution and Independence" and the close of Coleridge's "Dejection: An Ode," storm has been followed by a clearing of the air. But Bowles knows only the terror of the howling blast, not the terror of the divided self. He represents himself as musing in tranquility on a storm just past.

He gives us a picturesque scene, with the sun setting in calm on a ruin of pointed Gothic arches emblematic of an ancient religion eroded by time. He begins with a steep cliff and a recent storm; distance has converted fright into solemnity of response to the sublime. Art enables him, and enabled the readers he used to have, to contemplate the sublimity of a storm without being terrified by actual thunder and lightning.

Coming after Bowles, Wordsworth could be expected to write a poem about the picturesque ruin of Tintern Abbey. The ever-generous David V. Erdman has pointed out to me a precise example of what Wordsworth's poem could be expected to say. In the summer of 1792 Julius Caesar Ibbetson and two other painters journeyed along the Wye for the purpose of making preliminary sketches to be etched and sold to a public hungry for picturesque scenes. The report of Ibbetson, John Laporte, and John Hassell appeared promptly in London the next year as *A Picturesque Guide to Bath, Bristol Hot-Wells, the River Avon, and the Adjacent Country.* In search of the picturesque along the Wye one thanks God, Longinus, and Dr. Syntax that the "awful magnificence" of Tintern Abbey lies ahead: "The Wye, at Monmouth, does not exhibit such romantic scenes as about Chepstow. . . . By land, there is not a single object till we reach Tintern abbey, that deserves notice" (p. 245). The reference to the abbey in Wordsworth's title invites lovers of the picturesque to read on. The various engravings and photographs of Tintern Abbey that have been published with the poem, if collected in this volume, would provide a survey of technological changes in book illustration since 1800, but they have nothing to do with Wordsworth's text. Peter A. Brier has pertinently suggested that the poet designated Tintern Abbey in the title to "reidentify" Tintern with a pantheistically oriented natural religion,[3] but I would propose that the proferred irony is still greater. In "Simon Lee" the poet stops to scold the reader for expecting "Some tale will be related." The title of "Michael: A Pastoral Poem" promises to readjust the reader's conception of pastoral poetry. Aside from designating a particular segment of landscape along the Wye,[4] the force of the words "Tintern Abbey" in the title is to say "You have been misguided by Bowles and such; now let me introduce to you a better picturesque and the true sublime."

Bowles had begun, "As slow I climb the cliff's ascending side." Climbing, for a plump parson, had taken physical effort, the hard work of seeking the picturesque and the sublime in the hinterlands.

The poet revisiting the banks of the Wye says, "once again, / Do I behold these steep and lofty cliffs." I *behold.* By contemplation (as the derivation of *behold* implies) I make them mine to keep. By contemplation, I make them *mind.* What I perceive I can thus completely hold. Less objectively than it might seem, "The day is come when I repose here." The opening movement is slow, not to suggest physical effort, but partly to elicit questions from the reader, partly to emphasize the importance of the years passed, "five summers, with the length of five long winters,"[5] and partly because a poem dedicated to the spiritual effort of evaluation is not yet ready to say why this day is momentous.[6]

The first verse paragraph of 22 lines, which keeps some of its rhetorical devices unobtrusive, openly exploits a series of implied contrasts. England is a green and pleasant land, but the western area described in these opening lines is greener than most. The home counties near London are green, snug, and populous. The absent but normal scene that the reader of "Tintern Abbey" visualizes is rolling country, the hills near enough on each side to give neighborly comfort without crowding the traveler. Along the road, again on each side, neatly trimmed hedges sit in rectangles. They do not "run wild." Green, but less green than the banks of the Wye, the small squares are still hedged in as they continue, with occasional squares of beige or yellow, up the slopes toward the domesticated hills.

In this normal farmscape that Wordsworth imagines into the mind's eye of the reader, the English house, of brick or stone, seems to sit in a clearing, with a coach road or driveway, beds of flowers, perhaps raw dirt where the wagon sits. Chimneys on the steep roofs are often capped by ornamented chimney-pots, from which in Wordsworth's day smoke emerged the year round, for cooking and for warmth. From the road, the traveler saw that the family was at home, because smoke curled from the chimney.

In his *Guide through the Lakes*, which in general reverts to Burke's antithesis of the beautiful and the sublime, Wordsworth pays especial attention to chimneys. Here too he makes a contrast with the home counties. Following a "View of the Country as Formed by Nature," which is founded on uniformitarian geology but concentrates on the play of light over surfaces—the human eye experiencing permanence in the transitory—the second section provides a history of human habitation in the district, and the third advances a program for preserving "the joint work of Nature and time," with its blending of cottage life into the mountain scenery, against the intrusion of garish mansions that dispute Nature's primacy. In a way that illuminates the opening of "Tintern Abbey," he praises the cottages made of native stone, extended organically as needed by each generation, "so that these humble dwellings remind the contemplative spectator of a production of nature, and may (using a strong expression) rather be said to have grown than to have been erected;—to have risen, by an instinct of their own, out of the native rock—so little is there in them of formality, such is their wildness and beauty." Then he gets to the chimneys. Some "are of a quadrangular shape, rising one or two feet above the roof; which low square is often surmounted by a tall cylinder, giving to the cottage chimney the most beautiful shape in which it is ever seen. Nor will it be too fanciful or refined to remark, that there is a pleasing harmony between a tall chimney of this circular form, and the living column of smoke, ascending from it through the still air."[7]

Along the Wye, the poet looks down on farms that are not laid out in checks. The plots of cottage-ground are not divided by hedges into rectangles, but by wavering lines of unclipped trees, "little lines of sportive wood run wild." The region looks more like green woods than like populated farms. The farms are like pastures, "Green to the very door." People thrive in this unravished region. Their fathers lived here, and their children will live here; but the trees almost conceal all human activity. Wreaths of smoke are

> Sent up, in silence, from among the trees!
> With some uncertain notice, as might seem
> Of vagrant dwellers in the houseless woods,
> Or of some Hermit's cave, where by his fire
> The Hermit sits alone.

These lines make their point of contrast by negatives and abatements: "hardly hedge-rows," absence of a clearing "to the very door," smoke sent up "in silence" (a sublime deprivation, according to Burke), "vagrant," "houseless," and "alone"—yet not really houseless. In the home counties, the houses would give certain notice of busy lives; here the daily work of these families causes no more disruption to the processes of nature than a hermit would. Chimneys in the Lakes are the most beautiful to be seen (heard melodies are sweet); but chimneys along the Wye, not seen at all, are melodies unheard, sweeter and sublime: the unnoisy melody of human life.

Elsewhere as well Wordsworth commends for our admiration natural places that hide life and power beneath apparent calm, and similarly, the power hidden in cottagers, shepherds, or a nearly inarticulate, eloquent leech-gatherer. In the sea at Calais, and in the child at the poet's side. Nature speaks softly but carries a big stick. In the sleeping city seen from Westminster Bridge, as in the silence of those seemingly houseless woods along the Wye, sounds the unheard music of humanity. People seen seem puny, but those unseen are potent.

At first in "Tintern Abbey" Wordsworth barely hints at the

interchange of values between man and Nature in the act of human perception. In sketching the scene along the Wye, he understates the marriage between mind and Nature: The steep and lofty cliffs impress on a wild secluded scene thoughts of more deep seclusion. During the five years since he first saw these groves, draining himself in the muddy flow of existence in rented rooms, he has remembered from the seemingly houseless woods the still sad music of fellow sufferers, all, given such experiences as he has had, capable of little nameless acts of kindness and love. From this day of reaffirmation his companion and dearest friend need have less fear of lonely rooms. Instead of a ruined abbey, a green landscape giving a sense of solitude to gregarious human life becomes emblematic of that life, past, present, and to come.

The visit to the Wye five years earlier, recollected so fervently now, had been an extension of the days on Salisbury Plain, with their visions of savage ancient warfare and their scenes of human dereliction in the present. Indeed, the entire walking tour of 1793 either came hard upon or continued his nightmares

> of despair,
> And tyranny, and implements of death,
> And long orations which in dreams I pleaded
> Before unjust Tribunals, with a voice
> Labouring, a brain confounded, and a sense
> Of treachery and desertion in the place
> The holiest that I knew of, my own soul.
> (*The Prelude*, 1805, X:375–381)

These terrors and torments of experience and conscience, toned down until they became the *Guilt and Sorrow* of 1842, are both recapitulated and purged in "the still, sad music of humanity." These, again, are images that could have been expected had Wordsworth found sublimity in physical prowess. But the poem moves irreversibly toward an "aspect more sublime" (line 37), a "sense sublime of something far more deeply interfused" (lines 95–96), a true sublimity not dependent on physical vastness, roughness, darkness, loudness, or violence.

Burke had included an impression of solitude as a category of sublime deprivation. Kant, not in his *Beobachtungen über das Gefühl des Schönen und Erhabenen* (1764) but in his return to the subject in the *Kritik der Urteilskraft* (1790), emphasized the subjective state of mind put in motion by an object thereby regarded as sublime. In the same year (1790), Archibald Alison's *Essays on the Nature of Taste* shifted attention from the sublime object to the mind that perceives sublimity. Increasing (or recircling) emphasis on the perceiver was coincident with increased emphasis on the godliness of tranquility. Leigh Hunt published his distress at the storm and flames and noise at the end of Mozart's *Don Giovanni*. Assuming, as many critics and stage directors have, that Mozart was trying to achieve the sublime, Hunt thought that quiet should prevail.[8] A true ghost could do without the noise and smoke appropriate to a pretender like Horace Walpole. Hunt quoted 1 Kings 19:11–12, as Ruskin in a similar context did after him:

> . . . A great and strong wind rent the mountains, and brake in pieces the rocks before the Lord; but the Lord was not in the wind: and after the wind an earthquake; but the Lord was not in the earthquake: And after the earthquake a fire; but the Lord was not in the fire: and after the fire a still small voice.

That still small voice, the true sublime, is the divinity within the still sad music of humanity.

Probably much of the new emphasis on the sublimity of silence in solitude came indirectly from Johann Winckelmann's stress, notably in his *Geschichte der Kunst des Altertums* (1764), on the still spirit and tranquil eye reflected in Hellenic art.[9] Both the humanity and the tranquility are present in "Those green-robed senators of mighty woods" (Keats, *Hyperion* I:73); in preparation, the divinely majestic tranquility of "grey-haired Saturn, quiet as a stone, / Still as the silence round about his lair," has given way to awesome deprivation, not waiting for the lines on Saturn's nerveless, listless, unsceptered hand and realmless eyes (I:17–18) but apparent in the sympathetic quiet around him, the stirless air and voiceless stream (8–12). It is "more noble to sit like Jove" than "to fly like Mercury," Keats told Reynolds.[10] The Hellenic sublimity of "silence and slow time" comes immediately to the fore in "Ode on a Grecian Urn." Although the juxtaposition of external and internal sublimity can be seen in Shelley's work as early as the "Hymn to Intellectual Beauty" (1816)—the "awful shadow" is deeper in effect than any "voice from some sublimer world" (lines 1, 25)—the contrast is nowhere more forcefully made than in his notes and letters of 1819 on the gross inferiority of Michelangelo to Phidias, Praxiteles, and other Hellenic masters. The figures of Michelangelo, "rude, external, mechanical," communicate energy, terror, distortion of nature; Hellenic figures "combine the irresistible energy with the sublime & perfect loveliness supposed to have belonged to the divine nature."[11] Strong silence begets awe. Thus far the romantic internalization involves a movement from Hebraic obscurity to Hellenic linearity.

Apart from this movement, "Tintern Abbey" insinuates a similar silence to the ear, "quiet of the sky" to the eye, and to both ear and eye the smoke sent up "in silence" with "uncertain notice." The quiet comes no doubt partly from what Lionel Trilling described as

Wordsworth's rabbinical passivity.[12] But the new sublimity is above all epistemological. A poet coming in self-conscious unease after Locke, Berkeley, and Hume (and after Schiller's essay *Uber naive und sentimentalische Dichtung*), if he would speak on human life, had first to find nature in his own consciousness. It is inadequate to describe romantic subjectivity as J. R. Watson does: ". . . the romantics brought to the landscape their own pre-occupations: Coleridge's unhappiness, Byron's pride, Shelley's restlessness, Scott's sense of the past."[13] Albert O. Wlecke comes much nearer in arguing that "the 'sense sublime' refers to an activity of the esemplastic power of the imagination during which consciousness becomes reflexively aware of itself as an interfusing energy dwelling within the phenomena of nature."[14] Wlecke (p. 79) aptly quotes Coleridge: "I meet, I *find* the Beautiful—but I give, contribute, or rather attribute the Sublime."

One preposition in lines 93–102 has never been accounted for:

> And I have felt
> A presence that disturbs me with the joy
> Of elevated thoughts; a sense sublime
> Of something far more deeply interfused,
> Whose dwelling is the light of setting suns,
> And the round ocean and the living air,
> And the blue sky, and in the mind of man,
> A motion and a spirit, that impels
> All thinking things, all objects of all thought,
> And rolls through all things.

I have quoted the first edition, which, like Wordsworth's three other editions of *Lyrical Ballads*, has a comma at the end of line 99; from 1815 on, a colon ("the mind of man:") replaces that comma.[15] The punctuation here apparently troubled Wordsworth; the preposition *in* should have troubled the rest of us. How does it function grammatically? The solution, I think, lies in the proleptic appearance here of "spousal verse." Everything after the colon is within the mind, a reflection of the supposedly external world, of objects, and of other minds thinking objects, *in* the mind of the perceiver. To paraphrase Iago, " 'Tis in ourselves, that a thing is thus, or thus: our minds are gardens" in which we must will to replant what is natural, that there may be a correspondence between internal and external creativity and growth. The life abroad is the life within; the sublimity is from within.

Epistemologically, Shelley's "Mont Blanc" and the passage in "Tintern Abbey" could serve for exegesis of each other: "The everlasting universe of things / Flows through the mind. . . ." These are ruminations over the limits to human knowledge, but they are less cries of despair that the world has lost its props than exclamations of awe that the mind half-creates through interfusion with what it had once regarded as external to it. Each is tentative. Shelley's poem moves toward uncertainty; his what-if comes at the close. "Tintern Abbey" begins and ends with the phenomena most certain; the scene before the eye, and the poet's hope for his sister. His if-not and if-vain come deep in the center of the poem.

Yet he would find it still more majestically sublime if the ultimate sense of the one life in this active universe had no need of eye or ear. In remembering the banks of the Wye, he has concluded that we are in such moments "laid asleep in body, and become a living soul."

He makes here still another point against the "mimic rules" of the sublime and the picturesque. It is not the immediate sense of terror, awe, or pleasure that is most important, nor even one's previous associations with that sense, but what one does with the experience of awe or pleasure in later moments of quiet reflection. And what one does *after* reflection. The strength of landscape is realized by a strength of humanity and divinity within. William Empson led his many admirers to ask, "more sublime" than what? Even more sublime, the poem says, than little nameless acts of kindness, which are themselves sublime—as "beauteous forms" without "an eye made quiet" are not.

The philosophical function of that surreptitious preposition *in* is to say that all objects take definition and value only from the human mind. But the ultimate poetic function is to evoke such a direction of thought, rather than to state the thought. In his greatest philosophical passages Wordsworth is metaphysically, and even epistemologically, the most elusive of poets. *Why* he concealed or blurred the academic sources and rational explanations of his thought is debatable; *that* he did so is indisputable. He knows, and sometimes makes clear, what explanations of experience he regards as inadequate. As a poet he declines to be rationally paraphrased. The critic who gives a consistent epistemological interpretation equally to one of Wordsworth's great passages and to each phrase within the passage has invariably falsified some of the phrases and opened the larger interpretation to rebuttal because of the inevitable distortions. One way to begin an explanation is to say that Wordsworth knew poetry to be not only more philosophical than history but also more sublime than philosophy.

On the sublime itself he has left us a fragment in prose, with fewer appeals to Burke's physical categorization than in his *Guide to the Lakes* and fewer withdrawals into eighteenth-century aesthetics generally than in most of his prose and poetry after 1808. He asserts forcefully some of the points I have attributed to the romantics generally:

> To talk of an object as being sublime or beautiful in itself, without
> references to some subject by whom that sublimity or beauty is
> perceived, is absurd; nor is it of the slightest importance to mankind
> whether there be any object with which their minds are conversant
> that Men would universally agree (after having ascertained that the
> words were used in the same sense) to denominate sublime or
> beautiful. . . . The true province of the philosopher is not to grope
> about in the external world &, when he has perceived or detected
> in an object such or such a quality or power, to set himself to the
> task of persuading the world that such is a sublime or beautiful
> object, but to look into his own mind & determine the law by which
> he is affected. *(Prose Works,* II:357)

W. J. B. Owen has written valuably on the identification of sublimity
with power in Wordsworth's essay.[16] W. P. Albrecht has written
equally well on "the sublime of vision" in the romantic view of
tragedy: "The fullness of the imaginative process became more important to the sublime than visible size or the duplication of its
emotional impact."[17] Wordsworth's lines on revisiting the Wye were
an important force in this change; I do not believe that the phrase
"more sublime" appears in the poem by chance. "To this point was
Wordsworth come . . . when he wrote 'Tintern Abbey,' " said Keats,
"and it seems to me that his Genius is explorative of those dark
Passages" *(Letters,* I, 281).

Despite Lessing's *Laokoön* of 1766, Bowles had assumed that a
poem is like a painting. The scene in each is to be arranged by the
same rules. Wordsworth, like Constable and Turner, is concerned
with the value of landscape. Like them, he renders a scene more
deeply human by removing the human figures from the foreground
yet discovering, far more deeply interfused, the strengths of ordinary
human life, with its silent suffering and its quiet joys—in Constable's
vernacular, its wet planks. The unleashed, volcanic forces of the
French Revolution as well as the unleashed forces of the Gothic
villain, had found a worthy successor in the cottager whose emission
of smoke was no more obtrusive than a hermit's. According to the
Freudian economy advanced by Thomas Weiskel in *The Romantic
Sublime,* not only Wordsworth but Burke as well was attempting to
get something for nothing—a return without a deposit—but few have
gone emotionally bankrupt from Wordsworth's belief in the sublimity
of humble human feeling.

Notes

1. One of Gilpin's most popular books was *Observations on the River Wye and
Several Parts of South Wales* (1782). Gilpin appears in *The Cambridge Bibliography of
English Literature* (1940) only as a translator; *The New Cambridge Bibliography of*

English Literature has caught up with interest in the picturesque for literary studies to the extent of listing the two chief secondary sources: William D. Templeman, *The Life and Work of William Gilpin* (Urbana: University of Illinois Press, 1939); Carl Paul Barbier, *William Gilpin: His Drawings, Teachings, and Theory of the Picturesque* (Oxford: Clarendon Press, 1963).

2. Of many careful studies in this area, the standard works are Samuel H. Monk, *The Sublime: A Study of Critical Theories in XVIII-Century England* (Modern Language Association, 1935; Ann Arbor: University of Michigan Press, 1960); Christopher Hussey. *The Picturesque: Studies in a Point of View* (London: Putnam, 1927); Walter John Hipple, Jr., *The Beautiful, The Sublime, & The Picturesque in Eighteenth-Century British Aesthetic Theory* (Carbondale: Southern Illinois University Press, 1957); Elizabeth Wheeler Manwaring, *Italian Landscape in Eighteenth Century England: A Study Chiefly of the Influence of Claude Lorrain and Salvator Rosa on English Taste 1700–1800* (New York: Oxford, 1925; rpt. London, 1965); Edward Malins, *English Landscaping and Literature 1660–1840* (London: Oxford University Press, 1966); J. R. Watson, *Picturesque Landscape and English Romantic Poetry* (London: Hutchinson, 1970). For a deconstructionist Freudian view, discovering in attention to the sublime the rise of modern anxiety, see Thomas Weiskel, *The Romantic Sublime: Studies in the Structure and Psychology of Transcendence* (New Haven: Yale University Press, 1976).

3. "Reflections on Tintern Abbey," *Wordsworth Circle*, 5 (1974), 6.

4. Hardy appropriately called the poem "Wye above Tintern"—Florence Emily Hardy, *The Early Life of Thomas Hardy* (London: Macmillan, 1928), p. 267. In *Biographia Literaria* Coleridge calls it, *inter alia*, "his lines 'on re-visiting the Wye' " (London, 1817, p. 83). Wordsworth's surviving early references to the poem are few; on 9 December 1803, he called it "the Wye"; on 6 March 1804, he called it "Tintern Abbey"—*The Letters of William and Dorothy Wordsworth: The Early Years 1787–1805*, ed. E. de Selincourt, rev. C. L. Shaver (Oxford: Clarendon Press, 1967), pp. 425, 455.

5. Here Wordsworth exploits what he often defied, Pope's denunciation, "And ten low words oft creep in one dull line" (*An Essay on Criticism*, II, 147).

6. The interpenetrations of space and time in the poem have been much studied, perceptively but variously by Albert S. Gérard, "Dark Passages: Wordsworth's *Tintern Abbey*," in *English Romantic Poetry: Ethos, Structure, and Symbol in Coleridge, Wordsworth, Shelley, and Keats* (Berkeley: University of California Press, 1968), pp. 89–117; Geoffrey H. Hartman, *Wordsworth's Poetry 1787–1814* (New Haven: Yale University Press, 1964; rpt. 1971), pp. 26–30; Robert M. Maniquis, "Comparison, Intensity, and Time in 'Tintern Abbey,' " *Criticism*, 11 (1969), 358–382.

7. *The Prose Works of William Wordsworth*, ed. W. J. B. Owen and J. W. Smyser, 3 vols. (Oxford: Clarendon Press, 1974), II, 202.

8. *Examiner*, 17 August 1817, rpt. in *Leigh Hunt's Dramatic Criticism*, ed. L. H. and C. W. Houtchens (New York: Columbia University Press, 1949), pp. 146–152.

9. For some of the channels of Winckelmann's influence, see Bernard Herbert Stern, *The Rise of Romantic Hellenism in English Literature 1732–1786* (Menasha, Wisconsin: Banta, 1940), pp. 78–117.

10. *The Letters of John Keats*, ed. H. E. Rollins, 2 vols. (Cambridge: Harvard University Press, 1958), I, 232.

11. *The Letters of Percy Bysshe Shelley*, ed. F. L. Jones, 2 vols. (Oxford: Clarendon Press, 1964), II, 80, 88–89, 112.

12. "Wordsworth and the Iron Time," in *Wordsworth: Centenary Studies . . .*, ed. G. T. Dunklin (Princeton: Princeton University Press, 1951), pp. 131–152.

13. Watson, p. 196.

14. *Wordsworth and the Sublime* (Berkeley: University of California Press, 1973), p. 8.

15. I am obliged to Professor Stephen Maxfield Parrish for pointing out that a copy of *Lyrical Ballads*, 1805, at Cornell University has no punctuation after "man"; the absence of a comma (or colon) draws "All thinking things, all objects of all thought" more forcefully within the mind of the perceiver, who, in assuming the existence of thought in other minds, assumes also (after Bishop Berkeley) the existence of an impelling unity to account for the similarity between mind and mind.

16. *Wordsworth as Critic* (Toronto: University of Toronto Press, 1969), pp. 203–210.

17. *The Sublime Pleasures of Tragedy: A Study of Critical Theory from Dennis to Keats* (Lawrence: University Press of Kansas, 1975), p. 97.

Speaker as Questioner in *Lyrical Ballads*, 1798

Susan J. Wolfson°

"the fluxes and refluxes of the mind"

That many of the poems in *Lyrical Ballads* turn upon exchanges of question and response is nothing extraordinary in view of social custom and literary tradition. Wordsworth tunes such exchanges to a variety of purposes. Following the convention of pastoral dialogue, he may use a question to provoke a debate: "Why William, sit you thus alone, / "And dream your time away?" (*Expostulation and Reply*). Or as in the convention of the ballad, his speaker may begin with a query designed to arouse our interest:

> —Why bustle thus about your door,
> What means this bustle, Betty Foy?
> Why are you in this mighty fret?
> And why on horseback have you set
> Him whom you love, your idiot boy?
> (*The Idiot Boy*)

Sometimes he uses a question to engage our sympathy:

> Now, when the frost was past enduring,
> And made her poor old bones to ache,
> Could any thing be more alluring,
> Than an old hedge to Goody Blake?
> (*Goody Blake, and Harry Gill*)

° Reprinted from *The Questioning Presence: Wordsworth, Keats, and the Interrogative Mode in Romantic Poetry*. © 1986 by Cornell University. Used by permission of Cornell University Press.

At other times, a question produces an expansive lyric: "My friend / "What ails you? wherefore weep you so?" (*The Last of the Flock*). A speaker may exploit interrogative syntax to make a point—"Up! up! my friend, and clear your looks, / Why all this toil and trouble?" (*The Tables Turned*)—or to convey an agitated state of feeling—"For ever left alone am I, / Then wherefore should I fear to die?" (*The Complaint of a Forsaken Indian Woman*). Except for this last case, in which fact and feeling resist reconciliation, sooner or later an answer satisfies. We find out why Betty Foy frets, what this bustle means, what Johnny's mission is, why the friends weep so.

Yet if in these poems Wordsworth uses questions and responses in fairly conventional ways, he does so as part of an unconventional poetic program. Their speakers are not the invisible or purely per-functory rehearsers of traditional ballads but agents of "feeling" that "gives importance," Wordsworth says, to the poetic "action and situation" (*LB* 248). Indeed, in certain poems we see him locating "action and situation" in the play of voice itself. In *Old Man Travelling*, for instance, the speaker describes a figure of such "mild composure," that "patience now doth seem a thing, of which / He hath no need." Yet when the speaker "asked him whither he was bound, and what / The object of his journey," the Old Man's reply that he is "going many miles to take / "A last leave" of his son, who is dying of battle wounds in a hospital far away, at once belies the "perfect" peace his questioner may have hoped to understand. In the 1800 version Wordsworth substitutes indirect discourse for the original dialogue, with the effect of diminishing the rhetorical impact of the interview, and in the *Poems* of 1815 he drops the interview altogether, replacing it with a much less troubled fourteen-line, sonnet-like *Sketch* titled *Animal Tranquility and Decay* (the subtitle of 1798). Although such revisions reflect Wordsworth's later movement away from interro-gative drama, what is compelling about the 1798 poem is the way its entire action and situation are contained in an exchange of question and answer—an exchange, moreover, that confronts the speaker with his error of interpretation. In other poems in this volume, Wordsworth uses the interrogative mode to advance these dramas of interpretation into a confrontation with mystery. These are occasions when no satisfactory answer is forthcoming, the response often eluding the terms in which the question has been posed. Consider, for instance, the questions that interrupt the narrator of *The Thorn*:

> "But what's the thorn? and what's the pond?
> "And what's the hill of moss to her?
> "And what's the creeping breeze that comes
> "The little pond to stir?"

Despite their insistence, these petitions fail to clarify the report that provoked them: "I cannot tell; I wish I could; / For the true reason no one knows." Similarly, when Johnny, the Idiot Boy, is asked to tell "Where all this long night you have been, / "What you have heard, what you have seen," his answer fits the questions in syntax only: "The cocks did crow to-whoo, to-whoo, / "And the sun did shine so cold." As in *The Thorn*, an innocent appeal for information produces an unexpectedly enigmatic reply. When such questions and answers fail to link, when there seems to be no common frame of reference, our attention is drawn to the presence of a mystery beyond the reach of simple interrogation.

The 1798 volume shows Wordsworth's interest in probing these situations from a variety of angles, his willingness to entertain a troubling question or uncertain answer varying with the degree of apparent personal implication. In *We are seven* and *Anecdote for Fathers*, Wordsworth stages dialogues featuring distinct dramatic characters—an adult questioner and a contrary child—whose difference gives each poem its rhetorical force. In *The Thorn* he presents a single narrator who is less a character than a voice, and who engages not another character but a second disembodied voice by which he is relentlessly questioned. Yet the fact that there is less opposition than repetition in this dialogue places both questioner and narrator under a common burden of mystery that no answer can lighten completely. The most complex interrogative texture in the 1798 volume is that of its concluding poem, *Tintern Abbey*, where, in *propria persona*, Wordsworth asks no questions. The poem carries an interrogative charge nonetheless in several of its most crucial utterances, and the verse throughout seems constrained by unvoiced concerns—with the effect of making the poem's reader a sympathetic but skeptical questioner of the poem's speaker. Here especially, and implicitly throughout *Lyrical Ballads*, the play of questions voiced or resisted and answers proffered or denied requires the reader to participate in the rhetorical drama of the occasion.

ADULT QUESTIONERS, CHILD RESPONDENTS

The adult questioners in *We are seven, Anecdote for Fathers*, and *The Idiot Boy* attempt to impose logic on children who live under different, often "silent laws." *We are seven*, in fact, opens with a question that seems no question at all, but rather an invitation to share the speaker's bemused condescension:

> A simple child, dear brother Jim,
> That lightly draws its breath,
> And feels its life in every limb,
> What should it know of death? (1–4)

"Nothing" is the implied answer to a question whose tone blends marvel and annoyance. The occasion is a telling interview with an eight-year-old cottage girl:

> "Sisters and brothers, little maid,
> "How many may you be?"
> "How many? seven in all," she said,
> And wondering looked at me. (13–16)

The question seems simple enough and so does the reply. Yet the Maid's wondering poses a kind of baffled counterquestion—a signal of the gap that opens between the two when the speaker persists. "And where are they, I pray you tell?" and she replies:

> ". . . two of us at Conway dwell,
> "And two are gone to sea.
>
> "Two of us in the church-yard lie,
> "My sister and my brother,
> "And in the church-yard cottage, I
> "Dwell near them with my mother." (19–24)

The adult perceives death as division and subtraction; the Maid sees it as (at worst) displacement, as her syntax demonstrates: "in Heaven" seems no different from "at Conway" or "to sea." The Maid's claim that "we are seven" may be quite adequate to her experience, for the graves of her brother and sister offer more visible companionship ("they may be seen") than do her living but absent siblings:

> "My stockings there I often knit,
> "My 'kerchief there I hem;
> "And there upon the ground I sit—
> "I sit and sing to them."

But as his previous rhyme of "alive" with "five" may indicate, the adult resists the child's addition. He repeats his question, this time posing it as a testy test of logic: "How many are you then," said I, / "If they two are in Heaven?" The *should* of his opening question ("What should it know of death?") has by this point gained a resonance of moral obligation.

The Maid will not let herself be lessoned (and lessened) so, however, and persists with her refrain: "O Master! we are seven." Abandoning all questions to insist, "But they are dead; those two are dead! / Their spirits are in heaven!" the adult regards the child's tenacity as perverse willfulness: " 'Twas throwing words away; for still / The little Maid would have her will." His own tenacity at last provokes denial instead of mere reiteration: "Nay, we are seven!" The poem ends there. The adult can neither persuade nor bully the little girl with his logic; nor can her simplicity prevail. This standoff is again mirrored in Wordsworth's rhymes. The adult's final cry that a sister and a brother "are in *Heaven!*" is countered by the Maid's insistence that "we are *seven!*" And completely isolated from the ballad's rhyme scheme, as an odd fifth line in a poem of four-line stanzas, is the adult's final protest—"But they are dead; those two are dead!"—in which the word *dead* knocks against itself in a singular internal rhyme. These oppositions include the reader, for in the face of two orders of knowledge that are self-enclosed and irreconcilable, Wordsworth allows us no easy alignment. However "right" the adult may be, he is overbearing and humorless. Even so, the denial of death by a child who "feels its life in every limb" is something the most forgiving of adult readers knows is doomed to revision as she matures.[1] Moreover, without the relentless literalism of her opponent, the Maid's simple wit might cloy. Instead of making this conversation a mere occasion to endorse or reject childish sentiment, Wordsworth deftly exploits the gap between question and reply to provoke his reader to wonder at the mysteries of a child's sensibility and its complete insulation from one kind of adult intelligence.[2]

In *Anecdote for Fathers* Wordsworth again uses a conversation of question and reply to contrast the mysteries of a child's logic with the constraints of adult reason. While walking with his son at Liswyn farm, the adult is (once again) preoccupied with absences and presences. As he remembers the "former pleasures" of Kilve, their "pleasant home . . . A long, long year before," he entertains some fond regrets about their present home and decides to enlist his son's opinion. "My little boy, which like you more . . .

> "And tell me, had you rather be,"
> I said and held him by the arm,
> "At Kilve's smooth shore by the green sea,
> "Or here at Liswyn farm?"

Despite the avowed idleness of his inquiry, the father has his son "by the arm"—unwilling, it seems, to let go until he gets an answer. The son, perhaps discerning a preference for smooth shores and green seas and still feeling his father's hold on his arm, replies cooperatively, "At Kilve I'd rather be / "Than here at Liswyn farm." Not satisfied with mere indication, however, the father insists, "Now, little Edward, say why so; / My little Edward, tell me why; . . . There surely must some reason be." Obsessed with weighing, comparing, and analyzing the moods of his own mind, the father wants his son to do likewise, "To think, and think, and think again." But Edward's moods do not naturally yield to such negotiations; they are immediate and unified. He runs happily along, or, upset, he blushes and hangs his head. To the rush of *whys*, he responds the same way the confused narrator of *The Thorn* does: "I cannot tell, I do not know." Edward's evasion of the cause-and-consequence demands of his father's question invites only further harassment. "And five times did I say to him, / 'Why? Edward, tell me why?' " he persists, almost becoming Harry Gill to Edward's Goody Blake ("And fiercely by the arm he took her, / And by the arm he held her fast, / And fiercely by the arm he shook her" [89–91]). Edward succumbs: "At Kilve there was no weather-cock, / "And that's the reason why." On the surface this answer seems no reason at all, but it may betray a deeper emotional logic in its preference for something absent. At Kilve there was also no inquisition to plague a "careless mood"—a good enough reason for him to say he'd rather be there than here. The father, at least, understands this reason is no more than a convenience. In later versions of the poem, Wordsworth has him note that his son "eased his mind with this reply," and in all editions the adult concludes the *Anecdote* by claiming to have learned a lesson:

> O dearest, dearest boy! my heart
> For better lore would seldom yearn,
> Could I but teach the hundredth part
> Of what from thee I learn.

However tempting it is to credit such adult notices with humble acknowledgment of error, it is difficult to give an exact measure to the anecdote. What has the speaker really learned, and what fraction of lore still remains locked up in the child's mind? The way the *Anecdote* is framed gives some indication. The subtitle of 1798, *shewing how the art of lying may be taught,* supplies a seemingly self-aware piece of irony, but if it spells out a rueful lesson and the substance of what the speaker wishes he could teach, it is not free from error, for it assumes that the child's reply is an artful, cunning lie. The subtitle does not seem to recognize that for the boy, *any* answer would be a lie, a coercion of spontaneous feeling into the logic of cause and effect. Within the dialogue, the boy's resort to the gilded vane seems a contingency or pretext, but Wordsworth himself may have had an ulterior "reason." As an object that shows the direction of the invisible wind, the weathercock emerges as a sign that parodies all logic-minded attempts to apply instruments of analysis to the flow of obscure and elusive moods. In a letter written many years after the poem, Wordsworth records that his "intention was to point out the injurious effects of putting inconsiderate questions to Children, and urging them to give answers upon matters either uninteresting to them, or upon which they had no decided opinion" (*LY* 1:486). In 1845 he added an epigraph to the poem to emphasize the point—*"Retine vim istam, falsa enim dicam, si coges"* ("Restrain that force, for I will speak false, if you insist")—which was, according to Eusebius, Apollo's warning to those who would coerce the oracle.

The forced exercise in analysis in this poem parallels the arithmetic lesson conducted by the adult questioner in *We are seven*. But here the child proves vulnerable to the adult, while the adult, though still unaware of the basic limitations in the way he thinks, flatters himself that he has learned otherwise.

Such contrariety between adult and childhood orders of knowing is a fundamental Wordsworthian issue, and the absence of connection a perpetual Wordsworthian concern, negotiated most intensely through several drafts of *The Prelude*. In the first part of a two-part version he finished the year after he published *Lyrical Ballads*, Wordsworth finds himself able to "call to mind," even to feel again, the sensations of days he feared were "Disowned by memory" (445). But the opening verse paragraph of the second part produces two questions and a brief meditation that together subvert the illusion of recovery:

> Ah, is there one who ever has been young
> And needs a monitory voice to tame
> The pride of virtue and of intellect? (17–19)

In the dialogue poems, that monitory voice is nowhere heard, except perhaps in the limited apology of Edward's father. That coda, however, does not carry the tone of yearning the poet's next question does:

> And is there one, the wisest and the best
> Of all mankind, who does not sometimes wish
> For things which cannot be, who would not give,
> If so he might, to duty and to truth
> The eagerness of infantine desire? (20–24)

The question asks for our assent in imagining an ideal state that would blend adult orders of knowledge (virtue, intellect, duty, and truth) with the exuberance of a child's sensations, but its accents of regret and resignation suggest that this speaker, checked by the knowledge that it "cannot be," might wish to trade the one for the other.

Access to the sensations of childhood seems to require an almost magical or visionary telescoping of intervening vacancies:

> so wide appears
> The vacancy between me and those days,
> Which yet have such self-presence in my heart
> That sometimes when I think of them I seem
> Two consciousnesses—conscious of myself,
> And of some other being. (26–31)

The dialogues between adults and children in *Lyrical Ballads* display two consciousnesses, and the poet, like the autobiographer of *The Prelude*, stands somewhat outside, thinking of the difference with a sense and syntax that alternates uncertainly between heartfelt presence and the apprehension of a vacancy so wide that those days seem totally "other," not even of the self at all. That stance, like the dramatic format of the dialogues, promotes for the moment a poetry of disinterested speculation—the mode Keats consciously cultivates to explore the mysteries that play in his imagination. But Wordsworth is never entirely disinterested: to the extent that *We are seven* and *Anecdote for Fathers* show the worlds of adult and child to be qualitatively and mutually exclusive, Wordsworth necessarily shares the consciousness that views the child in question as "some other being." It is from the adult's point of view, however qualified, that each dialogue is reported. These dialogues, in fact, originated in his own experience. "The little girl who is the heroine [of *We are seven*] I met [in] 1793"; a conversation he had with a child who stayed in his household inspired *Anecdote for Fathers* (*LB* 285–86). Wordsworth's affinity with the adults suggests that these encounters are more crucial than their anecdotal tone indicates, for the questions betray disturbing evidence of a reduced, and reducing, imagination. Yet it is precisely such limitations that keep Wordsworth's own imagination tuned to the child's mysteries. Affinities with the adults' party notwithstanding, other poetic features and other notes suggest Wordsworth's "self-presence" in the child's voice. The title *Anecdote for Fathers*, as well as the early subtitle and later epigraph, implicitly credits the child's prerogative, and it is the child's logic that gives *We are seven* its title. Indeed, Wordsworth recalls of his own childhood, "Nothing was more difficult for me . . . than to admit the notion of death as a state applicable to my own being" (*LB* 286), and in the Preface of 1800 he includes us all in this difficulty. *We are seven* shows, he says, "the perplexity and obscurity which in childhood attend our notion of death, or rather our utter inability to admit that notion" (*LB* 247–48). In the 1802 Preface, in fact, he implicitly converts this difficulty to creative advantage by applying analogous terms to the general "disposition" of imaginative power. The "Poet," like the Maid, is especially prone "to be affected . . . by absent things as if they were present" (*LB* 256).

The most mysterious of Wordsworth's questioned children is the Idiot Boy. Sent into the moonlit night by his mother to fetch a doctor, Johnny is fortified with answers to all matters of possible importance: "What to follow, what to shun, / What to do, and what to leave undone, / How turn to left, and how to right" (64–66). His prolonged absence makes it clear that these prescriptions have failed their purpose, however, and the consequence registers in the questions that now beset the women at home: "How can it be he is so late?" (174); "Oh saints! what is become of him?" (232); "where's my Johnny?" (262). Yet these queries, despite the tone and atmosphere of mystery, do not write a poetics of mystery, for the world of this poem is essentially comic. Answers do emerge, however delayed for narrative effect, and the narrator can safely say, "Then calm your terrors, Betty Foy!" (373).

There are nonetheless certain gaps in his narrative and certain gaps between its questions and answers which directly confront the reader with the inadequacy of narrative logic to pre- or alogical modes of perception. Wordsworth's narrator is everywhere attentive to latent threats to his powers of telling. His opening stanza reports an owlet that "shouts from nobody knows where" (4), anticipating another more important mystery of origin: Betty Foy and Susan Gale "cannot guess" what ails the latter (36). These potentially tale-baffling mysteries are aggravated by the scant or nonexistent powers of communication in the protagonist of this tale, Johnny himself: "The moon that shines above his head / Is not more still and mute than he" (90–91); "How quietly her Johnny goes. / The silence of her idiot boy" (101–2). That silence encompasses Betty, too, as Johnny's delay stirs fears that she "to Susan will not tell" (150–51).

The narrator verges on this failure of voice himself, for in the face of Johnny's disappearance, he seems unable to produce anything more than a teasing set of questions that echo Betty's anxieties, as his tale recedes into the realm of a merely fantasized possibility:

> Oh reader! now that I might tell
> What Johnny and his horse are doing
> What they've been doing all this time,
> Oh could I put it into rhyme,
> A most delightful tale pursuing! (322–26)

He can pursue this unanswered *what* with no more than a series of conjectures, each, like Betty's earlier fantasies, prefaced by "Perhaps," and none solving the mystery of Johnny's "strange adventures" (327–51). The interrogative effort driving these supplements and surmises becomes explicit as they culminate in an exasperated petition, as if on our behalf, to the absent muses of this narrative of absences:

> Oh gentle muses! is this kind?
> Why will ye thus my suit repel?
> Why of your further aid bereave me?
> And can ye thus unfriended leave me?
> Ye muses! whom I love so well. (352–56)

At exactly this climax of unrequited questioning, however, the narrator relinquishes his complaints about the muses' (and Johnny's) absence to venture a necessary act of interrogative imagination, one that in effect summons his nearly defeated story and its wayward hero back into presence:

> Who's yon, that, near the waterfall,
> Which thunders down with headlong force,
> Beneath the moon, yet shining fair,
> As careless as if nothing were,
> Sits upright on a feeding horse? (357–61)

This question, unlike all the questioning by which it is preceded, is fully within the narrator's control. Through its agency, he returns his protagonist and reclaims his tale with mock-epic tones of victory.[3]

The narrator's emergence from confounded questioning to renewed powers of answering is given an ironic counterpart in the career of another potential narrator, Johnny himself. For most of the night, the Idiot Boy remains "still and mute, in wonder lost" (334), his bewilderment a more extreme version of the narrator's own bafflement. That opacity is hardly redeemed when he speaks, however, for his language defies interpretation. "Johnny burrs and laughs aloud, / Whether in cunning or in joy, / I cannot tell," the narrator reports (387–89). And when his mother asks the question to which all would like an answer—"Tell us Johnny, do, / "Where all this long night you have been, / "What you have heard, what you have seen, / "And Johnny, mind you tell us true" (448–51)—the answer that issues— "The cocks did crow to-whoo, to-whoo, / "And the sun did shine so cold" (460–61)—seems scarcely adequate to the experience to which it refers. The narrator's prefacing surmise that "Johnny all night long had heard / The owls in tuneful concert strive; / No doubt too he the moon had seen" (452–54) is a deliberate and knowing reduction, an affront to the expectations of any Idiot Questioner.

Wordsworth himself credited the scriptural expression that an idiot's *"life is hidden with God"* (EY 357), and in *The Idiot Boy* he allows Johnny's summary answer to remain enfolded in that benevolent and essentially mysterious rationale. Like the children of *We are seven* and *Anecdote for Fathers*, Johnny's intelligence is innocent of logic, particularly the logic of plot and argument. He forgets his errand (a logic imposed on him) as he burrs happily under the perpetual present of the "moon that shines above his head" (90); his answers to the questions "what?" and "where?" issue in language so self-enclosed as to defy certain translation—like the replies of Edward and the little Maid. The tone of impersonal declaration in all three speakers, in fact, gives their utterances a resonance of obscure symbolic import and leaves the reader with a corresponding sensation of exclusion. When Keats's speaker imagines the Grecian Urn meeting his questions with the quasi-oracular utterance, "Beauty is truth, truth beauty," we are struck by the sheer self-referential circularity of these terms and may wonder uneasily about the tone of the voice that tells us, "That is all . . . ye need to know." Keats had a precedent for this take-it-or-leave-it totality in Wordsworth's conclusion to *The Idiot Boy*, for the narrator there signs off gleefully, "—Thus answered Johnny in his glory, / And that was all his travel's story." If Johnny had told us "true," the mysterious "glory" of his answer remains radically private, hidden from adult (or perhaps any) inquiry, and the reader is left wondering at, but consigned to, its tantalizing periphery.

THE THORN: INTERROGATIVE DIALOGUE

However elusive its internal cause, the effect of Johnny's summary utterance as a creative cause is fully apparent. These lines were, so Wordsworth reports, "the foundation of the whole" poem (*LB* 292), and by placing Johnny's words at the poem's conclusion, he bestows their mystery on the reader. *The Thorn*, too, is founded on a mysterious circumstance, this time originating in a visual rather than a verbal event: "1798. Arose out of my observing, on the ridge of Quantock Hill, on a Stormy day, a thorn which I had often passed in calm and bright weather without noticing it. I said to myself, 'Cannot I by some invention do as much to make this Thorn permanently an impressive object as the storm has made it to my eyes at this moment?' " (*LB* 290). Wordsworth's answer to his self-addressed query is a poem that presents no direct encounter with "this Thorn," but treats that object solely in terms of the way it impresses the imagination of its observer. The poem begins plainly enough: an unidentified voice reports a simple fact, "There is a thorn." As the predicate develops, however, the world of fact begins to dissolve into shadows of imagination. It "looks so old"; it is a "mass of knotted joints, / A wretched thing forlorn," overgrown with a "melancholy crop" of mosses that "clasp it round," seeming "With plain and manifest intent, / To drag it to the ground"; this "mossy network" vibrates with strange and rich colors "Of olive-green and scarlet bright, / In spikes, in branches, and in stars, / Green, red, and pearly white." A nearby hill of moss is likened, curiously, to an "infant's grave," a comparison invoked twice more in the next ten lines and frequently throughout the poem. Perhaps the strangest detail of all appears six stanzas into the poem; it is a "woman in a scarlet cloak" who, we are told, "oft there sits," crying to herself, "Oh misery! oh misery! / "Oh woe is me! oh misery!" The intrigue is compounded by the speaker's repeated appeals to our assent: "In truth you'd find it hard to say"; "you see"; "Now would you see." He will soon exhort us to see for ourselves: "But to the thorn, and to the pond . . . I wish that you would go." In the meantime, to assist our efforts to visualize these objects, he gives their appearance in assiduous detail, as if to place his own subjective impression within a field of objective verification. He takes great care to fix size ("Not higher than a two-years' child, / It stands erect, this aged thorn"; the "hill of moss" is "Just half a foot in height," and "a little muddy pond . . . 'Tis three feet long, and two feet wide"); to map location ("Not five yards from the mountain-path, / This thorn you on your left espy"); even to diagram precise configuration ("to the left, three yards beyond").

The repetition and elaboration of detail might at first engage an audience "not accustomed to sympathize with men feeling in that manner," as Wordsworth intended (*LB* 288), but by Stanza 8, these oddly charged terms begin to tease too much—so much that when an unidentified voice interrupts, the questions seem both inevitable and appropriate:

> "Now wherefore thus, by day and night,
> "In rain, in tempest, and in snow,
> "Thus to the dreary mountain-top
> "Does this poor woman go?
> "And why sits she beside the thorn
> "When the blue day-light's in the sky,
> "Or when the whirlwind's on the hill,
> "Or frosty air is keen and still,
> "And wherefore does she cry?—
> "Oh wherefore? wherefore? tell me why
> "Does she repeat that doleful cry?"

This voice never disputes the narrator; it simply recasts a tentative report into interrogative form. Its echoing locution, as well as the anonymity of its identity and origin, suggests that it may even be expressing half of an internal dialogue between a self who reaches after fact and reason and a self burdened with a mystery.[4] Indeed in subsequent editions of the poem Wordsworth puts quotation marks around both voices (not just the questioner's, as above), blurring even further the distinction between the two. Instead of separate speaking characters, as in *We are seven* and *Anecdote for Fathers*, *The Thorn* presents two contraposed but curiously linked voices. These voices do not represent conflicting orders of experience, as in the dialogues between adult and child, but point instead to a shared mystery. In response to the many *wherefores*, the speaker can do no more than invoke the circumstances that provoked inquiry in the first place: "But if you'd gladly view the spot, / The spot to which she goes." However inviting his syntax, instead of a result clause, there follows only more amplification of the initial reference to the spot and its constellation of suggestive objects.

As in *Anecdote for Fathers*, the persistence of questioning summons an attempt to answer: "Perhaps when you are at the place / You something of her tale may trace." But one of the first things we notice is that this tale, like the report that provokes it, involves a variety of frustrated expectations. The woman referred to is Martha Ray, formerly betrothed to Stephen Hill, who reportedly seduced and then abandoned her on their wedding day to marry another. In the 1800 version of the poem, the local rumors prompt the narrator to pose a question himself, a coy suggestion: "What could she seek?— or wish to hide?" The lore of the village has it that she went mad, regained her senses over the course of her pregnancy, and gave birth to a child (stillborn? hanged or drowned by its mother?) who was then buried "Beneath that hill of moss." The legend that haunts about its shape is ultimately untraceable however, "For what became of this poor child / There's none that ever knew." Yet once the tale has been introduced, the speaker's protests to ignorance modulate into promises of interpretive assistance: "I'll give you the best help I can"; "I'll tell you all I know." These promises include a chorus of village testimony: "They say" or "Old Farmer Simpson did maintain" or "some remember well" or "I've heard many swear." At the center of this assemblage, in fact, is the speaker's own report of Martha at the spot: "I saw her face . . . and heard her cry."

But the fact that this testimony, with its edgy expansion of "There is" and " 'Tis said" into "I saw" and "I found," emerges only after Martha's attachment to the spot has been discussed suggests a mystery more crucial and immediate than the fate of Martha Ray. This is the unspoken question of her sheer presence at the spot. What has never before been available is an eyewitness; as the narrator himself says, "I never heard of such as dare / Approach the spot when she is there." Wordsworth's organization of his report allows us to wonder whether this narrator, alone on a mist-bound, stormy ridge "Ere [he] had heard of Martha's name," has really seen her at all. Confused in a storm, he looked for shelter and found Martha Ray; perhaps now, looking for shelter from a haunting recollection, he finds the tale of Martha Ray. Stephen Parrish has suggested in fact that "the point of the poem may very well be that its central 'event' has no existence outside the narrator's imagination," that in retrospect he has instead turned a bush covered with scarlet moss into Martha Ray hunched in her scarlet cloak, a hill into her infant's grave, and the sound of the wind howling through the branches into her cries of misery. Parrish's argument makes the speaker's report into a "dramatic monologue" exhibiting, in the language of Wordsworth's Note to the poem, "the general laws by which superstition acts upon the mind."[5]

That Note also ascribes to "Superstitious men" "a reasonable share of imagination, . . . the faculty which produces impressive effects out of simple elements" (LB 288)—a share that goes beyond superstition to extend the questionable affinity of the tale and the spot into a general inquiry about the procedures of the imagination as it tries to tease logic out of an impression. We may note for instance that as the speaker applies elements of the tale to his description of the spot, he enacts the basic operation of metaphor, "transfer." Moreover, the tale itself is produced only after the mysterious effects of the spot are detailed, suggesting that the imagination may actually make such effects into a cause for narrative. *The Thorn* begins with an effect—a seemingly haunted spot—and, under the pressure of questioning, works toward a cause in the history of Martha Ray. The virtue of that history is that it appears to answer the *wherefores* by unfolding a sequence of events that culminates at the spot and so explains its impressive effect on the eye of any beholder. To the extent the tale promises to supply "a cause / To solve the mystery,"[6] the speaker can transfer his obsession with the spot to Martha Ray: *she* haunts the spot, as a guilty soul might haunt the scene of a crime; he merely happens to be a witness. Thus his passive verbs—Martha "was often seen"; her cries "oft were heard"—both generalize his own experience and give her presence a priority over the fact of anyone's chance apprehension of her; indeed, Wordsworth's escalation of "woman" into "Woman" and "thorn" into "Thorn" in the 1800 version and after enhances that effect by seeming to ascribe an independent spiritual character to the spot. In answer to the question "why?" these presences spell a plain tale; a haunted imagination is the natural consequence of reading it. But Wordsworth's overall poetic organization implies an order of cause and effect different from this narrative one. The tale of Martha Ray is brought into play because a mystery demands an explanation. The speaker's experience at the mountain ridge is the psychological cause, and the tale is actually a psychological effect, emerging as a result of the questions that demand it. As he does with Edward's naming of the weathercock in response to his father's *whys*, Wordsworth makes the tale of Martha Ray less an explanation for a mystery than an expression of the imagination's reach after fact and reason in the face of a mystery. The repeated questions cannot clarify a report that remains suspended between what its speaker professes to know or swears is true and what he does not know and "cannot think or tell." What results, as Geoffrey Hartman puts it, is a poem with a "double plot" in which "the action narrated and that of the narrator's mind run parallel."[7] To transfer a phrase from *The Excursion* (4:1054–55), the speaker's imagination—"Stuffed with the thorny substance of the past, / For fixed annoyance; and full oft beset"—cannot unfix itself from the spot.

This double plot more than satisfies Wordsworth's originating question about how to impress a reader with what he saw on Quantock Hill. The force of an unusual isolated impression, rather than a village tale, is what inspires him to write and gives the poem its title; it compels the speaker's conversation, commands his attention, and entices his listeners. The legend of Martha Ray hovers over the spot, but neither speaker nor interlocutor can entirely connect the logic of the one with the mystery of the other. After all the speculation about why Martha Ray may haunt the spot, the poem returns to its founding enigma. "I cannot tell how this may be," the speaker wonders, finally absorbing that unanswered and unanswerable question into the only logic he can manage:

> But plain it is, the thorn is bound
> With heavy tufts of moss, that strive
> To drag it to the ground.
> And this I know, full many a time,
> When she was on the mountain high,
> By day, and in the silent night,
> When all the stars shone clear and bright,
> That I have heard her cry,
> "Oh misery! oh misery!
> "O woe is me! oh misery!"

Despite the speaker's "plain" incorporation of Martha Ray into his report of the spot, the poem's last stanza concludes not with a solution to the mystery but with an intensified repetition of the clues.

Wordsworth exploits such repetition as a verbal figure for mystery. In his Note he cites "repetition of words" as one way to convey an effort "to communicate impassioned feelings" crossed by "something of an accompanying consciousness of the inadequateness of our own powers, or the deficiencies of language" to do so. "During such efforts," he explains, "there will be a craving in the mind, and as long as it is unsatisfied the Speaker will cling to the same words." Sometimes, in fact, the mind's craving seems to be satisfied as it "luxuriates in the repetition of words which appear successfully to communicate its feelings" (LB 289). Wordsworth knew that the terms of his experiment were as difficult as they were radical. " 'The Thorn' is tedious to hundreds," he admits—or perhaps boasts—in response to a friend's displeasure (EY 367), and Coleridge's impatience is well known.[8] Yet however frustrating the effect, it does accord with the poem's interrogatives; repetition is after all "re-petition," reasking. Both repetition and repetitive questioning express that "craving in the mind" for answers, and both communicate only, finally, and insistently, the elusiveness of all certainty. Indeed the haunting cry that closes the poem—"Oh misery! oh misery! / "O woe is me! oh misery!"—itself repeated and full of internally repeated sounds, yields just the voice but not the "wherefore" of a radically self-enclosed passion. Mystery remains at the very center of the poem; it compels questions, it pressures forth response, and it persists past and despite all speaking.

If *The Thorn* emphasizes an effect over the questions that would grant the mind clear answers, the "Lucy" poems Wordsworth includes in the 1800 edition show his increasing interest in such situations. Like the spot that haunts the speaker's imagination in *The Thorn*, Lucy is a mystery and an occasion for questions and conjectures.[9] To take one case, we may consider the poet who confesses to recurring "Strange fits of passion," one of which is prompted by a "descending moon" that appears to race him to Lucy's cottage one night. He finds himself uttering an anxious half-question, "If Lucy should be dead!" But as even he realizes, this fit exceeds the evidence of anything so simply objective as the descending moon. Like the self-enclosed cries of Martha Ray and the Idiot Boy, there is something private and utterly mysterious about his cry "to myself." The whole sequence of "What once to me befel" remains latently interrogative, strung as it is from the wayward tendencies confessed in the present perfects of the opening line ("Strange fits of passion I have known"); to the penultimate and falsely offhand exclamation, "What fond and wayward thoughts will slide / Into a Lover's head," itself a suppressed question; to the surreal premonition of the final line. Neither this speaker's fixation on the "descending moon" nor the "very words" of the Idiot Boy's exuberant report nor the "sworn" truth of the narrator's description of what he saw and heard in *The Thorn* yields the intelligible, translucent signifiers Coleridge identified with the operation of symbolic language. These scraps of language and intense, momentary impressions (which include the answers of Edward and the cottage Maid) at once tempt and defeat any such interpretation.

In the Preface of 1800 Wordsworth describes his lyrical ballads as "experiments" in representing "the fluxes and refluxes of the mind when agitated by the great and simple affections of our nature" (*LB* 241, 247). Many of these experiments involve images of the poet himself—with the questions voiced by their speakers seeming to reveal the fluxes and refluxes of Wordsworth's own mind as he wonders about the debility of imaginative power in adulthood or the inaccessible life of the child's imagination or the true import of strangely impassioned moments of perception. Indeed, the full title Wordsworth gives to *Tintern Abbey* recalls the scrupulousness with which the narrator of *The Thorn* details the spot that inspires his speech; Hartman's comment that the latter is "a caricature of Wordsworth's own imagination-in-process" is persuasive.[10] The aspect of caricature is, of course, as crucial as that of reflection, for if these experiments yield questions of an emergent personal consequence, Wordsworth detaches himself from potential points of identity by means of deliberate distortions and fictional contexts. The speakers who question children may echo Wordsworth's own interviews, but they are cast as dramatic characters of exaggerated tendencies; the narrator of *The Idiot Boy* is a parody of a poet in difficulty; and Wordsworth carefully announces that *The Thorn* is not a poem in his own voice but rather that of a character whose imagination is helplessly "adhesive" (rather than merely responsive or recollective) and unequivocally "credulous" and "prone to superstition." The "adhesive" mind of this speaker may produce the style "adhered to" by the poet (*LB* 288), but Wordsworth's poem makes the superstition that excites that monologue a significantly more eccentric influence than, say, the "powers in the great and permanent objects" that the Preface of 1800 tells us agitate the Poet's affections and inform his verse (*LB* 249). Although such devices and strategies seem to effect differences primarily of degree rather than of kind, that degree is critical, for it enables Wordsworth to stand back from various acts of interrogative imagination so that he may frame them, ponder their operations, and explore their implications.

That these poems tend to suspend certain answering may actually secure the "truth" of imagination, one "not standing upon external testimony, but carried alive into the heart by passion" (*LB* 257). In the dialogues with Edward and the cottage Maid, that truth is perplexing or obscure; in *The Idiot Boy*, it emerges with comic glory. But the absence of external testimony and the essential incommunicability of impassioned imagination can have a less than glorious effect, as it does for the troubled narrator of *The Thorn* or for any speaker seeking the import of his own moments of liveliest perception. As we shall see, the difficulty of accommodating mysterious impressions to an argument of more than fitful certainty stirs behind the questionings of *The Prelude* and the *Intimations* ode, and those of the poem that precedes them both, *Tintern Abbey*. Here, Wordsworth's "I" is an autobiographical figure in a landscape charged with immediate personal significance, rather than a credulous character speaking of a spot enhanced by village gossip. The poetic result is an intense constraint on the voice of questioning.

TINTERN ABBEY: INTERROGATIVE SYNTAX

Wordsworth gives no indication that the closing poem of *Lyrical Ballads* is "not supposed to be spoken in the author's own person." He presents *Tintern Abbey* in his own voice as a record of an actual occasion. The poem's interrogative mode is powerfully affected by this transparency of self, for though a fretful stir of qualifications, hesitations, and perplexed recognitions trouble the address, such potentially interrogative moments never gain full, independent expression. We hear instead passionate affirmations of faith, as the poet feels himself rediscover and renew his bonds with those places and times when "the joy / Of elevated thoughts; a sense sublime / Of something far more deeply interfused" has moved him to acknowledge "In nature and the language of the sense, / The anchor of my purest thoughts, the nurse, / The guide, the guardian of my heart, and soul / Of all my moral being" (94–112). He dedicates himself to this "chearful faith" and its corollary claims: that change is growth, that whatever is "no more" has "Abundant recompense," that there is an underlying continuity of self and affect as Nature leads him and his sister "Through all the years of [their] life . . . From joy to joy" (125–26). Yet the flow of speech is by no means effortless. Expressions of joyful trust are crossed from the very start by contrary intuitions and contrary evidence. Far from a simple credo, *Tintern Abbey* is a peculiarly strained utterance; its impassioned testimonies are limited and sometimes subverted by interrogative tendencies of syntax, and these in turn are suppressed or contained by the urgencies of declaration. Wordsworth habitually revised to clarify and organize intended meanings, but he revised *Tintern Abbey* very little. "Not a line of it was altered" between inspired composition and subsequent transcription, he claims (*LB* 296), and afterward, only a few minor substitutions and adjustments of syntax were made. He allows *Tintern Abbey* to remain a poem of declaration under stress, a drama of contrary vocal moods interplaying with an argument that proceeds by fits and starts, as if responding to an undertow of questions denied a full voice and hearing. We might describe *Tintern Abbey* as a radically lyricized version of interrogative dialogue: not a monologue but half of a dialogue with a questioning voice that, though silent, affects the way the poet speaks—as if he were answering, or answering back.

Walter Pater has remarked that Wordsworth's poetry "stimulat[es] one always to look below the surface" and "begets . . . a habit of reading between the lines."[11] Readers of *Tintern Abbey* often find themselves doing this at the poem's opening: "Five years have passed; five summers, with the length / Of five long winters!" The exclamation and the subjective distortion of the calendar seem to say that more than mere time has passed. What that is remains unstated, but the way the poet speaks of his return suggests silent inquiry, for the expansive array of definite pronouns he summons to register what he sees and hears ("These waters"; "these . . . cliffs"; "these pastoral farms"), together with his repeated claims of renewed participation ("and again I hear . . . Once again / Do I behold . . . I again repose / Here . . . Once again I see"), seem meant to deny apprehensions of possible difference—either in the scene itself or (more significantly) in its beholder. The verse paragraph that follows this salutation shows what is at stake, for the poet hopes to say what he has owed to previous visits to the Wye Valley and the persistence of its "forms of beauty" in his mind even through a long absence; he hopes, by implication, to project present impressions into future blessings. Yet the interrogative latency of the repetitions in the opening paragraph remains. The poet finds that he can only suggest that these forms may "perhaps" have had "no trivial influence" on the "little . . . acts" of his life (32–36). Even the most important debt he hopes to acknowledge is prefaced by caution and hesitation: "Nor less, I trust, / To them I may have owed another gift, / Of aspect more sublime" (36–38). His voice does become more confident as it moves into a full and feeling description of this other gift: "that serene and blessed mood, / In which [we] . . . become a living soul." The unsteady private conviction conveyed in the first person ("I may have owed") yields to declarations of a plural, transpersonal confidence about those experiences in which "we are laid asleep" and "we see into the life of things" (42–50). Perhaps the initial tones of hesitation and the halting movements of voice show no more than the difficulty of finding words for such "quiet" powers of joy and harmony, especially in their "blessed" emergence from "hours of weariness."

But the sudden suspicion, "If this / Be but a vain belief," interrupts this meditation to force the verse into a new paragraph, and so suggests a more complex restraint. For this is an uncertainty not about *what* may be owed but about whether it is possible to attribute such effects at all. The "burthen of the mystery" may have been lightened in the past, only to disclose an even more unintelligible mystery now. It is the same kind of uncertainty that besets the narrator of *The Thorn:* can chronology argue cause and effect? That speaker looks for a past cause (local history) to explain a present effect (his haunted imagination); the poet of *Tintern Abbey* looks to future effects ("tranquil restoration") from past and present causes in this landscape. But for both, the question "what cause?" can be answered only by conjecture: "perhaps" and "may" and "if"—potentially (or even pre-) interrogative terms that anticipate the suspicion of "vain belief." To prevent that murmur, however, Wordsworth summons impassioned counterdeclaration to insist on the primary fact of his response: "yet, oh! how oft, . . . How oft, in spirit, have I turned to thee / O sylvan Wye! . . . How often has my spirit turned to thee!" (51, 56–58). The turn to apostrophe is important, for this is a figure that elides temporal issues in favor of the power of present speech.[12] And as for the speaker of *The Thorn*, the repetitions that shape this figure are to be "weighed in the balance of feeling" (*LB* 289); they are active and efficient statements that revive feeling, even as they assert its felt truth. The poet underscores this turn of faith by modulating the present tenses with which he had greeted the Wye Valley into the present perfect: I have turned.[13] Like "I have owed" in the second verse paragraph, both the verb and verbal tense write the past into the present.

Yet even this apostrophe, fervent as it is, is strained by what it must frame and contain: a vivid memory of "darkness" and "the many shapes / Of joyless day-light . . . the fretful stir / Unprofitable, and the fever of the world" (54–58). The appearance of a new verse paragraph and a sudden shift of voice suggest that the question of "vain belief" has not been resolved; nor can it be. For when the poet resumes, he must again claim revival against unspecified recognitions and perplexity:

> And now, with gleams of half-extinguish'd thought,
> With many recognitions dim and faint,
> And somewhat of a sad perplexity,
> The picture of the mind revives again. (59–62)

Once again, intervening clauses impose a burden, which as Richard Onorato remarks, requires a second set of *with* clauses "to balance, answer, or cancel the earlier ones in an almost rhetorically antithetical way" (43):

> here I stand, not only with the sense
> Of present pleasure, but with pleasing thoughts
> That in this moment there is life and food
> For future years. (63–66)

Even so, the pressure of "vain belief" remains, and continues to exert its force. For as the poet attempts to sum up—"And so I dare to hope / Though changed, no doubt, from what I was" (66–67)—the initially subordinate *though* clause usurps the syntax. Despite the seemingly casual tone, this deflection of voice reveals an undercurrent of inquiry. Though meaning to read recognitions of change as evidence of recompense, the poet equivocates. "Not for this / Faint I, nor mourn nor murmur," he says of "aching joys" and "dizzy raptures" that are "now no more" (85–87). Whether he means that he does not mourn (nor murmur) at all or that he does (but "Not for this"), the effect of the statement is to display what it disclaims. The contrariety of tones informs yet another effort to conclude: the statement "for such loss, I would believe, / Abundant recompense" (88–89) implicitly questions belief with a tentative auxiliary verb in the midst of its rhetoric of belief.

Even as such syntaxes disclose a questioning presence, other syntaxes develop an answerable style in a voice of emphatic denial: "Not for this / Faint I, nor mourn nor murmur"; "Nature never did betray / The heart that loved her"; "nor wilt thou then forget" (86–87, 123–24, 156). Disarming a question by negative containment is visibly evasive action, however; it is not the same as putting doubt to rest. And Wordsworth senses the difference, for he continues to negotiate counter-claims: "Nor, perchance," he says, turning to his

Sister, "If I were not thus taught, should I the more / Suffer my genial spirits to decay: / For thou art with me, here" (112–15). The doubt flickering and half-extinguished within "If this / Be but a vain belief" rekindles in this *if* clause, now as declarative denial: "Nor . . . Should I." He reiterates his faith—"Knowing that Nature never did betray / The heart that loved her; 'tis her privilege, / Through all the years of this our life, to lead / From joy to joy"—yet still admits impediments to this path of joy. "Never did betray" is qualified at best, as both Paul Sheats and Richard Onorato have remarked.[14] In this poem, however, such locution is perfectly characteristic. We may notice, too, the array of negatives the poet seems to require to express his trust that Nature guarantees

> that neither evil tongues,
> Rash judgments, nor the sneers of selfish men,
> Nor greetings where no kindness is, nor all
> The dreary intercourse of daily life,
> Shall e'er prevail against us, or disturb
> Our chearful faith that all which we behold
> Is full of blessings. (129–35)

What he excludes emerges with fuller descriptive power than what he owns, in effect making the effort to evade the matter of questioning as visible as the faith that would prevail against it.[15]

Like the poem's manner of speech, the uneven progress and perplexed methods of its argument suggest Wordsworth's willingness to show the pressure of questions within the designs of affirmation. The verse everywhere implicates its speaker's desire to express belief with his need to contain intuitions of vain belief. Despite the frequent signals of "And so" or "For" or "Therefore," the transitions from topic to topic are often obscure, the turns of verse abrupt, the logic strained, and the management of evidence frequently complicated and at times of dubious effect. In a note he added to the poem in 1800, Wordsworth implies that the "transitions," at least, may be legitimized by the conventions of the "Ode," but his tone of hesitation ("I have not ventured to call this Poem an Ode; but . . ." [*LB* 296]) suggests that there is more in these *Lines* than can be ascribed to that formal rationale.[16] Indeed, most readers feel like the interlocutor in *The Thorn:* we find ourselves interrogating the directions and indirections of speech. One such opportunity arises as the poet presents his initial catalogue of evidence—what he again sees, hears, beholds—for that enthusiastic inventory unexpectedly halts before one questionable shape:

> wreathes of smoke
> Sent up, in silence, from among the trees,
> With some uncertain notice, as might seem,

> Of vagrant dwellers in the houseless woods,
> Or of some hermit's cave, where by his fire
> The hermit sits alone. (18–23)

The obscure origin of these wreaths of smoke recalls those uncertainly engendered "Thoughts of more deep seclusion" (7) the poet finds impressed in the landscape.[17] And what "might seem" to be the import of this "uncertain notice" does "disturb / The wild green landscape" (14–15). Wordsworth later deleted "disturb" from line 14, even though its prefacing "Nor" and its agent, "orchard-tufts," seem safe enough. Nevertheless, the disturbance remains, for shading the poem's optimistic first paragraph, and just below the "green and simple" plane of the landscape, the poet's voice half creates the presence of vagrants or "some hermit"—different analogues for a life anchored in nature, "houseless" or "alone." These figures of isolation, in fact, yield the transition to the next verse paragraph, in which Wordsworth remembers himself withdrawn from the world, remembering Tintern Abbey in London's "lonely rooms." Doubts previously denied a voice now invade the verse as the ostensibly new topic revives some further uncertain notices. We hear that the feelings of pleasure that arise in this world-weary self may themselves have an unremembered source, and the acts they "may have" influenced are likewise unremembered. This consequence is perhaps a bit too self-effacing for one who will urge his listener to "remember me, / And these my exhortations!" As we have seen, the intuition of vain belief and the counterturn of the spirit erupt from this memory. So when the poet returns to a "sense / Of present pleasure" (63–64), he sets up what he hopes is a reassuring analogy, projecting a remembering self into the future and framing the present as a hypothetical memory: "in this moment there is life and food / For future years" (65–66). The proleptically remembered picture of this moment can now be placed side by side with the "forms of beauty" remembered "mid the din / Of towns and cities." By referring to the "tranquil restoration" afforded then, the poet can grasp the present scene in all its immediacy, and simultaneously know its value for whatever future hours of weariness there may be. Looking ahead to looking back, he modulates his evidence in such a way as to "prove" the continuity of present affect into the future, while avoiding the urban memory on which these claims had been based.

   And yet this strategy proves unstable. Although the long middle paragraph of *Tintern Abbey* does conclude with the seeming assurance that begins, "Therefore am I still / A lover of the meadows and the woods, / And mountains; and of all that we behold / From this green earth" (103–6), the poem does not end there. Another sudden indentation of verse dissipates both the passion and the argument:

"Nor, perchance, / If I were not thus taught, should I the more / Suffer my genial spirits to decay: / For thou art with me, here," the poet says to his "dear, dear Sister," in effect raising the originating question of loss and recompense all over again. That such a question persists can be seen in the way he summons her as an agent of recovery and in apparent desperation:

> in thy voice I catch
> The language of my former heart, and read
> My former pleasures in the shooting lights
> Of thy wild eyes. Oh! yet a little while
> May I behold in thee what I was once,
> My dear, dear Sister! (117–22)

For a poet who has said "I cannot paint / What then I was" (76–77), the sister offers "gleams / Of past existence" (149–50) enhanced by the values of present thought. Yet even as that act of recovery synthesizes a lost past with present gains, it brings further strains to the argument. One has to do with the poet's differing assessments of his sister's importance to him. She is, in part, a "thinking thing" that represents his former self. But as a *record* of the past, she is converted into one of the "objects of [his] thought," a figure whose very difference from him is the basis of her value. Indeed, to read in his sister's eyes an unchanging text of his own past, the poet has to avoid the consequence of treating her as a thinking human being, for as he has revealed, thought cannot escape knowledge of change. The urgency of the poet's plea, "Oh! yet a little while / May I behold in thee what I was once," turns on this instability. If his sister grows and develops as he has, what sort of language will she offer? This question is not voiced—indeed, it is begged—but its force emerges in the contradictory terms with which the poet composes his sister's future remembering mind. He imagines her at once as a lively agent like himself, capable of "healing thoughts," *and* as a passive, unchanging register: "thy mind / Shall be a mansion for all lovely forms, / Thy memory be as a dwelling-place / For all sweet sounds and harmonies" (140–43). If these two sets of terms (mind as agent or mind as artifact) seem incongruous only in logic but not in effect (each retains the past), even that effect is not secure, for it has to be asserted against contrary evidence the poet has felt on his own pulses. After another five years, might not she change, feeling the new presences and absences to which her brother has just admitted? Though he announces that her "wild ecstasies shall be matured / Into a sober pleasure" (139–40), we have seen how really sober that pleasure can be. Indeed the "prayer" that follows barely deflects the interrogative force of "with what healing thoughts" into the desired exclamation:

                                              Oh! then,
          If solitude, or fear, or pain, or grief,
          Should be thy portion, with what healing thoughts
          Of tender joy wilt thou remember me,
          And these my exhortations! (143–47)

These exhortations admit no more than urgent desire (prayer in a high key); they are speech acts premised on uncertainty.

That "me, / And these my exhortations" are what the poet urges his sister to remember discloses an even deeper concern. In the catalogue of present gifts, the poet had assigned the language of joy a dual residence: in "nature" and "in the mind of man." But now, the mind, as the agent of both future memory and present exhortation, emerges as the sole healing power. Might this shift from nature to a moment of joyful speech reflect a doubt about where nature leads— to sad perplexity as well as pleasing thoughts? Though the question is never directly voiced, the turn of exhortation from revisiting a place to remembering an utterance suggests its shaping influence. The poet urges a "dwelling-place" in his sister's memory not so much for the present scene per se as for the whole filtered through the singular medium of his own interpretations. The truly sweet sounds and harmonies turn out to be poetic rather than natural creations— not the landscape "a few miles above Tintern Abbey" but the *Lines written a few miles above Tintern Abbey*. This new emphasis involves the interrogative stir of "with what healing thoughts" with a second, even more urgent inquiry, even more faintly registered: "wilt thou remember me . . . !" Though the final exclamation point denies a question, the poet's plea that his "dearest Friend" not forget his voice or presence seems to raise one. The whole concluding movement is cast as if to answer a question about how he will affect future years. Assuming the character by which he hopes to be remembered (the giver of benediction, the priest of natural piety), the poet preordains healing thoughts with the force of present assertion. He exhorts his sister to forget neither the occasion ("on the banks of this delightful stream / We stood together") nor his presence ("I, so long / A worshipper of Nature, hither came") nor his dedication (his "far deeper zeal / Of holier love") nor the very words that will preserve the whole through whatever "years / Of absence" follow (150–58).

The poet's turn to his sister eases the "weary weight" of mortality and mutability by impressing upon her the power of his voice at this "unwearied" moment of service and renewal. Fixed within his sister's memory, the voice of loving worship and exhortation will abide. This article of faith extends even to anticipations of absence ("Nor, perchance, / If I should be, where I no more can hear / Thy voice" [147–49]) and, by implication, the final absence of death. Death affords release from change, and the constancy of his sister's memory promises a stable afterlife. We have only to recall the little Maid in *We are seven*, who defies change with her insistence that her dead siblings are alive (and whose refusal to admit loss in a sense makes them so), to find an analogue for the poet's sister in the future he imagines for her. If her present self shows what he "was once," her future mind becomes a screen upon which he fervently projects himself as he is now and upon which the effect of the present can be staged as if it were already a memory: "We stood together"; "I . . . hither came."

The "wordsworthian or egotistical sublime" described by Keats finds no more telling instance than in this shift from landscape to self. When his prayer ends in a return to the original landscape, it is one organized around his own central presence. Just as he had framed a "picture of the mind" for his own memory, so now he frames and bequeaths this picture to the mansion of his sister's mind and contains any doubt about his preservation there with quiet counterassertion:

> Nor wilt thou then forget,
> That after many wanderings, many years
> Of absence, these steep woods and lofty cliffs,
> And this green pastoral landscape, were to me
> More dear, both for themselves, and for thy sake. (156–60)

Inscribed on his sister's mind with the permanence of an epitaph, the poet's benediction provides a moving summation for his entire argument, expressing the vital interrelation of the shared occasion, his presence there, and the enduring value of both through whatever distance or absence.

Throughout *Tintern Abbey*, the poet's voice negotiates the questions by which it is informed by summoning the power of insistent, impassioned reiteration of faith—in much the same way as the "answers" to the questions in *The Thorn* insistently, passionately, and merely, reiterate that speaker's belief in what he saw. When the poet of *Tintern Abbey* states, "here I stand," it is as if he means to make a stand—a nineteenth-century anticipation of the "momentary stay against confusion" Robert Frost claims all poetry devises.[18] As a counterpoise to the flow of time and the dissolution of confidence, his argument "answers" unspoken questions about the very nature of the self in time—questions of memory, of expectation, of death— by willfully delivering the present moment from the flux into which it constantly threatens to disintegrate. Much as the speaker of *The Thorn* invokes a tale in an attempt to appease his questioner and elucidate a mysterious circumstance, the speaker of *Tintern Abbey* plots a narrative of self against the impress of mystery; both begin in the present with the impassioned feeling, and both then construct a history as if to deduce a cause. In *The Thorn*, Wordsworth renders the feeling primary and the cause problematic, hinting that what may be at the center is a superstitious reaction to a highly charged occasion. In *Tintern Abbey*, however, both feeling and cause are primary issues, and Wordsworth never suggests that what his autobiographical "I" perceives and half creates has anything to do with superstition. On the contrary, the poet implies a sublime interfusion of the "presence that disturbs" with the beholder's "elevated thoughts." Nevertheless, the vacillations of voice, the halting locution, the uneven progress and perplexed logic of the argument all point to a disturbing mystery—the "Thoughts of more deep seclusion" at the very heart of the poem. The barely expressed questions that force the burden of this mystery onto the occasion are, perhaps, the primary "cause" behind this urgent and strenuous composition of belief.

Notes

1. De Quincey remarked that the Maid "is yet (for the effect upon the reader) brought into connection with the reflex shadow of the grave: and if she herself has *not*, the reader *has*, and through this very child, the gloom of that contemplation obliquely irradiated, as raised in relief upon his imagination, even by *her*" (Jordan, *De Quincey as Critic*, pp. 404–5).

2. Ferry finds its irony in the way this poem "mak[es] us read it two ways at once, either to show the obstinate naïveté of the child, who refuses to understand that her brother and sister are really dead, or to emphasize the obstinate sophistication of the speaker, who refuses to recognize the superiority of the child's wisdom" (p. 84).

3. Jordan has detailed the poem's mock-epic qualities ("Wordsworth's Humor") and Jacobus has studied it as a "burlesque of the supernatural ballad" (pp. 250–61).

4. Christensen brings interesting attention to the role of the questioner-interlocutor in "Wordsworth's Misery, Coleridge's Woe."

5. Parrish, *The Art of the "Lyrical Ballads,"* pp. 100–101. Parrish's reading is virtually an allegory for that process Iser describes when the mind confronts "some kind of blockage"; we are then provoked "to bring into play our own faculty for establishing connections—for filling the gaps in the text itself" ("The Reading Process," pp. 284–85).

6. The phrase is from the "Companion" poem to *Love Lies Bleeding* (PW 2:167), composed sometime between 1833 and 1845 and included by Wordsworth among the "Poems of the Fancy" in 1845. For a discussion of the paradoxical transformations of cause and effect in narrative logic, see Culler, "Story and Discourse in the Analysis of Narrative," in *The Pursuit of Signs*, pp. 169–87.

7. WP 148. Hartman has given some brief but valuable attention to the quality of mental action displayed by the narrator. The " 'loquacious narrator' exposes a mind shying from, yet drawn to, a compulsive center of interest. . . . we suspect that his mind cannot free itself of some *idée fixe*. As he warms up to his tale he fluctuates more obviously between disclaiming firm knowledge and thirsting for it" (WP 147–48). See also Griffin, "Wordsworth and the Problem of Imaginative Story." For Griffin, the

real concern of *Lyrical Ballads* "is tale-telling and tale-listening, in confused conflict with the poetic imagination" (p. 393). Related to Griffin's interest is Iser's claim that "without the elements of indeterminacy, the gaps in the text, we should not be able to use our imagination" (p. 288).

8. See especially *BL* 2:49. Coleridge was himself given to some qualified experiments in voice however. In an 1817 headnote to *The Three Graves* (a poem he says he published with "some doubt," despite "the decisive recommendation of more than one of our most celebrated living Poets"), he explains that the "language was intended to be dramatic; that is, suited to the narrator," an old Sexton. Coleridge confesses that this is not really "poetry, and it is in no way connected with [his] judgment concerning poetic diction. Its merits, if any, are exclusively psychological" (*Poems*, pp. 267, 269).

9. For a sustained consideration of this issue, see Ferguson, who argues that these poems evince "a radical ambiguity about the status of the object of poetic representation" ("The Lucy Poems: Wordsworth's Quest for a Poetic Object," in *Wordsworth*, pp. 174–75).

10. *WP* 148. See also Owen, " 'The Thorn' and the Poet's Intention": "the superstitious man . . . in so far as his superstition is defined primarily by his obsession with insoluble questions and his resulting uncertainty . . . is an image of Wordsworth's own questioning imagination, which also pursues insoluble questions and receives only uncertain answers" (p. 14).

11. Pater, "Wordsworth," p. 40. For a compelling discussion of the tension between "poetic effects" and "the apparent declarative sense of poetic statement" in *Tintern Abbey*, see Onorato, pp. 29–87. Onorato reads the poem as an attempt "to express, contain, and resolve a doubt . . . in order to suppress a deeper experience of it" (pp. 39, 42).

12. Culler remarks that apostrophe "makes its point by troping . . . on the circuit or situation of communication itself"; apostrophe "works against narrative and its accompaniments: sequentiality, causality, time, teleological meaning"; "by removing the opposition between presence and absence from empirical time and locating it in a discursive time," apostrophe displaces an irreversible temporal sequence in which "something once present has been lost or attenuated," and "makes the power of its own evocativeness a central issue" ("Apostrophe," in *The Pursuit of Signs*, pp. 135, 148, 150).

13. See Boyd and Boyd, "The Perfect of Experience," for a study of how the poem's present perfect tenses imply a continuity of response, connecting past feelings to the present moment of composition.

14. Sheats, *The Making of Wordsworth's Poetry*, p. 241; Onorato, p. 34.

15. One earlier signal of this simultaneous acknowledgment and evasion is Wordsworth's uncertain surmise of "vagrant dwellers" in the landscape below, while he himself remains "a few miles above," not having to confront the challenge that such outcasts might post to his argument about the value of living a life anchored in nature. Contemporary guidebooks remark on the fact that the ruins of Tintern Abbey and the neighboring area were inhabited by vagrants, transients, gypsies; it "was a dwelling-place of beggars and the wretchedly poor," reports Moorman (*William Wordsworth*, pp. 402–3). For a fuller discussion, see Johnston, "The Politics of 'Tintern Abbey,' " esp. pp. 7–9. McGann, although he overstates Wordsworth's submission to "the power / Of harmony" and understates the conflicts by which he remains beset, also studies the dynamics by which Wordsworth seems to be displacing "material reality" into an immaterial "spiritual economy" dominated by "the landscape of Wordsworth's emotional needs" (*Ideology*, pp. 86–88).

16. Coleridge found "Impetuosity of Transition" to be one of "the *essential*

excellencies of the sublimer Ode" (*Letters,* 1:289). Robert Potter thought such lyrics "not only allowed, but even required sudden and bold transitions" (*An Inquiry into Some Passages in Dr. Johnson's . . . Observations on Lyric Poetry, and the Odes of Gray* [1783], p. 14, cited by Maclean, "From Action to Image," pp. 427–28). But a less sympathetic assessment is offered by Hugh Blair, who suggests, in a widely read lecture, that the "digressions," "disorder," and "incoherence" of the ode yield "abrupt . . . transitions; so eccentric and irregular . . . that we essay in vain to follow" ("Pastoral Poetry—Lyric Poetry," 2:354, 356). Given the general agreement about the intimacy of the ode form with discontinuity and disjunction, Wordsworth's reference to this "species of composition" serves merely to restate rather than accommodate the effects of the verse it would explain. Hartman connects Wordsworth's attraction to this form to the "vacillating calculus of gain and loss, of hope and doubt" that operates on the poem's "thematic level" (*WP* 27). Ferry wonders whether the poem shows a "confusion of feeling" or expresses "a complexity of feeling, a contemplated and contained ambivalence" (pp. 110–11). See also Sheats: "the balance of positive and negative forces changes from line to line and often from word to word" (p. 244, and see pp. 228–45).

17. Reading these lines, Wimsatt comments, "always something just out of sight or beyond definition" (p. 111).

18. Frost, "The Figure a Poem Makes," *Complete Poems,* p. vi.

Works Cited

Blair, Hugh. "Pastoral Poetry—Lyric Poetry." In *Lectures on Rhetoric and Belles Lettres* (1783), edited by Harold F. Harding. 2 vols. Carbondale: Southern Illinois University Press, 1965, 2:335–60.

Boyd, Julian, and Zelda Boyd. "The Perfect of Experience." *Studies in Romanticism* 16 (1977): 3–13.

Christensen, Jerome. "Wordsworth's Misery, Coleridge's Woe: Reading 'The Thorn.' " *Papers on Language and Literature* 16 (1980): 268–86.

Coleridge, Samuel Taylor. *Biographia Literaria.* Edited by James Engell and W. Jackson Bate. 2 vols. Princeton, N.J.: Princeton University Press, 1983. Abbreviated "BL" in text.

———. *The Poems of Samuel Taylor Coleridge.* Edited by Ernest Hartley Coleridge. London: Oxford University Press, 1912; reprinted 1960.

Culler, Jonathan. *The Pursuit of signs: Semiotics, Literature, Deconstruction.* Ithaca, N.Y.: Cornell University Prsss, 1981.

Ferguson, Frances C. *Wordsworth: Language as Counter-Spirit.* New Haven, Conn.: Yale University Press, 1977.

Ferry, David. *The Limits of Mortality: An Essay on Wordsworth's Major Poems.* Middletown, Conn.: Wesleyan University Press, 1959.

Frost, Robert. *Complete Poems of Robert Frost.* New York: Holt, Rinehart, and Winston, 1967.

Griffin, Andrew L. "Wordsworth and the Problem of Imaginative Story." *PMLA* 92 (1977): 392–409.

Hartman, Geoffrey. *Wordsworth's Poetry, 1787–1814.* 1964. Reprint. New Haven, Conn.: Yale University Press, 1975. Abbreviated "WP" in text.

Iser, Wolfgang. "The Reading Process: A Phenomenological Approach." *New Literary History* 3 (1972): 279–99.

Jacobus, Mary. *Tradition and Experiment in Wordsworth's "Lyrical Ballads" (1798).* Oxford: Clarendon, 1976.

Johnston, Kenneth. "The Politics of 'Tintern Abbey.' " *Wordsworth Circle* 14 (1983): 6–14.

Jordan, John E. "Wordsworth's Humor." *PMLA* 73 (1958): 81–93.

———, ed. *De Quincey as Critic.* London: Routledge and Kegan Paul, 1973.

McGann, Jerome J. *The Romantic Ideology: A Critical Investigation.* Chicago: University of Chicago Press, 1983.

Maclean, Norman. "From Action to Image: Theories of the Lyric in the Eighteenth Century." In *Critics and Criticism,* edited by R. S. Crane. pp. 408–60. Chicago: Chicago University Press, 1952.

Moorman, Mary. *William Wordsworth, A Biography: The Early Years, 1770–1803.* 1957. Reprint. Oxford: Clarendon, 1965.

Onorato, Richard J. *The Character of the Poet: Wordsworth in "The Prelude."* Princeton, N.J.: Princeton University Press, 1971.

Owen, W. J. B. " 'The Thorn' and the Poet's Intention." *Wordsworth Circle* 8 (1977): 3–17.

Parrish, Stephen Maxfield. *The Art of the "Lyrical Ballads."* Cambridge, Mass.: Harvard University Press, 1973.

Pater, Walter. "Wordsworth." In *Appreciations,* pp. 37–63. New York: Macmillan, 1901.

Sheats, Paul D. *The Making of Wordsworth's Poetry, 1785–1798.* Cambridge, Mass.: Harvard University Press, 1973.

Wimsatt, W. K. *The Verbal Icon: Studies in the Meaning of Poetry.* Lexington: Kentucky University Press, 1954.

Wordsworth, William. *The Letters of William and Dorothy Wordsworth: The Early Years, 1787–1805.* Edited by Ernest de Selincourt. 2d. ed., revised by Chester L. Shaver. Oxford: Clarendon, 1967. Abbreviated "EY" in text.

———. *The Letters of William and Dorothy Wordsworth: The Later Years, 1821–1850.* Edited by Ernest de Selincourt. 2d. ed., revised by Alan G. Hill. 3 vols. Oxford: Clarendon, 1978. Abbreviated "LY" in text.

———. *Lyrical Ballads.* The text of the 1798 edition with the additional 1800 poems and the Prefaces. Edited by R. L. Brett and A. R. Jones. 1963. Revised. London: Methuen, 1965. Abbreviated "LB" in text.

———. *The Poetical Works of William Wordsworth.* Edited by Ernest de Selincourt. 2d. ed., revised by Helen Darbishire. 5 vols. Oxford: Clarendon 1952–1959. Abbreviated "PW" in text.

———. *The Prelude, 1799, 1805, 1850.* Edited by Jonathan Wordsworth, M. H. Abrams, and Stephen Gill. New York: Norton, 1979.

ODE: INTIMATIONS OF IMMORTALITY FROM RECOLLECTIONS OF EARLY CHILDHOOD

Wordsworth's Severe Intimations   Paul H. Fry[*]

As I arrive at the period when genres begin to be "naturalized" along with poetic diction, my continuing to read odes as odes may call for a few further words of defense. In the eighteenth century the genres still comprised a "cosmic syntax"[1] that had its place in an articulate and more or less legible universe. Generic thinking prevailed in most quarters, even though there was often disagreement about the proper hierarchy of the genres: epic was still highest in the criticism of Pope's followers, but a lively minority from John Dennis to Watts and Bishop Lowth placed the "sacred lyric" highest. Johnson was rather unusual in viewing the genres with some disapproval. He opposed the strict decorum of any generic approach to poetry for fear of encouraging insincerity and distorted observation. As one pieces together his strictures on pastoral and the ode, his defense of Shakespeare's mixed genres, and his attention to the local rather than the larger structural features of poetry in all the modes, one realizes how fully he anticipates Wordsworth (though, of course, in behalf of a far more generalized sense of reality) in viewing poetry as the "real language of men."

The challenge to the taxonomic view of literature arose from a resurgence of epistemological trust in what Gray had contemptuously called the "language of the age." A genre, from Aristotle onward, had always been understood to be a fictive solution to the problem of untidiness in the real world, but no one had ever claimed that "history" is not itself far tidier than life. History was more accurate, perhaps, than poetry; but no critic in the line of Aristotle ever confused verbal representation with objective presentation. As Aristotle himself put the matter in his seminal grammar, the *Categories*, "Substance cannot be predicated."[2] Discourse, in other words, always defers and specie-fies the thing in itself, proceeding necessarily in referential categories. Since generic thinking is therefore inescapable,

[*] Reprinted from *The Poet's Calling in the English Ode.* © 1980 Yale University Press. Used by permission of Yale University Press.

the Aristotelian might argue, it may as well be cultivated, especially because it does seem to correspond to the several great forms that inhere in nature. Although in the Neoplatonic variant of this tradition that Sidney follows, the generic fictions were understood to merge with a transcendental ground (the Ideal) insofar as they purged the dross of their material ground (the phenomenal apparitions that Plato was right to abuse poets for imitating); and although even among empiricists opinions differed concerning the degree to which genres should realign the nature of things, there was still an implicit belief at the root of every generic theory until 1800 that poetic space is what we largely perceive and moderately re-create according to received models given either by nature or by nature's best metonym, Homer, whose *Margites* and "Homeric Hymns" made him the father of every genre that exists.

A Wordsworthian poetics leads to the new conclusion that poetic space is what we half perceive and half create on the basis of an ad hoc symbiosis of mind with nature. Thus the cosmic syntax or taxonomy formerly given ready-formed to the creative faculties of the poet becomes in Wordsworth a unitary principle that appears in changing ways, according to the pressure of the moment, at the joining place of mind and nature. This powerful reduction to "the one Life within us and abroad" (Coleridge) undermines all gross classification even as it promotes the unique selfhood or substance of "the meanest flower that blows" within the imagined unity of things. The atomistic and the cosmic fuse under the pressure of imagination, leaving the illusion of difference to linger only among intermediate quantities:

> the one interior life
> That lives in all things, sacred from the touch
> Of that false secondary power by which
> In weakness we create distinctions, then
> Believe that all our puny boundaries are things
> Which we perceive and not which we have made.[3]

On this view, symbolism is available to all the arts of expression, symbolism being the making-present of some universal power that is universally absent until by magic the *nomen* grows numinous. This faith in the symbol is meant to quiet our obstinate questionings, whether of sense or of the supersensuous, by waiving altogether the question of the existence or nonexistence of the physical referent. The triangulation of word, thing, and spirit by the "symbol" effaces the thing by sublating its newly glorified selfhood.[4] Only the symbol, as Coleridge might say, "is that it is," an articulate Presence, like the Word. This antigeneric faith, be it said now, is none other than— the faith that typifies the genre called the ode. Were it not antinomian, defiant of determinacy by externally given origins, this faith would attach itself to the office of prayer.

When genre theory reappears in the organization and the Preface of Wordsworth's 1815 *Collected Poems*, it is based in good part on subjective distinctions. The cosmos is still one, but our different faculties (e.g., fancy, imagination) with their different predilections (affection, the need to name, and so on) and phases of perception (e.g., "early youth") will present the "one Life" in various guises that truly are different from each other. Not absolutely but in tendency, Wordsworth transfers the science of genres from cosmology to psychology.[5]

It is only very recently that the idea of a random field of signification, irreducible to any well-ordered syntax of faculties in the conscious subject, has challenged classification of all kinds. According to this view, both objective *and* subjective generic thinking are attributes of a naïve epistemology, or rather of the naïve faith that an epistemology is possible. I think that this Pyrrhonism has always been perceptibly registered by the presentational lyric, despite its generally idealistic aims. The ode, that Great Auk among the birds that are themselves objects of the obsolete science of ornithology, the ode of all forms, has always known the ruptures of dissemination. The sheer textuality of the ode, its re(com)pression of alien generic structures as the daemonic traces of lyric metaphor, yields a skepticism about the contentments of form that belies both occasion and vocation.

Perhaps there is room for yet another sentence in the current debate about periodization, a sentence that would defend my own approach to literary history: *The theoretical discourse of any period lies waiting and implicit in the discursive forms that precede it.* Thus one could support the observation of Fredric Jameson, for whom origins are material and diachronic agencies, that "the new is to the old as latent content working its way to the surface to displace a form henceforth obsolete."[6] Periodization might properly map the passing over of knowledge from its encodement in structure to the discourse about structures: from code to statement, which in turn becomes a new code, harboring anxieties that will force their way into the open in yet later statements. This dialectic would somewhat exaggerate the incidence of change in the series of poems I am studying, however. The knowledge I am tracing in the ode remains partly encoded and partly discursive knowledge in any ode to this day, but periodic changes in the ode can nevertheless still be recorded as topological shifts, irreducibly different, in the near-utterance or dissemination of the repressed. Thus, concerning the great Romantic odes to which I now turn, it will gradually become apparent that in them the sublime, here understood as the uncanny element of lyric inspiration, has been conceived in a way that differs wholly from its conception in the eighteenth-century ode.

I

Wordsworth's early "Remembrance of Collins"[7] reflects a complex and alert reading of Collins's odes. Beginning as Collins once did with Spenser, Wordsworth's "Glide Gently, thus for ever glide, / O Thames!" recognizes Collins's desire to write the poem of his own chaste marriage. Very possibly, therefore, Wordsworth numbers among the motives of the mad "Poet's sorrows" (20) the epithalamic failure of Collins's odes. Interweaving images from the Death of Thomson Ode and the "Ode to Evening" (and also from Thomson's "Hymn on Solitude": "Descending angels bless thy train"), Wordsworth tries to purify Collins's typically mysterious haunted moment by arming it with holiness and scattering the daemonic, as did Milton in the Nativity Ode, with a militant poise:

> How calm! how still! the only sound,
> The dripping of the oar suspended!
> —The evening darkness gathers round
> By virtue's holiest powers attended.

Wordsworth's prayer that the "child of song" (19) be attended by a vision that lightens our falling toward darkness, a vision of the high birthplace both of ourselves and of our virtue, is offered in order to restore the otherness and innocence of the past to the odes of Collins; and, on a far more difficult occasion, it is also the prayer of the Intimations Ode.

The happier past, as a sign of poetic election and of life after death, can be recovered only through that most ontologically treacherous of faculties, memory. Recollection in "calm weather" can never be facile; indeed, it may be wise to assume, upon careful reading, that recollection in the Intimations Ode is recognized to be an exhilarating but futile exercise. In itself, however, the quality of difference between present and past that is given by memory as a newly refined poetic topic[8]—"and, oh! the difference to me!"— enables the odes of Wordsworth and his major contemporaries to represent change more plausibly than any of Gray's or Collins's resources had permitted. But only *more* plausibly. The Romantic ode writer hopes that one change—from past to present—will imply the coming of another, the redemption of the present. But the disappointment of that hope cannot be avoided, owing to the continued necessity of repetition, which insists upon the immutability of the present. No naturalizing of vocative devices can ever completely suppress this immutability because, after all, the presupposed existence of some indivisible and unchanging power is just what an ode is written to celebrate. The ode bends the quality of difference in all experience to its mono-myth, which is only speciously genealogical.

All the great odes I shall discuss from now on are evening odes.[9] The veils of Gray and Collins are taken over by the Romantics as a sober coloring of clouds and tropes at sundown that still conceals the "wavy bed" (Wordsworth's "mighty waters") of the sun-poet's origin. That the sense of evening in the Romantic ode is yet more intense than in earlier odes can be shown in a rough way even by comparative biography. Whereas eighteenth-century poets, even Swift, began their careers by assaying the vocational challenge of Pindarism, Wordsworth and Coleridge "began" (if we disregard their school exercises) in the quieter keys of the topographical poem and the slighter lyric modes. M. H. Abrams's inclusion of the Intimations Ode and "Dejection: An Ode" in his persuasively described unifying genre, "the greater Romantic lyric" (encompassing the common themes and structure of the sublime ode and the Conversation Poem), may be questioned simply by appealing to dates. Nearly all the major Conversation Poems of both Wordsworth and Coleridge were written well before the Companion Odes that were begun in 1802, begun in response to growing intimations of loss.[10] If the eighteenth-century poet proved himself to be a poet by writing an ode, the Romantic poet proved himself *still* to be a poet by writing an ode, but no longer a poet gifted with unmediated vision. The turning of Wordsworth and Coleridge to the unnatural conventions of ode writing is itself a farewell to the natural holiness of youth.

II

L'ode change l'éternité, l'épopée sollenise l'histoire, le drame peint peint la vie. Le caractère de la première poésie est la naïveté, le caractère de la seconde est la simplicité, le caractère de la troisieme, la vérité. . . . Les personnages de l'ode sont des colosses: Adam, Caïn, Noé; ceux de l'épopée sont des géants: Achille, Atrée, Oreste; ceux du drame sont des hommes: Hamlet, Macbeth, Othello. L'ode vit l'idéal. . . .
—Victor Hugo, *Preface de Cromwell* (1827)

From its publication to the present, the Intimations Ode has had the reputation of being Wordsworth's most confused poem.[11] In this respect it is appropriately an ode or, more precisely, an irregular Pindaric. What Wordsworth dictated to Miss Fenwick, "To the attentive and competent reader the whole sufficiently explains itself" (*Poetical Works* IV, 463), curiously recalls Gray's "vocal to the intelligent alone." As we have seen, from Jonson through Collins, the

Pindaric form is a refuge for confusion; it both reflects and deepens uncertainties that will not lend themselves to forthright treatment. As a final preface to the Romantic ode, we may review here, in the form of a summary typology, the confusions that lie beneath the unending hope of the ode to stand purely, through invocation, in the pure presence of what its presentation always stains and darkens.

Here, then, is the normative course of an ode. Some quality of absolute worth is traced back to its conception, where it appears as a fountainhead, sunrise, or new star. But the landscape of dawning, inescapably twilit, is instinct with regional spirits that misbehave and will not be reduced to order. It is impossible for the compressions of syntax and figure to avoid implicating these dark spirits in the ur-conception of the ode and of its numen alike. Such spirits are "kept aloof" at first, like Collins's "dangerous passions," by the ode's shifting of its etiology from the spiritual to the sublunary plane—from theogony, in other words, to the earliest stages of recorded history or childhood. This descent from the divine is halted and in some measure reversed by the poet's location of a primitive society or early selfhood in a region that he still calls sacred (the magic circle, garland, manger, shrine, or temple). The history of poetry, meanwhile, is imagined as one great ode, sacralized by the analogy between the holy place the ode describes and the circle of its own form. Hence, the transcendent pastness of the past is lost almost completely in the defensive act of exorcizing its false, daemonic, and generically diverse oracles. Once great Pan is pronounced dead, the oracle grows nearly silent, and the vocal occasion of the ode, consecrated to the celebration of the present, is mediated and muted by all the formal defenses that writing ritualizes.

In violent denial of this loss, the ode now loudly reasserts its divine calling: it hazards the frenzied tropes of identification that we call "enthusiastic"[12] and then quickly collapses into self-caricature. This is the brief noontide phase of the ode, envisioned as a Phaeton-myth of flight followed by blindness and a fall into or toward the sea. The sun has been placed once more too squarely in view, so that the excessive bright of its cloudy skirts becomes an ominous darkness, like the darkness of dawn. To avoid the bathos of Phaeton's death, the poet reins in ("Stop, stop, my muse," exclaims Cowley in "The Resurrection," "allay thy vig'rous heat!") and adjusts himself to the light of common day. In the decline of this light toward evening, the ode accepts a diminished calling, often movingly and even cheerfully embraced as the hymning of a favorite name, and never reasserts its enthusiastic mission. Even this dénouement is marred, however, by the regathering and haunting of twilit forces.

We may adapt some of these outlines to the Intimations Ode in order to establish a viewpoint from which its confusion may then be reconsidered more carefully. Wordsworth's ode opens with the recollection of a pastoral dawn[13] when the sun, in place of the poet, had a "glorious birth." This happy scene is peopled by the usual denizens of the vernal ode—songbirds, frolicking animals—from whose jubilee the speaker is excluded. In content the scene is that of the "Sonnet on the Death of West" abused by Wordsworth in his 1800 Preface. In earlier life the speaker's spontaneous vision helped "apparel" the scene he now adorns more conventionally. In order to make himself present to his own childhood, as he attempted to do by evoking the Boy of Winander in *The Prelude*, Wordsworth now invokes and petitions the happy voice of the Shepherd-boy. His identification with a better self, which is wholly fitting in an ode, seems for the moment to yield rewards. The Babe leaps up, as Wordsworth's heart had leapt up the day before, to nestle closer to Mother Nature. But—and here the voice of the original four-stanza ode turns downward after the blindly exclamatory "I hear! I hear!"— but, the poet seems to wonder, does paradise have a mother only? The lost Tree and single Field suggest an Eden that was begotten by a Father, and the adult poet can only partly keep from knowing that his visionary birth, though too noble for pastoral, was nevertheless still erotic. The Pansy at his feet recalls Milton's Pensive Nun, who always keeps her head pointed toward, if not in, the sand. Thus far Wordsworth's expression of loss has simply followed the convention of the amorous vernal ode whereby the speaker looks about frantically for his absent mistress.

Wordsworth does have a glimpse of her, though, and is not pleased, as the fifth stanza reveals. The maternal earth from which he feels alienated has "pleasures of her own," and it is her natural yearning to possess her foster child and make him forget his epic and patriarchal origins, "that imperial palace whence he came." Following exactly the scenario presented by Otto Rank,[14] she interferes, in her lowly role, with the poet's myth of his birth as a hero, and her interference is as erotic as that of the Nurse in *Romeo and Juliet*. Even as we pass the poem thus schematically in review, we should note that there is a degree of voluntarism, even relief, in the adult's alienation from his childhood. The "Child of Joy" is given pause in so designating himself, and feels a hint of Gray's "fearful joy."[15] We shall see in the long run, however, that this impure intimation is vastly preferable to those purer ones that come to replace it. From stanza five onward, the poet will strive to imagine a self-conception that is not an earthy anecdote from the pastoral tradition, to imagine a birth-myth that is not an earth-myth or failed autochthony. At first this seems a good idea. By bringing about a reconciliation of his mortal being with "the light of common day," with the ordinariness of earth, the poet can once more invest with the appearance of dialectical truth the assumption that his immortal being must derive from a region that is *not* common; the animation of the soul seems to depend on the disinspiriting of earth.

The figure of the imperial palace carries the sun's "glorious birth" across the increasingly dualistic chasm of the poet's logic while alienating the sun from the landscape it formerly graced. The poet remembering himself as a bright-haired youth or sun-child now identifies with the Father, through the metalepsis "God, who is our home," in a higher region that is set apart from natural kindness as the sublime is set apart from the beautiful. This brief intimation (his first of immortality) makes up the subsumed epic phase of the ode. In Victor Hugo's terms, Adam has become Orestes. Shaking off the mother, by whose possessive kisses he is fretted (like a brook fretting in its channel [1.94]), the hero descends from his epic to his dramatic phase, recalling Aristotle's derivation of theatre from child's play in the *Poetics:* "As if his whole vocation / Were endless imitation." Here the Father stands back, the one apart from the many, no longer identified with the son but still tendering the sunlight of his gaze. Now the child becomes the chameleonic Hamlet, trapped in a "prison-house" (68) of nature and changed into a different player by each attention from the mother whose yearnings in her natural kind have caused him so much anxiety. Little actor though he is, however, he is still a solitary and a soliloquist, like John Home in Collins's Scottish Superstitions Ode: "unto this he frames his song." He acts odes.

Hamlet calls the world a "prison" (II. ii); but in *Hamlet* the world is only one of two prisons, the other being identified by the ghost of Hamlet's father: "I am thy father's spirit . . ."

> But that I am forbid
> To tell the secrets of my prison-house,
> I could a tale unfold whose lightest word
> Would harrow up thy soul.
>
> (I.v.9, 13–16)

This discordant intimation Wordsworth records in his next stanza:

> Mighty Prophet! Seer blest!
> On whom these truths do rest,
> Which we are toiling all our lives to find,
> In darkness lost, the darkness of the grave;
> Thou, over whom thy Immortality
> Broods like the Day, a Master o'er a Slave . . .

For the child's domination by Mother Earth, then, there is an equivalent master-slave dialectic between son and father.[16] Immortal regions are suddenly as much like prisons as mortal ones; and the ode's noontide, its most high-flown rhetoric, having seen too much reality, falls back to the theme of blindness, which could be an ode's address, thus stated, to its own self-blighted celebratory mandate:

> Thou little child, yet glorious in thy might
> Of heaven-born freedom [as a Slave?] on thy being's height,
> Why with such earnest pains dost thou provoke
> The years to bring the inevitable yoke,
> Thus blindly with thy blessedness at strife?

In singling out the main point of repetition in this poem (crucial repetition being typically revealed, as we saw in the "Ode to Duty," by a stutter or gaffe like this one about the slave's heaven-born freedom), we have perhaps come to see why no blessedness is visible that is not in some wise tainted. The child must be admitted to know what he is doing in choosing blinders.

Having absorbed the rival genres in the child's progress toward his earthly prison and then reacted frantically back toward its displaced theme of originary magic, only to discover a different prison in that theme, Wordsworth's ode now lapses into its final, elegiac phase, giving notice of this change with a verbal allusion to "Lycidas": "Not for these I raise / The song of thanks and praise." Here begins Wordsworth's evening retrospect and its attempt to overbalance the heavy weight of custom with the philosophic mind's conversion of remembered joy into "natural piety." The ode becomes a song in praise of sublimation, and it has some sublime moments remaining. It distances the Deluge (into which an ode, like Phaeton, is always falling) from the standpoint of calm weather, thus belatedly justifying the suggestion of a covenant in the rainbow that comes and goes; it returns to the vernal festival of earthy childhood "in thought" only; and finally it returns to the landscape of the first line, adding the word "Fountains" to the initial list because, through the sublimation of dangerous waters, the philosophic mind is now able to recognize a seminal source as well as an Edenic foster mother. All these qualified returns make up Wordsworth's "Stand." The irregularity of all the previous stanzas is reduced to uniformity, with the exception of an odd line out that refuses the eclipse it appears in: "Is lovely yet." Wordsworth's hymnic epode, like Collins's homiletic harvest at the end of the "Ode to Evening," joins the common produce of the common day in an order serviceable. The necessary sacrifice of godlike autochthony for natural piety brings on silence, an unutterable pathos that is vastly different from the shouts of the Child of Joy. The question of immortality is mooted in the end, and we must reconsider it if we are to discover why this is so.

III

that dubious hour,
That twilight when we first begin to see
This dawning earth. . . .
            —*The Prelude* V:511–13

Is the Intimations Ode, in Lionel Trilling's deft phrase, about growing old or growing up?[17] It is hard to know how or where to enter this dispute. It seems to me that the poem is about not knowing whether childhood, adulthood, or yet a third state of complete disembodiment is best; that it is, in short, about confusion. In the Fenwick note Wordsworth confesses having experienced the opposite "subjugations" of idealism and materialism in childhood and adulthood, respectively, and seems to imply that the purpose of his poem is to thread its way between prisons, or rather to find a restful expansiveness in their mutual collapse. In this modest aim I think it succeeds, despite serious flaws of coherence that will appear. Deliberately an ode, the poem experiments with presentation, the presentation in this case of an elusive nimbus called a "glory." The experiment fails, but in place of ecstasy the poet gains knowledge, a new awareness of the role played by determinacy in consciousness.

Wordsworth's apology in the Fenwick note for his chosen myth of a prior existence reflects the etiological anxiety of any ode, the fear of dark places, and also recalls the antinomian relation of an ode to orthodoxy. His myth, he says, "is far too shadowy a notion to be recommended to faith." Still, however, as he also clearly implies in the note, he knows no proof of immortality that is not in some way shadowy; this despite the fact that for Wordsworth, as for Coleridge, autonomy of thought cannot be demonstrated without proof of the mind's original participation in an eternal cause. This necessary priority of the spirit is termed by Wordsworth in the note an Archimedean "point whereon to rest" what would be, otherwise, the dreary machine of Associationist psychology.

Although the lack of such proof may cause some anxiousness, it is not really the belief in immortality, however founded, that the ode questions, but rather the nature of immortality. By allusion and repetition, Wordsworth's ode clouds over what in religion are foregone conclusions about the sources of life and death. It is disturbing, for example, that "Nor man nor Boy, / Nor all that is at enmity with joy, / Can utterly destroy . . ." alludes to the speech of Moloch in *Paradise Lost* that calls the Creator a destroyer, like Collins's Fancy. Or again, it is difficult to understand what blindness is if the Child is at once "an eye to the blind" and "blindly with his blessedness at strife." As was also apparent in Collins's "Ode on the Poetical

Character," a poet cannot merely decree a difference between Vision and vision that his poem fails otherwise to sustain.

To cite another troublesome passage, where is the guilt and on what ground is the misgiving in the following lines?

> Not for these I raise
> The song of thanks and praise;
> But for those obstinate questionings
> Of sense and outward things,
> Fallings from us, vanishings;
> Blank misgivings of a Creature
> Moving about in worlds not realized,
> High instincts before which our mortal Nature
> Did tremble like a guilty thing surprised. . . .

The solipsism of the child is obstinate, and his experience of a lapse is the opposite of Adam's: not a corruption of soul but a falling away of the flesh. Immortality is intimated by the child as a state of emptiness and vertigo, a Melvilleian blankness that is duplicitous for all its vacancy, since it has more than one habitation ("worlds")— perhaps a true and a false zone of antimatter. The bodily "Creature" would appear to have been created as a companion for the soul's loneliness. The song that is raised, in sum, shows every sign of being a song of thanks for the gift of mortality.[18]

This is not to imply, however, that the entire burden of the song is a foolish critique of immortality. The main point is, rather, that memory harbors phantoms. Whatever immortality may be like, mortal discourse is confined to what a child can know about it, or, yet more mediately, to what an adult can remember of childhood knowledge.[19] The child's recollections are indeed "shadowy," both because adult memory is busy securing the present by darkening the past (in this sense the poem *is* "about growing up" and being happy with the present) and also because, as "be they what they may" rather sheepishly concedes, what the poet remembers is not really the "high instincts" of childhood but the phantom Underworld of the Greeks. The confessed Platonism of Wordsworth's preexistence myth comes chiefly from the Myth of the warrior Er, who "coming to life related what, he said, he had seen in the world beyond" (Plato's *Republic* 614b). Er describes souls struggling to be born between two worlds, governed, like Wordsworth's Slave, by the Spindle of Necessity. But the feeling of Wordsworth's intimations is, in fact, more Homeric than Platonic; it is "impalpable as shadows are, and wavering like a dream" (*Odyssey*, tran. Fitzgerald, XI). Wordsworth's ode may be seen as a moving failure of perspective; called forth to be condemned, mortal Nature reasserts its vital strength and beauty.[20]

By comparison, immortality is a dream. In the third stanza there is a crux of remarkable compression, "The Winds come to me from the fields of sleep." Many a hapless recitation of this line has produced "fields of sheep," a slip that is prompted by the surrounding gleeful pastoral in which no creature sleeps during the rites of spring. The fields of sleep belong to an earlier time and place, the threshold of birth which is, later, "but a sleep and a forgetting." Wordsworth's winds bring news of birth, then, yet seem imagistically to recall an even earlier moment, the classical fields of asphodel and poppy.[21] In contrast with the jollity of a child's landscape, the winds of adult memory recollect the stupor of immortality, or what Homer calls the "shores of Dream" (*Odyssey* XXIV).

In approaching the designedly binding and blinding symbol of the ode, that of the "glory," we must pause over metaphysics a little longer. The prolepsis that the ode never moves beyond is the ambiguous apposition of line 5. Presumably "the glory and the freshness of a dream" modifies "celestial light" in the previous line; but the grammar does not prevent reading the line in apposition to "every common sight." One's total impression of lines 1–5 is that the glory summarily modifies both the common, with which the poem concludes, and the celestial, with which it has begun. Hence either the common itself is glorious, properly viewed (like the cuckoo and the lesser celandine of the 1802 period), or else the glory is a nimbus, a frame of celestial light that leaves the framed common object unilluminated in itself. This sliding apposition looks forward to the confusion of the whole text. The word "dream" belongs to the rhyme group "stream-seem,"[22] and thus its presumptive modifying power over "sight" and "light" is further weakened. Having been spread too thin, the glory is only faintly visible. To parrot the inescapable question of Wordsworth interpretation, does the glory come from without or within?

Since the glory is now absent, and since it is recalled by an *ubi sunt* that is also, at the same time, an indirect invocation, this question is doubly difficult. To disregard for the moment where the glory comes from, even though that is the motivating question of any ode and plainly an important one, it may profit to go on asking what it is. Here an answer is forthcoming. The glory is an "Apparel," a dressy appearance that is Wordsworth's equivalent of Gray's tapestries and Collins's veils.[23] It is worn by every common sight as a covering for nakedness: "not in utter nakedness, / But trailing clouds of glory do we come." The glory screens out the indecent as well as the quotidian commonness of things and poses an obstacle to the kindness of natural yearning. Perhaps it is already clear where the glory comes from. Once more the Fall proves indeed fortunate, as it lends a needful covering to an original state of nakedness. In this poem death is not only the context of intimation, but also, it seems, the context of intimacy. By allusion to Collins's "sallow Autumn fills thy lap with

leaves," Wordsworth's imagery of mortality turns autumnal long before his evening ear takes command of the ode. "Earth fills her lap
with pleasures of her own" is a covering of Eve's nakedness that
unites the pleasures of life and the glory of afterlife in a common
veil. Man *wears* "Earth" even before we are told that he is her
inmate, exchanging as he grows up "the glories he hath known" for
new apparel.

If we compare the mortally colored imagery of the celestial that
the adult remembers from the time of glad animal movement in early
childhood with the otherworldliness of the celestial that he remembers
from the time of solipsism in later childhood, we can see the distance
between two glories, between the festive dress of a young world and
the phantom light of interstellar vacancy. Concerning this second
glory: Wordsworth could love a clear sky, and in the second stanza
we cannot yet feel uneasy about the sky's undress, as "The Moon
doth with delight / Look round her when the heavens are bare." But
the region of the Moon is absolutely separate from that of man, and
her delight cannot be merged with Earth's pleasures. Later, when
pleasure has palled, the bare sky will mirror a blank misgiving. In
"Dejection," Coleridge will seem to narrow this gulf by giving the
moon her own nimbus from the outset, "a swimming phantom light,"
and he will transfer Wordsworth's earthly pleasure to the sphere of
the moon's delight: "I see the old moon in her lap." In "Dejection,"
as we shall see, it is not the immortal skies that are lonely, but the
poet.

Both "Dejection" and the Intimations Ode sometimes touch upon
subjects that are too intimate to remain within a shareable sphere of
reference. For both poets, but for Wordsworth especially, the daemon
of an ode is an unreconstructed and thus far "strong" egoism. What
poet before Wordsworth admitted to being relieved and made strong
by his own timely utterance? As we have seen, Akenside read Milton
for inspiration, Gray Spenser, and so on. Although the position of
the sounding cataracts between "I am strong" and "No more shall
grief of mine" might indicate that Wordsworth has found his timely
utterance in Revelation,[24] one feels that too many more griefs succeed
this one to confirm any gospel. Earlier odes have mottoes chosen
from the classics; Wordsworth's utterance and his motto (starting in
1815) are all his own. The drawback of this strength is that Wordsworth's allusion to his own uncanonized oeuvre leaves the ordering
of his present text in a muddle. It is not possible to say with certainty
what Wordsworth's timely utterance was, nor what his thought of
grief was. But if a note on the subject in Wordsworth's own hand
were discovered, that would be a positive harm. In the text, the grief
and the thought are significant because they are unspecified. They
remain simply implied presences, emblems of what Coleridge termed

the "flux and reflux" of the whole poem. They are impure signifiers—
symptoms. Perhaps their presence in the text can be understood,
then, as a near-utterance about the idea of repression, about the
apparel of the repressed that veils an ode. To refer again to the
Fenwick note, what Wordsworth most vividly remembers about writing his ode is frustration. He needed a fulcrum, a prior content
without which his form, "the world of his own mind" (*Poetical Works*
4; 464), would follow its own irresolute course. The preexistence
myth provides inadequate leverage, but the timely utterance, because
unspecified, can stand behind and beneath the text as a buried
originary voice.

One may wonder about the deference of sound to sight in this
ode,[25] noting that elsewhere Wordsworth explored aural areas that
have more profound mystical roots than does the (mainly Western)
visionary idea. Like Dionysus "disguised as man" in Euripides, this
written ode travels daily farther from the East because pure voice
would be naked, a too immediate experience of "God, who is our
home." This is the experience an ode cannot risk. The prophetic
child must be "deaf" in order to read "the eternal deep." The visual
blankness of eternity is also an "Eternal Silence," and sound is
relegated wholly to "our noisy years": birdsong, the labor that syn-
copates the vernal heartbeat,[26] the outer-ance of speech that relieves
solitude, the trumpets sounding from the Salvator-fringes of the re-
generate landscape, the shouts of happiness. After this outburst, there
are no more sounds until the pygmy turns actor; however, even his
"song" is not sung but written down, "a little plan or chart."

Sound resonates beyond the setting for pastoral joy only once
in the poem, at the end of the ninth stanza, in the song of praise
for the adult's recollection of the child's recollections:

> Hence in a season of calm weather,
>   Though inland far we be,
> Our souls have sight of that immortal sea
>   Which brought us hither,
>   Can in a moment travel thither,
> And see the Children sport upon the shore,
> And hear the mighty waters rolling evermore.

This magnificent passage, the pivot (or fulcrum) of the poem, culminates in another unspecified utterance. It is also the key to Wordsworth's version of Milton's resurrected Lycidas, the "genius of the
shore." It *is* a pivotal passage, yet it is not easy to discover a context
for it. It is not clear by what logic the celestial descent has become
an aquatic emergence; nor is it clear, though we happily accept the
transit, just how we are carried from sight to sound.

I have suggested that the genealogical phase of the ode before

Wordsworth leaves out, or tries to leave out, the Deluge, which appears in nearly every scriptural cosmogony in the history of culture and recurs in Jung's belief that the materials of the dream-work are oceanic.[27] Until his personal tragedy concerning a death by water in 1805, Wordsworth, unlike his predecessors in the ode, was a willing voyager in strange seas of thought and loved sonorous waters. The dream-vision of *Prelude* V (88–97) offers up the sort of apocalyptic "Ode" that Wordsworth could have been expected to write:

> "This," said he,
> "Is something of more worth;" and at the word
> Stretched forth the shell, so beautiful in shape,
> In colour so resplendent, with command
> That I should hold it to my ear. I did so,
> And heard that instant in an unknown tongue,
> Which yet I understood, articulate sounds,
> A loud prophetic blast of harmony;
> An Ode, in passion uttered, which foretold
> Destruction to the children of the earth
> By deluge, now at hand.

One might then certainly expect the Intimations Ode, considering its subject, also to leave the shore for deeper waters. But the "Waters" at line 14 are merely lacustrine, and the jolly "sea" of "Land and sea" (30) is, one suspects, only present for the sake of rhyme. For the most part, the movement of this ode is inland and downward, until it comes to rest in a place that is "too deep for tears." Traditionally, the ode takes an aspiring flight but fears Phaeton's plunge, and with partial success avoids the risk of drowning by curbing its flight. Wordsworth's ode bows to this tradition, with the result, however, that this passage, with its seaward direction, seems isolated from the argument of which the passage is meant to be the center.

"Lycidas," not an ode but an elegy, makes room for a drowning. Milton recalls a happy pastoral setting, "by fountain, shade, and rill," to which Wordsworth alludes in lines 1 and 189; but with the death of its pastor, the *locus amoenus* will have fallen silent except for mournful echoes unless Milton can reanimate the strain. Wordsworth's first revision of "Lycidas," then, is to fill his own pastoral site with noise and to locate the noise only there, hoping to imply that the silence of higher places is preferable. However, the errancy of his intimations points to some awareness on his part that Milton was right, as was Sophocles in the *Coloneus:* if the vital and benign genius cannot be given a home within the budding grove, its possible course among the stars can offer little consolation. "Lycidas" announces the return of the genius from water to land through the intercession of one who could not drown. Wordsworth describes the return of memory from land to the shoreline where genius had been left behind.

Or rather, where genius *appears* to have been left behind. Wordsworth's ninth stanza, with its key in "Not for these," begins to look homeward, back toward the starting places of the ode that will be reviewed in stanzas ten and eleven. Wordsworth's journey to the shore begins this review of inland places because, in fact, the journey only seems to have been undertaken. He is and remains inland far; it is only in moments of vacancy, seasons "of calm weather,"[28] that he counteracts his fear of the eternal abyss with memories of "sport" among a community of children who have nothing in common with the solitude of infinite space. The children emerge *from* the "immortal sea," happy to be born, and steadily move inland themselves toward the pleasures of the Shepherd-boy.[29] Immured in our adulthood, our souls seem to want something else, something other than what children want, when they listen to the conch shells of their inner ear. They zoom directly back to the sea itself, and only afterward notice the children playing with their backs to the water. Unlike the ignorant child, the soul of the adult has intimations of death; they are not quite the intimations he was meant to have, but they still induce a state of mind that is preferable, as Jonson's Cary-Morison Ode also insisted, to "listlessness" and "mad endeavour."

The soul's hearing death for the first time, then, is an intimation of voice, of aural immediacy, not as a beginning but as an end. The children's audition, which is permitted by the grammar if not by the parallelism of syntax, is quite different; it is not nostalgic but strains forward, and smooths their passage from the deafening roar of death, which they no longer hear as such, to the companionable shouts of their coming joy. Lycidas our Shepherd-boy is not dead, because the morning star of his return replaces the evening star of his having sunk elsewhere. For Wordsworth's Child we rejoice, as in "Lycidas," because he has been born, not because he was previously drowned:

> The Soul that rises with us, our life's Star,
> Hath had elsewhere its setting.
> And cometh from afar.

The child has returned, fortunately, to be Nature's Pastor once more. His "vision splendid" arises from his own glorious birth, when Heaven is no distant bareness of the sky but an immediate environment that "lies about us in our infancy."

"Our birth is but a sleep and a forgetting," the line that precedes those just quoted, wavers uncertainly between two famous counterstatements about life and death in *Measure for Measure*. One of them, Claudio's "Ay, but to die, and go we know not where" (III. i. 118–31), is worth quoting at length, not only because it juxtaposes the two prisons of both *Hamlet* and the Intimations Ode, but also because it expresses the fear that Wordsworth's frostlike weight of life is, in fact, a condition of the afterlife as well:

> or to reside
> In thrilling region of thick-ribbèd ice,
> To be imprisoned in the viewless winds
> And blown with restless violence round about
> The pendant world. . . .
> . . . .
> The weariest and most loathèd worldly life
> That age, ache, penury, and imprisonment
> Can lay on Nature is a paradise
> To what we fear of death.

This is the body of imagery that Wordsworth's shadowy recollections cannot dissolve, however much his ode may aspire to the other-worldly viewpoint of the Duke's counsel about sleep and forgetting:

> Thou hast nor youth nor age,
> But as it were an after-dinner sleep
> Dreaming on both.
>   (III. i. 32–34)

The Duke's utterance is not strong enough to be "timely," though; it is merely Stoical, and itself contains the repetition that negates transcendence: "thy best of rest is sleep, / And that thou oft provok'st, yet grossly fear'st / Thy death, which is no more" (III. i. 17–19). Among these less than reassuring attitudes Wordsworth must himself have felt compelled to waver, "when having closed the mighty Shakespeare's page, / I mused, and thought, and felt, in solitude" (*Prelude* VII: 484–85).

The conclusion seems inescapable that Wordsworth's Intimations are best forgotten; and forgetting is what the last two stanzas in effect achieve. Stanzas ten and eleven seek images for the continuity that was hoped for in "The Rainbow":

> The Child is father of the Man;
> And I could wish my days to be
> Bound each to each by natural piety.

In these lines, the wish for existential continuity is weakened by having been spoken conditionally, and also by the impious bid for autochthonous independence of being that here and elsewhere undercuts Wordsworth's homage to the adult father.[30] Perhaps these slight discords are enough to warn us that an ode for which such a passage is the best available motto will not be smooth going; but they are nothing to the discords that any ambitious presentational ode will engender in itself. In any case, the poet's days are bound each to each at the close of the Great Ode in an altogether "natural" way that is *pius* if not pious; but his piety is *not* founded in any visionary or eschatological intimation.

From his and Coleridge's Conversation Poems, perhaps from the Meditative Lyric of the seventeenth century,[31] and certainly from instinct, Wordsworth had formed the habit of concluding with a benediction, which typically, as in "Tintern Abbey" or "Dejection," transmits the boon of gladness in nature to a beloved friend who is less burdened than the poet with the heavy weight of adulthood. The hesitation with which the pronoun "my" is introduced in "The Rainbow" may itself imply the replacement of the self by another in a benediction: *my* days and perceptions may prove disjointed, but perhaps yours will not. So in stanza ten of his ode, Wordsworth confers his generalized blessing on unself-conscious youth from the detached and newly acquiescent standpoint of "thought." However successful the tone of this blessing may be thought to be, it must still be stressed that there is no scope for benediction in the cult hymns after which odes model themselves. The ending of a hymn leads by nature in quite another direction, toward a petition. In a hymn the petition may possibly involve the blessing of others,[32] but in an ode it is primarily for the self, a request that the poet's egotistically sublime vocation be confirmed. Not just Wordsworth's but nearly all thoughtful odes, however, swerve away from the formula of petition toward benediction and other forms of self-sacrifice that are all essentially vocational disclaimers. At least in this last respect, then, the endings of hymns and odes are similar.

Wordsworth's heart no longer leaps up; rather it goes out, in "primal sympathy," to others, to the whole sphere of those Creatures whom Coleridge's Ancient Mariner learned to "bless" (see the Intimations Ode, 1:37). Henceforth there is little to be heard of the immortality theme and nothing of substance about the "one delight" (192) of joyous childhood that the poet has now "relinquished"— pretending, with the active verb, to have given it up voluntarily. What now appears, rather, is the severer compassion of the Eton College Ode, the "Ode to Adversity," and Wordsworth's "Ode to Duty": "the soothing thoughts that spring / Out of human suffering." As in the "Ode to Duty," the healing power of Nature is itself now hallowed as routine, as Nature's "more habitual sway," and the sober coloring of the clouds no longer needs to serve as a repressive veil, since the troubled mysticism of the poem is now silenced, apparently by choice. Until the final line of Wordsworth's evening ending there is no hint of immortality, no effort even to carry over or restate the phantom imagery of immortality. Natural piety in these lines is a secular reverence moved by the pathos of mutability:

> The clouds that gather round the setting sun
> Do take a sober coloring from an eye
> That hath kept watch o'er man's mortality;
> Another race hath been, and other palms are won.
> Thanks to the human heart by which we live,
> Thanks to its tenderness, its joys and fears,
> To me the meanest flower that blows can give
> Thoughts that do often lie too deep for tears.

This is a grave ending, full of allusions to Gray: to the "race" and the "fearful joy" of the Eton College Ode, to the frail blossoms in the Death of a Favorite Cat. Also, as in so many great odes, there is a final "gathering" of the mind's humbled thoughts now rendered as congregational homilies, a gathering that willingly stands far below the cosmic gathering of clouds or twittering swallows. A conclusion of this sort is a service rendered, a graveside hymn to man's mortality, without intimation but with something that would seem to achieve collective intimacy were it not for "To me," a last gift of special knowledge awarded to the self by the odic voice.[33] To the famous question, "Where is it now, the glory and the dream?" we may answer in behalf of Wordsworth's "me": Aye, where is it? Mortality alone has its music.

Intimations apart, then, the question remains, Which is better, childhood or being grown up? It may be of use to measure the Intimations Ode in this respect against a passage from "In Desolation," by a poet whom Wordsworth would have been less than human not to have reperused attentively in the summer of 1803, his new acquaintance Sir George Beaumont's Renaissance ancestor Sir John Beaumont:

> If solid vertues dwell not but in paine,
> I will not wish that golden age againe,
> Because it flowed with sensible delights
> Of heavenly things. . . .
> (Chalmers, X, 25)

Like Beaumont, Wordsworth is never quite easy about the glad animal movements of his little pagan selves, though it would be an exaggeration to insist that his nativity ode exorcises them; early childhood, for him, is simply incomplete. The later stages of childhood, however intense, are already projected by present memory toward the double imprisonment of the adult, the state of being shuttled to and fro between the burden and the absence of the flesh; but the difference remains that late childhood lacks the solace of adulthood's deliberative resources. At bottom, as it seems to me, the speaker of the Intimations Ode prefers himself grown up, or just as he is, in fact, at the moment.

Wordsworth's choice of the Pindaric format would mean that he could scarcely have composed the poem on his customary walks, chanting aloud. In attempting the vocality of an ode, Wordsworth would have needed to stay at his desk, weighing meters and blocking stanzas in writing. In facing this paradox, a highly relevant passage may be enlisted from Jacques Derrida: "Writing is that forgetting of the self, that exteriorization, the contrary of the interiorizing memory, or the *Erinnerung* that opens the history of the spirit."[34] Wordsworth's ode is more crucially a forgetting than an attempted reconstitution of any earlier self; it celebrates forgetting in celebrating birth, its own birth ultimately, and does so by entering a poetic shape that imitates the constant discontinuity of being alive and suffering. "Pain," says Nietzsche, "always raises the question about its origin while pleasure is inclined to stop with itself without looking back."[35] Childhood has no myth of childhood, and no fund of suffering to be projected as a benediction. (It goes without saying, I hope, that concerning actual childhood these assertions are probably false; we are speaking here, though, of what the overstrained figures of memory can know about a child's memory in an ode.) The failing powers of adulthood are necessary, like the fading of Shelley's coal and the secondariness of Coleridge's secondary imagination, for the dissemination of voice in the writing of poetry, which starts, like a mortal stroke, as a severance from the Logos, and then, over that very fissure, takes its stand against the "severing of our loves."

IV

To the last point of vision, and beyond,
Mount, daring warbler!—that love-prompted strain

. . . .

Thrills not the less the bosom of the plain:
Yet might'st thou seem, proud privilege! to sing
All independent of the leafy spring.
            —"A Morning Exercise" (1828)

The Intimations Ode is uncharacteristic of Wordsworth. It is a poem that appears openly to espouse the attitudes that partisans of the sophisticated Wordsworth take to be important but only covertly present in his poetry (longing for apocalypse, hatred of nature), but that actually favors, presumably against the poet's design, the wise naturalism that partisans of the Simple Wordsworth take to be everywhere intended: faith in and through nature without clear revelation, whatever "faith" in this context may mean. The Great Ode loses the power of grounding spiritual knowledge in physical experience, the power which had made "Tintern Abbey" a less confused poem, "well pleased to recognize"

> In nature and the language of the sense
> The anchor of my purest thoughts, the nurse,
> The guide, the guardian of my heart, and soul
> Of all my moral being.

This passage, which redeems even the troublesome foster mother of the Intimations Ode, represents what can with most propriety be called Wordsworth's "unified vision," though needless to say there are rifts in the ground near the Wye as well. Speaking only of "vicious" poetry in his "Essay, Supplementary" (1815) to the 1800 Preface, Wordsworth identifies the quality of "confusion" that Cleanth Brooks was the first to emphasize in the Intimations Ode itself: "the realities of the Muse are but shows, and . . . her liveliest excitements are raised by transient shocks of conflicting feeling and successive assemblages of contradictory thoughts."[36] Wordsworth seems to have felt that bad poetry is full of contradictions in terms—oxymorons—yet his own most contradictory poem is his Great Ode. In these concluding remarks I want to reconsider the oxymoron "natural piety" from the standpoint of Wordsworth's lesser odes[37] in order to show that the confusion of all his odes is peculiar to what he would have termed the "mould" in which they are cast (1815 Preface).

It may be remarked, though, before turning to other odes, that Wordsworth could always handle intimations of immortality more positively in poems that were not odes. Unless "The Mad Monk" was written by Wordsworth himself,[38] the clearest forerunner of the Intimations Ode (as of "A Slumber did my spirit seal"), doubtless printed as the first poem in the 1849 edition for this reason, is not an ode but a quieter sort of poem, "Written in Very Early Youth":

> a Slumber seems to steal
> O'er vale, and mountain, and the starless sky.
> Now, in this blank of things, a harmony,
> Home-felt, and home-created, comes to heal
> That grief for which the senses still supply
> Fresh food.

This passage affirms a "blank" vision without being troubled about its blankness; it is quite possibly referred to directly in the compromised affirmation of the Great Ode, lines 145–51, where a blank misgiving condemns the eternally dead to roll round earth's diurnal course with shadows. Another convincingly positive treatment of "this blank of things" appears in an untitled poem of 1800, in which a Solitary forsaken by his beloved exclaims:

> I look—the sky is empty space;
> I know not what I trace;
> But when I cease to look, my hand is on my heart.

This is indeed an intimation, lesser than, but comparable to, the moments of surprised revelation in lassitude that are featured in *The Prelude.* An intimation thus suggestive cannot appear in an ode because its quiet tenor openly founds knowledge in ignorance and avoids afflatus. Perhaps this distinction alone is enough to indicate that an ode can never be characteristic of Wordsworth.

Wordsworth's odes and ode-like poems constantly reject mysterious knowledge. The apostrophe called "To H. C. Six Years Old" (1802), for instance, offers an unambiguous view of the semi-transparent "glory" that confuses the Great Ode:

> O Thou! whose fancies from afar are brought;
> Who of thy words dost make a mock apparel,
> And fittest for unutterable thought . . .

Here the "glory," like Wordsworth's "home-created" harmony of 1786, is the opaque apparel by expression of sights both common and uncommon. "To a Skylark" (1805) summarizes without reversing the values of the Great Ode: strength of song in despondency, joy divine, the "banqueting place in the sky," "Joy and jollity," and the "hope for higher raptures, when life's day is done." This slight poem, which may play in the background of Keats's Nightingale Ode, petitions the bird to "Lift me, guide me, till I find / That spot which seems so to thy mind," but then admits failure, lacking as it does "the wings of a Faery," and at last reposes solely in hope.

In "To the Cuckoo" (23–26 March 1802), which plays in the background of Shelley's Skylark Ode, the poet asks, "shall I call thee Bird, / Or but a wandering Voice?" Clearly the latter, since only when invisible does the bird bring back childhood; the poet listens, "till I do beget / That golden time again." This poem, like the Great Ode, deprives spiritual knowledge of any material ground:

> O blessèd Bird! the earth we pace
> Again appears to be
> An unsubstantial, faery place;
> That is fit home for Thee!

Metric stress drives home the point: for thee, but not for me, and never for both of us at once. Only a much later bird poem, now fully shackled by the sense of "Duty" that overrides an ode's wish for immediacy, can return, though weakly, to the balanced tropes of earthbound freedom that sustain "Tintern Abbey." "To a Skylark" (1825; very possibly written in response to Shelley's "Skylark") concludes with the sort of nonvisionary emblem of continuity that characterizes the later Wordsworth: "Type of the wise who soar, but never roam: / True to the kindred points of Heaven and Home!" Here Donne's compass is lamentably overstretched, as Wordsworth's figure pays homage to the elastic metaphysical grounding that was available to Donne but is now unavailable, given the dualism on which the dialectic of presence and absence in an ode depends.

In the "Vernal Ode" (1817), a lumbering Pindaric, a "Stranger" descends from the sky and is compared to "the sun, / When it reveals, in evening majesty, / Features half lost amid their own pure light." Hence we are not surprised at his apparel: "there the Stranger stood alone; / Fair as a gorgeous Fabric of the East." This angel then delivers a homily to the harp that exactly recalls the dilemma of perspective in the Intimations Ode; what should have been a condescending account of mortality by an Immortal takes itself by surprise and gives way to envy of the lesser condition:

> Mortals, rejoice! The very angels quit
> Their mansions unsusceptible of change,
> Amid your pleasant bowers to sit,
> And through your sweet vicissitudes to range!

This passage is yet further sullied by its evocation of the tarnished angels (as interpretations of Genesis 6 often made them out to be) who wooed "the daughters of men" before the Flood. The poet tries in vain to undo what the Stranger, perhaps one of those angels himself, has done, and hopes to evoke a "golden time again" by studying the providential anatomy of the bee. But since that time *has*, after all, departed, man's intimations of any higher state are now a mockery, and the angels are perhaps a little too cozy when they appear even in man's least postlapsarian memories:

> We were not mocked with glimpse and shadow then,
> Bright Seraphs mixed familiarly with men;
> And earth and stars composed a universal heaven!

Nothing could confess more clearly what was missing from the "glimpse and shadow" of Wordsworth's earlier intimations.

The last line of the "Vernal Ode," like that of the 1825 Skylark poem, effects a clumsy and confessedly conjectural liaison of ground and sky that is amplified, again within the pleasing chains of Duty, in the long ode "On the Power of Sound" (1828):

> Ye wandering Utterances, has earth no scheme,
> No scale of moral music—to unite
> Powers that survive but in the faintest dream
> Of memory?—O that ye might stoop to bear
> Chains, such precious chains of sight
> As laboured minstrelsies through ages wear!
> O for a balance fit the truth to tell
> Of the Unsubstantial, pondered well!

This passage concedes the necessary failure of vocal poetry to unite the material and the immaterial worlds in the single liberating prison of a secular scripture, a minstrelsy "laboured" as writing but still not absent from vocal sources. The ode concludes hymnically, as the poet defers to a single and inimitable Maker, denying once and for all the priority of vision—which is nevertheless the only intuitive sense at the disposal of man, bounded as he is by space and time:

> A Voice to Light gave Being,
> To Time, and Man his earth-born chronicler;
> A Voice shall finish doubt and dim foreseeing,
> And sweep away life's visionary stir;
>
> . . . .
>
> O Silence! are Man's noisy years
> No more than moments of thy life?
>
> . . . .
>
> No! though earth be dust
> And vanish, though the heavens dissolve, her stay
> Is in the WORD, that shall not pass away.[39]

This poem is yet another critique of the hopes that Wordsworth now imagines his Intimations Ode to have embodied. His critique leads him to give up the idea of an ode altogether and to welcome in its stead the idea of a hymn. Wordsworth plainly understood a hymn to be a collective service, inspired only by faith in common and commonly shared truth. His two "hymns," "Hymn for the Boatmen" (1820), which begins "JESU! bless our slender boat" and ends "All our hope is placed in thee; / Miserere Domine!" and his "Labourer's Noon-Day Hymn" (1834), are both written as if for rote use by the unpoetical faithful. In Wordsworth, as in most other ode writers, the idea of a hymn is confined to the end of an ode. So "To the Small Celandine" (30 April 1802) ends by pledging a duty: "I will sing, as doth behove / Hymns in praise of what I love"; and since this flower or its equivalent is the "meanest flower" of the Great Ode, the decision in that poem's close for the renunciations of hymnody may be seen yet more clearly.[40]

In "Composed upon an Evening of Extraordinary Beauty and Splendour" (1818), called an "ode" in Wordsworth's headnote, aural childhood and an obscurely visionary present once more appear contrasted. The "Time"

> when field and watery cove
> With modulated echoes rang

is now supplanted by

> This silent spectacle—the gleam—
> The shadow—and the peace supreme!

On the present evening, the speaker claims to have had an unqualified renewal of Joy, at which he is too surprised not to wonder peevishly about the purpose of the experience: "This glimpse of glory, why renewed?"[41] To prepare him (he may suspect) for some unappareled horror? Or is it rather that he has grown accustomed to his earthly prison, to the "precious chains of sight" required for "laboured minstrelsies," so well accustomed in fact that he actively resents the recurrence of the boundless, of the unutterable sublime that mocks the ever-narrowing boundaries of his craft? Plainly he considers the Intimations Ode, not this one, to have been peevish, and he now accepts visionary loss as a wise Providence protecting him, perhaps, from a dangerous and heretical possession: "Oh, let thy Grace remind me of the light, / Full early lost, and fruitlessly deplored." The Great Ode's lament as much as its petition, he now feels, was fruitlessly undertaken for what already, in "Peele Castle" (1805), he had called "the gleam, / The light that never was."

If, as we now have seen, the dualism of a Wordsworthian ode is given as part of its "mould," so that its oxymorons cannot be sustained or illustrated without turning hymnic, we may reconsider "natural piety" as a gloss on the Intimations Ode, assuming that the oxymoron can be resolved only in ceasing to be a contradiction in terms.[42] Perhaps a literary source for a piety that *is* "natural" can be suggested: *The Aeneid*, by the author from whom Wordsworth took his punning and evasive first motto, *paulo majora canamus*. Wordsworth's sober coloring is quite Virgilian; it consists in the discovery of personal strength through reverence for an absent father who can *only* be revered in strength when he is absent. Wordsworth's tears (still tears, though "too deep" for them) are tears for the passing of *things* in their gay "apparel." In the conversion of spiritual loss to earthly sympathy, Wordsworth's Great Ode stages its limited triumph—and triumph of limits. The watch it keeps over mortality betrays its calling but recovers humanity. The moment when the ode writer crosses from the heroism of *pius Aeneas* to the profounder but far more melancholy heroism of *pater Aeneas*, having left the originary father forever among the Shades, is also the moment of relieved self-conception that purifies the earthly nature of Aeneas's mother, Venus.

Notes

1. Earl Wasserman, *The Subtler Language: Critical Readings of Neoclassic and Romantic Poems* (Baltimore: Johns Hopkins University Press, 1959), p. 11. The phrase is unfortunate, perhaps, since *kosmos* and *taxis* are synonyms; but that redundancy may be useful, on the other hand, for showing the fitness of things for the outlook in question.

2. See chapter 5 of the *Categories* in *The Basic Works of Aristotle,* ed. Richard McKeon (New York: Random House, 1941), p. 9.

3. *The Prelude or Growth of a Poet's Mind,* ed. Ernest de Selincourt and Helen Darbishire (Oxford: Clarendon Press, 1959), p. 525 (quoted by the editors from an early notebook, and closely related to *Prelude* 2: 215–21 [1805, 1850]).

4. As Paul de Man has pointed out with respect to the Coleridgean symbol, which is meant to have the "structure . . . of the synecdoche," Coleridge in fact deprives the symbol of "the materiality that had been used to distinguish it from allegory" by referring it to a transcendent totality ("The Rhetoric of Temporality," *Interpretation: Theory and Practice,* ed. Charles S. Singleton [Baltimore: Johns Hopkins University Press, 1969], pp. 176–77). On the symbol as synecdoche, "assuming a sort of *participation mystique,*" see also Angus Fletcher, *Allegory: The Theory of a Symbolic Mode* (Ithaca: Cornell University Press, 1964), p. 17. The reader will be startled to find the "symbol" stressed in a discussion of Wordsworth; I have in mind merely the totality of reference or resonance, featured in his work as much as in Coleridge's, that is meant to supervene "puny boundaries."

5. Frances Ferguson, who has many valuable things to say on this subject, quotes Crabb Robinson's remark that the 1815 classifications were "partly subjective, partly objective" (*Wordsworth: Language as Counter-Spirit* [New Haven: Yale University Press, 1977] p. 37).

6. *Marxism and Form: Twentieth-Century Dialectical Theories of Literature* (Princeton: Princeton University Press, 1974), p. 327.

7. My text for Wordsworth's poetry will be *Wordsworth's Poetical Works,* 5 vols., ed. Ernest de Selincourt (Oxford: Clarendon Press, 1969; hereafter referred to by volume and page as *Poetical Works*).

8. What is novel is the refinement, not the topic. Memory is a Pindaric topic as early as Congreve's "Daughters of Memory" (1706), and the mid-neighteenth-century lyrists wrote odes to Memory nearly as a matter of course. The association of the lyric with the past (and with childhood) is common to many of the tripartite German *Gattungsunterscheidungen,* most notably those of Heidegger and Emil Staiger. See René Wellek, "Genre Theory, the Lyric, and 'Erlebnis,'" *Festschrift für Richard Alewyn* (Cologne: Böhlau-Verlag, 1967), p. 400. Only Käte Hamburger, in fact, with whom Wellek undertakes to disagree, associates the lyric with the *present* on the grounds that it is the transcribed experience of an "Ich-Origo" ("Die lyrische Gattung," *Die Logik der Dichtung,* 2nd ed. [Stuttgart: Ernst Klett Verlag, 1968], p. 188). I follow Hamburger in proposing my notion of the self-constitution of an ode. (See also her distinction [pp. 192–93] between the "Gemeinde-Ich" of the hymn and the "Ich-Origo" of what I am calling the ode.)

9. This is not to disagree with Thomas McFarland, who says that *all* lyrics are evening lyrics, and that "the ultimate poetic theme is the elegiac theme. Great poems are monuments to our lost selves" ("Poetry and the Poem: The Structure of Poetic Content," *Literary Theory and Structure,* ed. Frank Brady, et al. [New Haven: Yale University Press, 1973], p. 104). The past and the past self in the ode, though, are as transparent as shadows.

10. See Abrams, "Structure and Style in the Greater Romantic Lyric," in F. W. Hilles and Harold Bloom, eds., *From Sensibility to Romanticism* (New York: Oxford University Press, 1965), p. 527.

11. Cleanth Brooks pioneered this reputation in *The Well-Wrought Urn* (1947; reprint ed., New York: Harvest Books, 1975), p. 125. A. Harris Fairbanks has suggested that "ambiguity is inherent in the form of the Romantic ode" ("The Form of Coleridge's Dejection Ode," *PMLA* 90 [1976]: 881).

12. This most odic of moments is what justifies Leo Spitzer in saying, "According

to the pattern fixed by Pindar, an ode must be rhapsodic, since this genre in contrast to others calls for the perpetuation, by the work of art, of the poet's original fervor" *(Linguistics and Literary History* [New York: Russell & Russell, 1962], p. 207).

13. Appropriately identified by Ferguson as "the classical *locus amoenus"* *(Wordsworth*, p. 108).

14. *The Myth of the Birth of the Hero*, pp. 65–96. Several critics have noticed the folkloric material in the fifth stanza; Jared R. Curtis has inferred from the Earth's substitute status that she is probably to be imagined as an old nurse (*Wordworth's Experiments with Tradition: The Lyric Poems of 1802* [Ithaca: Cornell University Press, 1971], p. 131).

15. See Lionel Trilling, "Wordsworth and the Iron Time," in *Wordsworth: A Collection of Critical Essays*, ed. M. H. Abrams (Englewood Cliffs, N.J.: Prentice-Hall, 1972), on the consequences of the sexual repression effected by Wordsworth's logic of the "unitary reality." Barbara Garlitz explains the appeal of the ode as an appeal to an age-old cultural belief that conception is a divine gift ("The Immortality Ode: Its Cultural Progeny," *Studies in English Literature* 6 [1966]: 648).

16. See the remarks on this anomaly by Abbie F. Potts, "The Spenserian and Miltonic Influences in the Immortality Ode and The Rainbow," *Studies in Philology* (1932): 221, and Ferguson, *Wordsworth*, p. 119.

17. Lionel Trilling, *The Liberal Imagination: Essays on Literature and Society* (Garden City, N.Y.: Anchor Books, 1953), p. 127.

18. In an argument strongly opposed to my own, Florence G. Marsh takes this passage for a transcendentally affirmative point of departure: "Wordsworth's *Ode: Obstinate Questionings," Studies in Romanticism* 5 (1965–67): 219–30. As Curtis points out (*Wordsworth's Experiments*, p. 133), the appositions in the passage were heaped on sometime between 1804 and 1807, thus only deepening its ambivalence (I would say) in underlining its importance. For troubled readings of the passage that are related to mine, see: Helen Regueiro, *The Limits of Imagination: Wordsworth, Yeats, and Stevens* (Ithaca: Cornell University Press, 1976), p. 69; Ferguson, *Wordsworth*, p. 123; Geoffrey Hartman, *Wordsworth's Poetry, 1787–1814* (New Haven: Yale University Press, 1964), p. 276; G. Wilson Knight, *The Starlit Dome: Studies in the Poetry of Vision* (New York: Barnes & Noble, 1960), p. 41.

19. There are two fine articles on memory's loss of immediacy in this poem: Stuart M. Sperry, Jr., "From 'Tintern Abbey' to the 'Intimations Ode': Wordsworth and the Function of Memory," *Wordsworth Circle* 1, no. 2 (1970): 40–49; and Kenneth R. Johnston, "Recollecting Forgetting: Forcing Paradox to the Limit in the 'Immortality Ode,' " *Wordsworth Circle* 2, no. 2 (1971): 59–64. I am surprised, however, to find Johnston (pp. 61–62) reading the "obstinate questionings" as a forgetting not of sensation but of immortality. Elswhere Johnston himself quotes a passage from *The Recluse* (1. 1. 781–83) that could gloss this one against his own reading ("The Idiom of Vision," *New Perspectives on Coleridge and Wordsworth*, ed. Geoffrey Hartman [New York: Columbia University Press, 1972], p. 2). Paul de Man puts the relation of memory and absence dialectically in saying, "nostalgia can only exist when the transcendental presence is forgotten" ("Intentional Structure of the Romantic Image," in Harold Bloom, ed., *Romanticism and Consciousness*, [New York: W. W. Norton, 1970], p. 69).

20. Cf. E. D. Hirsch, *Wordsworth and Schelling: A Typological Study of Romanticism* (New Haven: Yale University Press, 1960), p. 161.

21. Mario D'Avanzo plausibly suggests *Aeneid* 6: 739–45, in "Immortality's Winds and Fields of Sleep: A Virgilian Elysium," *Wordsworth Circle* 3, no. 3 (1972): 169. See the conclusion of the present discussion.

22. This is pointed out by Brooks, *The Well-Wrought Urn*, p. 127.

23. Brooks was, I believe, the first to define the "glory" thus precisely. See ibid., pp. 127–28.

24. This is the suggestion of Geoffrey Hartman, in *The Unmediated Vision: An Interpretation of Wordsworth, Hopkins, Rilke, and Valéry* (New York: Harbinger Books, 1966), p. 41; and in *Wordsworth's Poetry*, p. 275.

25. Wordsworth's epigraph for the 1807 Intimations Ode, *paulo maiora canamus*, was also used as an epigraph in several MSS of the later ode "On the Power of Sound" (see John Hollander, "Wordsworth and the Music of Sound," in Hartman, *New Perspectives*, p. 67); the Virgilian phrase, thus conceived, would deepen the irony of the silence that pervades the present in the Intimations Ode.

26. I suspect that Wordsworth's pastoral scene owes something to a poet who shares his grounding in the Psalms, Giles Fletcher, in *Christ's Victory in Heaven*, where after Easter, with immortality now guaranteed, the lambs hear the birds "piping grief away," and begin to "dance and play" (Alexander Chalmers, *The Works of the English Poets from Chaucer to Cowper*, 23 vols. [London, 1810] 10:76). See Ferguson on "the ancient instruments provoking the lambs' dance" (*Wordsworth*, p. 110).

27. The prominence of the rainbow may suggest that it is a talisman to keep off future floods. See Kenneth R. Lincoln, "Wordsworth's Mortality Ode," *Journal of English and Germanic Philology* 71 (1972): 217. On the immanence of the Flood and its Miltonic provenance in Wordsworth, see Neil Hertz, "Wordsworth and the Tears of Adam," in Abrams, *Wordsworth*, p. 122. The Flood is still more prominent in the argument of Hartman, *The Unmediated Vision*, esp. p. 30.

28. F. W. Bateson compares Wordsworth's "calm weather" to the tranquility with which, in the "Preface," emotion is recollected, in *Wordsworth: A Reinterpretation* (London: Longmans, 1965), p. 162.

29. See John Jones's fine evocation of this passage, differing from mine, in *The Egotistical Sublime: A History of Wordsworth's Imagination* (London: Chatto & Windus, 1954), p. 96; and the equally fine discussion by W. K. Wimsatt, "The Structure of the Romantic Nature Image," *The Verbal Icon: Studies in the Meaning of Poetry* (New York: Noonday Press, 1964), pp. 114–15.

30. See Ferguson on what she calls the "heuristic language" of the poem (*Wordsworth*, p. 99); and William Heath, *Wordsworth and Coleridge: A Study of Their Literary Relations in 1801–02* (Oxford: Clarendon Press, 1970), pp. 64–65.

31. On the use of meditative formats in the Romantic Period, see Reeve Parker, *Coleridge's Meditative Art* (Ithaca: Cornell University Press, 1975).

32. See the conclusion of "To the Small Celandine" (a Poem of Fancy written in the spring of 1802) quoted later in the body of my text: "I will sing, as doth behove, / Hymns in praise of what I love!"

33. In *The Starlit Dome* (p. 38), Knight has argued that since "immortality" can simply mean "death negated," Wordsworth's ode is "a vision of life victorious," which "need have nothing to say about life-after-death."

34. Jacques Derrida, *Of Grammatology*, trans. Gayatri C. Spivak (Baltimore: Johns Hopkins Press, 1976), p. 26. Later in this work, Derrida understands the evil of writing for both Rousseau and Lévi-Strauss as the rupture of the self-presence of childhood innocence.

35. *The Gay Science*, trans. Walter Kaufmann (New York: Vintage Books), p. 86.

36. *The Prose Works of William Wordsworth*, 3 vols., ed. W. J. B. Owen and J. W. Smyser (Oxford: Clarendon Press, 1974), 3:63.

37. I shall have nothing to say of the pseudo-laureate odes of 1814–16 that crow over the fall of Napoleon; the reader is referred to Byron's immensely superior and more genuinely ode-like ode on the same subject.

38. For the fullest discussion of this possibility, see Thomas McFarland, "The Symbiosis of Coleridge and Wordsworth," *Studies in Romanticism* 11 (1972): 267–68.

39. For discussion of this passage, see Hartman, *The Unmediated Vision*, p. 41, and Hollander, "Wordsworth and the Music of Sound," p. 79.

40. As Alan Grob has pointed out, Wordsworth experimented often in the spring of 1802 with "the lyric apostrophe to nature's more familiar and common objects" ("Wordsworth's *Immortality Ode* and the Search for Identity," *ELH* 32 [1965]: 33).

41. See Hartman on this passage in *Wordsworth's Poetry*, p. 275.

42. In stressing what remains natural in "natural piety," I follow Harold Bloom, *The Visionary Company* (Garden City, N.Y.: Anchor Doubleday, 1963), p. 173.

Wordsworth's Intimations Ode and Its Epigraphs

Peter J. Manning*

At the outset of his essay on "The Immortality Ode" Lionel Trilling observes:

> Criticism, we know, must always be concerned with the poem itself. But a poem does not always exist only in itself: sometimes it has a very lively existence in its false or partial appearances. These simulacra of the actual poem must be taken into account by criticism; and sometimes, in its effort to come at the poem as it really is, criticism does well to allow the simulacra to dictate at least its opening moves.[1]

Trilling was concerned with the tradition of critical interpretations that comes to encase a canonical text, but with the Ode the encasing begins with Wordsworth himself. Who now can read the poem without an intervening consciousness of the poet's own glosses on his work, those later simulacra of its meaning: the Isabella Fenwick note of 1842–43, with its invocation of Enoch, Elijah, and Platonic myth, and its reminiscences of childhood trances of idealism, also recorded by R. P. Graves and Bonamy Price, or the 1815 letter to Catherine Clarkson explaining the poem? And who can separate the poem from the three lines from "My Heart Leaps Up" which became its epigraph only in 1815, or from its title, also added in that year, habitually shortened (as in Trilling's essay), with unexamined consequences upon our understanding, to "The Immortality Ode"?[2]

* Reprinted from *Journal of English and Germanic Philology* 82, no. 4 (October 1983). © 1983 by the Board of Trustees of the University of Illinois. Used by permission of the University of Illinois Press. An earlier version of this essay was presented to the Wordsworth-Coleridge Association at the 1980 convention of the Modern Language Association. The author thanks the organizer of the session, Professor Gene Ruoff, and the other members of the panel for encouragement and criticism.

In 1807, however, when the poem we know as "Ode: Intimations of Immortality from Recollections of Early Childhood" first appeared as the last work in *Poems in Two Volumes*, it was headed simply *Ode*, and its epigraph was "Paulo maiora canamus," taken from Virgil's fourth eclogue. If, as Wordsworth later asserted, "to the attentive and competent reader the whole sufficiently explains itself," the first reviewers appear to have been, at least by Wordsworth's standards, neither attentive nor competent. One critic thought that the poem was a second "Ode to Duty," another complained that "the reader is turned loose into a wilderness of sublimity, tenderness, bombast, and absurdity, to find out the subject as well as he can," and Jeffrey proclaimed in the *Edinburgh Review* that the ode was "beyond all doubt, the most illegible and unintelligible part of the publication. We can pretend to give no analysis or explanation of it."[3] Jeffrey noted the Virgilian motto as the "title," but noticing did not lessen his bafflement. That introduction, however, provided an interpretive signal that might have led readers to recognize the genre of the poem. I should like in this essay to explore the continuities and contrasts suggested by reading the Ode in the light cast by Virgil's poem, and to consider the effects Wordsworth brought about when he replaced the original epigraph with lines from "My Heart Leaps Up."

Virgil's fourth eclogue is an account of the birth of a wonder child ushering in a new golden race and age, with a famously provocative elision of exact historical reference. The theme appealed to Wordsworth, whose own poem offers a mythic paean to the child he once was, incorporating a nativity within it as well. The appearance of Virgil's "let's sing a nobler song" at the head of Wordsworth's poem shows, too, that the mixture of pastoral and prophetic modes accorded with the Ode's thematic interests.[4] The allusion to the eclogue, and to the rich tradition that arose from its interpretive crux of the babe as either a particular, real child or a mythic symbol, announces the puzzles of the Ode as deliberate and rooted in convention. Even the hyperbolic praise of the infant in the eighth stanza ("Thou best Philosopher . . .") that so troubled Coleridge is prepared for in the tender, comic exaggeration of Virgil's mode.

But if the eclogue was in many ways suitable to Wordsworth's purposes, he rejected its most distinctive feature. Though miraculous, Virgil's babe realizes his identity in mortal life, and matures by modeling himself on his father. Beneath the extravagance is visible a familiar pattern of psychological growth, the stages of which Virgil clearly marks:

> But first, child, earth's uncultivated gifts
> Will spring up for you . . .

Your crib itself will shower you with flowers. . . .
But when heroic praise, parental deeds
You read and come to know what manhood is,
Plains slowly will turn gold with tender grain . . .

Later, when strengthening years have made you man,
Traders will leave the sea, no sailing pine
Will barter goods: all lands will grow all things.

The prophesied golden age is concomitant with the achievement of
manhood in the paternal image: the child will rule "the world calmed
by his father's hand."

The son's relationship with his mother is equally untroubled. The
poem concludes with a striking image:

Come now, sweet boy: with smiling greet your mother
(She carried you ten long and tedious months)
Come now, sweet boy: who smiles not on a parent
Graces no god's carouse nor goddess' bed.

This tableau, its ceremonial function underlined by the repetition of
"incipe, parve puer," harmoniously unites the generations, and blends
the familial and the divine. The infant's smile is the meet repayment
of his mother's labor in his own birth, an acknowledgment of the
inextricably dependent status of his origin; in turn, however, the
smile is the passport to the world of adult sexuality, the ground that
will make possible his later active participation in the erotic life of
"gods" and "goddesses" (and so the adults appear to the child).

In affording the child such an optimistic plot and such providential
models, Virgil was actually rewriting his own precursors. As Renato
Poggioli pointed out, in placing the Golden Age in the future, "Virgil
had already paradoxically reinterpreted the most important of all
pastoral myths. While the whole of antiquity . . . had relegated the
dream of mankind's happy state to the beginning of time, Virgil here
projected that dream into the age to come."[5] Wordsworth's ode
restores the myth of antiquity, once again placing paradise at the
origin, Heaven "in our infancy."[6] This alteration is perhaps not as
absolute as it first appears, for a paradise located in the past is the
mirror image of one projected into the future.[7] The reversal, however,
alters the representation of the family and the child's development
within it.

Indeed, Virgil's idyllic portrait of a fulfilled adulthood following
easily from the child's position within the family triangle is quite
different from the tensions that pervade the situation of the child in
Wordsworth's Ode. The "growing Boy" finds himself enclosed by the
"Shades of the prison-house"; the "Youth" who still is "Nature's
Priest" is succeeded by the "Man" who perceives his "vision splen-

did" die away. Wordsworth's mythic account of the stages of human decline is followed in the seventh stanza by a satiric portrayal that is its bitter complement.[8] The "light upon him from his Father's eyes" inadequately recompenses the playing child for the loss of the "celestial light"; adult roles appear only as "parts" on a "humourous stage,' " his emulation of them no more than a self-debasing "imitation," not a process of genuine growth. His mother's love disturbs rather than comforts: he is "Fretted by sallies of his Mother's kisses."

Such a satiric dismissal of the parents, however, is enfranchising: it frees the child from any obligation to them. The previous stanza of the Ode, by defining the child's alienation as that of a "Foster-child," degrades his parents into mere foster-parents. The true home of the child is not the prison-house of mundane existence, but "else-where."[9] This family romance, however, entails its own problems, because the child is "blindly with [his] blessedness at strife," eager to assimilate into the world whose authority Wordsworth derogates. The absent, lost heritage with which he aligns himself intensifies his unease: his "Immortality" "broods" over him, "a Master o'er a Slave, / A Presence which is not to be put by."

Through its vision of transformation Virgil's poem effortlessly reconciles the roles of son and parents, pastoral harmony and heroic glory, and this world with the divine. In Wordsworth's poem these pairs are split apart, and the son is torn between two allegiances. "Oh evil day! if I were sullen / While the Earth herself is adorning," the poet confesses in the fourth stanza, and the conditional seems intended to disguise his state, and his responsibility for it, from himself: it is his own myth of otherworldly origin that converts the earth into a mere "homely nurse."

The ninth stanza brings the attempted resolution:

> Not for these I raise
> The song of thanks and praise;
> But for those obstinate questionings
> Of sense and outward things,
> Fallings from us, vanishings;
> Blank misgivings of a Creature
> Moving about in worlds not realiz'd,
> High instincts, before which our mortal Nature
> Did tremble like a guilty Thing surpriz'd.

If these childhood recollections are, as Wordsworth claimed, the core of the ode, the attempted recuperation is brilliant: the child's uncertainties are reinterpreted by the adult as "the fountain light of all our day, / . . . A master light of all our seeing." The "Fallings from us, vanishings; / Blank misgivings," however, are traces of the home elsewhere and the original abandoned self, betrayed by the child's own avid maturation. Behind Wordsworth's "High instincts, before which our mortal Nature / Did tremble like a guilty Thing surpriz'd" lies Horatio's description of Hamlet's father's ghost—"it started like a guilty thing / Upon a fearful summons"—hinting at the Oedipal contest of Shakespeare's play, the son's obligation to his absent father, his duty to punish his "foster" father/uncle and his derelict mother, his allegiance to a home in comparison to which the present one is a prison, even as Wordsworth's allegiances make the world a prison-house. "Mortal nature" would repress those allegiances, but remains troubled by the "high instincts" that are a problematic parallel to Virgil's "higher things."

The crisis the poem explicitly describes, that of the fading of the celestial light, thus discloses itself as a myth concealing another conflict, between resistance to the everyday adult world that the transformative myth reduces to sterility, and assimilation to that same world. "Listlessness" and "mad endeavour" are the alternate, depressive and manic, phases of this unresolved dilemma. The child who cooperates with his own absorption by the everyday world is not simply "blindly with [his] blessedness at strife" but seeking to escape the conflict of loyalties by burying the self in "custom" "Heavy as frost, and deep almost as life." Willful blinding is preferable to continued division.

The question "Whither is fled the visionary gleam? / Where is it now, the glory and the dream?" had forced the breaking-off of the poem in 1802. The myth of the universally vanishing vision is the first response formulated by the 1804 resumption, which approaches the question of where the vision has fled by asking where it originated. A deterministic myth, with its generalized picture of decline from infancy to manhood, thus comes into being as a consoling formulation.[11] The lament contains a comfort: it places the vision safely in the past and represents its dissolution as an inevitability rather than as a matter of individual fallibility. It is the Child, the Youth, the Man who experiences these losses, not the first-person narrator of the beginning and the very end of the poem: the "I" of the 1802 opening yields to the inclusive "he," "we," and "our" of the 1804 continuation. Thus doubly distanced—by time and by generalization—from a personal crisis, the narrator can declare his fidelity to the vision while remaining removed from its demands. Trilling's avowedly "naturalistic" interpretation of the Ode invokes a version of Freud to legitimate Wordsworth's account of maturing: for all three figures the loss is an ineluctable one. Yet before we accept as merely "true" or "natural" this movement from the "eagerness of infantine desire" to "duty and to truth," in the words of The Prelude (1805, II:25–26),[12] we might ask what purposes this presentation serves in the psychic economy of the poem.

One advantage, surely, is that the poet may mourn the loss of vision in experience, but secure it in the mind by an act of memory:

> O joy! that in our embers
> Is something that doth live,
> That nature yet remembers
> What was so fugitive!

Abrupt transitions, like this one from the melancholy prospect of the eighth to the ninth stanza, reversing bare or gloomy narratives into revelations of strength, are not uncommon in Wordsworth, and always signal moments of particular intensity. Such a discontinuity, a characteristic formal feature of the sublime ode, here manifests those urgent grounds of his imagination that remain unspoken in, otherwise effaced by, the discourse of the Ode. The last of the 1802 stanzas concluded as the Tree and the Field "speak of something that is gone" and the Pansy "Doth the same tale repeat"; in 1804 that tale of absence is redefined as memory, as the tale of the knowledge of absence, as it were. As Kenneth Johnston observed some time ago, "what Wordsworth gives thanks for in his memories of childhood is something that even then he experienced as a loss, a 'vanishing.' "[13] It is memory alone that stabilizes this experience of disappearance, which is to say that in the poem Wordsworth reconstitutes himself as an historical being. The mythic history of decline from an ahistorical origin is in turn replaced by the history of the individual, the unique experience already anticipated by the *single* tree, the *one* field, the specific Pansy. Even while declaring that "nothing can bring back the hour / Of splendour in the grass, of glory in the flower," Wordsworth affirms continuity by a transference of his own memorial powers to a nature that at once provides an external ground for the self and seems to include it: it is "Nature [that] yet remembers / What was so fugitive." What vanished can now be interpreted as the human beginning of a deepening life in time that offsets both the sublime claims of infancy and youth and the guilt of falling away.

Wordsworth thus survives to speak the elegy over his own youthful narcissism, to record the chastening of the grandiose childhood "indisposition to bend to the law of death as applying to our own particular case" that he recalled to Catherine Clarkson in the letter referred to at the beginning of this essay (*LMY*, p. 189). He survives, in fact, by speaking that elegy, by defining himself as the elegist of that narcissism. Nativity and elegy are not unrelated forms, as Milton's *On the Morning of Christ's Nativity* and still more his *Lycidas* had shown: the drowned shepherd of *Lycidas* is reborn "In the blest Kingdoms meek of joy and love." Wordsworth, through the image of life continuing in its own ashes,[14] is reborn as the poet of "the human heart by which we live," committed to the songs of his own loss, the Virgilian "puer" become the Virgil of "sunt lacrimae rerum."

The union with the past is not only consoling, it is also fecundating: "The thought of our past years in me doth *breed* / Perpetual benedictions" (emphasis added). The poet appears as a mother, inseminated by thoughts of the past and thus able to "see the Children sport upon the shore." This parent is not a foster-parent, a deceptive homely nurse, or an exigent master brooding over a slave, but a true cherisher. Wordsworth counters the sense of a killing truancy from the past by mothering it, thus converting its monitory power into beneficence: as he preserves them, so the thoughts of the past now "uphold" and "cherish" him. The vision of the Babe leaping up on its mother's arm that provoked the poet's fears of alienation in the fourth stanza is now internalized, and so becomes sustaining: hence the innocent brightness of a newborn day will be lovely yet.[15]

The contrast between this image of self-begetting fertility, however, and the sexuality of the conclusion of Virgil's poem forcefully indicates how private is the world of the Ode. Virgil's poem, addressed to a consul, looks through an image of adult sexuality to the renovation of an entire social and natural order; Wordsworth's turns inward. Absent from this tableau is the world of action and of mature sexuality of Virgil's poem—the figure of the father. Manhood appears in Wordsworth's poem only through the narrator as a figure of contemplation, caught between the myth of pre-existence he imagines and the future promised by "the faith that looks through death." His position in this world remains threatened by anxiety: "And oh ye Fountains, Meadows, Hills, and Groves. / Think not of any severing of our loves!" In that line invocation yields immediately to supplication, and in the next to assertions of loyalty: "Yet in my heart of hearts I feel your might; / I only have relinquish'd one delight / To live beneath your more habitual sway." Wordsworth seems in the ambiguities of that last phrase to accommodate himself to the two conflicting demands upon him, the sense of an imperious immortality brooding over him like a master over a slave, and the "custom" of ordinary adult existence. Able to join the pastoral world before him only "in thought," Wordsworth strives to make of such "Thoughts that do often lie too deep for tears" the source of his final power. The "eye / That hath kept watch o'er man's mortality" can give a "sober colouring" to the landscape to set against the lost visionary gleam. So too in the fourth eclogue the poet's own prayer briefly reveals the mortal conditions that make the vision of a golden age precious: "O that a remnant of long life be mine, / Giving me breath to celebrate your deeds. . . ." In both poems this separation of speaker and vision provides the deepening that in Wordsworth becomes the poetry of the "philosophic mind."

Yet Virgil's poem is a celebration that largely steps outside of time. From the beginning, in which the foretold birth of the babe is hailed as a return, through the description of the stages of his growth, which in the lines quoted above suspend the question of agency (making uncertain whether the babe is the cause of the golden age or its emblem), to this glimpse of the mortal poet and the final lines of the poem in which the babe is yet to be born, Virgil creates out of the political conditions of contemporary Rome a prophetic vision, a wish, independent of ordinary chronology. Wordsworth's Ode is linear, or at best chiastic, combating loss only by human understanding. Wordsworth celebrates too, but what he celebrates, as he moves toward the "Thoughts that do often lie too deep for tears" that are the final words of his poem, is mourning. Deeper things, rather than Virgil's higher things, are his concern. "The soothing thoughts that spring / out of human suffering" are the emblems of his choice: the suffering is the penalty of his renunciation and the badge of his authenticity, the soothing quality from the presentation of this choice as an inevitability.[16]

A brief look at another of the Ode's contexts illuminates this situation. The first mention of the poem comes in Dorothy Wordsworth's journal entry of 27 March 1802: "At Breakfast Wm wrote part of an Ode."[17] As Paul Magnuson has observed, the form of the poem was fixed from the outset, well before Wordsworth had worked out its argument.[18] Even as Virgil began his eclogue by announcing a more exalted subject, so Wordsworth from the beginning elevated pastoral to the gravity of an Ode. Some of the sublime connotations of that form for him may be seen on another, contemporary occasion on which Wordsworth employed the term. In the Arab Dream portion of Book V of The Prelude, on which Wordsworth was working at about the time he completed the Ode in March 1804, the narrator, acknowledged in the 1850 text to be Wordsworth himself, hears "An ode in passion uttered, which foretold / Destruction to the children of the earth / By deluge now at hand" (1805 Prelude, V:97–99). The stone which utters this apocalyptic ode, however, is also "a god, yea many gods, / Had voices more than all the winds, and was / A joy, a consolation, and a hope" (ll. 107–109). This paradoxical joining of destruction and consolation is only one of the many doublings that mark the scene: Wordsworth and his "studious friend"; the Arab who is and is not Don Quixote; the stone and shell, which are both also books, and which must seemingly be buried in order to be preserved; the desert and the ocean; the bond between the Arab and the narrator, who finds that "A wish was now engendered in my fear / To cleave unto this man, and I begged leave / To share his errand with him" (ll. 115–17). The Arab travels onward while looking behind him at the approaching deluge:

And looking backwards when he looked I saw
A glittering light, and asked him whence it came.
"It is," said he, "the waters of the deep
Gathering upon us." Quickening then his pace
He left me; I called after him aloud;
He heeded not, but with his twofold charge
Beneath his arm—before me in full view—
I saw him riding o'er the desart sands
With the fleet waters of the drowning world
In chace of him; whereat I waked in terror,
And saw the sea before me, and the book
In which I had been reading at my side.
                                    (ll. 128–39)

The ambivalence of the moment, already attested by the numerous splittings, reaches such intensity as to disrupt the narrator's sleep.

Several features of this passage recur in the Ode: the glittering light that is also the engulfing flood matches, at one end of the poem, the "celestial light" of Wordsworth's myth of otherworldly origin, and, at the other, the "immortal sea / Which brought us hither." The linking of these two images thus makes evident the tension between the visionary world and ordinary human experience that the Ode seeks to reconcile. Wordsworth's uneasy position is revealed in the narrator's mixture of "wish and fear" toward the Arab knight, whose abandonment of him despite his call parallels the fading of the visionary gleam lamented in the Ode. At the same time, in this dream where all the split, reversed, and merged identities are fantasies of a single mind, one might read this abandonment as Wordsworth's relinquishment of the dangers of commitment to the visionary quest, self-protectively represented by its opposite: the knight's heedlessness of him.

The continuing fascination exerted by the "semi-Quixote," to whom Wordsworth acknowledges returning "Full often" in thought, epitomizes the temptations that the Ode is concerned to discipline:

And I have scarcely pitied him, have felt
A reverence for a being thus employed,
And thought that in the blind and awful lair
Of such a madness reason did lie couched.
Enow there are on earth to take in charge
Their wives, their children, and their virgin loves,
Or whatsoever else the heart holds dear—
Enow to think of these—yea, will I say,
In sober contemplation of the approach
Of such great overthrow, made manifest
By certain evidence, that I methinks

> Could share that maniac's anxiousness, could go
> Upon like errand.
>
> (ll. 149–61)

The cost in human connectedness required by this identification must have been apparent to Wordsworth in the spring of 1804, when his wife was pregnant with their second child. The questing knight whose grandeur is inseparable from his ode foretelling "destruction to the children of the earth" writes at large the dilemma the child faces in the Ode. That child experiences "A Presence" (eighth stanza) which is less like the benign "beloved presence" of the Blest Babe passage (1805 *Prelude,* II:255) than like the sublime "presence" of "Tintern Abbey," which *"disturbs . . .* with the joy / Of elevated thoughts" (ll. 94–95, emphasis added); it is a presence, in the words of the Ode, "which is not to be put by." Wordsworth chooses to forgo the quest, to place himself at a remove from the brooding Master and the haunted child, rather than to endure their demands.

The resolving image of the ninth stanza precisely stations the poet:

> Hence, in a season of calm weather,
> Though inland far we be,
> Our Souls have sight of that immortal sea
> Which brought us hither,
> Can in a moment travel thither,
> And see the Children sport upon the shore,
> And hear the mighty waters rolling evermore.

"Calm" here is to temperament as "inland" is to geography: calm because inland, because safe from the apocalyptic ocean that wells up before the dreamer of *Prelude* V, the "eternal deep" of the Ode. This watcher, merely traveling to see and hear the ocean, is in no danger of being swept away by it. In his influential analysis of these lines in "The Structure of Romantic Nature Imagery" William Wimsatt noted that in logic the children do not belong on the seashore: "they are not strictly parts of the traveler-space vehicle, but of the soul-age-time tenor, attracted over, from tenor to vehicle."[19] This "imposition of image upon image," as Wimsatt termed it, is a metaleptic transformation that marks Wordsworth's freedom from the regressive impulses risked by the Ode's lament for the past. The children become only figures generated within the poet's tropes, creatures of metaphor and myth. The immediacy urged in the third stanza—"Shout round me, let me hear thy shouts, thou happy Shepherd Boy!"—and the intimate address of the eighth stanza to "Thou little Child" give way to the mere seeing of children on the shore; the child who reads the eternal deep in the eighth stanza is himself read in the ninth, and that the children of the latter stanza can be said to "sport" marks the allaying of anxiety won by the tactic of distancing. Unlike Virgil's, sung to an approaching rejuvenation, Wordsworth's "song of thanks and praise" in the ninth stanza arises in, and is made possible by, the space left by the lost immediacy of vision. Like the Arab, Wordsworth looks backward in order to travel forward, and buries in order to preserve.

This stance gains an aura from another aspect of the allusion to the fourth eclogue, the way traditional interpretation had seen the poem as prophesying the birth of Christ.[20] Wordsworth later suggested to Miss Fenwick that "the fall of man presents an analogy in . . . favour" of the notion of pre-existence, and the preservation of the past in memory emerges as a private spiritual analogue to the Christian's keeping alive the presence of Christ in his heart: the Kingdom of God is within you. The Christian resonance accords with the language of transcendence running throughout the poem: it strengthens, for example, the echoes in "Another race hath been, and other palms are won" of I Corinthians 9:24–25: "Know ye not that they which run in a race run all, but one receiveth the prize? So run, that ye may obtain. And every man that striveth for the mastery is temperate in all things. Now they *do it* to obtain a corruptible crown; but we an incorruptible."

I would argue nonetheless that the indirectness of the reference to Scripture is as important to the success of the poem as the reference itself. To introduce the poem with an epigraph from the fourth eclogue is to recall a poet whose "Christian" allusions are always subject to debate; the Christianity of Wordsworth's language is also ambiguous. It is noteworthy that although the ode is replete with declarations of the "truths that wake, / To perish never," such assertions are absent from the final stanza. If the concluding movement of elegy is consolation, then it is the restraint of Wordsworth's final affirmations that is remarkable. The inclusive self-portrait that emerges from the disparate pictures of the Ode is that of "A meditative, oft a suffering man," to borrow the contemporaneous words of the *Prelude*,[21] "temperate in all things," as in the Pauline exhortation. The closing emphasis is on the continuing "joys and fears" of this meditative mind, and not on a heavenly resolution. The poem exploits the resonances of Christian faith without committing itself to belief, to the conviction that would lessen its human uncertainty.[22] Virgil, the virtuous pagan moving toward revelation but never vouchsafed it, thus makes a poignant figure for Wordsworth.

It is just such strong ambiguities that the alterations to the poem between 1807 and 1815 reduce. Dismayed by the reviews, urged by Crabb Robinson to provide a title for the Ode "to guide the reader to a perception of its drift," and seeking more urgently for consolation himself, Wordsworth replaced the merely formal heading of "Ode" with "Ode: Intimations of Immortality from Recollections of Early Childhood."²³ The change, like the earlier conversion of "The Leech-gatherer" upon publication into "Resolution and Independence," was an act of interpretation, a subsequent "clarification" by the poet that limited the rich equivocations of his original text. In the Ode immortality is a concept inseparably linked to experiences of mortality: the title shifted the emphasis to the former.²⁴ The substitution of three lines from "My Heart Leaps Up" for "Paulo maiora canamus" had similar effects. The Virgilian epigraph, as we have seen, was appropriate in signaling an interpretive complexity, and infelicitous in the contrast it brings forward between the discords of Wordsworth's own work and Virgil's prophecy of a general fertility based on an infant in an harmonious family. The assertion that "The Child is Father of the Man" tries to complete the family romance, obliterating the strains of dependency that the poem witnesses. The unambivalent celebration of the child as father in the lyric does not betray the cost of such a backward-facing gesture, whereas the original epigraph pointed to the loss of the active paternal model in Virgil's eclogue, the man who marks the emergence of a new civic order. The political hopes of Wordsworth's earlier years are not to be found in the Ode.²⁵ The conditional form of "I could wish" is the only trace in the lyric of the gaps between the sublime self and the world around him in the Ode: the celebration of "natural piety," with its double allegiances to the natural order and the complex of paternal, social, and religious values contained in the concept of *pious*, places such piety above the hints of rebellion that the poem illustrates.²⁶ The new epigraph, taken from a poem "more confident"²⁷ than the Ode itself, evades in its epigrammatic density the conflicts acted out by the Ode. The Ode proceeds from pastoral elegy in 1802 to an elegy for pastoral in 1804; the lyric reinstalls at the head of the text the constant relation of man and nature, affirming at the outset the continuity that the poem must labor to establish. The man's heart leaps up to the rainbow in the same phrase and hence as certainly, joyfully, and naturally as the Babe leaps up on his mother's arm.

To begin the Ode with "The Rainbow" is, moreover, to write in the language of divine sanction rather than of nature, to throw the emphasis on the enduring presence of that covenant against destruction rather than on the Ode's experience that "The Rainbow comes and goes." In the unbroken sequence "So was it . . . So is it . . . So be it" that his new epigraph summons up, Wordsworth under-represents the pathos of change and separation in the Ode itself, the difficulty of its progress from the irregular lines and abrupt transitions of the beginning of his poem to the steadily meditative blank verse of the conclusion.²⁸ In placing as the epigraph to the final poem of his collection an excerpt from the poem that stood first in the collection, Wordsworth sought to impose on his writings a closure, a completeness that obscures the powerful tensions within the Ode.[29] If in 1807 the Virgilian epigraph raised the question of career, of Wordsworth's further poetic growth toward "higher things," the symmetry established by the substitution of "The Rainbow" in 1815 suggested rather that the canon was now closed. The history of the poem mediates the debate between Trilling and Raysor over its meaning: whereas the Ode may have begun in 1802 as a poem about growing up, it is completed in 1815 as a poem about the possibilities of immortality. The acts of giving a title to the poem and changing the epigraph shed light on what is most moving in the poem: Wordsworth's need continually to interpret himself, to try yet again to rewrite into permanence the self he had written into being from that primary "forgetting," those elemental "vanishings."

Notes

1. "The Immortality Ode," in *The Liberal Imagination* (1950; rpt. Garden City, N.Y.: Doubleday/Anchor, n.d.), p. 125.

2. Alan Grob, in *The Philosophic Mind* (Columbus: Ohio State Univ. Press, 1973), endorses the opinion of Thomas M. Raysor ("The Themes of Immortality and Natural Piety in Wordsworth's Immortality Ode," *PMLA*, 69[1954], 861–75) that the later views "reinforce rather than conflict with views already present in the poem in 1804" (p. 275), but even a "reinforcement" can constitute a significant alteration in balance.

3. Donald H. Reiman, ed., *The Romantics Reviewed* (New York: Garland, 1972), Part A, Vol. 1, p. 20, A:1:337, and A:2:436, respectively.

4. In January 1816 Wordsworth wrote to Wrangham that "The Ecglogues of Virgil appear to me, in that in which he was most excellent, polish of style and harmony of numbers, the most happily finished of all his performances" (*The Letters of William and Dorothy Wordsworth: The Middle Years, Part II, 1812–1820*, ed. Ernest de Selincourt, 2nd ed. rev., eds., Mary Moorman and Alan G. Hill [Oxford: Clarendon, 1970], p. 276; hereafter cited as *LMY*). Three years later he repeated the praise: "I think I mentioned to you that these Poems of Virgil have always delighted me much; there is frequently in them an elegance and a happiness which no translation can hope to equal" (*LMY*, p. 523). I have made use of the translation and interpretation of the eclogues by Paul Alpers, *The Singer of the Eclogues: A Study of Virgilian Pastoral* (Berkeley: Univ. of California Press, 1979). For an astute discussion linking Wordsworth's ambivalence to pastoral with his attitudes toward the past, see Thomas McFarland, "Creative Fantasy and Matter-of-Fact Reality in Wordsworth's Poetry," *Journal of English and Germanic Philology*, 75 (1976), 1–24.

5. Renato Poggioli, *The Oaten Flute* (Cambridge, Mass.: Harvard Univ. Press, 1975), p. 19.

6. The text of the Ode cited throughout is from *Wordsworth: Poems in Two Volumes 1807*, ed. Helen Darbishire, 2nd ed. (Oxford: Clarendon, 1952).

7. On the link between elegy and prophecy see Michael Cooke, "Elegy, Prophecy, and Satire in the Romantic Order," pp. 1–54 of his *Acts of Inclusion* (New Haven: Yale Univ. Press, 1979).

8. Helen Vendler contrasts "the Child in his immensity of soul" in the eighth

stanza with the satiric portrait of "the Child wholly in exterior semblance" of the seventh stanza in her finely detailed "Lionel Trilling and the *Immortality Ode*," *Salmagundi,* 47 (1978), 66–86.

9. In the fullest psychoanalytic study of Wordsworth's poetry, *The Character of the Poet: Wordsworth in "The Prelude"* (Princeton: Princeton Univ. Press, 1971), Richard J. Onorato examines the recurrent conflict between the "opposed demands on child and man of the external world and its reality, on the one hand, and of a greater inner reality being sought regressively, on the other" (p. 69).

10. This interpretation accords roughly with David Ferry's account of Wordsworth divided between "mystic" and "sacramental" visions (*The Limits of Mortality* [Middletown, Conn.: Wesleyan Univ. Press, 1959]), and Geoffrey Hartman's antithesis of apocalypse and akedah (*Wordsworth's Poetry 1787–1814* [New Haven: Yale Univ. Press, 1964]).

11. The source of this myth may well have been suggested to Wordsworth already in 1802, however, by conversations with Coleridge about Proclus and other philosophers. See John D. Rea, "Coleridge's Intimations of Immortality from Proclus," *Modern Philology,* 26 (1928), 201–13, and Herbert Hartman, "The 'Intimations' of Wordsworth's *Ode*," *Review of English Studies,* 6 (1930), 129–48.

12. All quotations from *The Prelude* are from *The Prelude 1799, 1805, 1850,* ed. Jonathan Wordsworth, M. H. Abrams, and Stephen Gill (New York: Norton, 1979).

13. "Recollecting Forgetting: Forcing Paradox to the Limit in the 'Intimations Ode,'" *Wordsworth Circle,* 2 (1971), 59–64.

14. On the possible alchemical sources of this image, see John D. Rea, "Wordsworth's Intimations of Palingenesia," *Review of English Studies,* 8 (1932), 82–86.

15. I am uncertain precisely how much weight should be attached to the suggestion of the poet as mother carried by the imagery: certainly the metaphor should not be forced into a rigid identification. I do believe, however, that in regarding his potentially terrifying otherworldly allegiances with tenderness instead of suppressing them, Wordsworth endeavors to incorporate the powers represented in his earlier work as belonging to a maternal Nature (cf. the sixth stanza of the Ode). The description of those powers as including "Severer interventions" (1805 *Prelude,* I:370) indicates the disquieting aspects that must be (re)interpreted into beneficence. I note too that the famous lines on the "obscure sense / Of possible sublimity" in the 1805 *Prelude* (II:331–41) come in the verse paragraph immediately following lines that seem to allude to the death of the poet's mother: "I was left alone / Seeking the visible world, nor knowing why" (II:292–93). The language of the former passage—"I deem not profitless those fleeting moods / Of shadowy exultation; not for this, / That they are kindred to our purer mind / And intellectual life, but that the soul . . ."—is echoed in the ninth stanza of the Ode: "Not for these I raise / The song of thanks and praise; / But for those obstinate questionings / Of sense and outward things, / Fallings from us, vanishings: / Blank misgivings of a Creature / Moving about in worlds not realiz'd. . . ." The parallels suggest a sequence: the *Prelude* (and here 1805 is mostly unchanged from 1799) marks the loss of the mother as the "cause" that "now to Nature's finer influxes / My mind lay open" (II:297–99); the Ode traces the internalization of such a past relationship with nature, itself the successor of the world made harmonious for the Blest Babe by the mother's presence (I:237–80).

16. In "Resonances of Joy," Chapter 4 of *Wordsworth and the Human Heart* (New York: Columbia Univ. Press, 1978), John Beer suggestively compares these lines to Oswald's speech in *The Borderers:* "Suffering is permanent, obscure and dark, / And shares the nature of infinity." The conjunction underlines the progress made in the Ode: it is suffering, as much as joy, that links man to man and discloses infinity, suffering that gives the philosophic mind its sublime authority.

17. *Journals of Dorothy Wordsworth,* ed. Mary Moorman (London: Oxford Univ. Press, 1971), p. 106.

18. Paul Magnuson, "The Genesis of Wordsworth's Ode," *Wordsworth Circle,* 12 (1981), 23–30.

19. William Wimsatt's essay, originally published in 1949, is reprinted in his *The Verbal Icon* (Lexington: Univ. of Kentucky Press, 1954).

20. John Ogilby's translation of Virgil, which Wordsworth owned, places this "Argument" at the head of the fourth eclogue: "Here Sibil is apply'd to Pollio's son, / Her Prophesis his Genethliacon: / But Christs birth by happy errour sings, / The Prince of Poets crowns the King of Kings." Frances Ferguson touches on the relation of the Ode to "the Christianized Pollio tradition" and also discusses its relation to the canon in *Wordsworth: Language as Counter-Spirit* (New Haven: Yale Univ. Press, 1977), pp. 96–125.

21. 1805 *Prelude* XIII:126. According to Mark Reed (*Wordsworth: The Chronology of the Middle Years* [Cambridge, Mass.: Harvard Univ. Press, 1975]), this part of XIII was composed during the interval of January to March 1804 (p. 15); the last seven stanzas of the Ode were "probably composed, and the poem completed, probably early 1804, by 6 Mar." (p. 27).

22. Cf. Harold Bloom's observation that "the logic of the *Ode* only *plays* at being a logic of concepts" (*The Visionary Company* [Garden City, N.Y.: Anchor Doubleday, 1963], p. 183). In *A Map of Misreading* (New York: Oxford Univ. Press, 1975) Bloom contrasts the ending of the Ode with that of *Lycidas:* "The Wordsworth of the Ode will not present himself as an 'uncouth swain,' and the sober coloring imparted by his mature eye substitutes for the blue of the Miltonic mantle" (p. 149). Though Bloom's emphasis on this nonpastoral conclusion is fruitful, his restriction of the poem to "a misprison or powerful misreading of *Lycidas*" (p. 144) narrows its concerns.

23. Robinson claimed his influence in the affixing of a title in 1861 (*The Correspondence of Henry Crabb Robinson with the Wordsworth Circle 1808–1866,* ed. E. J. Morley [Oxford: Clarendon, 1927], II, pp. 838–39).

24. On the linking of immortality to mortality, see Kenneth R. Lincoln, "Wordsworth's Mortality Ode," *Journal of English and Germanic Philology,* 71 (1972), 211–25.

25. Compare the role of the fourth eclogue in the Ode with the political implications of the echoes of it in Wordsworth's 1793 *Descriptive Sketches,* as noted by M. H. Abrams in "English Romanticism: The Spirit of the Age," in *Romanticism Reconsidered,* ed. Northrop Frye (New York: Columbia Univ. Press, 1963), pp. 50–51.

26. On "piety" in the Ode see also Paul Fry, *The Poet's Calling in the English Ode* (New Haven: Yale Univ. Press, 1980), pp. 133–61.

27. The phrase is Raysors; see n. 2 above.

28. I owe to Paul Sheats this observation on the significance of the changes in the verse.

29. Yet note how already in 1807 the Virgilian motto of the Ode seems to complete the epigraph on the title page of Vol. I: "Posterius graviore sono tibi Musa loquetur / Nostra: dabunt cum securos mihi tempora fructus."

The Intimations Ode: A Timely
Utterance
Marjorie Levinson°

In his great essay "English Romanticism: Spirit of the Age," M. H. Abrams exposes the profoundly political interests of a group of poems which, in their mythic ideality, appear to refuse categorically topical analysis. Abrams explains that the English poets of the 1790s employed the panoramic procedures of epic and ode—procedures closely associated with Milton's political visions and invoked under that aspect—by way of focusing contemporary political meanings.

In a second landmark essay, published in 1965, Abrams defines the apolitical character of a central Romantic form which he designates the greater Romantic lyric.[1] My adjective, "apolitical," isolates the leading tendency of Abrams's implicitly contrastive formal description. The greater lyric—a private meditation born of the speaker's non-specific, existential malaise—reaches articulation through his response to a present, particular, and precisely located natural scene. The meditation concludes with the production of a consolation which is valorized by the private and disinterested character of its motivation and development.

Abrams includes in this category a number of odes and odal forms unrelated in his analysis to the panoramic odes of the nineties. He derives poems such as the Intimations Ode and "Dejection" from the eighteenth-century local poem and, further back, from the seventeenth-century religious meditation. The Romantic lyric is said to lack, however, both the "historical and political" dimension of the former and the "public symbolism" of the latter. To describe the "crisis" upon which the lyric turns, Abrams uses the language of the Intimations Ode; it would seem that he regards Wordsworth's poem as exemplary of the form inasmuch as the lyric's motivation and procedure are so closely aligned in his analysis.

In several important ways, however, the Intimations Ode, read in the spirit which it and most of its readings recommend, fails to approximate Abrams's model. One cannot by any stretch describe the pastoral landscape of the Ode as "particularized and localized," nor is the narrator developed as a historically determinate authorial presence. The dominant stylistic mode of the poem is that of sonorous, lofty oratory, just about the opposite of Abrams's "fluent vernacular." The Ode's verbal resources consist of stylized iconographic representations and generic, typologically resonant allusions. The syntax fails to effect that blending of subjective and objective moments

° Reprinted from *Wordsworth's Great Period Poems: Four Essays.* © 1986 Cambridge University Press. Used by permission of Cambridge University Press.

which distinguishes the Romantic lyric; it vigilantly discriminates perceiver and perceived and their respective loci: psyche and nature. Finally, the Ode features a discursive intellectual speculation which is not qualified by a fiction of spontaneous overflow nor offered as an enabling surmise.

I enumerate these discrepancies not to undermine Abrams's model but to illuminate the Ode by an observation Abrams himself advances in the earlier essay "Spirit of the Age." There, he notes that the great Romantic poems, most of which were written in the post-Revolutionary period of "disillusionment or despair," exhibit "in a transformed but recognizable fashion" a number of terms developed in the activist, republican periods, terms which "assume a specialized reference to revolutionary events." Among these "leitmotifs," Abrams includes "the dawn of glad day [and] the awakening earth in spring-time." Although Abrams discusses the place of another such figure ("hope") in Wordsworth's so-called quietist or post-nineties period, he does not remark the occurrence in the Intimations Ode of the first two topoi, perhaps because he formally classifies the poem in a way inconsistent with a topological and a topical reading.[2]

To my mind, Abrams's oversights signify his respect for the rhetorical instructions encoded in the poem. For while the Intimations Ode, like the panoramic or nineties ode, introduces "history, politics, [and] philosophy," it does so to expose them as apparitional and to denounce the apparitions as mental enthrallments.[3] Hence the greatly transcendent and interiorized character of the poem. One may, however, account for the Ode's resemblances to the politically interested nineties ode without violating that lofty character by proposing that the object of the poem was precisely to pose and answer political questions at the level of abstract idea, and thus to command formally as well as intellectually a disturbing political prospect. Or, the Intimations Ode carries out its repudiation of politics on two levels, the level of argument and the level of style.[4]

These procedures and objectives are not unique to the Ode. We have seen, of course, how they define and distort the workings of Wordsworth's "Tintern Abbey" and his "Michael." And, as Jerome McGann has argued, they locate the center of the Romantic ideology, one of whose chief illusions is the triumph of the inner life over the outer world. Where the ode is unusual is in its adoption of a representational style closely associated with that outer world: that is, with the particular history the poem refuses. This is to say that the idealizing action of this poem is a two-handed engine; it develops a determinate, topical polemic and, at the same time, veils that polemic in clouds of glory.

Early-twentieth-century criticism seems to have grasped something of the Ode's referential character. One encounters in the literature wayward attempts to anchor the poem's generalized and ideal allusions to objects and events that figured or might have figured in Wordsworth's life and thought.[5] This scholarship was not fruitful because the concept of referentiality on which it was based was, as we shall see, too narrow. The Ode offers a historical rather than a naturalistic particularity; its topography is ideologically and emblematically specific; and the speaker voices the unique but collective experience of a generation. The place to look for the meaning of Wordsworth's "Tree" or "Field" is not in a universe of natural objects but rather among ideas of Nature, ideas structured and colored by contemporary conditions and obtaining for Wordsworth as for others of his time, place, and position. Rather than ask of the text, "which Tree?" one might instead try to reconstruct the nexus of associations informing that image and word for the poet and his early readers.

This procedure is familiar to students of *Coopers Hill* and "Windsor Forest." Critics of these poems explain the ways in which landscape compositions represent not just or primarily particular persons and events but the ideas and values which inform and, as it were, occasion that topical material. One reason these ratios are, to most readers, nearly imperceptible in the Ode is that Wordsworth sets them under the sign of conflict and incommensurability rather than harmony.

The allegorical methods of the meditative and local poem as well as the political odes of the nineties derive, of course, from an analogical concept of the order of things: an assumption of systematic (i.e., motivated) symmetry obtaining between moral and phenomenal Nature. This concept was not simply unavailable in the central Romantic period, as Abrams suggests; in the case of the Intimations Ode, its "evanishment" is the poetic subject.[6] What is harder to see is that the narrator attributes his reluctant skepticism—a very personal dereliction and dismay—to a very public, an ideological treachery. A doctrine which had identified Nature with mankind's best interests had been seen to engender an irremediable catastrophe in human affairs. The results of that political, moral, and semiotic betrayal are depicted in the Ode, stanzas 1 and 2, a 'paysage *demoralisé*.'[7] Throughout the poem, Wordsworth uses the devices of allegory to discredit that form's projection of an analogically organized universe, confirming in this way the terrible vision of stanzas 5–8: the morbidity of Nature and history.[8]

What makes the Ode so Romantic a poem, then, is not that it lacks the public symbolism which Abrams attributes to its formal precursors, but that it repudiates that publicity *which it introduces* through its images and allusions. In Wordsworth's poem, history acquires its meaning through its bearing on one man's life. The failure of the French Revolution is represented as exclusively the poet's loss, and as a strictly emotional, epistemological loss: "To me alone there came a thought of grief." The meaning of this representation resides in its originary function: to transfer ideologically *possessed* material from public to private domain.

Hazlitt, whose comments on the Ode imply that he construed the work as an allegory addressed to the intellectual powers, provides us with a convenient point of departure. Here is an excerpt from his review of *The Excursion:*

> But though we cannot weave over again the airy, unsubstantial dream, which reason and experience have dispelled,
>
> > "What though the radiance, which was once so bright,
> > Be now for ever taken from our sight,
> > Though nothing can bring back the hour
> > Of glory in the grass, of splendour in the flower":—[sic]
>
> yet we will never cease, nor be prevented from returning on the wings of imagination to that bright dream of our youth; that glad dawn of the day-star of liberty; that spring-time of the world . . . when France called her children to partake her equal blessings beneath her laughing skies; when the stranger was met in all her villages with dance and festive songs, in celebration of a new and golden era; and when . . . the prospects of human happiness and glory were seen ascending . . . in bright and neverending succession. The dawn of that day was suddenly overcast; that season of hope is past; it is fled with the other dreams of our youth . . .[9]

Hazlitt's quotation of the Ode in the context of an explicit political reflection, and his pronounced stylistic imitation of the poem, suggest that he read in it a commentary on the French Revolution and its metamorphoses. In Wordsworth's description of an abstract and timeless Innocence, Hazlitt found a reference to that "bright dream" of his own and of Wordsworth's youth—a social and political dream. In Wordsworth's generic and greatly aestheticized May jubilee, Hazlitt discerned the rural fete which figured so prominently in the early days of the Revolution and in Wordsworth's experience of it.[10] In a characteristically telling analysis, E. P. Thompson identifies phrases from Hazlitt's review as "stale libertarian rhetoric" cast into "nostalgic rhythms."[11] In that the passage self-consciously imitates Wordsworth's Ode, Thompson effectively underlines the conventional and political character of the odal materials as well. Of course, Wordsworth's own description of his sojourn in France and her politics—"Bliss was it in that dawn to be alive, / But to be young was very Heaven!"— should amplify the political overtones of the Ode's celestial nostalgia and of the metaphysic thereby introduced, as should the following excerpt from *The Prelude*, where the poet, recalling the glad dawn of the Revolution, observes the present political twilight:

> . . . the sun
> That rose in splendour, was alive, and moved
> In exultation with a living pomp
> Of clouds—his glory's natural retinue—
> Hath dropped all functions by the gods bestowed,
> And, turned into a gewgaw, a machine,
> Sets like an Opera phantom.
>
> (*The Prelude*, XI:363–69)

When Hazlitt described his own enthusiasm for the Revolution by way of evoking the spirit of the nineties, he again adopted the idiom of the Ode, from which he again quoted:

> . . . at this time the light of the French Revolution circled my head like a glory, though dabbled with drops of crimson gore: I walked comfortable and cheerful by its side—"And by the vision splendid / Was on my way attended."[12]

Here, too, Hazlitt indirectly but unequivocally identifies Wordsworth's "vision splendid" as a reference to the worldly renewal heralded by the French Revolution.

To suggest that Wordsworth's general theme—the terrors and *longueurs* of Experience—gets focused through a topical issue is not to trivialize or in any way depreciate that high theme. The Ode *is* about the inevitable loss of that celestial light which makes of everyone's childhood a "visible scene / On which the sun is shining." I propose only that the archetypically radiant state of Innocence remembered and recreated in stanzas 1–4—a touchstone for the Ode's emotional and intellectual argument—was embodied for Wordsworth and his readers in the memory of a briefly enlightened epoch in human history. When the odal narrator observes, "There was a time," a reader such as Hazlitt may have recalled the opening phrase of Coleridge's "Religious Musings"—"This is the time"—itself an echo of Milton's "This is the month." In Coleridge's ode (1794), the phrase designates the millennium once glimpsed in the French Revolution. To read Wordsworth's general elegiac lament against Coleridge's (and Milton's) fiercely specific proclamation is to identify the occasion of that lament as the passage of a *particular* time, say, 1790–93.

The poet's nostalgia, then, for a vivid experience of Nature, must be the reflex and expression of his nostalgia for the particular idea of Nature which informed the Revolution and its philosophic discourse. The Nature addressed as a *dea abscondita* in stanzas 1–4 (and demystified in 5–8) is the concept personified in eighteenth-century libertarian art: fierce goddess of the Revolution, incarnation of freedom, ground of sociality, and guarantor of the meaning of mundane experience.[13] It is, moreover, and as I argue below, the Nature conceived by Holbach and the philosophic school he exemplified. The Child Wordsworth addresses in the strophe as a lost power— the power to feel Nature's meanings—is a displacement of the poet's own young manhood with its unconflicted attachments to Nature and mankind. And the child he celebrates in stanza 8, "best philosopher," is a negation of the ratiocinative methods and analytic values so famously associated with the French *philosophe*—implicitly, "worst philosopher."

Mary Moorman has remarked Wordsworth's habit of "telescoping" incidents which occurred at different times, and her metaphor aptly describes the method of the Ode.[14] There, in a single field of vision, Wordsworth interweaves his and his generation's political and philosophic disillusion with his private memory of a season of "glad animal spirits." These two themes—the one derived from a recent, specific, and social experience, the other an eternal, existential fact— meet in Wordsworth's awareness that by negating the structure of ideas which had formed his young manhood, he renounced as well the vital self which he had experienced through that conceptual structure and in the era of its social hegemony.

By reconstructing the occasion, private and public, of this awareness and its expression, I hope to elucidate the function of the vision elaborated in stanzas 5–8, a vision sharply inconsistent with Wordsworth's canonical statement, as the poet himself acknowledged in 1843.

The first extrinsic factor to address is the immediate compositional situation. The odal strophe (stanzas 1–4) was written on a day of national significance, March 27, 1802, the day which concluded the negotiations for the Peace of Amiens. Wordsworth could not have known *on* the twenty-seventh that the peace with Napoleon was achieved that day, but the press had been full of the business for months. On March 15, the dispatches from Amiens arrived by special courier and the cabinet council hastily convened to examine them. The papers were returned for signing as reported in *The Times* of March 17, and on the thirtieth, the arrival of the definitive treaty was proclaimed.[15] Wordsworth, an avid reader of *The Times*, could not have been ignorant of the imminent conclusion to the negotiations. The perfect coincidence of national events with Wordsworth's poetical calendar is sheer serendipity. But the fact that the Ode was conceived in mid to late March 1802, the season of the final talks, strongly urges a causal explanation. The ode is, of course, the traditional formal choice for a poem on the occasion of a major national event.

The treaty officially marked the end of the season of conflict for Wordsworth, the season which began in 1793, when he could hope only for a divorce between "him who had been" and "the man to come."[16] With the end of hostility between his two early allegiances, Wordsworth could begin to reintegrate his experience. The treaty, which vastly favored France's imperialistic regime, underlined the perfidy of the Revolution and the faultiness of its guiding principles. (Sheridan called the treaty "a thing of which every man must be glad but no man can be proud.") Thus while the Peace brought to Wordsworth a welcome end to his divided loyalties, it also impressed on him once and for all the error of his "first affections."

Moreover, spring 1802 was the season of Wordsworth's projected marriage to Mary Hutchinson and of his visit to and emotional divorce from Annette Vallon.[17] Wordsworth had, of course, given up Annette long before 1802; he had also emerged from his Jacobin enthusiasm at least two years before he began writing the Ode. But it is one thing to "pass insensibly," as it were, from one position to its "contrary," feeling all the while that "things revolve upon each other."[18] It is quite another to find that not altogether perspicuous decisions and / or circumstance have enjoined upon one a position sharply antithetical to a former structure of belief. Wordsworth's engagement to Mary not only cast the involvement with Annette as a digression from what had come to seem his domestic destiny, it officially marked the period of the romantic phase of the affair.[19] In the same way, the Peace of Amiens, by formalizing France's role as imperialist aggressor, had to figure a major breach in the poet's carefully integrative self-chronicle. The closures thus defined for Wordsworth by the peace and by his betrothal could well have compelled him to revise more deliberately than he had yet done his sense of the past.

By 1802, Wordsworth was well established in the country of his boyhood and in the domain of a remembered Nature associated with eternally recurrent revolutions, as opposed to violent, political, and singular Revolution. He had engaged to marry an old family friend, a countrywoman. At such a time, the gap between Wordsworth's childhood and his present maturity would have seemed especially wide. The closing of that gap—which is to say, the reinterpretation of those "noisy years" of political passion—is a major objective of the Ode, as its headnote implies:

> The Child is Father of the Man;
> And I could wish my days to be
> Bound each to each by natural piety.[20]

Hence, I suggest, the indirection of Wordsworth's ideological revisions, by which he avoids the discontinuity of a recantation in the style of Coleridge's "France: An Ode" (1798; reprinted October 1802).[21]

The poems written in closest proximity to the Ode—"To the

Cuckoo," "The Rainbow," and the Sonnets Dedicated to Liberty—
betray Wordsworth's preoccupation with what seemed to him the
fragmented condition of his life, a condition foregrounded by personal
and political developments. In the two little lyrics, the narrator, who
inhabits a bleak and tedious Experience, seeks through the agency
of the natural mnemonic, bird and rainbow, to enrich his present
being with feelings from "that golden time" of childhood, when
Nature was a living sacrament.

The Sonnets to Liberty, most of which were written in 1802–3,
many of them based on Wordsworth's 1802 visit to France, articulate
in full voice some of the themes which are rendered *sotto voce* in
the Ode. Whereas "To the Cuckoo" and "The Rainbow" treat ab-
stractly of existential discontinuities, the sonnets anchor these sensations to the dispiriting view of Napoleonic France. In that several
of the sonnets contrast England's moral decline to the glorious era
of *her* Revolution, readers have associated the republican rhetoric of
the series with a lofty Miltonic eloquence. This rhetoric had, however,
become the stylistic exponent of the Jacobin position, and, in terms
of referential priority, the French Revolution clearly took precedence
over the Puritan. Moreover, the preponderance in both the sonnets
and the Ode of certain key words and verbal effects evoking the
classical naturalism of Enlightenment rhetoric strongly imputes to the
Ode the political themes developed in the sonnets.[22] When one reads
in Sonnet 11, "Inland, within a hollow vale, I stood; / And saw, while
sea was calm and air was clear, / The Coast of France . . ."—prelude
to a depressing political reverie—it is difficult not to think of the
meta-physical prospect seized by the narrator toward the end of the
Ode:

> Hence in a season of calm weather
> Though inland far we be,
> Our Souls have sight of that immortal sea
> Which brought us hither,
> Can in a moment travel thither,
> And see the children sport upon the shore,
> And hear the mighty waters rolling evermore.

To attend that echo means historicizing the Ode's ideal and imagined
scene by associating the narrator's indefinite *accidie* with the spiritlessness infecting all those children of the Revolution who lost their
Innocence and their Eden when France lost her virtue.

The third sonnet of the series, with its extended depiction of
France's political springtime, presents some suggestive parallels to
the pastoral festivities represented in the Ode. Wordsworth describes
the French countryside, 1790, as "like the May / With festivals of
new-born Liberty" (1837 revision). "The antiquated earth / Beat like

the heart of Man," and the narrator recalls the joyous expressions of this new rhythm: "songs, garlands, mirth, / Banners, and happy faces." Then, reductively and in rueful retrospect, he acknowledges the irrecoverability of "these things." Here, as in *The Prelude* (Books VI and X) and the Ode (stanzas 1–4), Wordsworth elegizes that perfect harmony of man with Nature, singular with social existence, which defined for the poet and through his experience of "the gorgeous festival era of the Revolution" the meaning of that tremendous event.[23]

Wordsworth's style ultimately tells us more about his referential universe than do his representations per se. Moorman, in characterizing the Ode's pastoral landscape as that of Spenser, Shakespeare, and Milton, evidently observed that the Nature depicted in stanzas 1–4 differs significantly from the intimate, particular, and impressionistic landscapes far more frequent in and typical of the Wordsworth canon.[24] The landscape of the Ode is a stylized, static, and ideal affair. Wordsworth's manner clearly invokes a tradition; Moorman emphasizes the literariness of that tradition whereas Hazlitt's extrapolation (and Wordsworth's epigraphic allusion to Virgil's Fourth Eclogue, see below) highlights for us the political motives of the pastoral. The Ode, like "To the Cuckoo," "The Rainbow," and many of the Sonnets to Liberty, features a figurative mode best described as abstract and emblematic; commonplace and general nouns are pressed into service as lofty, even mystical and numinous universals. The Cuckoo, the Rainbow, "Fair Star of Evening," "Rising Sun in May"; these 'naturalistic' materials function in the sonnets and lyrics as classical and biblical emblems denoting transcendent ideas that are nonetheless accessible to human understanding and capable of influencing historical development. Abrams, in a discussion of the *Lyrical Ballads* Preface, identifies "the essential, the elementary, the simple, the universal, and the permanent" as Wordsworth's controlling norms. Marilyn Butler, who has discriminated the political meaning of these qualities in the work of Blake, Gillray, and Wordsworth, exposes the modishness of these effects in certain contexts.[25]

The simplicity of the Ode is, then, quite unlike the experiential and idiomatic inflection of "Tintern Abbey," despite the initial tonal and thematic resemblances. The Intimations Ode develops an austere, monumental, and self-conscious simplicity—a *philosophic* simplicity denoting the purity of a language and iconography purged of the topical, the local, the particular, the adventitious.[26]

Consider, with reference to the history of styles and their ideological meanings, Wordsworth's portentous isolation of common— and commonplace—nouns (Rainbow, Rose, Moon, etc.); the pointedly archaic, hieratic pronominalization (thy, ye, thou) and phrasing (and cometh from afar, behold the Child); the oratorical expressions of pathos (stanzas 1 and 2); the conspicuous use of parallelism; the idealized simplification of Nature.[27] In his work on the art of the Revolution, D. L. Dowd has described the character of David's painting as follows:

> The form . . . was "classical" . . . [or] characterized by an emphasis upon line rather than color, upon static composition rather than movement, and upon the imitation of Greek and Roman sculpture. On the other hand, the treatment of his subject matter was highly "realistic" in its imitation of nature. Finally, the content of his art was essentially romantic, if by "romantic" we mean . . . an admiration of an enviable and idealized past, and an emphasis upon an emotional message.[28]

To read these comments in the light of the Ode is to recognize in the opening movement of that poem the look of a particular painterly school. It is to materialize the *meaning* of Wordsworth's style: the pictoral but highly abstract representation of an ideologically charged object (the organic community) focused through emblematic tableaux (babe leaps up, children culling flowers) and suffused with nostalgia for an enviable and idealized past.

Wordsworth not only organizes his imagery in an ideologically specific fashion, he draws his denotative and iconic materials from the dictionary of eighteenth-century libertarian discourse. Rather than gloss these materials individually, let me bring out the relevant correspondences by sketching the argument developed allegorically in the Ode.

There was a time when Nature, conceived as goddess of the Revolution, was instinct with providential omens signifying human fulfillment in time. During this season and by virtue of a certain widely held belief structure, the common was sublime and quotidian life a recurrent sacrament. The individual felt himself to be a member of a vast human family: then, "joy of one / [was] joy for tens of millions." The pastoral community so poignantly portrayed in stanzas 3 and 4 gives us the displaced representation of that defunct ideal. Those "things" (line 9)—the dreams of a particular time, place, and culture—have vanished. The narration *does* imply that man's power to perceive existing realities has also fallen off, but it presents that cognitive debility as the *result*, not the cause, of a more primary and a political disillusion. The syntax of the first two stanzas is clear, even insistent, about this: "The things which I have seen"; "There hath past away a glory from the earth." The lines unambiguously denote an external depletion.[29] Nature, the product of a historical moment and its modes of perception, no longer houses the glorious meanings which had endeared physical and social reality. The narrator faithfully records the presence, even in an unhallowed Experience, of illuminations, most of them secondary or reflective sources: rainbow, moon, glittering waters, stars. The conceptual and therefore organizing effulgence, however—the light of Reason and Nature as kindled by the Enlightenment, that "master-light"—has faded, rendering all other sources of light dubious, unreliable, or simply insufficient.

The word glory, so hardworking a noun in the Ode, seems to have been something of a code word during the Revolutionary era. Hazlitt, in both the excerpts quoted above, employs the word, and, in the idiom of the day, glory apparently signified something like the classical and Renaissance virtù. Brissot, leader of the Girondins, the party which briefly won Wordsworth's loyalty, proudly exclaimed, "j'ai prodigieusement aimé la gloire." Marat, describing the ancient Greek republics, asserts that "glory, that fruitful source of whatever men have done that is great or beautiful, was the object of every reward."[30] In "France: An Ode," Coleridge adorns his personification of Revolutionary France with "clustering wreathes of glory," and, in his Lectures on Politics and Religion, he refers repeatedly to that "small but glorious band" of "thinking and disinterested Patriots," a theoretically defined Jacobin group.[31] In a substantial passage of The Prelude treating of Wordsworth's involvement with the Revolution, that interval is designated "a glorious time, / A happy time" (VI: 754–55), and in two major passages, from The Excursion and The Prelude, the one somewhat sincere in its remembered political enthusiasm, the other openly derisive, the narrator recurs to the word glory.[32] Finally, Wordsworth's decision to render his phrase, "great and glorious birth"—a phrase describing France's upsurge of Revolutionary energy—as "lovely birth" in his revision of "Descriptive Sketches" argues his sensitivity to the political nuance of the word.[33] When the narrator of the Ode recalls, then, "the glory and the freshness of a dream," he remembers that vision of individual, social, and natural harmony which was the ideological center of the Revolution. ("Dream," here, is used in its high-Romantic, realized character.) When he laments, "there hath past away a glory from the earth," he observes Nature's lack of personal meaning to him now that its public and ideological meaning has been discredited.[34]

The explanation of Wordsworth's original epigraph—"paulo majora canamus"—seems to reside here, in the poet's memory of a golden age in its dawning. The quotation is the first line of Virgil's Fourth Eclogue. The eclogue is generally assumed to have been composed "to announce the Peace [of Brundisium and] to anticipate the natural and desired consequences of the wedding of Antonius and Octavia." The Peace of Amiens, and Wordsworth's recent betrothal to Mary Hutchinson, might seem to present a debased or parodic occasional analogy (or a particularly egotistical sublime), but the resonance is not implausible. In the Fourth Eclogue, Virgil ushers in a new era, a golden age, "to be fulfilled or at least inaugurated by a child soon to be born," the child of an actual Roman father and matron. Or, Virgil's "child of destiny" images a spiritual regeneration effected through the political actions of a temporal leader.[35]

By transforming the "golden hours" of the Revolution (*Prelude*, VI: 340) into a psychic and metaphysical postulate, Wordsworth adapts to his purposes the pre- and trans-figurative logic so often applied to Virgil's celebrated eclogue, but he suppresses the militant, apocalyptic thrust of that traditionary reading. (The dynamic which the Ode dramatizes is Abrams's "paradox of spiritual quietism.") Moreover, the Virgilian allusion situates the whole business of temporal and spiritual renovation in the discourses of poetry. The French Revolution and the Roman wars both begin to look like leitmotifs. Thus the Ode's epigraph supports its transcendental and interiorizing themes and, at the same time, identifies the factual original of those themes, in this, operating in much the same way as the poem's other images and allusions.[36]

The fiction of stanzas 1-4 is that the narrator's own inevitably evocative utterance reminds him how concrete a thing his loss is. His attempted escapes into poetic pastoral ("Now, while the birds thus sing . . .") repeatedly fail, and he is compelled to confront the form and meaning of his despair. "To me alone there came a thought of grief." That grievous thought, so emphatically particularized, announces the narrator's recognition of the occasion of his *Angst*: his memory of a vision of earthly delight, a vision which was political in both the widest and the narrowest sense of that word.

The strangely specific allusion to a "timely utterance" is usually glossed as a reference to one of the two lyrics written on March 26, "To the Cuckoo" and "The Rainbow" ("My heart leaps up"). The narrator's cryptic reassurance of recovery from his thought of grief—as I have suggested, a political memory—implies a political antidote. The narrator confesses that the conception of Nature developed in "To the Cuckoo" and "The Rainbow"—healer of existential breaches and eternally available mnemonic system—"solves" the historical problem: the invalidation of the Enlightenment idea of Nature. Yet as the narrator strives to consolidate experientially this ahistorical notion, symbols of that other, ideological Nature intrude, giving us a peculiarly Wordsworthian *et in Arcadia ego*.

"But there's a Tree, of many, one, / A single Field which I have looked upon, / Both of them speak of something that is gone." Of all the symbols generated by the Revolution, none was more prominent than the Tree of Liberty. Wordsworth was, of course, familiar with this commonplace symbol; in the passage from *The Excursion* cited above, the Solitary paraphrases the "prophetic harps" as follows: "Bring garlands, bring forth choicest flowers, to deck / The tree of liberty!" Wordsworth spent the summer of 1790 enjoying the Federation, a month of celebration to be encountered throughout France.[37] "C'est probablement vers les premiers jours de l'année 1790 que l'on commença dans les campagnes à planter des mais que l'on appela arbres de la liberté." Wordsworth was back in France, in residence, during the great Federation Feast, July 1792. Carlyle, in *The French Revolution,* describes the feast: "There are tents pitched in the Champ-de-Mars; . . . There are Eighty-three symbolic Departmental Trees-of-Liberty; trees and *mais* enough." He describes the great *mai* in the 1790 celebration: "All lamplit, allegorically decorated; a Tree of Liberty sixty feet high; and Phrigion Cap on it."[38]

By associating Wordsworth's Tree and Field (Champ de Mars) with the emblems and events of a glorious and irrecoverable era, one is in a better position to explain the abrupt intrusion of these images and the disproportionate emotion which the narrator brings to them, as well as their extreme specificity. The narrator thus indicates that his attempt to liberate the fond, pastoral memory from its original, political context ("There was a [that is, *some, any*] time . . .") has failed. The historicity of the imagery is as a return of the repressed.

In the Revolutionary context, Tree and Field had signified an apocalyptic idea and its imminent fulfillment. In the Ode, these natural objects assume, for a moment, their former and symbolic character; they remind the narrator of something that is gone. With that loss, all those natural objects which had been raised into social symbols through the corporate conviction that Nature meant Liberty and a culture redeemed, lapse back into the unhallowed commonplace.[39] Wordsworth's blazon, stanzas 1 and 2, is a cold pastoral, enumeration of signs denoting vacancy where once there was meaning. The Pansy that had risen to prominence by virtue of an "analogically meaningful" notion of Nature becomes in stanza 10 "the flower." The subsequent designation, "meanest flower," a negative valorization, suggests the christological and otherwordly tendency of "the philosophic mind." The narrator protests that *nature* yet lives for him and by his redemptive acts, but he also confesses that *Nature*—the historical idea which had endeared the Creation by binding mankind's happiness to her tutelage—is dead and cannot be resurrected.[40]

What emerges from the elegiac strophe is the narrator's reluctance to yield up the mental categories of the Enlightenment along with their content. The project which the Ode takes up in its antistrophe (composed in 1804) is that of emptying those structures—Nature and Reason—of their inherited, perfidious meanings. By endowing them with a new content, Wordsworth could heal the breach defined for him by the events of March 1802.[41] Stanzas 5–8 bespeak the poet's unequivocal interest in devaluing historical experience. These stanzas have always been read across an ideology: Platonic and Stoic.

It is important, however, to identify the immediate object of Wordsworth's critique and thus the stanzas' primary ideological commitment. By representing life in time as irremediably and radically circumscribed, inimical to man's happiness, and spiritually degenerative, Wordsworth exposes the Enlightenment as a misconstruction of the very order of things. Against Rousseau's proposition "I saw that everything was radically connected with politics, and that . . . no people would ever be anything but what the nature of its government made it," Wordsworth sets the perniciousness of man's investment in the structures that shape his mortal life.[42] To read the following proposition from Holbach's *Système de la nature* in the context of Wordsworth's antistrophe is to see that section of the Ode as a far more pointed statement than it appears.

> The source of man's unhappiness is his ignorance of Nature. The pertinacity with which he clings to blind opinions imbibed in his infancy . . . renders him the slave of fiction, . . . [and] doom[s] him to continual errour. He resembles a child destitute of experience. . . . Let us then raise ourselves above these clouds of [errour and] prejudice, . . . let us consult Nature, . . . let us fall back on our senses . . . let us . . . examine the visible world, and let us try if it will not enable us to form a tolerable judgement of the invisible territory of the intellectual world: perhaps it may be found that there has been no sufficient reason for distinguishing them.[43]

Holbach's treatise includes a long section entitled "The Soul and Its Faculties," and another, "The Doctrine of Immortality"—both, of course, materialist critiques. Wordsworth had certainly read Holbach (a copy is listed in the catalogue of his library) along with Godwin, his English counterpart.

Tenet by tenet, phrase by phrase, image by image, Wordsworth deconstructs the Enlightenment's "vision splendid."[44] To each of the *philosophes'* idols—freedom, individuality, joy, progress, Reason, illumination, Nature—Wordsworth opposes a bleak other: imprisonment, uniformity, sadness, accommodation, degeneration, memory, darkness, mind.[45] To suggest that our greatest power, clearest amplitude, was in a past we can barely recall, much less recover, is to set a regressive ideal for mankind. Politically, the Ode advances a radical conservatism; ethically, a doctrine of consolation and compromise; intellectually, a curriculum grounded in memory. When, in the epode, the narrator gives thanks for those "obstinate questionings / Of sense and outward things," he celebrates his inability to see those "things" of stanza 1, a reference to the material expressions of the Revolution and to his own believing endowment. This is to say, Wordsworth constructs his counterfaith from the very materials of Enlightenment thought.

A serviceable formulation of the negated position might go as follows. We are born into the light of Nature, a light we perceive by our inner light, Reason, which participates in that visible light; our earthly experience can be a progressive exercise in self-enlightenment rewarded by enhanced vitality and worldly control. Against this program, Wordsworth develops a vision of mankind not just as Nature's "foster" (rather than 'natural') children, but as Inmates of her indomitable "prison-house," a phrase which, eighteen lines preceding a reference to "that imperial palace," must bring to mind the Bastille. The prison, we learn, is life itself; Nature, which had meant Liberty in the context of the Enlightenment, is represented in the Ode as the supreme jailer. In characterizing mankind's native dimension (its being's heart and home) as an imperial palace, Wordsworth not only appoints the protective enclosure over imaginative expansion (so-called Romantic Nature), he adopts the language of the Royalist position. Although he undercuts the elitism of the phrase by representing this mansion as a universal source, universally inaccessible, the allusion identifies Wordsworth's vision as a critique of the Revolution's millennial thrust. Likewise the epithet "Nature's priest" at once inscribes and negates the Revolutionary program.

As we know, a great deal of Wordsworth's poetry and that of his contemporaries develops its Edenic, Experiential, and Paradisal visions with reference to the Child, symbolically and naturalistically invoked. This is not to rule out, however, more typical uses and derivations of the image in particular poems. In the Intimations Ode— as we can now see, a very timely utterance—the representation of childhood draws its meaning from several contrastive relationships. In the context of 1807, apostrophes to a Child could not but conjure Rousseau, he who *made* the child father of the man. The Rousseauvian child, empowered by his ignorance of the coercive categories of social life and by his undefended instinctual life, was, of course, a political as well as a psychic postulate. The construct of a former (but historical) sublimity serves in Rousseau as sanction of a future, and a historical, renaissance.

It is under this politicized aspect that Wordsworth presents his *Lyrical Ballads* "wise child," an essentialist, Enlightenment figure. In the ballads, this figure typically converts a complacent (read, "conservative") narrator to a perception of a universe instinct with apocalyptic energy. The *Lyrical Ballads* child seizes the authority traditionally (paternalistically) accorded to age; his unclouded intellect grasps the simple, subversive truths which we are toiling all our lives not to find.

The wisdom with which the odal Child (a far more sublime and generalized representation) is credited is that of the removed seer. He is the passive possessor of a vision "into the life of things"; his metaphysical penetration is incommunicable and, but for the pleasure and memories it yields him, without effect. Whereas the *Lyrical Ballads* child, something of an *enfant terrible,* performs a monitory (and minatory) function, the odal Child develops a critique of pure reason which amounts to a lesson in "wise passiveness." There is a devilish irony in all this. The French *philosophe* had invented the child as a symbol of unfettered Reason, powerful to see and to act on its clear visions. Wordsworth not only restricts this power to a period of physical and political impotence, he enlists it in the service of Enlightenment critique.

> Childhood is the cornerstone of the philosophy of [Wordsworth's] great Ode. The child's joyous acquiescence in the free spirit of life and his indomitable instinct for the unseen and eternal make him humanity's best philosopher.[46]

This observation by Helen Darbishire may sound dated, but its substance would not be rejected by most modern Romanticists. Once we appreciate, however, the extent to which the Ode is informed by political associations and anxieties writ large elsewhere in Wordsworth's canon and illuminated by the discourses of the day, we perceive the developmental and psychological themes as a device for (dis)figuring a specifically treacherous vision.

The dark determinism of the mythic stanzas is reinforced by the suggestion that active resistance to Nature's deadening influence only hastens the inevitable enslavement. Since self-affirmation implies acquiescence in the categories, hence the reality of natural life, even Prometheanism ultimately constitutes a self-betrayal: betrayal of the eternal by the earthly self. The Enlightenment commitment to exertion in the service of personal, intellectual, and social liberty is opposed in the Ode to the spiritual freedom passively realized by the Child in his possession by the immortal Mind, which is to him "a Master o'er a Slave."

The Ode associates "delight and liberty"—the "simple creed" of the Revolution—with the nonreflective condition of childhood. According to the Ode, adult wisdom, such as it is, begins in the memory of an Edenic infancy, proceeds by inference (intimation) to the hypostasis of a more blessed, prenatal state, and concludes in the certainty that "natural life is the history of the acceptance of loss."[47] This is an epistemology based upon normatively contrastive acts; present perception and historical memory live, move, and have their being through shadowy recollection of a noumenal world.

This scheme is what is meant by "thoughts that do often lie too deep for tears." The phrase divests 'philosophic thought' (rational, inductive problem solving: a communicable process and product) of the supreme value it had acquired during the Enlightenment. Such thought—Reason in its most, or least, exalted mood—had failed Wordsworth dramatically. In the Ode, he develops a context wherein to redefine Reason, thereby preserving a shade from his past. The canceled passage (lines 121–24) where the narrator postulates an intellectual life in death was more clearly in the service of this de- and re-valuation—a salvaging action.

Those grand and pitiful concluding lines ("To me the meanest flower that blows can give / Thoughts that do often lie too deep for tears") are not nearly so devoid of polemic as they seem. With this announcement, Wordsworth denies a correspondence essential to the whole structure of Enlightenment rationalism: a consensus corre-spondence between objects of thought (meanest flower) and the conceptual object (thought). Wordsworth clearly intends this denial; the expected phrase is "feelings" too deep for tears. The narrator's affirmation brings out his independence of Nature, any indifferent piece of which "means" insofar as it awakens a private memory of a consecrating past. Moreover, a thought that lies too deep for tears is also too deep for words. One might observe that a thought which cannot be formulated cannot be disconfirmed and, further, that such thought is the stuff of ideology. With the final line of the Ode, Wordsworth installs a definition of thought not just independent of Reason and Nature but inimical to them. We can, at this point, look back to "Tintern Abbey" and its epistemological workings, and glimpse in that grammar yet another historical imperative.

In sum, Wordsworth's myth of the soul, a pragmatic narrative never assimilated into his thinking, situates his grief over the failure of the Revolution and the invalidation of its ideology within a vision so vast and impersonal as to 'disappear' that pain. Those "noisy" or politically passionate and "restless" years are contextualized by the sobered narrator as but "moments in the being / Of the eternal Silence."[48] The "truths" to which mankind should cling are those, we learn, "that wake, / To perish never," decidedly *not* those which were born of historical immediacies and which maintain their relation to those lived truths. Wordsworth celebrates the sort of truths that no amount of "listlessness, nor mad endeavour"—one might say, no attempts at implementation—can destroy. History is exposed in the Ode as an unworthy object of human interest and involvement, its challenges nugatory. "Another race hath been, and other palms are won"; there are victories, the narrator's Pauline allusion suggests, far greater than those once anticipated from the French Revolution. Rather than grieve over those mundane losses, the reader is exhorted to set his sights on those other and spiritual palms. The heroism that Wordsworth ultimately defines is the capacity to live in the absence of a "consecrating dream," a "dream of human life"—by the end of the poem exposed as a belle dame sans merci.

In place of that treacherous dream or "gleam," the narrator recommends the "soothing thoughts that spring / Out of human suffering." By this substitutive reemphasis, Wordsworth rejects the hectic, hopeful fellowship promoted by the Revolution. He derives the authentic human community from a common pathos, which is to say, from a shared knowledge of irremediable human defect and deficiency. The object of Wordsworth's Ode is, like Gray's, to "teach [us we] are men."

Let me ask once again the question framed at the outset: why would a writer concerned to empty out history structure his statement by way of political allegory? I have argued that a dominant motive of the Ode is to expose the fallacy of those analogical assumptions which had governed Enlightenment thought and Revolutionary action. By his allegorical efforts to bridge the abyss separating Nature from Mind ("clouds" from "colour," "meanest flower" from "thoughts"), Wordsworth at once defines that abyss and identifies Mind as the source and stuff of Nature's meaning.

In that the Ode develops a metaphysics of absence punctuated by individual projective acts:

> Not for these I raise
> The song of thanks and praise;
> But for those obstinate questionings
> Of sense and outward things,
> Fallings from us, vanishings;
> Blank misgivings of a Creature
> Moving about in worlds not realized,

it behooves us to notice the tension between the poet's "act of mind and the material acted upon."[49] Of course, the narrator's triumph in the Ode is his concluding, symbolic act: his vision of a 'paysage consacré', its meanings ineffable and consubstantial with its appearances. Since, however, the value of this achievement is predicated on its factitiousness—on the special motives and acts that produce it—we read most sympathetically by refusing the symbolic, the Romantic option.

This is one reason why I have elaborated here a " 'knowledge' of the text"—what Terry Eagleton has defined as a reconstruction of "the conflicts and dispositions of its specific historical codes . . ."[50] I agree with Eagleton that this is not always and necessarily the most important thing to do. But with a poem like the Ode—one which has been so securely seized as "literary," which has been "detached by a certain hermeneutic practice from its pragmatic context and subjected to a generalizing reinscription"—it does seem to me most important right now and for the politics of Romantic scholarship to nudge the work toward a less literary register.[51]

Notes

1. This essay, "Structure and Style in the Greater Romantic Lyric," and the above in Harold Bloom, ed., *Romanticism and Consciousness* (New York: Norton, 1970), pp. 90–118, 201–29.

2. Above quotations from Abrams, "English Romanticism: The Spirit of the Age," in Bloom, *Romanticism and Consciousness*, p. 107.

3. Abrams, "English Romanticism," p. 103.

4. For an extended definition and critical history of this phenomenon, see Jerome McGann, *The Romantic Ideology* (Chicago: University of Chicago Press, 1983).

5. McGann, *Romantic Ideology*, p. 88.

6. Abrams, "Structure and Style in the Greater Romantic Lyric," pp. 210, 211.

7. Ibid., p. 209.

8. Hegel knew Romantic art by its indifference to "the sensuous externality of form" which assumes in the work an "insignificant and transient" character. ("Introduction to the Philosophy of Art," in *Hegel Selections*, ed. and trans. J. Loewenberg [New York: 1929], pp. 326, 327). What we observe in the Ode is the deliberateness of this indifference and this assumption.

9. References to Wordsworth's poetry are to the following editions: *The Poetical Works of William Wordsworth*, ed. Ernest de Selincourt, Helen Darbishire, Thomas Hutchinson, 5 vols. (Oxford: Clarendon Press, 1940–49); *The Prelude, 1799, 1805, 1850*, ed. Jonathan Wordsworth, M. H. Abrams, Stephen Gill (New York: Norton, 1979). William Hazlitt, "On Mr. Wordsworth's Excursion," in *The Collected Works of William Hazlitt*, ed. A. R. Waller and Arnold Glover, vol. 1 (London: Dent, 1902), p. 119.

10. Charles Cestre, *La révolution française et les poètes anglaises* (Paris: Hachette, 1906), p. 29. "Ils [Wordsworth and Robert Jones] arrivèrent à Calais la veille du jour où fut célébré dans toute la France cette fête splendide, qui sembla exalter la nature humaine au-dessus d'elle-même, la Première Fédération, la fête de la fraternité. Ils virent 'dans un petite ville et chez quelques-uns comme les visages deviennent radieux, quand la joie d'un seul est la joie de dix millions.' . . . Tout le long de la route, ils trouvèrent des vestiges de la grande fêtes, des guirlandes, et des arcs de triomphe, et ils assistèrent aux réjouissances de la liberté. . . ."

11. E. P. Thompson, "Disenchantment or Default? A Lay Sermon," in Conor Cruise O'Brien and William Dean Vanech, eds., *Power and Consciousness* (London: University of London Press, 1969), p. 178.

12. Hazlitt, *Collected Works*, 12: 236.

13. I refer to such artists as Peyron, Barthélémy, Jeaurat de Bertry—painters of allegorical works wherein topical and ideological argument is developed by a specifically charged classical style. For an apt literary representation of Liberty in the 1790s, see "Invocation to Liberty," anonymous, in *The Watchman*, March 25, 1796, in *Collected Works of Samuel Taylor Coleridge*, ed. Lewis Patton and Peter Mann, *The Watchman*, vol. 2 (London and Princeton: Routledge and Kegan Paul and Princeton University Press, 1970), p. 130.

14. Mary Moorman, *William Wordsworth: A Biography. The Early Years, 1770–1803* (London: Oxford Univ. Press, 1957; rpt., 1968).

15. This research executed by Rick Halpern, Department of History, University of Pennsylvania.

16. Moorman, *Early Years,* p. 223.

17. Wordsworth became engaged to Mary Hutchinson probably during mid-November 1801; they planned a spring wedding (Moorman, *Early Years,* p. 518). Toward the end of March, however, two or three days after composing the strophe of the Ode, Wordsworth decided to take advantage of the peace and visit Annette at Calais. The rapidity with which the visit was conceived and executed suggests that Wordsworth had cherished the idea for some time, presumably while he was conceiving the first part of the Ode. We do know that on March 22, Wordsworth heard from Annette and resolved both to see her and to visit Mary (Mark Reed, *Wordsworth: The Chronology of the Middle Years, 1800–1815* [Cambridge, Mass.: Harvard University Press, 1975], p. 155). According to Moorman (p. 158), "a long exchange of letters with Annette Vallon occupied the spring months." The sojourn with Annette interfered with Wordsworth's marriage plans; the wedding was postponed until October 1802. One cannot know, of course, but one could confidently surmise that the engagement to Mary and the interest in renewed contact with Annette were not unrelated.

18. William Wordsworth, "Essay upon Epitaphs," in *The Prose Works of William Wordsworth,* ed. W. J. B. Owen and Jane Smyser, vol. 2 (Oxford: Clarendon Press, 1974), p. 53.

19. Wordsworth maintained a correspondence with Annette until the war interrupted it again. Upon the marriage of his and Annette's illegitimate daughter, Caroline, Wordsworth settled £30 a year upon her until 1834, when he gave her the sum of £400 (Moorman, *Early Years,* p. 565). The closure I discern in Wordsworth's relationship with Annette (as prompted by his marriage to Mary) refers to an internal, intellectual and emotional shift rather than to an active expression of detachment.

20. The headnote was added in 1815, and it replaced the Virgilian epigraph. The new extract, with its existential generalities, obviously discourages the sort of pointed, politically sensitive reception invited by the original epigraph. The substitution suggests Wordsworth's interest in deemphasizing, even obscuring, the Ode's topical and allegorical dimension. The emergence of this interest, or its gradual ascendancy, is consistent with what we know of Wordsworth's political and social development.

21. Spoken by the Solitary: "Such recantation had for me no charm, / Nor would I bend to it." Like the Solitary, Wordsworth would not declare, with others, " 'Liberty, / I worshipped thee, and find thee but a Shade!' " or "dream" (*The Excursion,* III: 776–79). He did, however, say just that in the Ode, but through a subtler language than, say, Coleridge's.

22. "Star," "splendour," "glory," "Man," "hope," "master-spirit." Of course, the most elaborate metaphor in the Ode is that of light, and the political resonance of this word and image would have been obvious to Wordsworth's early readers. Here is Paine's celebrated elaboration of the figure: "The revolutions of America and France have thrown a beam of light over the world, which reaches into man . . . when once the veil begins to rend, it admits not of repair . . . the mind, in discovering truth, acts in the same manner as it acts through the eye in discovering objects; when once any object has been seen, it is impossible to put the mind back to the same condition it was in before it saw it" (Thomas Paine, *Rights of Man,* ed. Henry Collins [New York: Penguin, 1979], p. 140). James Boulton, in his *Language of Politics in the Age of Wilkes and Burke* (London: Routledge and Kegan Paul, 1963), p. 206, quotes Priestley, *Letters to Burke:* "Prejudice and error is only a mist, which the sun, which has now risen, will effectually disperse." For additional examples of these and related, shared metaphors of the day, see Boulton, *Language of Politics in the Age of Wilkes and Burke,* pp. 75–249.

23. "Wordsworth, it is well known to all who know anything of his history, felt himself so fascinated by the gorgeous festival era of the Revolution . . . that he went over to Paris and spent about one entire year between that city, Orleans, and Blois" (De Quincy, quoted in Leslie Chard, *Dissenting Republican: Wordsworth's Early Life and Thought in Their Political Context* [The Hague: Mouton, 1972], p. 70).

24. Moorman, *Middle Years*, p. 23.

25. M. H. Abrams, ed., *Wordsworth: A Collection of Critical Essays* (Englewood Cliffs, N.J.: Prentice-Hall, 1972), p. 1; Marilyn Butler, *Romantics, Rebels and Reactionaries* (Oxford: Oxford Univ. Press, 1981), pp. 11–16.

26. "But if I am to tell the very truth, I find . . . the great Ode not wholly free from something declamatory." Thus does Arnold distinguish the Ode from Wordsworth's best and most characteristic poems, those which "have no style." Matthew Arnold, "Wordsworth," 1879.

27. These also define the Pindaric ode. The Intimations Ode is, however, predominantly Horatian in its private, contemplative, and tranquil character. One could think of the poem as representing an attempt to marry the two traditions, but this is to treat the work as an academic exercise, or to situate it in a rather narrow aesthetic space. I have been trying to ascertain the meaning of particular styles and formal decisions during a particular interval.

28. David Lloyd Dowd, *Pageant-Master of the Republic: Jacques-Louis David and the French Revolution*, University of Nebraska Studies, no. 3 (June 1948), p. 22.

29. The received readings of this stanza indicate, more than any other single fact, the idealist character of so much Romantic criticism. The lines which conclude the first and second stanzas of the Ode—"The things which I have seen I now can see no more" and "There hath past away a glory from the earth"—are typically taken as statements of spiritual exhaustion, perceptual debility, and decrease in personal power to consecrate the objective contents of vision. The literal meaning of these lines—the expression of an external and imposed impoverishment—is consistently overlooked.

The language of several critics, however, seems to expose unacknowledged associations and assumptions of the sort I have isolated above. Mary Moorman describes Wordsworth's political disillusion in 1795 (viz., the increasingly unmistakable reign of violence in France): "Then came the great crisis; the human tragedy breaking into the bright vision of his youth; the sharp suffering, and the desperate search for a philosophy that would make life possible again" (*Early Years*, p. 279). Moorman's metaphors as well as her psychological reconstruction ("search for a philosophy") appear to derive from the Intimations Ode. One might observe that Moorman's phrase "bright vision" refers not to Wordsworth's childhood but to his young manhood with its political and social visions. Cestre, in his *Révolution française*, characterizes Wordsworth's post-Revolutionary resolve as follows: After the crisis of the Revolution, Wordsworth hoped to project upon reality "une lumière de réve" (p. 548). More recently, Clifford Siskin discerns in the Ode the essentially revisionist and dehistoricizing procedures I address here: "This strategy is most familiar to us as enacted in the 'Intimations Ode,' the poet becomes philosophic hero as change felt as loss is transformed by revision into intimations of the unchanging . . . the apotheosis of the 'Poets' entails the repression of history under the weight of transcendent continuities" (Siskin, "Revision Romanticized: A Study in Literary Change," *Romanticism Past and Present* 7, no. 2 [1983]: 1–16). And George Watson, while he offers no critical observations, characterizes the period in question as follows: "Wordsworth had lost two paradises by . . . the years between 1799 and 1805: a political paradise in revolutionary France, and a sensory paradise of youth as well. He is a twofold Adam" (Watson, "The

Revolutionary Youth of Wordsworth and Coleridge," *Critical Quarterly* 18, no. 3 [Autumn 1976]: 57.

30. Harold Parker, *The Cult of Antiquity and the French Revolution* (New York: Octagon Books, 1965), pp. 47, 48.

31. Samuel Taylor Coleridge, "A Moral and Political Lecture" and "Conciones ad Populum," in *The Collected Works of Samuel Taylor Coleridge. Lectures 1795 on Politics and Religion*, ed. Lewis Patton and Peter Mann (Princeton and London: Princeton University Press and Routledge and Kegan Paul, 1971), pp. 12, 40.

32. From *The Excursion*, III: 711–26:

> Fell to the ground . . .
> A golden palace rose, or seemed to rise,
> The appointed seat of equitable law
> And mild paternal sway. The potent shock
> I felt: the transformation I perceived,
> As marvellously seized as in that moment
> When, from the blind mist issuing, I beheld
> Glory—beyond all glory ever seen,
> Confusion infinite of heaven and earth,
> Dazzling the soul. Meanwhile, prophetic harps
> In every grove were ringing, "War shall cease:
>
> . . . .
>
> Bring garlands, bring forth choicest flowers, to deck
> The tree of liberty,"—my heart rebounded . . .

From *The Prelude*, 1850, XI: 236 ff:

> How glorious! in self-knowledge and self-rule,
> To look through all the frailties of the world,
> And, with a resolute mastery shaking off
> The accidents of nature, time, and place,
> Build social freedom upon personal Liberty,
> Which, to the blind restraints of general laws
> Superior, magisterially adopts
> One guide, the light of circumstances, flashed
> Upon an independent intellect.

The derisive excess evident in the passage above measures Wordsworth's early investment in that "dream of human life"; his rude awakening from that millennial dream figured to the poet a second Fall.

The narrator of Sonnet 15 ("Great men have been among us") reflects upon France's decline by way of comparing the character of her Revolution to England's redemptive revolt, the Puritan Revolution. The English "master-spirits" taught us "how rightfully a nation shone / In splendour." "They knew how genuine glory was put on." One might observe that beyond the shared diction, the sonnet and the Ode develop the concept of a "glory" which is not the necessary expression of an inalienable nobility ("glory" in its religious and painterly connotations) but the historical manifestation of an elevated and conditional state of the soul: a majesty assumed, "put on," an "apparel." As James Chandler has argued ("Wordsworth and Burke," *ELH* 47, no. 4 [Winter 1980]: 741–71, 756), Wordsworth, as early as 1799, had adopted Burke's wryly literal characterization of "habit" or prejudice as moral clothing. "Burke's related figure of reason's 'nakedness' also appears in the 'Essay' ('bald and naked reasonings') as well as, more prominently, in *The Prelude*." Chandler argues that "such figures are properly called Burkean . . . because, though Burke did not invent them, he did invest them in the 1790s with an ideological power distinctly his own." To accept Chandler's very sound reasoning is to read the Ode's representation of Nature and the Child—respectively appareled in celestial light and trailing clouds of glory— across Burke. Again, like Burke, Wordsworth characterizes the condition of the strictly rational creature—which is to say, he who has lost his "intimations"—as that of a nakedness signifying poverty and weakness. "Not in entire forgetfulness, / And not in utter nakedness." To learn that Wordsworth recommends the healing properties of memory and that he celebrates the habitual, instinctual character of childhood wisdom is no surprise. But the Burkean polemic of these moves—the denigration of a particular and politicized idea of Reason—is a less commonplace critical inference.

33. Abrams has set Wordsworth's famous account of the imagination (Simplon Pass episode) against his earlier, political "prophecy of a new earth emerging from apocalyptic fires," by way of establishing the poet's post-nineties "spiritual quietism." Abrams isolates from the passage the "leitmotif," hope, and centers his contrastive analysis on that word ("English Romanticism," p. 109). I would add to Abrams's discussion that in the Simplon Pass section, it is individual imagination which rises up and, "awful Power," assumes a "glory"—not Liberty and not a militant populace.

34. Nature's fall into historicity is explicitly represented in the Sonnets Dedicated to Liberty as the result of a historical treason: the failure of the French Revolution. The Ode's representation of an abruptly profane experience of Nature can be illuminated with reference to that theme in the sonnets (see Sonnet 19).

35. Peter Manning, "Wordsworth's Intimations Ode and Its Epigraphs," *Journal of English and Germanic Philology* 82, no. 4 (October 1983): 526–40. And see Sir Ronald Syme, *The Roman Revolution* (Oxford: Oxford University Press, 1939), pp. 218, 219 (on the Peace of Brundisium and Virgil's Fourth Eclogue). Manning takes an interesting psychoanalytic approach. I thank Mac Pigman, California Institute of Technology, for identifying the classical, political meanings embedded in Wordsworth's allusion.

36. As I noted above, Wordsworth's 1815 decision to replace the Virgilian epigraph with a headnote quotation from "The Rainbow" suggests his wish to suppress the originally political burden of the Ode, and to emphasize the priority of what has been treated here as instrumental: the metaphysical, psychological argument. In the absence of the new headnote, stanzas 1 and 2 need not be construed as a reference to childhood. Although the indeterminacy of the phrase "there was a time" conjures a mythical past, the line could have been read as a reference to the Revolutionary era; the new headnote makes such a construction more problematic.

37. Alan Liu, "Wordsworth: The History in Imagination," *ELH* 51, no. 3 (Fall 1984): 505–48.

38. Thomas Carlyle, *The French Revolution*, 2 vols (London: Dent, 1906), II: 102, I: 285. See Abbé Henri Grégoire, *Essai historique et patriotique sur les arbres de la liberté*, 1794. Wordsworth's phrasing echoes St. Augustine's reference to

> ". . . the fields and spacious palaces of memory . . . where are the treasures (thesauri) of innumerable images, brought into it from things of all sorts perceived by the senses. There is stored up, whatever besides we think, either by enlarging or diminishing, or any other way varying those things which the sense hath come to; and whatever else hath been committed and laid up, which forgetfulness hath not yet swallowed up and buried. (St. Augustine, *Confessions*, X, 8 [Pusey's translation], quoted in Francis Yates, *The Art of Memory* [Chicago: Univ. of Chicago Press, 1966], p. 46 [my emphasis]).

To hear this echo is not, of course, to yield up one's sense of the Ode's topical gestures, but to appreciate the ambivalence of those gestures. Such two-toned statements underline for us the difference between a "consumption of the text and a revelation of a text through a deliberated distance" (John Goode, *George Gissing, Ideology in Fiction* [New York: Barnes and Noble, 1979], p. 32). Or, it is to actualize historically the Derridean postulate of writing as *pharmakon:* poison and remedy, a "complicity of contrary values" (Jacques Derrida, "Plato's Pharmacy," in *Dissemination,* trans. Barbara Johnson [Chicago: Univ. of Chicago Press, 1981], p. 125). Finally, it is to recognize in the Intimations Ode the project defined through "Tintern Abbey" and more critically, to glimpse the internal limits of that project—a problematic.

39. Nature meant Liberty and accordingly, when Liberty in its historical incarnation proved itself a false god, Nature too was emptied out. The clearest expression of the symbology which married Nature and Freedom is Coleridge's "France: An Ode." The poem, prompted by France's invasion of Switzerland, 1798, was published in that year and later reprinted in the *Morning Post,* October 14, 1802, with the addition of a note and Argument. Coleridge explains that "the present state of France and Switzerland give it [the Ode] so peculiar an interest at the present time that we wished to re-publish it." The poem was originally titled "The Recantation: An Ode."

David Perkins, ed. (*English Romantic Writers* [New York: Harcourt Brace and World, 1967], p. 423) summarizes the thought of the first stanza: "That natural objects ceaselessly inculcate the idea of liberty." Thus, the great disillusion addressed by Coleridge in his ode (and by Wordsworth in his) rendered Nature, which had been a semiotic system promoting specifically humanitarian meanings, a chaos. One of Wordsworth's Sonnets Dedicated to Liberty crystallizes the sentiment: "I find nothing great: / Nothing is left which I can venerate; / So that a doubt almost within me springs / Of Providence, such emptiness at length / Seems at the heart of all things" (Sonnet XII on Independence and Liberty). In order to sustain his libertarian posture and, more important, to preserve Nature's meaningfulness in the face of this ideological earthquake, Coleridge locates "God in Nature." Wordsworth's strategy, far more radical than Coleridge's pantheism, is first to denounce Nature as a great confiner (and thus oppose the literary and political association of Nature with Liberty) and then to divest Nature of all public or consensus meaning. When the narrator asserts, "I love the Brooks which down their channels fret, even more than when I tripped lightly as they," he not only characterizes Nature as a private amour, he attributes his love to the "vanishings" which Nature inscribes, and which invite his valorizing acts.

40. He implies, moreover, through the changes he rings upon the word "dream," that the death of that idea calls into question the fundamental mechanism and thus all the products of human vision. In stanzas 1–4, "dream" denotes either a preview of reality or the essence of reality (that is to say, "dream" in its high-Romantic, subjectivist character). When the narrator asks, "where is it now, the glory and the dream," he refers to, in Keats's phrase, an "existence." Specifically, he remembers the Revolutionary vision of a collective and liberated imagination. This Blakean premise, however, is quite literally discredited in the Ode's antistrophe. Here, "dream" ("a sleep and a forgetting," a "dream of human life") assumes its more pedestrian and prudential aspect: the delusive, fantastic, and dangerous escape from or ignorance of the real. An apposite usage occurs in *The Prelude,* 1850, XI: 125; "Fed their childhood on dreams" (i.e., of the Revolution).

Hazlitt, in "On Mr. Wordsworth's Excursion," professes his sustained belief in the essential truth of that "airy, unsubstantial dream" of his youth. He implicitly characterizes the fictive status of that dream as conditional, a vision of reality in that finer tone man will one day experience directly. For Wordsworth, apparently (from the evidence of the Ode and, more important, of his political evolution) the despair induced by the failure of his Enlightenment dream was too profound for any response but total abjuration. "Hence, perhaps, the flatness of the word 'Flower'—Wordsworth does not even give the daisy its specific name—which may be taken to signal the intuition that we may as well give up trying to find the *word* which does ample justice to the *thing,* and points us back to the immediacy of an experience outside language, which language at its most efficient can only tentatively indicate" (David Simpson, *Wordsworth and the Figurings of the Real* [London: Macmillan, 1982], p. 25). Simpson's subject here is Wordsworth's "The Daisy." The "intuition" with which he credits the poet can be detected as well in the Intimations Ode and in the same device: the abstention from concrete and particular designation (Pansy to Flower). In the Ode, however, Wordsworth's intuition seems a more interested or motivated determination whereby he reinforces his critique of reason (the intellectual processes which transform perception to communicable thought) and of Nature, which, in her necessarily specific and fixed manifestations tends to reduce and immobilize imagination.

41. This might remind one of Coleridge's advice to Wordsworth, 1799: "I wish you would write a poem in blank verse addressed to those who, in consequence of the complete failure of the French Revolution, have thrown up all hopes for the amelioration of mankind, and are sinking into an almost epicurean selfishness, disguising the same under the soft titles of domestic attachment and contempt for visionary *philosophes*" (from E. P. Thompson, *The Making of the English Working Class* [New York: Pantheon Books, 1964], p. 176). In one major passage of *The Prelude*, Wordsworth responds specifically to Coleridge's analysis. Here, he articulates what one scholar has called the "moral depression, not to say hopelessness . . . which weighed upon Englishmen not only up to the beginning of the Peninsular war but . . . until the English successes in Spain attracted the attention of the whole world. This spiritlessness [was] caused by the continued triumph of Buonaparte" (A. V. Dicey, *The Statesmanship of Wordsworth* [Oxford: Clarendon Press, 1917], pp. 72, 73). But it is the Intimations Ode which explores that cultural depression and which describes by enacting a way to transcend without trivializing that collective and personal despair. At the same time, Wordsworth both implements and subverts Coleridge's rebuke to those who would offset their bitterness and rationalize their self-centeredness through "contempt for visionary *philosophes.*" Wordsworth *assumes* that mantle in the Ode—what are stanzas 5–8 but a philosophic vision—but in such a way as to repudiate its historically specific character. Wordsworth's myth of the soul is a pointed rebuttal of the doctrine, program, and methods associated with the French philosophy—in the poet's phrase, "pestilential philosophism" ("Convention of Cintra").

42. Jean-Jacques Rousseau, *Oeuvres Complètes*, 5 vols., eds. B. Gagnebin and Marcel Raymond (Bibliothèque Pléiade, Paris, 1959–69), I: 404, 405. From *The Confessions.*

43. Baron d'Holbach, *The System of Nature*, trans. H. D. Robinson (New York: Burt Franklin, 1868, rpt. 1970), pp. viii, 15.

44. Two years intervened between the composition of the strophe and that of the antistrophe. One might conjecture that in 1802, Wordsworth's emotional commitment to "the vision splendid" and to his quondam involvement in it was still too intense to permit the thoroughgoing repudiation enacted in stanzas 5–8. The admission of loss was candor enough. By 1804, Wordsworth was more firmly consolidated in every way; whereas 1802 found him on the verge of marriage, by 1804 he had been established with Mary for two years. Moreover, Wordsworth's return to France on "Buonaparte's natal day" in 1802 and the bitterly ironic pall cast over the lengthy visit, as well as the resumption of the war soon after, had to destroy any lingering attachment to France, or it had to sever once and for all in Wordsworth's mind the France of 1789–92 from Napoleon's France.

In the eight weeks following Coleridge's departure for Malta, Wordsworth wrote the "Ode to Duty," completed the Intimations Ode, and Books 3, 4, and 5 of *The Prelude*. He had originally planned *The Prelude* as a five-book work, ending with his return to Cambridge at the end of his first long vacation (described in Book 4), *before* his momentous sojourn in France. Wordsworth's sudden decision to include his experiences in France argues his achievement of a sufficiently dispassionate attitude toward those experiences and their meanings as to permit their aesthetic resolution. That distance could well have been the chief factor in Wordsworth's decision to resume work on the Ode.

45. Although I lacked the opportunity to read Ronald Paulson's recent study, *Representations of Revolution, 1789–1820* (New Haven: Yale University Press, 1983), before or during the composition of this essay, I would like to note here its consonance with my line of argument, and its confirmation of some local matters (see pp. 22, 24, 27, 46, 47, 149–50, 190, 192, and 206).

46. Helen Darbishire, ed., *Wordsworth: Poems in Two Volumes, 1807* (Oxford: Clarendon Press, 1952), p. xlvii.

47. Kenneth Eisold, *Loneliness and Communion: A Study of Wordsworth's Thought and Experience, Salzburg Studies in English Literature, Romantic Reassessment,* ed. James Hogg (Salzburg, 1973), p. 130.

48. Truths "do rest" upon the child, whereas the man vainly "is toiling all [his] life" to recover those early wisdoms. He is restless in pursuing them and the more desperate his pursuit, the more he estranges himself from its object. "Restlessness," in the context of Wordsworth's canon, denotes political anxiety, the condition which came to a head in Wordsworth's London experience, 1793.

49. Simpson, *Figurings of the Real,* p. 113.

50. Terry Eagleton, *Walter Benjamin or Towards a Revolutionary Critique* (London: Verso and NLB, 1981), pp. 122, 123. And see pp. 6–10, 22, 117.

51. Eagleton, *Walter Benjamin,* p. 123.

THE PRELUDE

Wordsworth's *Prelude* and the
Crisis-Autobiography [Excerpt]

M. H. Abrams*

In the Prospectus to *The Recluse* and its associated poems Wordsworth announced his intent "to weigh / The good and evil of our mortal state." This was his version of Milton's undertaking to "justify the ways of God to men." Wordsworth's argument, like Milton's, is a theodicy which locates the justification for human suffering in the restoration of a lost paradise. In Milton's view, this event will not occur "till one greater Man / Restore us, and regain the blissful Seat." Wordsworth's paradise, however, can be achieved simply by a union of man's mind with nature, and so is a present paradise in this world, capable of being described "by words / Which speak of nothing more than what we are"—without recourse, that is, either to an intervenient deity or to a heavenly kingdom to redress any imbalance between the good and evil of our mortal state.

In Wordsworth's *Prelude*, the autobiographical preliminary to *The Recluse*, the ultimate goodness governing the course of his life is brought into question by his suffering and crisis of spirit, then is established by the outcome of his experience, which is represented as prototypical for the men to whom he addresses himself. Wordsworth's assumption, like that of all writers of theodicies, whether of universal scope or of the private life, is that if life is to be worth living there cannot be a blank unreason or mere contingency at the heart of things; there must be meaning (in the sense of a good and intelligible purpose) in the occurrence of both physical and moral evils. The Christian theodicy of the private life, in the long lineage of Augustine's *Confessions*, transfers the locus of the primary concern with evil from the providential history of mankind to the providential history of the individual self, and justifies the experience of wrongdoing, suffering, and loss as a necessary means toward the greater good of personal redemption. But Wordsworth's is a secular theod-

* Reprinted from *Natural Supernaturalism: Tradition and Revolution in Romantic Literature* by permission of W. W. Norton & Company, Inc. © 1971 W. W. Norton & Company, Inc.

icy—a theodicy without an operative *theos*—which retains the form of the ancient reasoning, but translates controlling Providence into an immanent teleology, makes the process coterminous with our life in this world, and justifies suffering as the necessary means toward the end of a greater good which is nothing other than the stage of achieved maturity:

> Ah me! that all
> The terrors, all the early miseries
> Regrets, vexations, lassitudes, that all
> The thoughts and feelings which have been infus'd
> Into my mind, should ever have made up
> The calm existence that is mine when I
> Am worthy of myself! Praise to the end!
> Thanks likewise for the means!
>
> (I: 355–62)

In other words, the Wordsworthian theodicy of the private life (if we want to coin a term, we can call it a "biodicy"), belongs to the distinctive Romantic genre of the *Bildungsgeschichte,* which translates the painful process of Christian conversion and redemption into a painful process of self-formation, crisis, and self-recognition, which culminates in a stage of self-coherence, self-awareness, and assured power that is its own reward.

On the one level Wordsworth tells this story in terms of his literal experiences of terror, pain, error, and misery, climaxed by his crisis of doubt and despair after the failure of the French Revolution; and he justifies these experiences (as he says in a revision of the passage just quoted) as "bearing a part, / And that a needful part" in making him a man, in making him a poet, and in making him exactly the kind of man and poet he was. But throughout *The Prelude* there is a double story being told—a story of Wordsworth's life in the world and a correlative story of his life in nature. And on this second narrative level Wordsworth incorporates the problem of suffering within his overarching myth of the interaction between mind and nature, in which fostering nature conducts the mind through successive stages of growth, while speaking nature defines and communicates to the mind that degree of self-knowledge which its stage of cumulative experience has prepared it to receive.

No sooner does Wordsworth begin the story of his life as a child engaged in the ordinary activities of bathing, basking in the sun, and running through the fields and woods, than he turns to the correlative presentation of his soul in direct engagement with nature, as it is formed by contrary influences of the external scene:

> Fair seed-time had my soul, and I grew up
> Foster'd alike by beauty and by fear.
>
> (I: 305–6)

Throughout the earlier books of *The Prelude* Wordsworth repeatedly represents his mind as developing by a sustained interchange with "these two attributes," the "sister horns that constitute [nature's] strength," whose "twofold influence . . . of peace and excitation" instills in the mind a union of "emotion" and "calmness," of "energy" and "happy stillness."[1] Of one type are the gentle and "fearless" aspects of nature—the calm and ordered prospect, small-scale objects, "quiet Heavens," "tranquil scenes," "gentle breezes," "a garden with its walks and banks of flowers," all of which manifest "love" and "tenderness," act by effecting "pleasure and repeated happiness," and move the mind "by feelings of delight." But "Nature . . . when she would frame / A favor'd Being" alternates her "gentlest visitation" with "severer interventions, ministry / More palpable." Of this opposite type are the awe-inspiring and terrifying aspects of nature—vast scenes of wildness and majesty, the "awful" and the "grand," elements "in tumult," "the midnight storm," "the roaring ocean and waste wilderness," which act on the mind by "terror" and by "pain and fear" and manifest not nature's "love" but her punitive actions: her "impressive discipline of fear."[2]

In this natural polarity of "beauteous forms or grand," or of "forms sublime or fair,"[3] as Samuel Monk pointed out more than three decades ago, Wordsworth adapted the two primary categories—that of the beautiful and that of the sublime—into which earlier eighteenth-century theorists had apportioned the aesthetic qualities of the natural scene.[4] By and large the beautiful is small in scale, orderly, and tranquil, effects pleasure in the observer, and is associated with love; while the sublime is vast (hence suggestive of infinity), wild, tumultuous, and awful, is associated with pain, and evokes ambivalent feelings of terror and admiration. But behind this familiar eighteenth-century aesthetic dichotomy lay centuries of speculation about the natural world—speculation whose concerns were not aesthetic but theological and moral, and which in fact constituted a systematic theodicy of the landscape. For on the Pauline ground that "the invisible things of Him from the creation of the world are clearly seen," the problem had early arisen, how to justify the goodness of an omnipotent Creator who has brought into being an earth which, in many of its aspects, is not beautiful and beneficent, but wild, waste, ugly, perilous, and terrifying?

This is precisely the question put to God by Dorigen in Chaucer's *Franklin's Tale* when, her husband away on a distant voyage, she looks with terror from the brink of a cliff upon the sea and its "grisly feendly rokkes blake,"

> That semen rather a foul confusion
> Of werk than any fair creacion

Of swich a parfit wys God and a stable,
Why han ye wroght this werk unresonable? . . .
I woot wel clerkes wol seyn as hem leste,
By argumentz, that al is for the beste—

But having thus displaced the burden of theodicy from human evil and suffering, with its backdrop of Eden, Calvary, and the New Jerusalem, to the ugly and terrifying aspects of what should be the best of all possible physical worlds, Dorigen helplessly resigns all disputation on the matter "to clerkes," while her friends, to distract her from the "disconfort" of the wild sea, escort her to conventional places of ordered and agreeable beauty:

They leden hire by ryveres and by welles,
And eek in othere places delitables.

(lines 856–99)

The "clerkes" proposed a variety of answers to this question, but a standard one was that a perfect, wise God had originally created a perfectly smooth, orderly, useful, and beautiful world. Mountains and other wild, waste places were the product not of divine benevolence but of human depravity, for they had been wreaked by the wrath of a just God at the original fall of man in Eden, or alternatively (in some commentators, additionally), they had been effected by the devastating flood with which He punished the all-but-universal corruption of mankind at the time of Noah. Henry Vaughan expressed the common opinion in his poem *Corruption;* when Adam sinned

He drew the Curse upon the world, and Crackt
The whole frame with his fall.

Mountains, therefore, and other vast, chaotic and frightful aspects of nature, as Marjorie Nicolson has said, were looked upon as "symbols of human sin" and of the consequent wrath of a justly punitive God.[5]

A late and circumstantial document in this tradition was Thomas Burnet's *The Sacred Theory of the Earth*, of which the first Latin version was published in 1681–89. On the one side, this immensely popular book fostered the development of "physico-theology," which undertook to demonstrate the existence and attributes of God, and especially the justice of His ways to men in the creation, entirely by reasoning from the phenomena of nature; on the other side, it served as an influential model for translating theological and moral concepts into an aesthetics of landscape. Burnet was often compared to Milton (Coleridge described *The Sacred Theory* as "a grand Miltonic Romance"[6]), and not merely because of the baroque magnificence of his style. As Burnet's subtitle to the expanded version in English describes his subject, it is "an Account of the Original of the Earth, and of all the General Changes which it hath already undergone, or is to undergo, till the Consummation of all Things." The span of his work, then, from creation to apocalypse, coincides with that of the plot of *Paradise Lost;* and although Burnet tells the story primarily in terms of changes in the physical universe which were effected by natural law, or "second Causes," these causes operate in preestablished harmony with what he calls the "first Cause"—that is, with the underlying purpose and providence of Milton's God.[7]

According to Burnet the perfect God had originally brought into being a perfectly beautiful world; and this, by Burnet's Palladian standards of beauty, was a world "smooth, regular, and uniform; without Mountains, and without a Sea" (I: 72). Earliest mankind dwelt in perfect innocence and ease in an unchanging springtime, in a region of the flawless world which was even more perfect than the rest. This region was the paradise which is described in Genesis and is also dimly remembered in pagan myths of *"Elysian* Fields, Fortunate Islands, Gardens of *Hesperides, Alcinous,* etc."—a passage Wordsworth may well have recalled when he wrote in the Prospectus of "Paradise, and groves Elysian, Fortunate Fields. . . ."[8] The providential cause of the destruction of this perfect world was God's wrathful judgment on "the Wickedness and Degeneracy of Men" at the time of Noah, when "the Abyss was open'd" and "the Frame of the Earth broke and fell down into the *great Abyss";* the resulting flood and cataclysm transformed all nature into its present state, "wherein it must continue till the Redemption and Restitution of all Things." The world we now inhabit therefore is only the wreck of paradise, with some remains indeed of its original beauty, yet overall "the Image or Picture of a great Ruin . . . the true Aspect of a World lying in its Rubbish" (I: 130, 90, 223, 148).

Toward the ruinous parts of the present world Burnet exhibits the complex attitudes which helped form the new aesthetics of the following century. For he finds positive values in those aspects of the landscape which are vast, misproportioned, terrifying, and by traditional aesthetic standards, ugly; but these values are both aesthetic and quasi-theological, for in them the speaking face of earth declares the infinity, the power, and the wrath of a just deity.

> As to the present Form of the Earth, we call all Nature to Witness for us; the Rocks and the Mountains, the Hills and the Valleys, the deep and wide Sea, and the Caverns of the Ground: Let these speak, and tell their Origin: How the Body of the Earth came to be thus torn and mangled? (II, 331–2)

Yet these same phenomena, "the greatest Objects of Nature," the "boundless Regions where Stars inhabit . . . the wide Sea and the Mountains of the Earth," seem to him "the most pleasing to behold."

> There is something august and stately in the Air of these things, that inspires the Mind with great Thoughts and Passions; we do

naturally, upon such Occasions, think of God and his Greatness: And whatsoever hath but the Shadow and Appearance of INFINITE, as all Things have that are too big for our Comprehension, they fill and over-bear the Mind with their Excess, and cast it into a pleasing kind of Stupor and Admiration.

And yet these Mountains . . . are nothing but great Ruins; but such as shew a certain Magnificence in Nature. (I, 188–9)

Inherent in precisely those ruined elements of landscape which manifest the terrifying wrath of God are the highest aesthetic values, because they also express God's infinite power, and so evoke from Burnet attitudes and emotions which men had earlier felt for almighty God himself.

Burnet's distinction between the beautiful and the "great" aspects of nature was developed by later theorists (with the help of a term imported from Longinus' treatise on the elevated style) into the distinction between the beautiful and the "sublime." Even in later naturalistic treatments of these categories, we recognize a consonance with the earlier theological context, in which the beautiful elements in nature are the enduring expression of God's loving benevolence, while the vast and disordered in nature express his infinity, power, and wrath, and so evoke a paradoxical union of delight and terror, pleasure and awe. Edmund Burke, for example, in his greatly influential *Philosophical Enquiry into . . . the Sublime and Beautiful,* bases the sense of beauty on the passion of love and associates it with pleasure, while "whatever is fitted in any sort to excite the ideas of pain, and danger, that is to say, whatever is in any sort terrible . . . is a source of the *sublime.*"[9] The sublime also has its source in the associated qualities of "power," "vastness," "infinity," and "magnificence," and its characteristic effects on the beholder are the traditional ones aroused by the conception of the infinite power of a stern but just God: "terror," "astonishment," "awe," "admiration," and "reverence."[10]

William Wordsworth, who in his writings showed an early and continuing interest in the antithetic categories of the beautiful and the sublime,[11] thus inherited a long tradition of finding moral and theological meanings in the aesthetic qualities of the landscape, as well as of conducting an inquiry into cosmic goodness and justice by reference to the contrary attributes of the natural world. From such hints he constructed his account of an individual mind in its developing capacity to respond to and interpret "whatso'er of Terror or of Love, / Or Beauty, Nature's daily face put on" (III: 132–3)—an achievement which in its subtlety and insight had no precedent either in the physico-theology, the aesthetics, or the psychology of his day.

We can most clearly follow Wordsworth's procedure in the biography of the Pedlar which he interpolated into the 1798 version

of his greatest narrative poem, *The Ruined Cottage*. Wordsworth told
Isabella Fenwick that he represented in the Pedlar "chiefly an *idea*
of what I fancied my own character might have become in his
circumstances,"[12] and he later transferred a number of passages from
this description into *The Prelude*. The biography of the Pedlar, then,
is the first sketch of what I have called the controlling "idea" of *The
Prelude*, and in it Wordsworth, in some 250 packed lines, describes
the growth of the Pedlar's mind from early childhood, through a
spiritual crisis (experienced "before his twentieth year was pass'd,"
in which "his mind became disturbed" and he turned "in vain . . . /
To science for a cure" in order "to mitigate the fever of his heart")
to the time in which he discovered his role in life and "assumed /
This lowly occupation." But though his outer occupation was that of
a pedlar, he had also been born to be a mute inglorious poet, for

> he was a chosen son
> To him was given an ear which deeply felt
> The voice of Nature in the obscure wind
> The sounding mountain and the running stream.
> . . . In all shapes
> He found a secret and mysterious soul,
> A fragrance and a spirit of strange meaning.[13]

The compactness of this biography allows Wordsworth to sustain
the narrative mode of the transaction between mind and nature in a
way not possible in the extended autobiography of *The Prelude*. In
early childhood the Pedlar's mind had been fostered by his solitary
experiences with the terror, power, and grandeur of the natural
sublime:

> So the foundations of his mind were laid
> In such communion, not from terror free.
> While yet a child, and long before his time
> He had perceived the presence and the power
> Of greatness, and deep feelings had impressed
> Great objects on his mind.
> (lines 77–82)

Though even at this time, in the "fixed and steady lineaments" of
the face of the landscape, he had "traced an ebbing and a flowing
mind," he had not yet been ready for a later stage of nature's teaching,
"the lesson deep of love" enciphered in the gentle aspects of the
outer scene.

> In his heart
> Love was not yet, nor the pure joy of love,
> By sound diffused, or by the breathing air,
> Or by the silent looks of happy things.

The passage to that stage at which he learns to decipher the lesson of love in nature is precisely fixed in time: it occurred "ere his ninth summer," when having for the first time been sent out alone to tend his father's sheep, he beheld the beauty of a mountain dawn.

> He looked,
> The ocean and the earth beneath him lay
> In gladness and deep joy. The clouds were touched
> And in their silent faces did he read
> Unutterable love. . . .
> His mind was a thanksgiving to the power
> That made him. It was blessedness and love.
> (lines 106–41)

Such were the experiences which fostered the development of his mature mind which, "in a just equipoise of love," had the psychic strength to participate with human wretchedness—"He could afford to suffer / With those whom he saw suffer."[14]

In a revealing passage Wordsworth says that the boy "had learned to read / His bible" while at school, before he came to discover the same meanings written more distinctly and impressively in the *verba visibilia,* the symbolic language of the landscape:

> But in the mountains did he *feel* his faith
> There did he see the writing—All things there
> Looked immortality, revolving life,
> And greatness still revolving, infinite;
> . . . nor did he *believe*—he saw.
> (lines 54–6, 146–55)

But it would appear that the Pedlar learned to transfer the divine attributes from the Book of Scripture to the Book of Nature with some help from the physico-theology of Burnet's *Sacred Theory;* for one of the revelations he found encoded in a scene of bleak sublimity was that of the cosmic vengeance which had loosed the mountain-making deluge in the age of Noah—in

> some peak
> Familiar with forgotten years, which shews,
> Inscribed, as with the silence of the thought,
> Upon its bleak and visionary sides,
> The history of many a winter storm,
> Or of the day of vengeance, when the sea
> Rose like a giant from his sleep, and smote
> The hills, and when the firmament of heaven
> Rained darkness which the race of men beheld
> Yea all the men that lived and had no hope[15]

In *The Prelude* (which also contains echoes of Burnet's *Sacred Theory,*[16] as well as of various eighteenth-century treatises on the aesthetics of landscape), after Wordsworth moves from the rural milieu of his boyhood into the variegated life of Cambridge, London, and France, he represents himself as coming to terms with his experience in periodic accountings with the natural scene. The mind finds in the scene what it has become ready to find, and what it finds is its own aspect. As Wordsworth put it, "from thyself it is that thou must give, / Else never canst receive" (XI: 333–4). And what the mind at such moments brings to nature is the hitherto inchoate product of its experience of men and the world since it had last come to an understanding with nature.

A central instance of this recurrent tactic constitutes a notable passage in Book VI of *The Prelude.* There Wordsworth describes his first pedestrian trip through France in the summer of 1790, when he participated joyously in that festival period of the Revolution. On his way through the Alps from France to Italy he crosses the Simplon Pass and descends into the narrow and gloomy ravine of the Gondo, there to read, inscribed in the physical properties of the scene, a revelation about man and nature and human life.

Burnet had long before incorporated in *The Sacred Theory* reminiscences of his trip across the "great Ruins" of the Alps,[17] and the description of Alpine sublimity had become a standard *topos* among eighteenth-century connoisseurs of pleasing horror, including John Dennis, Shaftesbury, Addison, and Thomas Gray, who had vied in representing prospects where, as Gray said, "not a precipice, not a torrent, not a cliff, but is pregnant with religion and poetry."[18] Wordsworth's description of the ravine below Simplon thus epitomizes a century of commentary on the religion and poetry in the sublime Alpine landscape, brought together by a poet of genius and endowed with an ominous life:

> The immeasurable height
> Of woods decaying, never to be decay'd,
> The stationary blasts of water-falls,
> And everywhere along the hollow rent
> Winds thwarting winds, bewilder'd and forlorn,
> The torrents shooting from the clear blue sky,
> The rocks that mutter'd close upon our ears,
> Black drizzling crags that spake by the way-side
> As if a voice were in them, the sick sight
> And giddy prospect of the raving stream. . . .

The grimness of the lesson this scene bespeaks is made even more emphatic in a manuscript addition which suggests Burnet's view that mountains and rocks are the ruins left by the wrathful destruction of the pristine world, and also indicates the implicit relevance of the prospect to the violent contingencies of human life:

> And ever as we halted, or crept on,
> Huge fragments of primaeval mountain spread
> In powerless ruin, blocks as huge aloft
> Impending, nor permitted yet to fall,
> The sacred Death-cross, monument forlorn
> Though frequent of the perish'd Traveller. . . .

Integral to Wordsworth's description of terrifying sublimity, however, is a contrary aspect of the scene: the light and serenity of beauty, exhibited in "the clear blue sky" and in "the unfetter'd clouds, and region of the Heavens." And this *coincidentia oppositorum* suddenly expresses a revelation which Wordsworth equates with the showing forth of the contraries of God in the Apocalypse, the Book of Revelation itself. There the Lamb of the gospel of love had manifested Himself as the terrifying deity of the *dies irae*, while men cried "to the mountains and rocks, Fall on us and hide us . . . from the wrath of the Lamb: For the great day of his wrath is come"; but the opening and closing chapters had insistently reiterated that the God of wrath and destruction is one and coeternal with the God who manifests his love in the creation at the beginning and in the redemption at the end of time: "I am Alpha and Omega, the beginning and the ending"; "Fear not; I am the first and the last"; "I am Alpha and Omega, the beginning and the end, the first and the last."[19] In Wordsworth's version:

> Tumult and peace, the darkness and the light
> Were all like workings of one mind, the features
> Of the same face, blossoms upon one tree,
> Characters of the great Apocalypse,
> The types and symbols of Eternity,
> Of first and last, and midst, and without end.
>   (VI: 551–72)

In consonance with Wordsworth's two-term frame of reference, the Scriptural Apocalypse is assimilated to an apocalypse of nature; its written characters are natural objects, which are read as types and symbols of permanence in change; and its antithetic qualities of sublimity and beauty are seen as simultaneous expressions on the face of heaven and earth, declaring an unrealized truth which the chiaroscuro of the scene articulates for the prepared mind—a truth about the darkness and the light, the terror and the peace, the ineluctable contraries that make up our human existence.

This recognition, however, is not the end but only a mid-stage in the evolution of the poet's mind. Book IX, which will begin the fateful record of his second visit to France and its aftermath, opens with a statement of Wordsworth's human reluctance to face the crisis of maturity, as he winds and doubles back like a river which fears

the way "that leads direct to the devouring sea"; the passage ominously echoes Milton's invocation to his ninth book, which narrates
the fall of man and his expulsion from paradise into "a world of
woe, / Sin and her shadow Death, and Misery."[20] After the failure of
the limitless initial promise of the French Revolution, the growing
divisions and conflicts in a world gone mad are reflected in Wordsworth's inner divisions and conflicts, until the integrity of his spiritual
development is shattered in what seems incipient madness. He suffers
from Kafka-esque nightmares, pleading

> Before unjust Tribunals, with a voice
> Labouring, a brain confounded, and a sense
> Of treachery and desertion in the place
> The holiest I knew of, my own soul.
> (X: 378–81)

He makes a desperate attempt to reestablish on abstract premises,
and by logical analysis and reasoning, what had originally been his
spontaneous confidence in life and his hope for man, but the attempt
leads only to utter perplexity about "right and wrong, the ground /
Of moral obligation," until he breaks down completely. In the context
of our discussion it is significant that Wordsworth describes his crisis
as involving, explicitly, his despair about a solution to the problem
of the good and evil of our moral state:

> I lost
> All feeling of conviction, and, in fine,
> Sick, wearied out with contrarieties,
> Yielded up moral questions in despair.
> This was the crisis of that strong disease,
> This the soul's last and lowest ebb.[21]

The account of the dark night of his soul—"I was benighted
heart and mind" (XII: 21)—is at once correlated, in Wordsworth's
double narrative, with an account of the paralysis of the earlier
reciprocative relation between his mind and nature. For his heart
"had been turn'd aside / From nature by external accidents" (X:
886–7), and the habit of "logic and minute analysis," infecting even
his perceptions, replaced the attitude of total receptiveness to all
that nature had to give—"I never thought of judging, with the gift
of all this glory filled and satisfied"—by an attitude in which the
mind sat "in judgment" on nature,

> disliking here, and there,
> Liking, by rules of mimic art transferr'd
> To things above all art.
> (XI: 126–55)

That is, he evaluated the scene according to the fixed and formal aesthetic categories of the picturesque which had been abstracted from the principles of composition in the art of landscape painting.[22] And in place of the earlier freedom in its negotiations with nature, his mind, thus weakened, became a slave to "the eye . . . / The most despotic of our senses," which rejoiced "to lay the inner faculties asleep" (XI: 171–99). The poet had succumbed to the "sleep / Of death" from which, in the Prospectus (60–61), he undertook to "arouse the sensual" by his evangel of the creative power of the liberated mind.

Wordsworth's eleventh book, which begins the systematic account of his "Imagination . . . Restored," opens with another extended parallel to *Paradise Lost*, this time echoing Milton's relief, in his invocation to the third book, at escaping the realms of hell, "though long detain'd / In that obscure sojourn." In Wordsworth's version:

> Long time hath Man's unhappiness and guilt
> Detain'd us; with what dismal sights beset
> For the outward view, and inwardly oppress'd . . .
> And lastly, utter loss of hope itself,
> And things to hope for. Not with these began
> Our Song, and not with these our Song must end:
> Ye motions of delight, that through the fields
> Stir gently, breezes and soft airs that breathe
> The breath of Paradise, and find your way
> To the recesses of the soul!

Thus having traversed his personal hell, he turns to the correspondent breeze which had blown in the glad preamble of his song—now specified as "the breath of Paradise" that finds its way "to the recesses of the soul"—to assist him in restoring the paradise within.[23] Wordsworth narrates the process of this recovery by his customary alternation between the details of his outer life (the influence of Dorothy, of Coleridge, and of the "uncouth Vagrants" and "lowly men" with whom he talked in his solitary wanderings) and his private intercourse with "Nature's Self, by human love / Assisted," which ultimately brings his mind back to what it had earlier been, but on the level now of deepened awareness, wider breadth, and firm stability. Nature's self

> Conducted me again to open day,
> Revived the feelings of my earlier life,
> Gave me that strength and knowledge full of peace,
> Enlarged, and never more to be disturb'd.

In a manuscript version of this passage Wordsworth remarks that in saying this much he feared "to encroach upon a theme / Reserv'd to close my Song."[24] This ultimate resolution of his crisis is reserved for the concluding book of *The Prelude*, and follows from the climactic revelation on Mount Snowdon in which, in a sudden burst of natural illumination, the poet sees the landscape as "the perfect image of a mighty Mind." Like the ravine below Simplon Pass, the prospect unites the contraries of tumult and peace, the darkness and the light— the terrifying dark chasm, "a deep and gloomy breathing-place through which / Mounted the roar of waters," while overhead the moon "naked in the Heavens . . . look'd down upon this shew / In single glory." Above all, the give and take of influence between the moon and the mist-shrouded scene shows forth the radical power of human minds to confront nature in a creative and life-giving interchange, "Willing to work and to be wrought upon," so that "in a world of life they live." From this power, Wordsworth says, follows "sovereignty within and peace at will," "truth in moral judgments and delight / That fails not in the external universe," as opposed to the tendency, from which he has finally freed himself, of "habit to enslave the mind . . . by laws of vulgar sense," and so to

> substitute a universe of death,
> The falsest of all worlds, in place of that
> Which is divine and true.
>   (XIII: 39–143)

That is, his mind has escaped back to "a world of life" from its experiential equivalent of the hell which Milton had described (in the phrase Wordsworth here dramatically echoes) as "a Universe of death, which God by curse / Created evil, for evil only good / Where all life dies, death lives" (*Paradise Lost*, II: 622–4).

There immediately follows the first part of Wordsworth's resolution of his long dialectic of good and evil:

> To fear and love,
> To love as first and chief, for there fear ends,
> Be this ascribed; to early intercourse,
> In presence of sublime and lovely Forms,
> With the adverse principles of pain and joy,
> Evil as one is rashly named by those
> Who know not what they say. From love, for here
> Do we begin and end, all grandeur comes,
> All truth and beauty, from pervading love,
> That gone, we are as dust.

And this love is a "higher love," a "love more intellectual" than maternal and sexual love, which are "human merely," for this "proceeds / More from the brooding Soul, and is divine" (XIII: 143–65). Patently Wordsworth's statement is in the traditional idiom of Christian theodicy, and is exactly equivalent in its place and function to Adam's climactic statement in the last book of Milton's epic when, upon hearing Michael foretell Christ's birth, death, resurrection, and

return to an earth which then "shall all be Paradise," he acknowledges
the justice of the ways of God to men:

> O goodness infinite, goodness immense!
> That all this good of evil shall produce,
> And evil turn to good; more wonderful
> Than that which by creation first brought forth
> Light out of darkness! Full of doubt I stand,
> Whether I should repent me now of sin
> By me done and occasion'd, or rejoice
> Much more, that much more good thereof shall spring,
> To God more glory, more good will to Men
> From God, and over wrath grace shall abound.
>
> (XII: 469–78)

In the passage in *The Prelude* of 1805, however, there is no
mention of the Incarnation, Crucifixion, or Second Coming, nor even
of a deity. The recognition Wordsworth describes is the end product
of a sustained intercourse between mind and nature, and in defining
it he collects and resolves the contrary qualities of the natural scene—
aesthetic, moral, and quasi-theological—with which he has been weav-
ing the complex design of his theodicy since his opening statement
that he grew up fostered alike by beauty and by fear. On the one
side is the "sublime" and its near-synonym, "grandeur"; and on the
other the "lovely Forms" of nature (the identification is sharpened
in the later revision of line 146, "In presence of sublime or *beautiful*
forms"). With the sublime are aligned "fear" and "pain," hence what
is mistakenly supposed to be "evil"; with the beautiful are aligned
the "adverse principles," which are "joy" and "love." And whereas
in the poet's earlier revelation in the Alpine ravine he had envisioned
the contraries of peace and fear to be equal as well as coeternal
attributes of the "first and last, and midst, and without end," he now
has progressed to the higher realization that love is "first and chief,
for there fear ends," and therefore is the last as well as the first
("from love . . . / Do we begin and end"), so that in this final
accounting not only the beautiful but the sublime turns out to issue
from love: "From love . . . all grandeur comes, / All truth and beauty."
Such is Wordsworth's naturalistic equivalent, in a theodicy transacted
between mind and nature, of the Miltonic doctrine that God's love
not only subsumes and justifies, but necessitates the pain and fear
imposed on man by God's wrath—a paradox put by Dante with a
starkness beyond Milton when he inscribed over the eternal gates of
his ghastly hell that primal love had made it:

> Fecemi la divina potestate
> La somma sapienza e'l primo amore.[25]

Not all readers of *The Prelude* attend to its conclusion with the care they devote to the earlier sections, and to some of those who do it has seemed that Wordsworth's shift from pain and evil to love and good has been managed by logical sleight of hand. A main undertaking in the later parts of the poem, John Jones has said, is to marshal "into consequential argument 'the history of a poet's mind,' " and the "optimism . . . of the late *Prelude* is a determined end towards which the poem must be manipulated, like the plot of a bad play."[26] But Wordsworth does not undertake to prove that good subsumes ill by consequential argument; in fact, he has told us that it was the attempt to apply "formal proof" to moral matters that precipitated the breakdown in which he "yielded up moral questions in despair." What Wordsworth attempts is to represent a mode of experience, in which the recovery from his spiritual crisis yields the vision of a nature transformed, and in which, conversely, what he now sees in nature is correlative with a radical change in himself.[27] "His attainment of intellectual love," Francis Christensen has said, is "a kind of secular conversion" marking "the poet's entrance into his maturity" and involving (as Wordsworth goes on to describe in some detail) "the taming of the daring, the turbulent, the violent, the wilful in his nature."[28] That is, it involves the taming of the equivalent in Wordsworth's inner nature to the sublime aspects of external nature; for his own "soul," as he puts it, had been framed at birth to be "a rock with torrents roaring" (XIII: 221–32). It is possible to read the slackened power of these passages as a sign that Wordsworth feels less than the total assurance to which he aspires, and it is also possible to infer, from our knowledge of his later fate as a poet, that he has given up too much for too little. The conclusion of Wordsworth's theodicy, however, is not an extemporized argument, but is grounded in the beginning. And if this conclusion exhibits "optimism," it is of a kind which, far from denying the reality of pain, terror, and suffering, insists not only that they are humanly inevitable but that they are indispensable conditions for developing the calm, the insight, and the power that is ours when, as Wordsworth put it, we are worthy of ourselves.

In *The Prelude*, then, the justification of seeming evil turns on a crisis and inner transformation, parallel to Augustine's agony and conversion in the garden at Milan. An important difference is that in Augustine's account, although his spiritual preparation has been long, the conversion is instant and absolute, an accession of grace which takes place at a precise point in time, "*punctum ipsum temporis,*" and effects at a stroke the destruction of the old creature and the birth of the new. In Wordsworth's secular account of the "growth" of his mind, the process is one of gradual recovery which takes three books to tell in full; and for the Christian paradigm of right-angled change into something radically new he substitutes a pattern (the typical Romantic pattern) in which development consists of a gradual curve back to an earlier stage, but on a higher level incorporating that which has intervened. "Behold me then," Wordsworth says, "Once more in Nature's presence, thus restored," although now "with memory left of what had been escaped" (XI: 393–6). But if in the overall accounting, by Wordsworth's calculation, the gain outweighs the loss, he does not deny that growth is change, and change entails loss. Nature, he says, "I seem'd to love as much as heretofore," and yet this passion

> Had suffer'd change; how could there fail to be
> Some change, if merely hence, that years of life
> Were going on, and with them loss or gain
> Inevitable, sure alternative.
>
> (XI: 36–41)

There remains a second stage in Wordsworth's elaborate resolution, in the concluding book of *The Prelude*, of the problem of human suffering. Having recognized the general truth that love is first and last, he turns to the evaluation of the particular life that he has lived. Typically, as we have seen, he transforms that life into a landscape over which he soars in metaphoric flight; and from this high perspective he is able to discern that all its parts are centered in love, and that all its earthly sorrows are ultimately for the best:

> Call back to mind
> The mood in which this Poem was begun,
> O Friend! the termination of my course
> Is nearer now, much nearer; yet even then
> In that distraction and intense desire
> I said unto the life which I had lived,
> Where art thou? Hear I not a voice from thee
> Which 'tis reproach to hear? Anon I rose
> As if on wings, and saw beneath me stretch'd
> Vast prospect of the world which I had been
> And was; and hence this Song, which like a lark
> I have protracted, in the unwearied Heavens
> Singing, and often with more plaintive voice
> Attemper'd to the sorrows of the earth;
> Yet centring all in love, and in the end
> All gratulant if rightly understood.[29]

This was, he says, the vision given him at the beginning of the poem, although what he now assays is his life as represented in his just-completed song, the work of art which is *The Prelude* itself. If we turn back to the poem's beginning, we find in its fifteenth line the first prominent instance of Wordsworth's carefully chosen and allocated allusions to *Paradise Lost*—a very striking instance, because in his opening he echoes the closing lines of Milton's epic, when Adam and Eve, between sadness and expectancy, leave paradise to take up their journey in this world of all of us:

> The World was all before them, where to choose
> Their place of rest, and Providence their guide:
> They hand in hand with wand'ring steps and slow,
> Through *Eden* took their solitary way.

"The earth is all before me," Wordsworth too says; but his mood is joyously confident, and he entrusts his guidance not to Providence but to nature:

> The earth is all before me: with a heart
> Joyous, nor scar'd at its own liberty,
> I look about, and should the guide I chuse
> Be nothing better than a wandering cloud,
> I cannot miss my way.
>
> (I: 15–19)

Critics who have noted this parallel interpret it to signify that *The Prelude* as a whole is a kind of sequel to *Paradise Lost;* "as if," Elizabeth Sewell has said, "Wordsworth meant to dovetail his epic directly into the very place where the Miltonic epic ends."[30] This, I think, is a mistake (although an easy one to make) for it overlooks the fact that, though the preamble comes first in the structural order of the *Prelude*, it inaugurates the stage of the narrator's life which comes last in its temporal order. It is not, then, *The Prelude* which Wordsworth meant to dovetail into the place in Milton's poem at which man, having lost paradise, sets out on his pilgrimage to recover it again, but the narrative which follows *The Prelude;* namely, the opening book of *The Recluse* proper, *Home at Grasmere*, in which the poet takes up the place of rest he has selected at the end of the preamble, when "I made a choice / Of one sweet Vale whither my steps should turn" (I: 81–2).

On his first glimpse of this happy valley when, as a "roving schoolboy," he had overlooked it from the verge of a "steep barrier," it had appeared as a "paradise before him" (*Home at Grasmere*, lines 1–14), and now that he has returned to this "dear Vale, / Beloved Grasmere," he describes it in terms which repeatedly echo Milton's description of Eden in *Paradise Lost* (e.g., lines 126 ff.). By "surpassing grace," however, his is an Eden happier far than Adam's original paradise, because it possesses an attribute which "among the bowers / Of blissful Eden . . . was neither given, / Nor could be given": it is a felicity that incorporates the memory of what it was to have lacked it (lines 103–9). Above all, his is a higher paradise than Milton's because it is inhabited by man as he is, exhibiting the mixed state "of solid good / and real evil"; that is, it possesses the solid advantage of reality over "all golden fancies of the golden Age," whether located "before all time" or in some distant future "ere time expire" (lines 405–6, 625–32). The point that Wordsworth repeatedly makes in *Home at Grasmere* is his personal experience of a truth which, in the Prospectus concluding that poem, he announces as the argument for all *The Recluse:* that in our life in this actual world, with its ineradicable evil and suffering, lies the possibility, and the only possibility, of achieving a paradise which serves him, as it did Milton, to justify the evil of our mortal state.

At the conclusion of *The Prelude* itself, in justifying the sorrows which had fostered the growth of his mind as "in the end all gratulant," Wordsworth has completed his private "history" of "the discipline / And consummation of the Poet's mind." But this poet, as he had said in the opening preamble, is a poet-prophet, "singled out, as it might seem, / For holy services." He has, that is, a public role; and at the close Wordsworth calls upon his fellow poet Coleridge, to whom the whole account has been addressed, to serve with him in a recreant age as, quite explicitly, an evangelist of a new redemption. Though "this Age fall back to old idolatry," we shall be to men

> joint-labourers in a work
> (Should Providence such grace to us vouchsafe)
> Of their redemption, surely yet to come.
> Prophets of Nature, we to them will speak
> A lasting inspiration. . . .

But the prophet of nature at once proceeds to a coda which is a *gloria in excelsis* not to nature but to the mind of man. We will

> Instruct them how the mind of man becomes
> A thousand times more beautiful than the earth
> On which he dwells, above this Frame of things. . . .
> In beauty exalted, as it is itself
> Of substance and of fabric more divine.
>
> (XIII: 431–52)

Thus he announces the end of his long preparation for writing his masterpiece. But in describing that preparation Wordsworth, no less than Proust, has achieved the masterpiece itself.

Notes

1. *The Prelude*, ed. Ernest de Selincourt and Helen Darbishire, 2nd ed. (Oxford: Clarendon Press, 1959), XII: 3–4; and p. 571.

2. See ibid., I: 362–71, 439–41, 490–501, 630–40; II: 320–6, 341–8, 389–93; III: 131–6; XII: 1–14; and the MS passages, pp. 572, 577–8.

3. Ibid., I: 573, and the 1850 version, I: 546. Also I: 635–6, "scenes . . . beauteous and majestic"; p. 578, "familiar things and awful, the minute / And grand"; and VI: 672–6: "whate'er / I saw, or heard, or felt . . . did administer / To grandeur and to tenderness."

4. Samuel H. Monk, *The Sublime: A Study of Critical Theories in XVIII-Century England* (New York, 1935), pp. 227–32. See also Herbert Lindenberger, *On Wordsworth's Prelude* (Princeton, 1963), pp. 23–29.

5. Marjorie Hope Nicolson, *Mountain Gloom and Mountain Glory* (Ithaca, N. Y., 1959), p. 83; and see chap. II.

6. Coleridge's annotation in Pepys' Diary, in *Coleridge on the Seventeenth Century*, ed. Roberta Florence Brinkley (Durham, N. C., 1955), p. 492. He classed Burnet's *Theoria Sacra* with the writings of Plato and Bishop Taylor as "undeniable proofs that poetry of the highest kind may exist without metre" (*Biographia Literaria*, ed. J. Shawcross, 2 vols. [Oxford: Clarendon Press, 1907], *Biographia Literaria*, II, 11). For Coleridge's high admiration for Burnet in the 1790's, see J. L. Lowes, *The Road to Xanadu* (Boston and New York, 1927), p. 16, and Index, "Burnet."

7. Thomas Burnet, *The Sacred Theory of the Earth* (6th edition; 2 vols., London, 1726), I, 142–4.

8. Ibid., I, 240; see also I, 349. A variant in a MS of the Prospectus is even closer to Burnet: "Paradise, and groves / Elysian, fortunate islands like those / In the deep ocean. . . ."

9. Edmund Burke, *A Philosophical Enquiry into the Origin of Our Ideas of the Sublime and Beautiful*, ed. J. T. Boulton (London, 1958), Part I, Sections 6–18.

10. Ibid., II, 1–13.

11. As early as the *Descriptive Sketches* of 1793 Wordsworth included a long note on the attributes of the sublime: *The Poetical Works of William Wordsworth*, Ernest de Selincourt and Helen Darbishire, 5 vols. (Oxford: Clarendon Press, 1940–49), I, 62. See also his careful discrimination between beautiful and sublime scenes in his *Guide to the Lakes*, ed. Ernest de Selincourt (London, 1906), e.g., pp. 21–6, 36, 69, 99, 102.

12. *Poetical Works*, V, 373 [my italics].

13. *The Ruined Cottage*, MS B, *Poetical Works*, V, 384–8 (II. 220–81).

14. Ibid., pp. 386–7. Like the Pedlar, Wordsworth in *The Prelude* underwent the natural discipline of terror "ere I had seen / Nine summers" (I: 310–11).

15. Ibid., p. 384; the last five lines of this passage are written on the verso of the MS page.

16. See, e.g., *The Prelude*, p. 53 (variant in MS B), and the editorial note, p. 522; also, p. 77 (variant in MS A)—an apparent recollection of Burnet's view that the ruined world in which fallen mankind lives retains traces of the beauty of its prime.

17. Burnet, *The Sacred Theory of the Earth*, I, 190–2. Burnet asks the reader to imagine the prospect he had seen from an Alpine mountain, "a Multitude of vast Bodies thrown together in Confusion . . . Rocks standing naked round about him; and the hollow valleys gaping under him," listening to "the Thunder come from below." On Wordsworth's route through the Simplon Pass and the ravine of Gondo, and his treatment of his experience in *Descriptive Sketches* as well as *The Prelude*, see Max Wildi, "Wordsworth and the Simplon Pass," *English Studies*, XL (1959), 224–32, and XLIII (1962), 359–77.

18. Thomas Gray, *Works*, ed. Edmund Gosse (4 vols.; New York, 1885), II, 45. For an account of eighteenth-century Alpine travelogues see Marjorie Nicolson, *Mountain Gloom and Mountain Glory*, pp. 276–9, 289–90, 304–7, 354–8. While actually on the tour he later reworked in accordance with his idea of *The Prelude*, Wordsworth in a letter to his sister had alluded to his Simplon crossing in the standard theological-aesthetic language of the natural sublime: "Among the more awful scenes of the Alps . . . my whole soul was turned to him who produced the terrible majesty before me" (*The Letters of William and Mary Wordsworth: The Early Years 1787–1805*, ed. Ernest de Selincourt and Chester L. Shaver, 2d ed [Oxford: Clarendon Press, 1967], p. 34).

19. See Revelation 1:8, 11, 17–18; 21:6; 22:13. Wordsworth may be recalling also the morning hymn of Adam and Eve, who praise in the qualities of the creation the "goodness beyond thought, and Power Divine" of "him first, him last, him midst, and without end" (*Paradise Lost*, V: 153–65).

20. Cf. *Paradise Lost*, IX: 1–12, with *The Prelude*, IX: 1–17, as well as the MS variant, pp. 314–15. De Selincourt and Darbishire remarked this significant parallel in *The Prelude*, p. 584.

21. *The Prelude*, X: 873–902; and in the edition of 1850, XI: 306–7.

22. See Martin Price, "The Picturesque Moment," in *From Sensibility to Romanticism*, ed. F. W. Hilles and Harold Bloom (New York, 1965), pp. 288–9.

23. The implicit parallel to Milton's invocation to Book III of *Paradise Lost* continues through Milton's plangent lament for his blindness, which no longer permits him to read in God's book of nature the symbolic significance of the return of day and of the revolving seasons. In Wordsworth's account, "The morning shines, / Nor heedeth Man's perverseness; Spring returns, / I *saw* the Spring return, when I was dead / To deeper hope"; so that, unlike Milton, being able to see, he found in nature's symbolism "a counterpoise . . . / Which, when the spirit of evil was at height / Maintain'd for me a secret happiness." Cf. *Paradise Lost*, III: 40–50 and *The Prelude*, XI: 22–34; also *Paradise Lost*, III: 26–38 and *The Prelude*, XI: 12–22.

24. *The Prelude*, X: 922–7, and MS version, p. 420.

25. *Inferno*, III: 5–6. T. S. Eliot's formulation, in the theodicy which concludes his *Four Quartets*, is even more succinct: "Who then devised the torment? Love" (*Little Gidding*, IV).

26. John Jones, *The Egotistical Sublime* (London, 1954), pp. 126–9.

27. A striking theological parallel to Wordsworth's secular form of experience is described in Jonathan Edwards' spiritual history, the *Narrative of His Conversion*. From childhood, he says, "the doctrine of God's sovereignty" in preelecting whom he pleased "eternally to perish, and be everlastingly tormented in hell," had appeared "like a horrible doctrine to me." But then he happened to read the text of I Tim. 1:17, and it brought him to "not only a conviction, but a *delightful* conviction" of the absolute sovereignty of God; and this inner conversion effected a correlative transformation of the external world: "The appearance of everything was altered; there seemed to be, as it were, a calm, sweet cast, or appearance of divine glory, in almost everything," and in "all nature." Edwards' experience of a glory in the landscape then led him, three-quarters of a century before Wordsworth, to solitary communings with the speaking face of nature. Jonathan Edwards, *Representative Selections*, ed. C. H. Faust and T. Johnson (New York, 1935), pp. 58–60.

28. Francis Christensen, "Intellectual Love: The Second Theme of *The Prelude*," *PMLA*, LXXX (1965), p. 70.

29. *The Prelude*, XIII: 370–85. Wordsworth, who tells us that he had memorized hundreds of lines of Pope's verse, may here be recalling the key statement in the theodicy of *The Essay on Man:*

All Discord, Harmony not understood;
All partial Evil, universal Good.
(I: 291–2)

30. Elizabeth Sewell, *The Orphic Voice* (New Haven, 1960), p. 342.

Wordsworth's *Prelude*   Ronald Paulson*

O *pleasant* exercise of *hope* and *joy!*
For mighty were the auxiliars which then
stood
Upon our side, us who were strong in *love!*
Bliss was it in that *dawn* to be alive,
But to be *young* was very heaven! O times.
In which the meagre, stale forbidding ways
Of *custom, law, and statute* took at once
The attraction of a country in *romance!*
(*Prelude*, XI: 105–12)

The emphasis falls on those by now familiar terms of the revolutionary experience outlined positively by Paine and Blake and negatively by Burke. Books IX–XI are the "revolutionary" books of *The Prelude*, in which Wordsworth recreates his experience of the 1790s. But his invocation to book I, although it never mentions the French Revolution, is couched in the vocabulary that will dominate the poem. It is a vocabulary of double meanings, strong and weak, manifest and latent, which designate the poem's most basic polarities of external and internal, political and poetic.

When Wordsworth starts a verse paragraph, "Dear Liberty" (l. 31), he cannot but introduce the two senses of *liberty*, including the French *liberté*, which he later contrasts in the episodes of boat-stealing and ice-skating: one is a challenge to social authority followed by retreat and internalization, the other a free play of private imagination in a form of art. He skates on ice that covers the waters of the lake into which he had been plunging the oars of the stolen boat.

So also the "correspondent breeze" (l. 35), the echo within him of the natural forces without, is both a metaphor for the creative process that emerges in the course of *The Prelude* and a memory of the political vocabulary associated with the Revolution. It is this "correspondent breeze" that is

* Reprinted from *Representations of Revolution (1789–1820)*. © 1983 Yale University Press. Used by permission of Yale University Press.

> gently moved
> With quickening *virtue,* but is now become
> A *tempest,* a redundant *energy.*
> Vexing its own creation.
>
> (ll. 35–38)

The poet moves from "breeze," the constructive poetic inspiration (as in the "Aeolian visitations" of l. 96), to "tempest," the breeze transformed into a destructive force that will "vex" its own creation (the central metaphor of book V); and also from "virtue" to "energy," the word used by both Burke and Fox for the revolutionary stimulus to liberation. Virtue/breeze becomes, in the actual experience of the Revolution, energy/tempest.

Thus at the end of the passage "A cheerful confidence in things to come (l. 58) refers both to the future of the poet now that he has moved beyond the political-social experience, away from the city and into the bower of nature, and also to the still hopeful future of the social organism as a whole. Or perhaps the second meaning has by this time been canceled out, or internalized, in the first—the tempest in the "gentle breeze" of the first line of the poem.

Other familiar revolutionary associations run through book I. Both the breeze and the tempest "join / In breaking up a long-continued frost, / Bring[ing] with them vernal promises": the imagery of winter breaking and dissolving into spring from Paine's *Rights of Man.* In a general way the epic invocation of book I is laid out on a pattern of *choice* (a word repeatedly used) between the threat/lure of the "tempest" of "this passion" and the withdrawal to a "green shady place," a locus amoenus where the poet will settle "into gentler happiness" (ll. 60–64):

> Content and not unwilling now to give
> A respite to this passion, I paced on
> With brisk and eager steps; and came, at length,
> To a green shady place, where down I sate
> Beneath a tree, slackening my thoughts by choice.
> And settling into gentler happiness.

This refuge from the "passion" of tempest/energy also reflects the transition Wordsworth works out in *The Prelude* between the sublime and the beautiful. The latter is "the sheltered and the sheltering grove / A perfect stillness," the "soft couch" of line 86 and the "hermitage" of line 107, all of which develop the associations of Burke and others with the beautiful experience that is being swept irretrievably away by the French Revolution.

Again, speaking of "hope" that "hath been discouraged," the poet introduces the familiar imagery of light: "welcome light / Dawns from the east [i.e., from France], but dawns to disappear / And mock me with a sky that ripens now / Into a steady morning . . ." (ll. 124–27). One possibility, or "choice," is to recall "the bold promise of the past," of the revolutionary years, and thus "grapple with some noble theme," but this possibility has been rejected for the reasons cited ("Impediments from day to day renewed"). Thus he is going to turn from "those lofty hopes" toward "present gifts / Of humbler industry," another transition from the sublime to the beautiful.

Here, addressing Coleridge, he makes a crucial equation:

> But, oh, dear Friend!
> The Poet, gentle creature as he is,
> Hath, like the Lover, his unruly times. . . .
> (ll. 134–36)

The poet, though a "gentle creature," is nevertheless compared to a lover with his "unruly times," and later linked to "his own / Unmanageable thoughts," his "passion." Into the ambience of political upheaval—the passionate and sublime experience Wordsworth has tested and somehow contrived to pass beyond—has now slipped the metaphor of the lover's passion, which will in turn have been transmuted by the end of the poem into the gentle love of his two "friends," his sister Dorothy and Coleridge.

The poet's "choice" of an epic subject then takes him back to traditional literary themes like those of Milton's *Paradise Lost,* even of chivalry, which he rejects, and thence at length back to his own youth. This originary time is both his chosen subject and the world of the locus amoenus seen as maternal solicitude ("a babe in arms," "infant softness," ll. 276, 278) and the world of Burke's aesthetic category the beautiful, though constantly threatened by the temptations to sublime "liberty."

In the passage that opens his recollection of childhood the opposing terms (public, private; political, poetic; sublime, beautiful) begin to intermingle. The images are mostly of maternal softness, peace, shelter, and love, but the "more than infant softness" appears "Amid the fretful dwellings of mankind" (l. 280), and the "smooth breast" of the mountain lies in the "shadow of those towers / That yet survive," the "shattered monument / Of feudal sway" (ll. 283–85). The passage describing the pleasures of a five-year-old boy leads from bathing in streams and basking in the sun to the view of "distant Skiddaw's lofty height," and finally to the first "spot of time," which follows from the formulation of the hints that have been gathering: that this "Fair seed-time" was "Fostered alike by beauty and by fear," by forces both beautiful and sublime. The poet goes out with bird-traps over his shoulder; his "visitation" now becomes "anxious," and as earlier in the presence of "Skiddaw's lofty height,"

> I was alone,
> And seemed to be a trouble to the peace
> That dwelt among [the moon and stars].
>   (ll. 315–17)

And in these "night wanderings," sometimes "a strong desire / O'-erpowered [his] better reason," and the birds became his "prey," his "captive." At this moment the "solitary hills" seem to rise and pursue him, his guilt materialized in an apparent retribution by the offended shapes of towers and mountains, the images of paternal authority ("Thou shalt not steal").

There is a strong sense in book I of indirection, of euphemism, even of writing in the presence of a censor whom the poet has to placate by using words with double or triple meanings. It is nevertheless possible to read Wordsworth's *Prelude*, in the manner of Burke's *Reflections* or Blake's prophetic books, as about the experience of coming to terms with the Revolution, not simply as a representation of the phenomenon itself. *The Prelude* draws upon the externalizing stereotypes of dawn, youth, love, and passion (as well as pleasure and bliss), but as secondary to the poet's own developing imagination, and as a retrospect, looking back from the end of the century and the end of the Revolution.

Burke and Blake had already set out the kind of progression we can call the revolutionary plot. It took two forms: a movement from circular to irreversible change with internalization of the fallen tyrant by the rebel, and a story about an observer at some distance from the conflagration but with a stake of his own and a progression from innocence to experience (or failure to make this transition and adjustment), involving an internalization (or transcendence) of the revolutionary experience. In Blake's later works, especially *Milton* and *Jerusalem* (1804), the general quest became a personal one, not altogether unlike Wordsworth's but with a crucial difference.

We can see this difference by noting the literary model for both writers: Milton's *Paradise Lost*. Blake took, revised, and criticized the revolutionary poet Milton, who was personally involved in a real revolution, suffered in its failure, and sublimated or internalized (or externalized) his experience of it in *Paradise Lost*, as an imaginary construct, essentially a vision. Blake's persona—his bard—is the poet who lives through revolution and is himself a revolutionary force, a prophet (of the Old Testament sort who speaks the truth against kings and anticipates the Messiah of the New Testament) who projects and in some sense *is* the revolution. In *Milton* Blake is trying to correct a revolutionary position in John Milton, and in *Jerusalem* he himself is the revolutionary who can no longer fight it out on the ground but must raise the battle to a higher, imaginary plane.

At a certain point, carefully defined, Wordsworth commits the revolutionary act. But he slips into and out of the role; in *The Prelude* he looks back on the French Revolution as a shaping force on his youth. It was something that kept him from writing poetry or offered him an alternative to poetry in action. But above all it forced upon him a new identity or a choice of identities. In *The Mysteries of Udolpho* M. St. Aubert told M. Quesnel that he preferred the "happiness" of monotonous constancy to "life" if the latter involved the risk of losing one's true self. Wordsworth's poem puts the "true self" in doubt; the Revolution produces a new self and questions the old one, whether it is a Roman identity or one involving (as with Emily St. Aubert) her property and her sex. Conversion is therefore one of the basic revolutionary plots, followed by disillusionment or an alternating ambivalence (once more a form of Burke's plot spread out in time).

The "I" is the person who is affected by the Revolution, not (like Ambrosio) an embodiment of it; and the essential elements now become psychological categories such as absorption, sublimation, displacement, and repression. We are entering with these writers a phase of spiritual autobiography but one markedly different from the Puritan tradition embodied in John Bunyan or Robinson Crusoe. Spiritual autobiography of the earlier dispensation universalized the private events of a life history: Crusoe was an Adam or a Prodigal Son whose experience was applicable to all his readers. Private life became public history. The people of Wordsworth's generation make history (the particular events of the French Revolution, its phases and aftermath) the structuring matter of their private lives. The moment of Revolution releases man's utmost potentialities, opening for him what he may become rather than what he has been; it sees him in terms of his ultimate desires and suggests that the outer reaches of historical man can be known only through his contact with a revolution of some sort, with its attributes of cataclysm as well as sunrise. The peripety or transformation of revolution in the public realm can produce definition of the private individual.[1]

The contemporary who wrote a spiritual autobiography of the Revolution internalized this public history as a crucial part of the structure of his life, either to transmute this public experience or to escape it. The Milton of *Paradise Lost*, whom Wordsworth adopted as his model, sublimated his experience in the writing of his great epic. But his epic plot was also applicable. The Revolution equaled the redemptive value of the Enlightenment—and so its failure could be regarded either as a Fall or as a false or failed Redemption following the Fall. Blake's was the second explanation. The first simply supposed a fallible mankind and a need after the Fall to work out, in the manner of Crusoe, your own redemption by means of Crusoe-like constructions, whether political, personal, or imaginary. In both cases, however, a new mode of redemption was sought outside the structure of the conventional Christian religion that informed   *Paradise Lost,* and this was itself a sign of the revolutionary representation.

The *Preludes* of 1805 and 1850 can be construed as Wordsworth's attempt to understand in an increasingly discursive way those child-hood memories he called "spots of time" first recorded in the 1799 two-book *Prelude.* The stealing of birds' eggs and boat, the skating scene, and the drowned man are simply divided off by a mass of explanation from the official "spots of time," the gibbet and the fatal Christmas homecoming. The primal scenes Wordsworth may have been screening with those memories seemed explicable to him only in terms of other subjects: his growth as a poet and the important events (personal and political) of 1790–94. The final 1850 version then suppressed the fictional lovers Vaudracour and Julia, who even in 1805 had served to conceal Wordsworth's real love affair with Annette Vallon.[2] If there was a five-book version ending with the experience of Mount Snowden,[3] book V of the full text must represent the beginning of Wordsworth's attempt to fill in a middle which bridges the earlier and later spots of time (the stealings and the punishings), or more specifically bridges his schooldays and the Mount Snowden revelation with his experience of the French Revolution.

In book V two public images emerge: the Revolution as deluge/holocaust and the Revolution as precocious child, the book-reader who does not grow up, does not use books properly. Both are related, however, to the overarching concern of the poet's vocation: the ends to which his writing can be used, that is, either as an alternative to experience or as an ability to render it. Book V comes to a climax in the alarming experience of the drowned man whose head shoots up out of the lake, and Wordsworth promptly adds (not part of the 1799 version) that this did not faze him as a small boy because he was able to assimilate such an experience to stories he had read of "faery." However convincing we may find this passage as adumbration of the larger thesis of *The Prelude,* as the point of intersection between the observation of the drowned man and its absorption into literature, there is nevertheless a discrepancy of feeling here that is not as noticeable elsewhere in the poem. This is the book where Wordsworth most obviously loses his way, as if grappling without total awareness, himself part of a process of discovery. The whole book seems to be written to explain that one experience of the drowned man, and just below the surface all the subjects and themes surge forward that will surface in book IX.

The process begins with the Arab dream, a "Revolutionary dream."[4] The elements of the dream are books and the products of intellect, a seaside, the poet's anxiety at the rising tide ("the fleet waters of a drowning world / In chase of him"), and the question of survival in the face of natural disaster. The natural disaster was introduced in the opening lines and much labored over in the various drafts. Wordsworth's effort to describe his response to this "deluge," and the effect it has on his writing, is the center of book V. "Deluge" was, of course, one of the stereotyped images applied to the French Revolution. If we look ahead to the consequences of the Revolution in the Terror, we find in book X (ll. 567–68) the same seaside setting ("the great sea meanwhile / Heaved at safe distance, far retired," as well as references to rocks, shells, and horses along the strand) that appears in the dream, this time summoning up the announcement of Robespierre's execution. The Revolution is described (ll. 477–80) as

> a terrific reservoir of guilt
> And ignorance filled up from age to age.
> That could no longer hold its loathsome charge,
> But burst and spread in deluge through the land.[5]

In the dream Wordsworth settles on deluge instead of on the apocalyptic fire and earthquake he had invoked in the opening passage of book V. The Deluge was what physically separated the human face from Eden, for (as Thomas Burnet, for one, argued in *The Theory of the Earth*) it was after the waters receded that the earth no longer bore any resemblance to the ordered landscape of Eden. It is appropriate that Wordsworth returns to the boundary between the fallen and unfallen worlds, experience and innocence, because his own theme is focused on childhood and on the losses and gains of maturity. But he has also turned back to the point at which the Fall and Deluge converge with the Tower of Babel. For as the Deluge carries out the geographical cutting off of the human race from Eden, the multiplicity of languages following the Babel experiment carries out (more important for the poet) the linguistic dislocation from the universal prelapsarian language. The ostensible subject, of course, is the function of writing in a world of experience and catastrophe. The shell, according to the dream, is the poetic symbol that explains that what is lost will be recreated by other words, images, and poems—which will be the language Wordsworth has to work out for himself in order to survive the Deluge.

We could argue that the elaborate discussion of water and perishable books, the stone and the shell, in book V essentially explains and rationalizes the scene in book I of the boy skating over the unmanageable water on a sheet of ice, retiring into an inlet and turning in circles, then stopping and letting the world seem to whirl around him. Those early "spots of time" were said to have

> Impressed upon all forms the characters
> Of *danger or desire;* and thus did make
> The *surface* of the universal earth
> With *triumph and delight,* with *hope and fear,*   •
> Work like *a sea*
>
> (I: 471–75)

I have emphasized the words denoting the polarities we have already discussed in book I, which here lead into the image of the sea. *Choice* is between the indeterminate, incalculable world of the sublime and the "determined bounds" of the beautiful, the memory of childhood comfort—life as a card game or as ice-skating, in which even the chase, to which war had been sublimated in Pope's *Windsor Forest,* has been transmuted to a mimicked chase on the icy surface of a lake (435), a very different situation from the "hope and fear" of the incomprehensible "sea."

It is probably significant that Wordsworth opens book V by turning from nature to man's reason (or in other versions, "reason and exalted thoughts," "reason or . . . faith," and "contemplation"), its triumphs and dangers. These are manifested in books, those that were alleged to have led men into the Revolution and those that he hopes will, through his intervention, lead at least himself out of it. The dreamer—in the 1805 version Coleridge, in the 1850 the poet himself—has been reading *Don Quixote* and dreams of a knight who by the end of the dream has become Don Quixote in relation to the deluge of the French Revolution. The dreamer's temptation is to follow Quixote with his books, pursued by the ocean's rising tide. (Quixote carried connotations of general book-learned folly and misguided chivalry as well as the particular reference to Edmund Burke, and a personal allusion to a nickname attached to Wordsworth himself.)

The next image after the dream is of the mother hen, the proper mother (Wordsworth's own mother) who guides her child according to nature, in effect, an un-Enlightenment/un-Revolutionary mother, whose child

> Was not puffed up by false unnatural hopes,
> Nor selfish with unnecessary cares,
> Nor with impatience from the season asked
> More than its timely produce; rather loved
> The hours for what they are, than from regard
> Glanced on their promises in restless pride.
>
> (V: 282–87)

Throughout book V Wordsworth seems to be talking about something else—skirting the subject that really interests him. This passage not surprisingly ends with a break, and in the 1805 version reads:

> My drift hath scarcely,
> I fear, been obvious; for I have recoil'd
> From showing as it is the monster birth
> Engender'd by these too industrious times.
> Let few words paint it: 'tis a Child, no Child,
> But a dwarf Man. . . .
>
> (ll. 290–95)

This "monster birth" (partly suppressed in the 1850 version) is obviously more than just the child whose book-learning perverts rather than opens his imagination. He is one of the Abbé Barruel's images of the Revolution as the consequence of the Enlightenment, the philosophes, and the illuminati—of too much reading and thought dissociated from contact with experience (or nature). The child believes, and thinks he represents, the ultimate perfectibility of man ("Know that he grows wiser every day"):

> For, ever as a thought of purer birth
> Rises to lead him toward a better clime,
> Some intermeddler still is on the watch
> To drive him back, and pound him, like a stray,
> Within the pinfold of his own conceit.
>
> (ll. 332–36)

The figure is then expanded from the prodigious child to Sin and Death building the bridge which will serve as a channel for these evils to enter the earth (ll. 347–50). Later in book X the child will be connected with the specific reference to the French Terror as a child who does not grow up, playing now with a guillotine (ll. 364–74). In much the same way Wordsworth in book X pinned down the deluge, ambiguously offered in book V, to its explicit referent, the French Revolution.

In retrospect a monstrous arrested child (a grotesque), at the time it seemed a (beautiful) "purer birth," conceived by the young. Wordsworth saw the Revolution as inextricably involved with his own youth, with young men like himself as its metaphorical progenitor. In *Descriptive Sketches* (1793), which recorded his first trip to France in 1790, Wordsworth had suggested a surprisingly close analogue to Blake's youthful Orc of about the same time: "Lo! from th' innocuous flames, a lovely birth!" (l. 782). In *The Prelude* he shows "What happens when the child fails to grow up. . . . The child's self-centeredness makes it by nature imperial," recalling for Wordsworth the absolutism of Robespierre and later Napoleon.[6]

This child is contrasted in book V with the Boy of Winander, who exemplifies the origin of poetry in the imitation of animal sounds to stimulate their response; who does not grow up either to play with a guillotine or to write *The Prelude* because he is arrested at this primal stage of give-and-take, when he is still at one with nature. He therefore does not progress to the next stage of development, toward which Wordsworth himself is for better or worse striving. On the one hand Wordsworth contrasts himself with the prodigious child, on the other with the boy who dies at the threshold of experience, and, in the final episode, with the drowned man.

The experience of the drowned man sums up the poet's fear of drowning and engulfment by the deluge, but it also recalls the spot of time at the end of book IV which described the discharged soldier the poet met during a school holiday. The soldier appears as the young poet takes a "sudden" turn in the road—"stiff, lank, and upright . . . ghastly in the moonlight . . ." (IV: 393–96); whereas the drowned man "bolt upright / Rose, with his ghastly face, a spectre shape / of Terror. . . ." The drowned man also anticipates the blind beggar of book VII ("London") who "with upright face, / Stood, propped against a wall." In the 1799 *Prelude* the drowned man was alone; the other two versions were added presumably to further explain him. He can be thought of by himself only as a bridge between the crimes of the first spots of time and the punishments (hanging and loss of father) of the last: here an ambiguous accident or suicide that is witnessed by the boy who has already been pursued by "low breathings" and by a mountain that "like a living thing, / Strode after me" (I: 323, 384–85). As I have already noted, the horror of the drowned man is now explained, understood, or in effect absorbed by being placed in the context of books the child Wordsworth has read. The old soldier explains himself in words ("From his lips, ere long, / Issued low muttered sounds, as if of pain / Of some uneasy thought. . . ."), and the blind beggar has a "written paper, to explain / His story" affixed to his chest.

The story of the soldier fighting for his country, only to be abandoned to destitution, sets him up as another victim of the government and society Wordsworth described in his poems of the late 1790s. Alongside this victim of society, and in the context of deluge and revolution, he helps to place the drowned man. The historical referent, the schoolmaster James Jackson, was drowned in 1779 while bathing in Esthwaite Water, but Wordsworth does not specify either accident or suicide. He is simply a man who immersed himself in water and drowned, and in that sense has been made a figure parallel to Quixote, the monstrous child, the Boy of Winander, and the poet himself. But none of this appears in the 1799 version. The passages about books and the additional "upright" figures are fixed in the context of Wordsworth's revolutionary experience.

He knows what has happened in both versions of the story by seeing "a heap of garments" on the lakeside. *Garments* was the word connected earlier in book V with books (the books lost in the deluge are "garments," l. 24) and with language as the "garment" of thought.[7] These "garments" now constitute the evidence that prevents the uprising of the drowned man from being so "sudden" or shocking as the appearance of the soldier: Wordsworth has seen the "garments" the day before and knows what to expect, as in the passage immediately following, he claims (somewhat lamely in fact) that the reading of stories had "hallowed the sad spectacle / With decoration of ideal grace." The "garments" seem in fact the more significant explanation: It was the "garments vexed and tossed" of the woman with the pitcher that fixed that figure in his memory, seen near the gibbet in the first designated "spot of time" that immediately followed the drowned man in the 1799 text. Books of "faery" are an attempt to explain that "garment."

I doubt if we shall ever know what that garment meant to Wordsworth in its earlier contexts, as opposed to the 1805/1850 *Prelude.* But this scene, whose resolution is more satisfactory as metaphor than as fact, is followed by his return to his father's house for the holidays—an anticipation of the later spot of time (bk. XII) that will involve his return for a holiday coincident with his father's death. His "impatience" as he waited to be taken home from school suffers the "chastisement" of his father's death. But "chastisement" obviously covers a deeper guilt, presumably a subconscious wish for his father's death, suggested by the reference to how God has "thus corrected my desires." The guilt felt for the discharged soldier (he is "from self-blame / Not wholly free") may be for the mistreatment of soldiers who serve their country, but more likely it reiterates the vague guilt of the first spots of time in book I. For this "uncouth shape," "Stiff, lank, and upright," suddenly appearing, carries with it the memory of the "huge peak, black and huge" that "Upreared its head" in the boat-stealing episode, and with it come also the associations of stealing and guilt. In the stealing episodes—of birds from traps, eggs from birds' nests, and of a boat—nature itself is in some sense being challenged by the boy, but in each case a more immediate antagonist appears: the man who set out the traps, the parent birds, and the man who owns the boat (as well as the boy's father, who taught him the injunction "Thou shalt not steal").

All these events and details seem gathered around some central, inexplicable, and terrible experience, which Wordsworth now chooses to label (or screen) as the French Revolution. Every spot of time he recounts connects in one way or another with a looming, uprisen figure of terror and the unknown, one dispossessed or killed, with whom a crime or guilt of some sort connects Wordsworth the experiencer. The issue in book V is this traumatic experience, on one level the French Revolution and the way the poet can cope with such an experience through his imagination—by using books or texts in a proper way to meet the demands of nature, rather than in an unnatural way that leads to monstrous intelligence and the Terror or to drowning in a sea of Babel.

One final way in which Wordsworth elaborates the drowned man in the later versions is to add to the first version, which read,

> At length the dead man, 'mid that beauteous scene
> Of trees and hills and water, bolt upright
> Rose with his ghastly face,—

the further words: "a spectre shape / Of terror" (ll. 278–81). He has recognized by this time that he can place his experience in a wider context in the contrast between the aesthetic categories of the beautiful and the sublime (the essence of which for Burke was terror).

The pattern set forth in book V is pursued in VI. The subject, the disillusionment in experience that is compensated for by imagination, is presented in Wordsworth's visit to France in 1790 at the moment of the first celebration of Bastille Day, followed by a visit to the Grande Chartreuse and finally to the Simplon Pass. The third summer of Cambridge, he says, "freed us from restraint." It sent him to the Continent: an experience that linked climbing the Alps ("mightly forms, seizing a youthful fancy, / Had given a charter to irregular hopes," ll. 334–35) with his stopover in revolutionary France, and that other sense of "hope." For

> . . . Europe at that time was thrilled with joy,
> France standing on the top of golden hours.
> And human nature seeming born again.
>
> (ll. 339–41)

He participates in the Fête de la Fédération, a mass performed joining the king, the Constituent Assembly, and the National Guard of the people, with everyone swearing an oath of federation that materialized once again the *Oath of the Horatii* and the *Oath of the Jeu de Paume*. This was a coherent structure of order, an ideal Wordsworth must have seen collapsing on his return trip two years later, but already in 1790 threatened in his sad passage on the destruction carried out by French revolutionary troops on the beautiful Grande Chartreuse.

But the way of political reason and the way of mountain climbing lead to the same failure. As the poet and his friend ascend the pass they learn that they cannot climb farther—they have already "crossed the Alps," and now they "must descend," for the path "was downwards, with the current of the stream." They are "Loth to believe what we so grieved to hear, / For still we had hopes that pointed to the clouds . . ." (ll. 575–87). "Hopes" again join the natural and political realms, and the book ends with the great passage on the power of imagination to compensate for these disappointments, its resolution found in experience through the imaginative transformation on Mount Snowden (bk. XIV). The passage is again colored by terms of overt political action. First the imagination's "hope that can never die" and "something evermore about to be"; and second:

> Under such banners militant, the soul
> Seeks no trophies, struggles for no spoils
> That may attest its prowess. . . .
>   (ll. 609–11)

The reference to "spoils" may be to the sacking of the Chartreuse, but the soul is rather "blest in thoughts / That are their own perfection and reward. . . ," and again the book ends with an overt paean to the Revolution:

>   a glorious time,
> A happy time that was; triumphant looks
> Were then the common language of all eyes;
> As if awaked from sleep, the Nations hailed
> Their great expectancy. . . .(ll. 754–58)

And yet Wordsworth is not yet himself "intimately" involved:

> . . . I looked upon these things
> As from a distance; heard, and saw, and felt,
> Was touched, but with no intimate concern. . . .
>   (ll. 767–69)

As yet he neither experiences nor needs the Revolution, which does not impinge upon him until book IX and his "Residence in France." But book VII, "Residence in London," represents the stage in which he "bade / Farewell for ever to the sheltered seats / Of gownèd Students . . ." and pitched "a vagrant tent among / The unfenced regions of society" (ll. 52–57). It is also the book where Burke makes his appearance, and while not specifically connected with his revolutionary writings, his appearance ("like an oak") would seem best explained by the hovering presence of the Revolution. Wordsworth sees him in the context of theatricals and the theatricality of London life, which lead him to think of oratory and so of Burke. "Like a hero in romance" (the Don Quixote figure of the Arab dream), he made the Revolution into a theatrical experience in his *Reflections*. He represents the power of literature to which a youth like Wordsworth is susceptible. Such words as Burke's allow him to absorb painlessly the drowned man, the soldier, and perhaps the blind beggar, and also the Maid of Buttermere, who is seduced and traduced and then transformed into a ballad.[8]

Jonathan Wordsworth has argued that the discharged soldier and blind beggar are naturalizations of eighteenth-century personifications of the Satan, Sin, and Death sort of which Burke makes so much in his *Enquiry*.[9] I am arguing that something else lies behind these images, but I would not want to deny the possibility that in their first manifestation in the 1799 *Prelude* they are already distanced to some degree by being seen as horror personifications in the manner of Collins; they also, however, pick up in revision the associations of Burke's sublime, and return to something like the allegorical denominations of Pity and Terror—another example of what Burke's *Enquiry* had taught him about the distancing that converts a troubling experience into pleasing art.

The most famous of such confrontations occurs in the *Lyrical Ballads* with "The Leech-Gatherer," who is in the technical sense of the term a grotesque, embodying a transitional state between human and natural or inanimate forms. All these figures (the prodigious child as well as the drowned man and the blind beggar) show the very close relation between grotesque and sublime. They appear grotesque, but for Wordsworth they are sublime: They terrify and move precisely because they are neither human nor other but both. These figures become in the "Revolution" book IX the hideous subhuman related to Gillray's John Bull or Burke's (or Wollstonecraft's) masculine women marching on Versailles—in effect the immeasurable wrong that the Revolution tried to correct and that the poet tries to comprehend: the "hunger-bitten girl, / Who crept along fitting her languid gait / Unto a heifer's motion." She and her heifer are a single entity moving down the road and "picking thus from the lane / Its sustenance" (ll. 510–14).

This is the ultimate degradation of the woman that begins with the Maid of Buttermere, transforming the beautiful woman seduced and deserted into the terrifying figure of the animal-woman. Wordsworth runs the gamut of the aesthetic categories as he tries to comprehend the phenomenon of the French Revolution. Like Milton, he tells us that he began by going through all the possible subjects for an epic and finding them all inadequate to the task of charting the development of his mind. This is the same procedure he follows in trying to describe the "Revolution" in book IX (which as in his model *Paradise Lost* is his book of the Fall). He is trying to fit the central experience of his public life into an aesthetic category, or a literary genre, in the manner of Burke's *Reflections*. The Revolution is in one sense the great subject matter that may explain to him his spots of time, and in another the great public subject matter he is turning *away* from as less suitable than the development of his own mind (or of his imagination). At the same time its complexity, its refusal to be formulated, demonstrates to him (and implicitly to Burke) that no literary form can be used to express or fathom the experience, any more than the inscription "Blind Beggar" can do justice to the human being who wears it.

Thus when he arrives at book IX, he first seeks imaginative solace in Paine's metaphor of pastoral beauty: "Even as a river" turns and twists (partly for fear that a direct way "would engulph him in the ravenous sea," he says, reviving the metaphor of drowning), "Or as a traveller" pauses on the brow of the hill "to review / The region left behind him," and this allows him to slip into London as into a pasture in which he ("a colt") ranges. He leaves the book-stalls ("hedge-row fruit") of London for a visit to the very unpastoral world of France.

Significantly, the reason he gives (in the 1805 text) for his trip to France is "To speak the language more familiarly" (1805, l. 37).[10] The language barrier leads him to *see* "the revolutionary Power," which (he still employs a locodescriptive mode) will "Toss like a Ship at anchor, rock'd by storms," and to *listen* to the "hubbub wild" "with a stranger's ears." Still detached from the Revolution, trying to frame the experience as a tourist does ("the sauntering traveller"), he "look'd for something that I could not find." The most telling evocation of the "temper of [his] mind" was that the Revolution in Paris moved him less than a painting, Le Brun's *Penitent Magdalen.* As it had done for Burke, visual art, moving him more, holds him at a distance from the raw reality of the Revolution, rendering it more comprehensible.

But the *Magdalen* also prepares us for the great absence in book IX, the story of his love affair with Annette Vallon, whose role Wordsworth gives to the male friend Beaupuy. And the soldier Beaupuy himself is absorbed into another fictional context, that of tales of chivalry (as Vallon is in the 1805 text in the tale of Vaudracour and Julia); he is, again alluding to Burke, part of "the chivalry of France," a knight on a quest.

Wordsworth evokes one genre after another. From line 94 onward he mingles the metaphor of theater with that of journey, the mode of tragedy with locodescriptive poetry. Like a painter the poet keeps trying to construct a manageable landscape: "the first storm was overblown, / And the strong hand of outward violence / Locked up in quiet." He does this in the face of an actual landscape becoming increasingly unmanageable: "all swarm'd with passion, like a Plain / Devour'd by locusts . . . earthquakes, shocks repeated day by day," he concludes, referring back to the holocaust at the beginning of book V and summoning up the category of the sublime. This transformation is taking place at the same time that he himself is being absorbed—and not altogether acknowledging it—into the scene as participant rather than tourist-observer. As the pastoral and locodescriptive categories fail him, he finds that the "Tales of the Poets" do not fit the circumstances in France and then that Beaupuy (who is killed in action) is a knight who does not survive his quest.

With the tale of Vaudracour and Julia (another fiction that veils a painful fact), Wordsworth says he is turning from romance to "a tragic Tale"—but still a "tale." Book X modulates from romance to stage tragedy: the king falls, is tried, and executed. In a room high in a building in Paris, the poet mediates on reports of the September massacres augmented by thoughts or dreams "conjured up / from tragic fictions or true history" of hurricanes and earthquakes—"Until I seemed to hear a voice that cried, / To the whole city, 'Sleep no more' "—the words of Macbeth after killing *his* king. And suddenly Paris seems to him (as it did to so many others) "unfit for the repose of night, / Defenceless as a wood where tigers roam" (ll. 93–94).

From one point of view these are outmoded literary forms, as inappropriate as Collins's Pity and Fear to the Leach Gatherer or as poetic diction to the lives of Simon Lee or Harry Gill. From another the Revolution is such a staggering experience that it simply (in Alan Liu's words) "refuses to obey an Aristoelian order of beginning, middle, and end and so juts out of the framing structures implicit in fictional idioms. Both its origin and 'end' (and *un*-ending succession of violence and betrayal) are unaccountable according to the poet's available languages."[11]

None of the formal ways of thinking succeeds for Wordsworth, and before the end of book X he has begun to recover himself and his subject by returning to a language closer to the everyday, as in the climactic account of Robespierre's death (once again on the edge of the sea, as in the Arab dream). He has learned a great deal since he came to terms, by an optimistic utilization of romance, with the drowned man. But his access of knowledge coincides with his turn from joy at the fall of Robespierre to disillusion again at the pragmatism of the Directory, the tyranny of the Pitt Ministry in his own England, and the ruthless conquests of Napoleon.

His return from the external, "tempestuous" world of politics to the internal "correspondent breeze" of poetic imagination is not, however, manipulated without benefit of the Burkean categories.[12] He follows a progression from a topographical landscape poem to a sublime one as his awareness of the Revolution grows, but he repudiates this dark and terrible landscape—both metaphor and historical phenomenon—for a more peaceful one (he has already associated with England) which he can dominate with his own imagination. This is consistent with his belief, expressed in his essay on "The Sublime and Beautiful," that temporally the sublime must be succeeded by the beautiful:

Hence, as we advance in life, we can escape upon the invitation of our more placid & gentle nature from those obtrusive qualities in an object sublime in its general character; which qualities, at an earlier age, precluded imperiously the perception of beauty which that object if contemplated under another relation would have been capable of imparting.[13]

In *The Prelude,* as Theresa Kelley has shown, a "spot" which the poet cannot control—"the terror of being confronted with the enormous failures and gaps in human experience"—is corrected by a further stage that Wordsworth designates as the beautiful.[14] This may be a second "spot" to succeed the sublime one "so as to make the mind momentarily safe for human habitation." It may be a closure of the sense of engulfment in the sublime experience (as in book V) with a determinate significance. On the level of the "spots" this is the addition of naming and explaining, and on a higher level the sort of signification the whole of *The Prelude* is attempting to impose on these intractable moments. The stealing of birds and boats, episodes concerned with the violation of known limits, are followed by the skating scene: A sublime experience is followed by a beautiful, and one of indeterminacy by one in which the child controls the unruly waters of the lake (into which he has aggressively plunged his boat and oars) by making patterns on its icy surface, an experience which replaces "visionary dreariness" with an access of joy. In the same way, the gibbet "spot" is followed by the still young Wordsworth's return visit with Dorothy and Mary, sister and wife, which blesses the scene, renaming and redefining all the elements from sublime to beautiful (as from illicit passion to domestic harmony). The "visionary dreariness" of the place is now closed by the human affections of the three friends, which (as Kelley says) "comprise the domesticated beauty of the Wordsworthian aesthetic. And, as clearly, this revisitation suppresses the sublime recognition that the poet once encountered there."

The nodal point, the hidden center of Wordsworth's revolutionary experience, comes in book IX, and this is the experience of Annette Vallon, their love affair, their child, and his desertion of mother and child. In his experience woman and revolution are interchangeable phenomena, both involving (as in Ambrosio-Matilda or even Mary Wollstonecraft-Gilbert Imlay) liberation and betrayal, involving a crime that is nevertheless necessary for the poet's transition from innocence to experience.[15]

The ballad recounted in the pre-Revolutionary residence in London (bk. VII) is "The Maid of Buttermere," a tale of love, childbirth, and desertion anticipating "Vandracour and Julia" in book IX. The poet writes a hopeful epitaph on the main enduring "In quietness, without anxiety," and her child buried near a mountain chapel "fearless as a lamb": "Happy are they both— / Mother and child!" outside the roar and rush of London and "the times." But the image of the dead child, the product of the maid's love affair and desertion by a "spoiler," is followed by the story of the "lovely Boy," another Boy of Winander who sits untouched in the center of "dissolute men / Like one of those who walked with hair unsinged / Amid the fiery furnace" (ll. 328–29, 360–70). Like the maid's child, this boy "by special privilege of Nature's love, / Should in his childhood be detained for ever!" (ll. 375–76).

The Maid of Buttermere was a final externalization of the figure Wordsworth tries to come to terms with in book IX. The revolutionary images of his earlier poems (besides the imagery of sun, fire, and deluge) consisted of stories of a female vagrant and a discharged soldier, leading eventually to the poor soldier of book IV and the hungry girl Beaupuy points to in book IX as the cause of the French Revolution.[16] These are images of the victims of tyranny which we might refer to as stimuli to revolutionary consciousness. The most significant element in the gestalt is the woman with child, deserted or widowed, perhaps as a displacement of the guilty image Wordsworth does not show. It is not simply that he invents the image, of course, for as Carl Woodring writes: "From the beginning of the war with the Colonies, such figures had been seen on the roads with increasing frequency. To the prevalence of actual derelicts, letters and journals of the poet and others in his family testify as eloquently as the poetry."[17] But Wordsworth's deserted women stand out in "Evening Walk," "The Thorn" and the poems of the Lyrical Ballads, in "Ruth," and in "The Deserted Cottage."

Wordsworth's own "grievances as a dislodged orphan" may have led him to read himself into "The Female Vagrant" and other victims of the old system prior to the Revolution. His experience with Sir James Lowther showed him how a nobleman can defraud his dependents.[18] At this point in 1792, the moment of grievance, Wordsworth went to France, but also with his memory of the experience of 1790, when he had arrived in France on the anniversary of Bastille Day and watched the French joyously celebrate the Feast of Federation. He goes to Paris and admits that he feels at the moment more emotion before Le Brun's Magdalen than the Revolution, which

> Less mov'd me, gave me less delight than did
> Among other sights, the Magdalene of le Brun,
> A Beauty exquisitely wrought, fair face
> And rueful, with its ever-flowing tears.
> (1805, IX: 76–79)

The Magdalen, with its echoes of the Maid of Buttermere and anticipation of Julia, was in fact thought to be a portrait of Louise de la Vallière, Louis XIV's mistress, looking up rapturously at a burst of sunlight from above, a Danae awaiting the Sun King's impregnation (the whole title was *Sainte Madeleine renonçant aux vanités de la vie).*

About the Revolution itself he was still, he says, "affecting more emotion than I felt." It is only after the affair with Annette Vallon that he becomes a "delighted" supporter of the Revolution. Mary Moorman puts it simply, speaking of the summer of 1792: "A double tension racked him: he was deeply and anxiously in love, and he was also becoming a proselyte of the Revolution."[19] He represses Annette, attributing his "conversion" to Beaupuy, and to Beaupuy's showing him a hungry, oppressed girl. And of course Annette could not have "converted" him to the Revolution because her sympathies were presumably royalist.[20] But the ambivalent feelings of books IX and X arise from his love of her.

Beaupuy is brought closest to the Wordsworth-Annette situation (with Burke's Marie Antoinette as with the Quixote of book V, who was "crazed / By love and feeling") by his associations with chivalry and "old romance, or tale / Of Fairy, or some dream of actions wrought / Behind the summer clouds." For romance seems to refer to

> A passion and a gallantry, like that
> Which he, a soldier, in his idler day
> Had paid to woman. . . .
> (ll. 300–03, 311–13)

He was covered, we are told, by "a kind of radiant joy" when "he was bent on works of love or freedom"; while Wordsworth himself at this time "was scarcely dipp'd / Into the turmoil." These are the words that carry the central revolutionary vibrations. But there is also the passage about satyrs "rejoicing o'er a female in the midst, / A mortal beauty, their unhappy thrall" (ll. 460–61), which recalls the less romanticized Maid of Buttermere. The poet moves on to thoughts of one of François I's mistresses "bound to him / In chains of mutual passion" (ll. 485–86), who recalls the Magdalen based on Louix XIV's mistress and introduces a discussion of droit du seigneur, royal (male) tyranny over a female. This is finally translated into the "hunger-bitten girl" Beaupuy shows Wordsworth—female beauty degraded into grotesque heifer-like servitude: " 'Tis against *that* / That we are fighting," he says; and this leads into the exemplum of ancien régime tyranny, "Vaudracour and Julia," with which book IX ends.

In the same way, the most enigmatic aspect of the gibbet "spot of time" is the girl with the pitcher, an image of beauty buffeted by the wind. Her blowing "garments" (that significant word, joining language and body) may beautify the sublime experience of the gibbet as it did earlier the experience of the drowned man. Or it may point to one center of the experience, the one linked with the abandoned Maid of Buttermere or Julia, and so with the Revolution.

As we have seen so often in the revolutionary literature of the 1790s, love itself is the symbol of revolution—even if the loved one happens to be a royalist. The act of love was (among other things) an act of rebellion, or at least a scandalous act, in the context of a society of arranged marriages, closed families, and decorous art and literature. In France the overt symbolism of sexual "liberty" in the early phases of the Revolution was succeeded by the suppression of the erotic in the later puritan phases. Wordsworth can be said to follow the same trajectory, but as we trace his own suppression of the story of his love from the text of *The Prelude*, we can also see the sexual love of woman being sublimated, as the sublime is sublimated by the beautiful, in a dedication to a supposedly higher, or at least more refined, goal first social and then poetic. In human terms, the "passion" and "love" of the revolutionary situation is replaced by the "Friend" to whom he repeatedly addresses himself in the final books.

But Wordsworth is the young student of Rowlandson's *The Milk Sop*, whose love has a consequence, and in the stories he retells love is followed by a birth and disillusion, by the child's death and the father's guilt. If in book V Wordsworth associates himself with the child, and in IX with the father, in the later books it becomes clear that he is the boy himself. He has displaced the object of guilt from the product of his love onto the mother/lover. This allows him to associate himself with the child: the Boy of Winander and even the potentially monstrous child who remains arrested in childhood but with an adult brain—and so with the sons of the "spots of time" who are waiting for something, for whom something unexpected suddenly appears—a soldier, a corpse, above all a father who, instead of appearing, dies. Thus although a father himself, Wordsworth can place himself invariably in the role of the rebellious son—as lover and as little boy who steals boats and wishes his father dead.

If we recall the story of Agnes the nun in *The Monk*, we will notice that in one revolutionary scenario the lover penetrates the woman's cell, liberating himself from his father and her from her imprisonment, and the child who follows from their union is a demonstration of their rebellion. It is, however, the woman, not the lover, who suffers the wrath of the Church and the child who invariably dies. The baby, says Agnes, was her lover Raymond's fault, and Vaudracour is said to have been responsible (through negligence perhaps) for his baby's death.

The story of Vaudracour and Julia moves the plot from revolution/love/betrayal back to the ancien régime and repression and betrayal of *both* lovers by the father. The fact remains that Vaudracour is guilty in much the same way as Wordsworth. Used to represent the paternal/contractual tyranny of the ancien régime about which Paine and others wrote, the story is a displaced paradigm of Wordsworth's experience of the Revolution: he falls in love with the alien woman (alien by class and nationality), challenges his father, runs away with her, but eventually succumbs to the external, paternal pressures. The act of loving with this slightly alien woman *is* the act of revolution— and in fact corresponds to it in Wordsworth's experience as well as in his poetry—and the total story of the Revolution is played out in their failed relationship. The Fall, like that of *Paradise Lost,* is both betrayal and liberation, on the public level the French Revolution (and Wordsworth's involvement with it) and on the personal the suppressed Adam-Eve affair. Both are presented as disobedience, as rebellion against a father—the England that declares war on France and Vaudracour's father who will not hear of a marriage with Julia— and behind this somewhere is Wordsworth's own dead father, who keeps cropping up in one form or another in the spots of time.

I am referring most generally to the masculine figure whom Wordsworth associates with guilt and retribution in the mountain that rears up and pursues him when he steals the boat,[21] and the startlingly phallic figure (the word *upright* is used in each case) he associates with terror, crime, and personal guilt or the figure who confronts or proclaims his guilt (ultimately Vaudracour's). The gap he is trying to bridge by dividing the spots of time, moving the crucial so-called spots back to book XII, is between those paternal figures and the death of his father, which he acknowledges in the memory of the holiday in which his impatience was punished with his father's death. The gibbet presumably refers to his own feelings of guilt. The crime is stipulated in the 1799 version: "A man, the murderer of his wife, was hung / In irons . . ." (I: 309–10), but softened to a more general murder in the later versions. Thus the sexual passion and guilt of the gibbet image, localized and refined in the cathected image of the girl with the pitcher and blowing garments, form a final—and perhaps the original—symptom of the revolutionary guilt against the father in the 1799 *Prelude.*

Following the Fall of book IX, book X had described the development of the Revolution and Wordsworth's involvement with it in terms of betrayal, murder, and guilt—of the revolutionaries and in particular Robespierre destroying the king. The sequence that is stressed in book X is a series of nightmare scenes: Wordsworth's "Sleep no more" dream (and the killing of Louis XVI); the Girondin who in the morning rises to the tribune and cries "I, Robespierre, accuse thee!" only to find himself abandoned and alone; Wordsworth's association with the Girondin in his own nightmare of delivering

"long orations, which I strove to plead / Before unjust tribunals";
and finally his hearing of the deaths of both his old schoolmaster
Taylor and of Robespierre as he walks on the seashore.

What disturbs him on his return to England is his homeland's
own entrance into the war against France. This, he tells us, was the
real stimulus to "revolution" for him (ll. 269–85). He means that
this was the frightening phenomenon, but also the event that turned
him into a revolutionary in the sense of an enemy of his own *father*land. And yet the English intervention coincides with the Terror
in France, summed up in the images of the monstrous child playing
with a guillotine and the deluge of burst contagion from the "terrific
reservoir of guilt." Robespierre is a "cruel son"; as the fierce winds
are to King Lear, a father-king, he is to his native city of Arras (l.
506). It is in this context that Wordsworth tells of his old teacher
Taylor (who had encouraged him to be a poet), whose parting words
to him were "My head will soon lie low" (l. 539), and of the stranger
who says to him, "Robespierre is dead!" (l. 573)—after which he
can say, "Come now, ye golden times" (l. 587).

As Jonathan Bishop has observed: "Taylor, his amiable foster
father, had predicted a death, and the prediction unexpectedly comes
true for a man with whom Wordsworth has for many years felt a
profound connection, a villain who acted out fantasies of murderous
rebellion in which Wordsworth, it is not too much to say, half-
consciously participated"[22]—though the point of Robespierre's fantasies was their fratricidal as well as patricidal flavor. Thus the re-
gicide/betrayer of the Revolution has been punished and the guilt
(including Wordsworth's) purged in the "river of blood." But the
death of the schoolmaster and surrogate father, followed by the death
of Robespierre, points toward the death of the father in the "spots
of time": Wordsworth wished Robespierre dead—he died; he wished
his father dead—and he died. The "terrific reservoir of guilt" is both
public (the French) and personal (Wordsworth's own). The political
books, in short, have a powerful effect on the final spots of time,
showing the relationship on a poetic level between the killing of the
king and of Robespierre and the death of Wordsworth's own father.

I do not mean that *The Prelude* can be understood merely by
finding the repressed subject but rather by recognizing a complex
cluster of subjects: love of a woman, political revolution, the son's
disobedience to his father, and the making of a poet. All these
represent one side of an exchange between what is acknowledged
and what is repressed, what is understood and what the poet does
not want to understand. For even if an oedipal conflict is thought to
be the repressed subject, it is only a sign for some larger sense of
loss which is not yet, and perhaps cannot ever be, defined.

Wordsworth produces both internalized and externalized versions of this plot—in the development of his own mind in *The Prelude* and in the history of the Solitary in *The Excursion,* books II–IV. The allegorical version in *The Excursion* is far less compelling than the autobiographical one in *The Prelude* but it does reveal interesting similarities. It progresses from Margaret's plight, deserted by her husband, to the Solitary's love affair followed by the tragic loss of both his bride and his children, and then the joy of the French Revolution followed by his disillusionment. In the background is the series of shorter poems like "The Thorn," even like "Nutting," in which the boy feels he has to rape/murder the trees before he can have his crop: he commits the crime, against the wood nymph, the father or the king, which is necessary for the increase of consciousness.[23]

Even in "Home at Grasmere," the fragment that was to connect *The Prelude* and *The Recluse,* Wordsworth repeats again the story of the man who seduces the maiden and is driven by his guilt to wander far and wide—but here

> he dies of his own grief
> He could not bear the weight of his own shame.
> (ll. 531–32, MS. B)

The whole passage was suppressed in the final version of the manuscript (MS. D) Wordsworth prepared in the 1840s, sharing the fate of the Vaudracour and Julia story.

These elements recall the prominent association of love, loss, and guilt with revolution in *The Prelude.* And as we follow their revisions from the 1790s to the 1840s we also see the same process of secondary revision or repression (the different versions of "Salisbury Plain" are a case in point). We can also, however, follow another progress within the poetry as a whole, analogous to that of *The Prelude,* from an early poem such as "Salisbury Plain," where the benevolent man is oppressed by the treatment of government and society until he is forced to commit murder, to book I of *The Excursion,* where Margaret responds to the same pressures with "weak endurance, without hatred or any thought of revenge for her undeserved wrongs."[24]

Something like Wordsworth's plot was already outlined by Coleridge in 1794 in "To a Young Lady with a Poem on the French Revolution." This is an allegory of his own poetic development and his youth (when in college he first "heard of guilt and wonder'd at the tale"), which are suddenly interrupted by the Revolution. He uses Pity and other figures that recall Collins's odes to produce a more pedestrian version of the opening of Blake's *America:*

> When slumbering Freedom roused by high Disdain
> With giant Fury burst her triple chain!
> (ll. 17–18)

Freedom (or Liberty) is a fierce Orc-like figure, a woman, but with Coleridge personally assisting her:

> Red from the Tyrant's wound I shook my lance,
> And strode in joy the reeking plains of France!
>   (ll. 25–26)

What connects the poem with *The Prelude* is the subsequent stage of the poet's disillusioned withdrawal:

> Fallen is the Oppressor, friendless, ghastly, low,
> And my heart aches, though Mercy struck the blow
> With wearied thought once more I seek the shade.
> When peaceful Virtue weaves the Myrtle braid.
>   (ll. 28–30)

A figure of love comes (or returns) to replace these public, social emotions, and so poetry can be written.

Immeasurably expanded and complicated, this is the plot Wordsworth weaves in *The Prelude*. But the lyric subject of the poet's inspiration has become epic; the poet, like Aeneas, still has to choose between duty and eros, between public and private desires, and he begins as Milton's Adam saying, "The earth is all before me" (I:14). In other words the 1799 *Prelude* is altered (or glossed) in two crucial ways in the 1805 *Prelude*: It is Miltonized into an epic, and it is given as its central crisis the French Revolution. The verse of the 1799 version is, of course, already Miltonized in diction, but the revision makes it explicitly an alternative to *Paradise Lost*. The French Revolution is already implicit in the 1799 version, and by making it explicit Wordsworth may only be offering one explanation for the spots of time in their original formulation. But perhaps more important the Revolution grows from a stimulus (as in Coleridge's poem) to a model, despite his ostensible rejection of it, for Wordsworth's career as a poet.

The Revolution is a model, first, for the artist's relationship to action, love, violence, and catastrophe ("deluge")—a scenario of which Rowlandson's artist satires were a comic version. As such it inevitably involves his disillusion and withdrawal. But second, and more particularly, it is a model for Wordsworth's writing this kind of an "epic of the mind of the poet," which is a struggle with (as Harold Bloom would put it) his poetic father John Milton reflecting in microcosm the oedipal conflict of the Revolution itself. As soon as he identifies himself with Adam, he turns to the choice of a subject for his great poem—which in fact becomes a Shandyan telling of how he would come to write the poem—and puts himself in the place of Milton, rejecting the idea of writing "some old / Romantic tale by Milton left unsung" (ll. 168–69). He will not write a chivalric romance of the sort he had used to understand the incident of the drowned man and seeks unsuccessfully to identify with the French Revolution.

The plot of the development of the poet's mind turns, like the Revolution, on incidents of personal violence: his betrayal of Annette or behind her of a parent and/or of a poetic father. As we have seen, Wordsworth censors the explicit crime, the Annette-Julia betrayal, transferring it in the version of "Vaudracour and Julia" to the relation of Vaudracour and his father, which on a public level is embodied in Robespierre and the Revolution, on a poetic level in Adam's defiance of God's will, and on a private but still essentially poetic level (though it may mask something about his natural father) in the Wordsworth-Milton relationship.

Looked at from the end of the century, the poet's view of the Revolution defines itself in progressions and personal odysseys: broken, circular, open-ended, or closed. Wordsworth forcibly accomplishes the last by the addition of Milton and the Revolution; this amounts to an assertion that the external, public life of the Revolution, the external, public story of Adam and Eve, have been internalized, and that the sublime must be followed by the beautiful, which means, in terms of his writing poetry, that he has transformed a sublime into a beautiful experience. He has gentled the most terrible part of the experience even while showing the progress itself from one category to the other. Surely Milton's *Paradise Lost* is the poetic equivalent of the Revolution in this context, the sublime action transformed into a beautiful and inward truth. Both *Paradise Lost* and the French Revolution represent for Wordsworth upheavals which have to be internalized/beautified in order for him to survive as a poet.

The Prelude involves types of progression very different from the old plot of action-consequence or even progress which may in fact be regress (as in the Hogarthian "progress"). It may well utilize old plots, perhaps the only ones available, and adapt them to its purpose. But there is a marked difference: The progression is characterized by trial and error, by the employment of this genre and that, by breaks and discontinuities, new and false starts, pauses ("my drift I fear / Is scarcely obvious"), and most importantly by a series of displacements of one realm of experience or subject onto another. Indeed in some cases it is achieved by an avoidance of the chief subject or a confusion as to what the main subject is, whether this proves ultimately to be personal or public, the writing of poetry, a guilty love affair, or the French Revolution. The progression, however, is at the end unambiguous. Wordsworth is saying what Blake said in *Milton* and *Jerusalem:* After the lesson of the French Revolution, one knows that change can be effected only within the individual personality or within the art of poetry. If art is the daughter of freedom, after the Revolution art must be used to subdue and control.

At the heart of *The Prelude* is the assertion of Wordsworth's own "revolutionary" art as freedom ("to be young was very heaven"), which refers back to the "revolutionary" stage of his poetry in the *Lyrical Ballads* or perhaps the 1799 *Prelude*. The art itself was more immediately overturning eighteenth-century ideas of poetry and poetic diction, while more generally replacing the great model of the Miltonic epic. Wordsworth's description of this process in *The Prelude* (VIII: 365 ff.) sounds like a description of the ancien régime—from which the poet like the politician feels the need to rebel. The two plots prove to be parallel: art like the Revolution overturns and starts anew but then returns after excess and disillusion to first things—to peace and closure, the imaginative experience of Mount Snowdon—in order to work out a perspective that infolds the experience of the Revolution itself.

There is, however, a difference. Rebellious action at the political level is sublimated into writing, but it remains on the level of writing itself in the rebellion against Milton (and more overtly against Pope and the Post-Miltonic tradition of poetry): a successful version of the Vaudracour-Julia story in which the father *is* defied.

The image of the poet has come a long way from the craftsman or the "vindicator of God's ways to man" to the revolutionary, a figure who grows with the potential of the French Revolution itself. By the end the model for the poet is a political one based on struggle, power, and desire, which expresses itself in the preface to *Lyrical Ballads*, but one which also includes the resolution in which the father-poet is internalized. This is the poet whom Bloom describes in *The Anxiety of Influence*, for whom power and priority are at issue (just as they were for the political revolutionaries), for whom poetry is a struggle with forebears, precursors, and poetic fathers. This is Bloom's way of explaining the tendency of late eighteenth-century poets toward self-consciousness and subjectivity and the writing of poems about the writing of poetry. They begin (as W. J. Bate has shown) to feel the "burden of the past," to revolt *against* tradition rather than living with it or using it as a norm (as Pope ostensibly did). The emergent poet, on the contrary, is left with only himself and his autonomous, solipsistic powers. I would not want to preclude the possibility that the sort of poetic sensibility that was developing under the "burden of the past" by Collins in poetry and Sterne in prose simply found a political analogue that expressed more clearly and forcibly its privately earned insights. But the Bloomian fight with the poetic father is, in one aspect, merely a historical phenomenon and a literary consequence of the internalizing of external sociopolitical experience, which has become that of the powerful tyrannic father and the rebelious son—a formula that was not so thinkable before the Revolution, or at least so charged with significance.[25]

In *The Prelude* Wordsworth comes to be the poet who joins the worlds of poetry and politics, connecting them by the common term *revolution*. The artist now not only depicts an ocdipal situation as the fiction for revolutionary violence; he himself is in an oedipal situation. Now that will and power are prime elements of existence, the poet sees himself (not as Pope did as a doomed Orpheus) as the sinner Adam or Oedipus the outsider chosen to take all the guilt upon himself, the one who suffers in order to atone for the violence of political revolution. How does he serve this function? By relating the private to the public Fall in a Wordsworthian version of the theme of *Paradise Lost*. He thereby gives art itself a new definition or emphasis: It is a response to catastrophe, to betrayal or loss and absence; by implication, it is now a less satisfactory reflector of plenitude or of God's ways to man.

Notes

1. A novelist-historian such as Sir Walter Scott takes as his subject, as the nodal point of his stories, the fact of a great reversal in human consciousness and human affairs. He displaces the experience of the French Revolution back to the English revolution/civil war of the seventeenth century and makes this the situation of a social revolution: the peripety, reversal, or fall which defines his major characters, the problem of the claims of opposing historical forces in revolutionary conflict. For Scott, as later in his different way for Carlyle, political revolution is the moment that releases man's potentialities. For Scott the revolution brings about definition and definable change in the individual; for Carlyle the revolution may be only a chaotic static presence which attenuates or confuses definition or difference. But in either case it is the great moment that settles the question central to the historian. See Donald Davie, *The Heyday of Sir Walter Scott* (London, 1961), and Hedva Ben-Israel, *English Historians and the French Revolution* (Cambridge, 1968), p. 19.

2. "Vaudracour and Julia" was published separately in 1820, harmless outside the context of book IX of *The Prelude*. Citations are to *The Prelude*. ed. Ernest de Selincourt and Helen Darbishire, 2d rev. ed. (Oxford, 1959). But cf. the 1799 edition, ed. Stephen Parrish (Ithaca, 1977), and *The Prelude, 1799, 1805, 1850*, ed. Jonathan Wordsworth, M. H. Abrams, and Stephen Gill (New York, 1979), which includes the 1799 text and critical essays. Unless otherwise noted, I quote from the 1850 text in de Selincourt and Darbishire.

3. Mark L. Reed, *Wordsworth: The Chronology of the Middle Years, 1800–1815* (Cambridge, Mass.), pp. 638–44. Jonathan Wordsworth ("The Five-book *Prelude* of Early Spring 1804," *Journal of English and Germanic Philology*, 76 [1977], 1–25) believes that in March 1804 Wordsworth wrote a "fifth book" which concluded a five-book version of *The Prelude* but bore little or no resemblance to what we now know as book V.

4. Mary Moorman, *William Wordsworth: A Biography. The Early Years* (Oxford, 1957), p. 250. See also J. Hillis Miller, "The Stone and the Shell: The Problem of Poetic Form in Wordsworth's Dream of the Arab," in *Mouvements Premiers* (Paris, 1972), 140; Michael Ragussis, "Language and Metamorphosis in Wordsworth's Arab

Dream," *Modern Language Quarterly*, 36 (1975), 148–65; Jane Worthington Smyser, "Wordsworth's Dream of Poetry and Science: *The Prelude*, V, *PMLA*, 71 (1956), 269–75; and Newton P. Stallknecht, "On Poetry and Geometric Truth," *Kenyon Review*, 18 (1956), 1–20. In Thomas DeQuincey's schema of knowledge versus power, often imputed to Wordsworth, the stone represents knowledge while the shell represents power or genius. See W. J. B. Owen, *Wordsworth as Critic* (Toronto, 1969), p. 192. I am also indebted to Theresa M. Kelley, "Spirit and Geometric Form: The Stone and the Shell in Wordsworth's Arab Dream," forthcoming.

5. The evocation of deluge remains in "swept away" by the "river of blood" (ll. 584, 586). Further evidence can be found in the specific connection of the imagery of fire and deluge with the French Revolution in *Descriptive Sketches*, ll. 774–83, 791–809.

6. Lawrence Goldstein, *Ruins and Empire: The Evolution of a Theme in Augustan and Romantic Literature* (Pittsburgh, 1977), p. 191; also pp. 184–95 on "The Child of Revolution." On the general subject of Wordsworth, youth, and the Revolution, see David Ellis, "Wordsworth's Revolutionary Youth: How We Read *The Prelude*," *Critical Quarterly*, 19 (1977), 59, 67; and John Beer, "The Revolutionary Youth of William Wordsworth and Coleridge: Another View," ibid., 79–87.

7. See Rosemund Tuve, *Elizabethan and Metaphysical Imagery* (Chicago, 1947), pp. 61–78. An essay, come to my attention since the writing of this chapter, connects the linguistic and psychoanalytic aspects of the Revolutionary books: Gayatri C. Spivak, "Sex and History in *The Prelude* (1805): Books Nine to Thirteen," *Texas Studies in Language and Literature*, 23 (1981), 324–60.

8. Jonathan Wordsworth, in criticizing Wordsworth's revisions of the gibbet "spot of time," misses the point that the addition of "the inscription of the murderer's name," the "monumental letters," is another case of Wordsworth's attempting to come to terms with experience through the use of words (another "garment"). See Wordsworth and Stephen Gill, "The Two-Part *Prelude* of 1798–99," *JEGP*, 72 (1973), 503–25.

9. "William Wordsworth 1770–1969," *Proceedings of the British Academy*, 55 (1969), 211, 28; also see Herbert Lindenberger, *On Wordsworth's Prelude* (Princeton, 1963), p. 23, where he divides these agencies of Wordsworth's mind's growth as beautiful and sublime.

10. I am indebted here to Alan Liu's " 'Shapeless Eagerness': The Genre of Revolution in Books IX–X of Wordsworth's *Prelude*," *Modern Language Quarterly*, forthcoming (originally "History and the Text: The Authority of Language," ch. 3 in his unpublished dissertation "The Darkness' in Language: Wordsworth's 'Prelude' and Metaphors for Speech," Stanford, 1979).

11. Ibid.

12. See Geoffrey Hartman, *Wordsworth's Poetry*, 1787–1814 (New Haven, 1964), pp. 242–46.

13. *Prose Works of William Wordsworth*, ed. W. J. B. Owen and Jane Worthington Smyser (Oxford, 1974), 2, 349.

14. I am indebted in this paragraph to Kelley's "The Economics of the Heart: Wordsworth's Sublime and Beautiful," *Romanticism Past and Present*, 5 (1981), 15–32 (the final quotation is on p. 27).

15. In Hartman's words this is a transition from "a prior, nature-involved and relatively blind state of consciousness to the enlightened pain of self-consciousness' (*Wordsworth's Poetry*, p. 134).

16. *Descriptive Sketches* is full of the familiar revolutionary imagery: light and fire: "Tho' Liberty shall soon, indignant, raise / Red on his hills his beacon's comet blaze . . ." (ll. 774–75); deluge: "Oh give, great God, to Freedom's waves to ride /

Sublime O'er Conquest, Avarice, and Pride. . . ." (ll. 792–93); "And grant that every sceptred child of clay. / Who cries, presumptuous, 'here their tides shall stay,' / Swept in their anger from th' affrighted shore, / With all his creature sink—to rise no more" (ll. 806–09).

17. Carl Woodring, *Politics in English Romantic Poetry* (Cambridge, Mass., 1970), p. 87.

18. Moorman, *William Wordsworth*, p. 169, also p. 189.

19. Ibid, p. 187.

20. Unless she was revolting against *both* her family's morals and politics when she took Wordsworth as a lover. We do know she was later a prominent member of the royalist "resistance movement," but she may have acted parallel to her cousins Charles and Claude, priests who took the oaths required of them by the Civil Constitution of the Clergy and welcomed the new order but later opposed the Convention's pressure to make the clergy give up their ministries. And, indeed, her attitude toward the Revolution could have corresponded to Wordsworth's own as the Jacobin excesses followed.

21. See Weiskel's analysis of this passage, *The Romantic Sublime* (Baltimore, 1976), pp. 101–02.

22. "Wordsworth and the 'Spots of Time,'" *ELH*: 26 (1959), 45–65; reprinted in *Wordsworth: A Collection of Critical Essays*, ed. M. H. Abrams (Englewood Cliffs, N.J., 1972), p. 142. Bishop comments on the girl and pitcher: "Can we read the extraordinary concentration upon the separate images of pool, beacon, and girl as a displacement of feeling from the evidences of crime and punishment to accidental concomitants of an experience too over-whelming to be faced directly?" (p. 145). This scene with which he associates the young girl and young love takes place close to the death of his mother.

23. It is possible that Wordsworth's suggestion to Coleridge for *The Rime of the Ancient Mariner* ("some crime was to be committed which should bring upon the Old Navigator . . . the spectral persecution") was another version of the trauma he was representing in his own poems of the time. See *Poetical Works*, ed. Ernest de Selincourt and Helen Darbishire, 2d ed. (Oxford, 1952), 1, 361, note to "We are seven."

24. Moorman, *William Wordsworth*, p. 316.

25. See Harold Bloom, *The Anxiety of Influence: A Theory of Poetry* (New York, 1973), and W. J. Bate, *The Burden of the Past and the English Poet* (Cambridge, Mass, 1970).

WORDSWORTH THE POET

"Home at Grasmere": Ecological Holiness

Karl Kroeber[*]

Two centuries after his birth William Wordsworth is a less significant figure to literary critics than his slightly older contemporary William Blake. For many, Wordsworth appears to have evaded the crucial issues raised by the political, industrial-agricultural, and social revolutions of the late eighteenth century. Unlike Blake, who attained prophetic relevance by meeting those issues head-on, Wordsworth retreated into quietistic meditation among the barren mountains and unprofitable lakes of Cumberland. I propose, however, that recent changes in our thinking about man, nature, and human life make it possible to recognize a special originality and relevance in Wordsworth's prosaic celebrations of serene egoism amidst remote mountain valleys.

Because everyone knows that Wordsworth is a "nature poet," we might consider first whether contemporary attitudes toward nature differ from those of our fathers and grandfathers, those who established the popular view of the poet as a simple-minded nature lover. To judge from what is happening among the most conspicuously active nature lovers of today, conservationists, attitudes toward nature are shifting radically. Government officials are tearing up roads that give access into National Parks. Many now believe that to preserve our humanness we must preserve as much as possible the natural world that is specifically inhumane, inhospitable to man. In the 1970's we try to conserve not just beautiful places but also wastelands—the title of T. S. Eliot's poem already sounds out of date. It used to be that an indisputably virtuous act was draining a swamp. No longer. Now there are defenders of the environment of alligators, water-moccasins, and leeches. Wordsworth, without the advantage of reptile-rich or insect-rich surroundings, foreshadows late twentieth-century conservation. He argues that man's humanity is completely realized only within nature's "inhumanity." He praises unspectacular places

[*] Reprinted by permission of the Modern Language Association of America from *PMLA* 89 (1974).

and usually unfecund ones. "Nature" to him is what we now call an ecological unity. What he celebrates, to use his own term, is a "region," a complexly interdependent, self-sufficient "place." Against the forces of agricultural and industrial progress he affirms the preciousness of "useless" territorial sanctuaries. He appears to have learned from the French Revolution that in the perspective of natural existence—the rhythmic continuity of an infinitely rich ecosystem— even the most epical of social events is trivial and fragmentary. He speaks for the profound, biologically rooted need for territorial security common to all men and against the conquest of space, most vividly apparent in the urbanizing of technological civilization which daily consumes more of our planet.

My thesis, then, is that today we may be able to appreciate certain purposes in Wordsworth's poetry as our parents, and their parents, could not. This is not a call to revalue his position in the hierarchy of British poets. But if we are in a position now to respond with sympathy to Wordsworth's aims and methods, we are also in a position to understand better our relationship both to the immediate and to the more remote past of our culture. I take such understanding to be a primary object of humanistic study.

The poet, his family, and his friend Coleridge agreed that the most complete expression of Wordsworth's philosophy was to be *The Recluse,* a poem of which *The Excursion* constitutes only the middle third, and to which *The Prelude* serves as a mere introduction. Of this proposed work only one book was composed, the lines known as "Home at Grasmere," first published more than three decades after the poet's death. Because "Home at Grasmere," became known only when Wordsworth's critical popularity was no longer waxing, and probably because the poet and his intimates had so frequently expressed dissatisfaction that *The Recluse* did not, somehow, get written, Wordsworthian scholars (secretly thankful on the evidence of *The Excursion* that there are not another 20,000 lines to edit and defend?) have paid relatively little attention to this "first book."[1] Yet the neglect is odd, because parts of "Home at Grasmere" that were published during the poet's lifetime have often been cited as major exemplifications of Wordsworth's "philosophy." I suggest that "Home at Grasmere" is *The Recluse.* Wordsworth could never "finish" *The Recluse* because he had already written it.

"Home at Grasmere" is a remarkably coherent work, and the truncation of *The Recluse* to one book is formally appropriate to the poet's ambition. The final lines proclaim the superiority of his theme to that of *Paradise Lost.* What could be more fitting than the accomplishment of this audacious purpose in one book instead of a dozen? At issue is not so much length or brevity but a new kind of esthetic unity. "Home at Grasmere" coheres, one may say, vertically rather than horizontally, the terminology suggested by Wordsworth's consistent emphasis on height-depth dimensions. Despite his concern with memory and time, he does not, as one might expect, organize linearly. Characteristically, he stands at one spot and tells of different or reiterated impressions associated with that place on diverse occasions. "The Ruined Cottage" and "Tintern Abbey" are "classic" examples of this art of superimposition.[2] Even *The Prelude,* the total structure of which is circular, and *The Excursion*—in more dramatic fashion, different speakers commenting on the same scene or situation—reveal Wordsworth's inclination to move through overlays and underlyings of impression, speculation, emotion. His wide-ranging, or loose, if one prefers, style in poetic meditation is possible because it is rooted to a single, fixed place. Thus the primary intra-referential system in "Home at Grasmere" is literally and metaphorically vertical: the linking of earth and sky is climactically imaged by the lake below reflecting the heavenly dome—between which the swirling birds rise and fall. The poet never moves, but his language "falls" and "rises," most dramatically in the final "Prospectus" lines, which repeat the structural patterns of the opening lines on, simultaneously, both a "higher" and a more "profound" level. Poetic form reproduces the "blended holiness of earth and sky" the poet cherishes; the shape of the poem is the shape of Grasmere Vale.

The unity of "Home at Grasmere" is inseparable from the topographical actuality of the valley, above all, its self-completeness. The valley needs nothing because it is indivisibly self-unified.[3] The self-sufficing unity of being which the poet holds forth as a human ideal is naturalistically embodied in the form and condition of Grasmere Vale.

Wordsworth begins by referring to himself in the third person, as a "roving School-boy" when he first saw the valley years before. This characteristic maneuver allows the poet to "objectify" his subjective experience, but then, with the confession of line 46, to transform the objective back into the subjective mode. The interchange establishes a fundamental pattern in the poem, the interplay between the poet's inner, imaginative life and his sensations, his impressions of external realities in the circumambient vale. By beginning with his younger self, furthermore, the poet introduces mnemonic dimensions into a poem focused on the present instant (in fact, though not calendrically, the first day of a new year) until it attains a climactic vision of the future. The high prophetic strain of the final lines is effective because it develops from earlier interfusings of diverse time relations. From its first lines the poem demonstrates how awareness of time liberates man from the prison of immediacy, the delightful yet dangerous actuality of sensation and impulse.

This liberation entails no escape to some other, more idealized realm of being. Consciousness of time is alertness to the *continuity* of actual existence. Hence Wordsworth stresses the somatic component of memory. Memory functions most effectively, most creatively, in an ambience of reiterated impressions. Where the body can in some measure repeat its responses, the psychic power not merely to recollect but also to explore and enjoy mental connections between temporally distinct experiences is enhanced. Repetition is the locus for that pleasure of finding similitude in dissimilitude and the reverse, which in the 1800 Preface to the *Lyrical Ballads* the poet represents as the most fundamental of human pleasures.

Wordsworth finds psychic freedom, then, within the restriction of a limited, familiar physical environment in which present sensations can be assimilated into an awareness of the flow of time. The same freedom appears in the final portion of the poem, where the present is illuminated by an envisagement of future felicity—in the same place. Because past and future literally, corporeally as it were, exist in the present, recollective and visionary language both enter easily into the poet's recording of immediate impressions. Paradise is not a place or condition "beyond" Grasmere Vale but its earthly actuality truly perceived. The contrast to Milton could not be more absolute. Wordsworth represents paradise by delineating the "little realities of life"[4] of an unimportant English valley whose most familiar inhabitants are a blind man, a paralytic, and a widow "withering in her loneliness."

The poet's retreat to Grasmere is no evasive action. The perfect spherical enclosure of the vale embodies the possibility of a wholeness of life, a joining of the psychic with the physical, of past with future in the present, which the innovations—economic, political, social— of the Napoleonic era in fact threatened, even though some originated in an ideal of such wholeness. Grasmere is no vacation spot, no mere place in respite from the fragmented restlessness of modern life. Nor is it a symbol of a utopian existence. It is an authentic alternative. It is a genuine alternative because it is a real home.

The Wordsworthian home is the opposite of a Yeatsian ancestral house. The poet and his sister are newcomers to the vale. Grasmere is a place they *choose* to live in and to love. "Home" for Wordsworth is a limited territory, adopted deliberately as a self-sufficing physical environment. He is indifferent to rootedness. He does not feel tied to an owned piece of property. The attractiveness of Grasmere to him is that it provides territory in which to roam, in which he can actively realize that which is most vital in his being. What he does in Grasmere is to fit himself to nature and fit nature to himself, not in the fashion of a farmer, a pastoral poet, or a modern exurbanite, but, strange as it sounds, in the fashion of a predator such as a wolf. I don't wish to press my animal analogy, but I know of no better way to define the poet's preferred relationship to nature, because it excludes many conventional attitudes toward possession and property in its emphasis upon territorial familiarity. Wordsworth's attitude, if a lycanthropic comparison is too farfetched, may be closest to that found in preagricultural societies, whose concepts of "land possession" are to us almost incomprehensible. Well-defined hunting territories among some American Indian tribes, for instance, do not consitute "communal ownership" as we, or the Soviets, understand the term. The relation between a preagricultural society and its home "territory" usually, in fact, is too subtle, intimate, and fluidly complex (too close, I believe, to animal territoriality) to be defined in the rigid, abstract terms of our postagricultural possessiveness. Preagricultural peoples seem to feel that they belong to their territory as fully as it belongs to them—although such "belonging" is entirely distinct from the "enslavement" of a serf to a piece of land.

Wordsworth, of course, knew no more about preagricultural societies than do most readers of literary criticism today, and he desired no return to a "primitive" way of life. He disliked "hunting." He claims simply that Grasmere Vale is a perfect place to love. To define love in terms of territoriality, emotional commitment to the unified complexity of a particular geographical-ecological entity, may be absurd. But it may also be a significant if neglected aspect of what is called in respectable academic circles Romantic "organicism."

The vale "swarms with sensation, as with gleams of sunshine, / Shadows or breezes, scents or sounds" and "solitude is not / Where these things are" (ll. 447–48 and 592–93).

> . . . Society is here
> A true Community, a genuine frame
> Of many into one incorporate.
> . . . .
> Human and brute, possessors undisturbed
> Of this Recess, their legislative Hall,
> Their Temple, and their glorious Dwelling-place.
> (ll. 614–24)

Because man and nature can so interpenetrate in the vale, its "true Community" must comprise "human and brute" and plant and topographic fact as well. The reality the poet praises surpasses "all Arcadian dreams, / All golden fancies of the golden age" (ll. 625–26), because it entails man's active involvement not with one segment of nature but, instead, with a microcosmic reproduction of its *wholeness.* The vale is a complete world in itself. Probably the most compelling image of its living unity is that of the spiraling birds, rising to the sky, dipping to the lake, engaged in a natural dance whose irregularity transcends the crude patterning of any human art, just as the scope of the birds' flight contrasts with the miniaturization intrinsic to all human art.[5] In their free yet vitally rhythmic activity the birds epitomize the liberating power latent in "this Recess," a literal hiding place of power.

Sensation "swarms" in Grasmere because, physically limited, it can be psychically familiar. Without familiarity the swarming of sensation would be unrecognized. What to the casual passerby is merely a tree is, to one familiar with it, perhaps a tree planted by an old acquaintance. Our feelings toward a wild animal are likely to depend on whether or not we know its burrow. So the vale is "enclosed" not just physically but also psychologically. The poet loves it because he is intimate with both its "little realities" and its wholeness as a self-sufficient entity. Grasmere, then, is much like the "little world" of a child. The analogy is encouraged by the poet's unabashed presentation of his relation to the valley as that of a child to its mother.

> Embrace me then, ye Hills, and close me in,
> . . . I feel
> Your guardianship; I take it to my heart;
> . . . .
> But I would call thee beautiful, for mild
> And soft, and gay, and beautiful thou art,
> Dear Valley, having in thy face a smile
> Though peaceful, full of gladness.
>
> (ll. 110–17)

The maternality of the vale is explicit, and much of the language of the poem works to feminize the landscape (even the sound of the words—note the liquidity of the sounds in the last line quoted) and to emphasize the poet's dependence on it. One need not interpret out a repressed psychic pattern. The poet overtly proclaims his relation to the vale as sexual, even infantile, celebrating a conscious regressiveness. He does not uncover submerged, archetypal patterns and disdains the support of concealed mythic significances. He speaks for the pleasure of deliberately fitting oneself into a natural organization consciously discerned and appreciated. He does not applaud, or appeal to, any simple release of that which is "primitive" within us. Indeed, what offends many twentieth-century readers of "Home at Grasmere" is its manifest discursiveness, that is, the poet's attempt to deal rationally with topics we tend to feel ought not to be represented in this manner—topics such as the love of a brother for a sister.

Originally, references to Wordsworth's sister were disguised by the use of the name "Emma," usually "my Emma," but this subterfuge was dropped in revision, principally, I believe, because "openness" is so essential to the poem.

> On Nature's invitation do I come,
> By Reason sanctioned—
> . . . .
>
> Mine eyes did ne'er
> Fix on a lovely object, nor my mind
> Take pleasure in the midst of happy thoughts,
> But either She whom now I have, who now
> Divides with me this loved Abode, was there,
> Or not far off. Where'er my footsteps turned.
> Her Voice was like a hidden Bird that sang.
> The thought of her was like a flash of light,
> Or an *unseen* companionship, a breath,
> Or fragrance independent of the wind.
>   (ll. 71–94)

I quote at length to illustrate that while it may be legitimate to describe Wordsworth's feelings as "incestuous," if "fraternal love" seems too feeble a term these days, it is less legitimate to claim that the poet is unaware of his "incestuous" feelings, that he inadvertently reveals repressed impulses. Whether or not one regards the poet's feelings toward his sister as too intense to be "normal," the important fact is that he treats openly a subject rarely so treated in poetry. The fact is important because, as F. R. Leavis has observed: "Sex is virtually absent from Wordsworth's poetry. . . .[But] there are . . . no signs of morbid repression anywhere in Wordsworth's poetry. And his various prose remarks about love plainly come from a mind that is completely free from timidity or uneasiness."[6] Nowhere in "Home at Grasmere" is there praise of merely instinctual behavior in man, of the undisciplined release of animalistic impulse. The sanction of reason is ever present. And Wordsworth's consciousness of loving his sister both exemplifies and reinforces his larger affirmation of the value of conscious love for nature.

Conscious love demands restraint, for it is disciplined affection. It controls aggressiveness, produces quiet receptivity, even passiveness, willingness to let things happen without trying to arrange them, without meddling. The poet does not feel that passivity (including yielding himself to nature as to a maternal being) derogates his manhood, because to him loving is both giving and receiving. Unlike sexual impulse, love requires surrender of the pleasure of mere aggressiveness. The yielding up of a masculine assertiveness implicit in his fraternal affection adumbrates the quality of the poet's love for Grasmere Vale, which is a cathexis directed to the complex totality of the life of the valley as a whole, and which depends, therefore, upon overcoming any impulse to "violate" it.

A difference between "Nutting" and "Home at Grasmere" is the poet's mature consciousness in the later poem. Full awareness enables him to accommodate himself to the "spirit" of a place (instead of "ravaging" it) by an act of deliberate regressiveness. The poet *lets* the vale "mother" him. It may be that only a man profoundly secure in his masculinity (Coleridge regarded Wordsworth as entirely masculine) can risk such conscious "infantilism." The most successful fathers I have known are men mature enough to behave unabashedly like children with their children. Perhaps more to the point, the ancient Greeks were unashamed of worshipping the earth as a mother, and their temples are evidence that such "regressiveness" is not incompatible with creative assertion of a high and enduring order.

"Home at Grasmere" culminates in a creative assertion of a most impressive kind. By giving himself up to the completeness of life in the vale, the poet attains a unique expressive power.

> . . . to me I feel
> That an internal brightness is vouchsafed
> That must not die, that must not pass away.
> . . . .
> Possessions have I that are solely mine,
> Something within which yet is shared by none,
> Not even the nearest to me and most dear,
> Something which power and effort may impart,
> I would impart it, I would spread it wide,
> Immortal in the world which is to come.
> (ll. 674–76, 686–91)

Through humble passivity the poet has nourished within himself a potency exceeding that of warriors and statesmen. It is this power that informs the "Prospectus lines," wherein the poet represents his theme as grander and more thrilling than that of his greatest predecessors, even Milton's

> All strength—all terror, single or in bands,
> That ever was put forth in personal form—
> Jehovah—with his thunder, and the choir
> Of shouting Angels, and the empyreal thrones—
> I pass them unalarmed.
> (Prospectus, ll. 31–35)

The audacity of the poet may be breathtaking, but the ambition to which it leads is even more astonishing.

> Paradise, and groves
> Elysian, Fortunate Fields—like those of old
> Sought in the Atlantic Main—why should they be
> A history only of departed things,
> Or a mere fiction of what never was?
> For the discerning intellect of Man,
> When wedded to this goodly universe

In love and holy passion, shall find these
A simple produce of the common day.
—I, long before the blissful hour arrives,
Would chant, in lonely peace, the spousal verse
Of this great consummation:—and by words
Which speak of nothing more than what we are.
(Prospectus, ll. 47–59)

The "produce of the common day" and "nothing more than what we are"—out of these, nourished by the spirit of Grasmere Vale, the poet will achieve an art undreamed of by great poets of the past. His confidence is founded on the earlier portion of the poem, in which he in fact describes "How exquisitely the individual Mind / . . . to the external World / Is fitted:—and how exquisitely too . . . The external World is fitted to the Mind." Thanks to the ecological wholeness of the vale in which he so consciously participates, he is able to envision "the creation . . . which they with blended might / Accomplish."

One may doubt Wordsworth's success at transcending the esthetic triumphs of his predecessors yet recognize the significance of his enunciating such a claim. To assert uncompromisingly the possibility of making the finest poetry out of the commonest and most everyday *beingness*, merely "what we are," of revealing reality to be intrinsically poetic, is to establish new potentialities for art. And the direction toward which "Home at Grasmere" moves, especially those parts which stress the poet's passive submergence into the quietly maternal embrace of the valley, is the flourishing of a *unique* power of Wordsworth's mind, a power that he believes can be "spread wide." The poem, in other words, redefines the "individual self" and attributes to the self so redefined far more than personal significance: "joy in widest commonalty" spreads from "the individual Mind that keeps her own / Inviolate retirement."

By insisting that a potent "self" is created through deliberate fitting of one's individuality to the external world and of the external world to one's mind, Wordsworth implicity rejects any ambition to change, to reshape the external world, to "improve" nature. Insofar as we now regard life on our planet as an interplay of ecosystems constituting a vast ecological totality, we, too, recognize that particular "improvements" are not "free," not independent of consequences throughout the complex of systems. Increasingly we perceive civilization as healthiest when most adroitly adapted to the necessities of the total framework of natural balances within which it must function. This is, in effect, Wordsworth's vision: no return to primitivism, but, instead, full utilization of trained consciousness so as to fit better into the unified interdependence that is nature.

The valley Wordsworth praises is not a "primitive" place, although it is not in the mainstream of the "progressive" agrarian-industrial society that was coming to dominate the life of Great Britain in his day. The "primitive mind," one deduces from the poet's affirmations, is inadequate because it has not developed to the point where it can positively and effectively work with the full requirements of ecological reality. Using Wordsworth's own terminology, one might say that the primitive mind can fit itself to the external world, but cannot fit the external world to the mind. Contrarily, the modern farmer, industrialist, or urbanite fits the world to his mind (usually with the aid of a bulldozer), but cannot fit his mind to the world. Both kinds of fitting are necessary. We know of many human societies that have weakened, even destroyed, themselves through misuse of nature. Wordsworth would not be surprised. To him civilized life is the fulfillment of natural life, not its antithesis, just as the ultimate result of his submergence in the commonalty of Grasmere Vale is the realization of the power of his special, unique individuality. His individuality completes the natural self-sufficiency of Grasmere, reintegrating the natural and the human on a higher plane, or, more simply, transforming nature into paradise.

"Beauty . . . Surpassing the most fair ideal Forms" exists as the poet's "hourly neighbour" within Grasmere because in its actuality it is "Paradise, and groves / Elysian, Fortunate Fields" since the poet's "discerning intellect" has been "wedded to this goodly Universe." What "Home at Grasmere" describes is the consummation of the union, the "making" of a microcosmic world. Wordsworth's relation to the valley, if my observations of children and my memory of my own childhood do not betray me, is very close to that by which a child fits himself to, and makes fit his "demands," the microcosmic environment of a garden, a farm, or a "country place." The child makes the limited environment into a self-sufficient, self-contained world, that is, a unity in which place and self are mutually defining. The peculiar poignancy (captured perfectly by the phrase in *The Excursion*, "familiar with forgotten years") of one's memories of such microcosms of early youth springs from the fact that *there* one simultaneously discovered both the external world and one's self—one through the other.

Whether or not I'm right about children, in "Home at Grasmere" Wordsworth certainly insists that his unique self is defined in terms of a place, *his* territory. In the "Prospectus lines" he describes the mind of man as the "haunt" and main "region" of his song, and the metaphors are significant. He treats the mind as a territory. In the final lines of "Home at Grasmere" we recognize that the shape and character of the valley mirror the form of a creative mind—self-contained, self-sufficient, profoundly at ease. Not only does the poem's form reflect its meaning, but also its meaning images its form, which is a linguistic realization of the loveliness of the vale.

"Home at Grasmere" praises the divinity of the world and gives joyous thanksgiving for the goodness of actual life, internal and external. The valley indubitably is Wordsworth's temple, his holy place. Just as indubitably it is also his home, his "Dwelling Place." And if it is reasonable to suspect angels of speaking matter-of-factly of the Heaven they inhabit, one may forgive Wordsworth some prosaicness. Living in paradise, he lives by ordinary standards "idly." Because the poet does not segregate home from holy place, the sacred from the profane, because to him commonplace living can be divine, his religiosity appears as a kind of indolence.

Because to Wordsworth it is only by opening himself to the unified wholeness of life that he can attain wholeness of individuality, it is to the abundance, the overflowing fullness of life in Grasmere that he persistently recurs. And in so doing, he implicitly derogates the conventional work ethic. Like Cowper, Beattie, Collins, and Gray before him, Wordsworth celebrates a life of sensations and sensibility that exclude purposeful industry—bluntly, earning a living. But by making Grasmere a microcosmic ideal world, Wordsworth raises the traditionalized indifference to industriousness of "nature-loving" poets to an absolute negation of "work" as we usually conceive it.[7] Grasmere Vale is not, as I have pointed out, a place of respite, a vacation spot, for by definition a "vacation" is a segment of life determined by a work routine, and the valley is self-sufficient. In it the poet's life can be successful only because he does nothing "useful" in the conventional sense—except praise, worship, write poetry. Wordsworth worked hard at his verse, even suffering physical anguish in its composition, but he does not in "Home at Grasmere" (or in any other poem) describe the making of poetry of praise as "work." Analogously, St. Francis did not treat praise of God and his creation as "work." The comparison ought not to be pressed, but it is useful in reminding us of how much of Wordsworth's best poetry is, simply, joyous worship.

Most of us, having little time for joyous worship, often complain that the "realities of life" are "cold . . . ready to betray . . . stinted in the measure of their grace." Wordsworth, happily withdrawn in Grasmere, observes that we, not the realities, are at fault. He is overwhelmed by the lavishness with which his life is enriched at every turn by the mere reality of a rather barren valley. His message is that our perverse commitment to aggressive "work" impoverishes us as well as the natural world. Being busy blinds us to the potentialities for fulfillment that surround us. We are sick because we are not at ease in the affluence available to us at the cost simply of being quiet. Yet Wordsworth has no ambition to eliminate "labor," and he explicitly decries mere sensual self-indulgence and self-gratification.

For all his passivity, he is convinced that it is his moral obligation to contribute to the well-being of mankind. By turning away not only from the madding din of urban life but also from aggressive impulses within himself the poet develops a power to "impart" (not impose) a gift of transcendent worth.

Of what the gift consists we may discern by attending to the poet's mode of bestowal, the form of his poetry. "Home at Grasmere" is usually described as a monologue or meditation, although neither term is entirely apt. In the earlier parts of the poem Wordsworth most often addresses the valley and the creatures in it (employing the intimate "thou"), and in the latter part he addresses himself, his own mind and spirit, but until the "Prospectus lines" his mode is exploratory. He speaks to the valley in order to relate fully to it, in order to participate entirely in its life, and he talks to himself in order to realize his complete psychic capabilities. The "Prospectus lines" are the reward for these explorations, in attaining of what before had been only possibilities. In the closing lines the poet asserts and expounds, but until then he repeats himself as if hesitant, qualifies affirmations, and often balances opposed possibilities. Through this tentativeness he achieves a special kind of rhetorical accuracy: the effect of a man literally talking to himself. Success in this rhetorical mode (beyond attention to how, in fact, one does "meditate," which is not in the elegantly conventionalized manner of Renaissance literary "meditations") probably depends upon recognition of the intimate connection between language and the individual "self." Communication, as animals prove, is often effectual without language. But the discovery and formulation of a "self" may be regarded as a function of our ability to speak to ourselves. Wordsworth uses language to explore relations between himself and the world and to define by those relations the power within him that otherwise would remain impotent. His attitude toward language is apparent in his characteristically long sentences of loose syntactic structure, which permit development of thought, expansive treatment of emotion, and—above all—a fluid interplaying of perceptual "fact" with mental "fancy."

Long sentences contribute to the continuous, accumulating movement of his blank verse. Fluidity of syntax is signaled by his fondness for the semicolon, which facilitates association of clauses treating diverse aspects of a central sight or intuition. Associative syntactical arrangements permit linked expressions of similitude in dissimilitude and the reverse, within which, for him, resides the essence of the dynamic tranquillity of living process. Wordsworth, moreover, tends to avoid rhetorical vividness and ingenious verbal play in order to create a subterraneous interaction between large and small repetitions, just as he links his sentences in such a manner as to elucidate underlying configurations, the essential organizing principles, within landscapes and moods. Thus his specific representation of Grasmere's "blended holiness of earth and sky" is composed of two sentences, the second literally repeating the first, because it describes a reflection. The large repetition is reinforced by quiet reiterations of detail that emphasize the vale's depth:

> And the clear hills, as high as they ascend
> Heavenward, so piercing deep the lake below.
> (ll. 578–79)

It is as a vertical "theatre" that the valley serves to embody the poet's vision of

> The boundary lost, the line invisible
> The parts the image from reality
> (ll. 576–77)

that is, the continuity between the "superficialities" and the "profundities" of life.

The entire passage, lines 560–79, illustrates not only how Wordsworth's apparently casual and unhurried syntax enables repetitions and contrasts to accumulate to a rich yet not overelaborate total effect but also the nature of his unusual semantics. Connotation is often self-contained, that is, he quietly exploits the concealed root meaning of a word, its underlying, original sense, which is usually more concrete and physical than its later, "surface" meaning.[8] A good example in line 560 is the word "compass," deriving from "to measure off by paces." The vale has been and will be "paced off" by the poet. Often, too, he employs a word that while echoing the signification of a preceding word is yet distinct: the relation of "pageant" in line 570 to "theatre" in line 560 is of this kind. Such diction accords with his predilection for associative syntax and assists the revelations of similitude in dissimilitude, but perhaps most important his word choices serve as a formalized parallel to the manner of actual speech. Unless I err grievously, most of us repeat ourselves endlessly when we talk, especially when we talk to ourselves. In conversation we overlook the extent of our reiterations because by tone, rhythm, pitch, gesture, and so on we bestow on a given word, or cluster of associated words, a wealth of signification that is not so much connotative as the power of concentrated emotion. It is this emotionally focused quality of living language, not idiosyncrasies of individual manner, that Wordsworth strives to "imitate."

"There neither is, nor can be," he asserted in the 1800 Preface, "any *essential* difference between the language of prose and metrical composition." The effectiveness of the description of the reflected scene depends on its *not* being a mere poetic effusion. Words as words are, as the poet insisted as late as 1829, "powers" and not "vehicles." Poetry consists in the realization of the intrinsic powers of individual words, not in the construction of "secondary" artifices of language (including even metaphor), which inevitably dilute the inherent power of the simple word in itself.

Not surprisingly, Wordsworth prefers similes to dramatic metaphors. The simpler, more literal trope suits his aim of realizing what Coleridge called unity in multeity, the harmonious interrelating of disparate elements whose disparateness is cherished as much as their coherence. The open and extended comparison, furthermore, suits the poet's interplaying of description (presentation of immediate sensations) with past impressions, possible future observations, and even purely imagined perceptions. The obvious sign of the intermingling of sensory "fact" with mental "fancy" is Wordsworth's fondness for the subjective and conditional, e.g., "And if this / Were otherwise" (ll. 648–49). When one contrasts "Home at Grasmere" to poems in the Genius Loci tradition within which he worked, one notices that what especially distinguishes Wordsworth is the extent and subtlety of his devices for making his record of immediate sensations interact with the representation of mental actions beyond perceptual responsiveness. The first two lines juxtapose "*yon* steep barrier" with the remembered vision to introduce the interplay of "fact" and "fancy," developed in the opening verse paragraph by the boy's remark to himself "if a thought of dying . . . could intrude" and by the older poet's assertion that the boy felt only "A fancy in the heart of what might be / The lot of Others," namely, an existence that "never could be his." This exploitation of language's power to evoke "the contrary to fact" in the very presence of the fact itself (e.g., what is, "never could be") is perhaps Wordsworth's most characteristic and significant poetic device. In diverse fashions it is central to poems such as "Tintern Abbey," "Resolution and Independence," "Peele Castle," and the Intimations Ode, but nowhere does he employ it with more skill than in "Home at Grasmere."

Briefly to indicate his skill, I point to the second verse paragraph, in which the poet blends the boy's actual sensations with his mental creations (ll. 25–35). And, as the poet goes on to make clear, the "unfettered liberty" that the vale now provides him derives from its simultaneous encouragement of delight in his perceptions and in his power to remember both what he had perceived and had imagined and to envisage what he will perceive and imagine. Possession of this multiple power convinces the poet that we are wrong to regard "the realities of life" as "stinted in the measure of their grace." Realities, the obstinacies, so to speak, of actuality, are what provoke mental activity, especially imaginativeness, and imaginativeness, as the Preface of 1800 had suggested, "colors," that is, transforms without distorting.

Because the vale as an entity permits the poet to experience the "unity entire" of an ecological "Whole without dependence or defect," his imagination is liberated rather than confined by the limitedness of Grasmere. He is not tempted to distort perceptual reality, to seek refuge either in solipsism or in Arcadian dreams, but, instead, is enabled to project visions, memories, speculations, evaluations upon perceptual realities as fulfillments of their actualness. Thus he affirms that the dwellers in the valley "require / No benediction . . . For they are blest already" because

> They who are dwellers in this holy place
> Must needs themselves be hallowed.

Yet the affirmation is balanced by the reservation:

> Thus do we soothe ourselves, and when the thought
> Is pass'd we blame it not for having come.
>   (ll. 277–78, 290–91)

And in subsequent lines he repeats the caution of lines 273–76 that he does not merely report perceptible reality, while demonstrating, as for example, through reference to the "reiterated whoop" of the shepherd, that he has not been "betrayed by tenderness of mind" into romanticizing the harsh truths of valley life. The shepherd's voice, "a Spirit of coming night," to "superstitious fancy" *might* seem "Awful as ever stray Demoniac uttered," and *may* "have reached mine ear / Debased and under profanation." Man can make of perceptions something different from their "literal" truth (else there would be no "making"), yet if a man's spirit be properly attuned through his participation in the wholeness of life's unity, his "makings," his imaginations, will be neither falsifications nor evasions of actuality.

This brings us to the core of Wordsworth's ideal of what poetry should be and do.

>   is there not
> An art, a music, and a strain of words
> That shall be life, the acknowledged voice of life,
> Shall speak of what is done among the fields,
> Done truly there, or felt, of solid good
> And real evil, yet be sweet withal,
> More grateful, more harmonious than the breath,
> The idle breath of softest pipe attuned
> To pastoral fancies? Is there such a stream,
> Pure and unsullied, flowing from the heart
> With motions of true dignity and grace?
> Or must we seek that stream where Man is not?
>   (ll. 401–12)

These interrogatives are finally transformed into the triumphant declaratives of the "Prospectus lines," for this ideal of poetry is what "Home at Grasmere" proclaims. Of all Wordsworth's poems it is the one in which most explicitly and at greatest length he articulates his fundamental "poetics." It is his longest poem about poetry. For him poetry is language that, without falsifying literal actuality, will liberate man from the prison of perceptual responsiveness, enabling him to be simultaneously a sensitive and a creative soul, being one because he is the other.

Liberation depends upon conscious participation in the living yet nonperceptible unity of the vale, in fine, in its ecological equilibrium. Such conscious participation only language can carry us toward and give expression to when attained. Language distinguishes us from the so-called "lower forms" of life. Used "poetically," language enables us to reintegrate ourselves with those lower forms (as well as with "inanimate" nature) without becoming imprisoned in sensory responsiveness, without becoming mere creatures of impulse. Animals inhabit environments apprehended almost entirely through immediate sensations; they do not appear to compare present with past perceptions nor to imagine how and why something perceived now might be different at another time or be responded to differently. Properly used, language permits us to do these things, and so live more richly and complexly the same life, the "one life," not only of animals but also of flowers, which, as we may imagine as they cannot, "enjoy" the air they breathe. What Wordsworth imparts is the power language bestows on us consciously to reintegrate our lives into the affluence of natural existence and thereby to exalt man and nature, rather than debasing one before the other.

Whether or not today one judges that Wordsworth's poetry embodies successfully the ideal of poetry articulated in "Home at Grasmere," one can recognize that his undertaking is more pertinent to our time than earlier critics could have anticipated. Wordsworth is, perhaps, the one "nature" poet whose vision is truly ecological. Furthermore, as I have tried to suggest but have not fully explored here, his manner of presenting his vision provokes thought about some fundamental presuppositions that have dominated criticism throughout most of this century, especially our assumptions about "the primitive." Insofar as one accepts Wordsworth's diction, vocabulary, and rhetoric as appropriate to a remarkably sophisticated conception of man, of nature, and of human life, one is compelled to wonder if, as has been so widely accepted, the fundamental and originating impetus of art is to be found in myth—to which Wordsworth is as indifferent as to sex. Art may not, after all, be so deeply rooted in those "archetypal patterns" which recently have attracted most attention. Possibly what we call myth-making is a relatively late cultural development. Perhaps that large body of "primitive" art that does not fit readily into the patterns favored by modern mythographers—I am thinking of a good deal of American Indian music, dance, and storytelling in particular—directly expresses what Wordsworth explores: the fundamental life processes which underlie, and upon which depend, the *power* of man's developed imaginative creativity. Conceivably a truly "primitive" response to nature consists less in aggressiveness or the free play of impulse than in a quieter yet more complex engagement with the environment as a totality, as a "world." The emergence of myth-making may signal the loss of this primal unity, the diminishment of an original, inborn sense of territorial integrity, of what might be termed innate ecological sensitivity. Maybe such speculations are absurd, and surely only extended study (not only of Wordsworth but also of the life sciences) could validate any part of them. But because it suggests the possible fruitfulness of such study, "Home at Grasmere" deserves attention that has been denied it in the past.

Notes

1. Two good commentaries, however, are those of Herbert Lindenberger, *On Wordsworth's Prelude*, 2nd ed. (Princeton, N. J.: Princeton Univ. Press. 1966), pp. 163–66; and Geoffrey Hartman, *Wordsworth's Poetry 1787-1814* (New Haven, Conn.: Yale Univ. Press, 1964), pp. 171–74.

2. Although Carlos Baker does not use the word "superimposition" in his introduction to the Rinehart Edition of *The Prelude* (New York: Holt, 1948), my term doubtless derives from his analogy of a photographic "double exposure" in that excellent essay.

3. "A Whole without dependence or defect, / Made for itself; and happy in itself, / Perfect Contentment, Unity entire." "The Recluse. Part First. Book First. Home at Grasmere," *The Poetical Works of William Wordsworth*, ed. Ernest de Selincourt and Helen Darbishire (Oxford: Oxford Univ. Press, 1949), Appendix A, 318, ll. 149–51. All may quotations from "Home at Grasmere" are from this edition, which prints what I call the "Prospectus lines" (the last 107 ll.) in their "final" form only in the Preface to *The Excursion*, v. 3–6. At least a portion of these lines probably was composed as early as 1798.

4. The quoted phrase is from the MS. B version of the "Prospectus lines," de Selincourt, v, 327. Hereafter quotations from "Home at Grasmere" are identified by line number only.

5. On art as miniaturization, see Claude Lévi-Strauss, *The Savage Mind* (Chicago: Univ. of Chicago Press, 1966), pp. 22–25.

6. Leavis' discussion appeared originally in *Revaluation*, but my quotations are from the reprint of his essay appearing in Jack Davis' handy collection, *Discussions of William Wordsworth* (Boston: Heath, 1964), pp. 90–108.

7. A tradition in which Wordsworth works in "Home at Grasmere" originates in Denham's "Coopers Hill," the first example of "local poetry," as Dr. Johnson named it. An aspect of this tradition is discussed by Geoffrey Hartman in "Romantic Poetry and the Genius Loci," *The Disciplines of Criticism*, ed. Peter Demetz, Thomas Greene,

and Lowry Nelson, Jr. (New Haven, Conn.: Yale Univ. Press, 1968), pp. 289–314. In a larger study, of which this essay is a part, I discuss not only literary but also graphic traditions of landscape art upon which Wordsworth drew.

8. Only after writing this comment on Wordsworth's diction and syntax did I encounter the late W. J. Harvey's "Poetic Vision in the World of Prose," *Inaugural Lecture, The Queen's University*, New Lecture Series, No. 29 (Belfast: Queen's Univ., 1966), which anticipates several of my observations; see esp. pp. 9, 11–12.

Wordsworth's Mirror Imagery and the Picturesque Tradition   Stephen J. Spector°

I

Though in some important ways Wordsworth is the most typical English Romantic poet, the more noticeable kinds of Romantic mirrors—the Narcissistic mirror of the demonic quest-romance, the mocking mirror-double of the tale of the divided self, the dark, cracked mirror of psychological disintegration[1]—are conspicuously absent from his poetry, except for his youthful Gothic play, *The Borderers*.[2] Nevertheless, aside from Shelley, mirror imagery plays a more important role in his work than in the poetry of any other major English Romantic. His mirror imagery looks back to the eighteenth century and to the kind of mirror imagery found abundantly in the period's topographical poetry, where reflections on water (typically pools in grottoes) usually symbolize a harmonious relationship between the mind and the world based upon the analogy of the reflecting water and the reflective mind. But the eighteenth-century tradition from which Wordsworth's mirror imagery springs most directly is the Picturesque, to which, like other young men of taste, he looked for guidance in matters of painting, poetry, landscape, architecture, aesthetics, and travel.

As is well known, the category of the Sublime played a crucial role in the Picturesque tradition; and Wordsworth, who in 1790 went to the Alps questing after the Sublime and the Beautiful, has always been acknowledged as a devotee of sublimity, even if many readers agree with Keats that Wordsworth is mainly a poet of the "egotistical sublime." Great mountains, especially the Alps, were naturally the most frequently mentioned examples of the sublime; and in his *Guide through the District of the Lakes*, Wordsworth takes it as a matter of

° Reprinted from *ELH*: 44 (1977). © 1977 The Johns Hopkins University Press. Used by permission of The Johns Hopkins University Press.

common knowledge that "A stranger to mountain imagery naturally on his first arrival looks out for sublimity in every object that admits of it."[3] Of course Mt. Blanc and Mt. Snowdon did not exhaust the category of the Sublime; indeed, as true sublimity became firmly associated with infinity, two other natural objects, the ocean and the sky, became the highest forms of the Sublime, and the two together, when the sky is reflected on the surface of the ocean, became the *ne plus ultra* of sublimity as well as one of the most frequently repeated instances of Romantic mirror imagery, not only in poetry but also in the great English seascape painting tradition from Constable to Turner.[4]

It is curious that in Wordsworth's poetry sublime sea/sky mirror imagery is almost totally absent; instead he repeatedly delights in the Picturesque reflections of pools, tarns, and lakes. While it could be argued that his preference for the circumscribed image is due to his residence in the Lake country, a more likely explanation is that the Sublime induced in him a genuine anxiety because he could not always confine it to the landscape or seascape he was contemplating; when the Sublime could no longer be anchored to Nature, Wordsworth was forced to come face to face with the autonomous power of his own mind, an anagnorisis that, as Geoffrey Hartman has argued, was almost unbearable,[5] even though in the Prospectus to *The Excursion* Wordsworth announced that he would brave the terrors of self-discovery. Wordsworth's own explanation is less complicated: "though it is impossible that a mind can be in a healthy state that is not frequently and strongly moved both by sublimity and beauty, it is more dependent for its daily well-being upon the love and gentleness which accompany the one, than upon the exaltation or awe which are created by the other" (*Prose Works*, II: 349).

II

Picturesque formulas for mirror imagery, where the inverted reflection on the water's surface is seen as a painting, originated in eighteenth-century travel literature and have since infiltrated all kinds of writing. One of the most impressive examples of Romantic mirror imagery is a text that conceals its debt to the Picturesque because its imagery is embedded in matter that every reader immediately recognizes to be deeply personal: Wordsworth's "There was a Boy," written in 1798 and first published in *Lyrical Ballads*, 1800:

> There was a Boy; ye knew him well, ye cliffs
> And islands of Winander!—many a time,
> At evening, when the earliest stars began
> To move along the edges of the hills,

Rising or setting, would he stand alone,
Beneath the trees, or by the glimmering lake;
And there, with fingers interwoven, both hands
Pressed closely palm to palm and to his mouth
Uplifted, he, as through an instrument,
Blew mimic hootings to the silent owls,
That they might answer him.—And they would shout
Across the watery vale, and shout again,
Responsive to his call,—with quivering peals,
And long halloos, and screams, and echoes loud
Redoubled and redoubled; concourse wild
Of jocund din! And, when there came a pause
Of silence such as baffled his best skill:
Then sometimes, in that silence, while he hung
Listening, a gentle shock of mild surprise
Has carried far into his heart the voice
Of mountain-torrents; or the visible scene
Would enter unawares into his mind
With all its solem imagery, its rocks,
Its woods, and that uncertain heaven received
Into the bosom of the steady lake.[6]

(PW, II, 206)

The reader's first response is that the text embodies a mode of consciousness central to Wordsworth when he walks the tightrope of Natural Supernaturalism. The picture on the surface of the water is a reflection in the natural element (the water) of the potentially supernatural (the "uncertain" heavens above). The union of the natural and the supernatural is extended by the mind of the poet as he meditates upon images of reflection: Wordsworth reflects upon the Boy of Winander's mind, which was a mirror of the lake, which in turn was a mirror of the earth and that "uncertain heaven." And mirroring water and reflective minds are not the only unifying reflectors in this series of interweavings; the mirror imagery has been prefigured by the mention of echoes, the aural equivalent of mirrors: the Boy's hoots are answered by the owls, and the hootings of both the boy and the bird are echoed by the hills. Wordsworth pictures a world of possibly infinite interconnection between the mind, nature, and the divine—each behaving as if it were a mirror imaging other mirrors.

Certainly the reader must feel that this passage describes a moment of authentic reflection. Even if Wordsworth's Boy of Winander were not the boy Wordsworth himself, as we know he is, the entire passage would be familiar as one version of the silent, meditative pause in which Wordsworth's mind spreads out in concentric circles until it reaches a midpoint between life and death, sense and transcendence, presence and absence, the natural and supernatural—that poised moment which is almost Wordsworth's signature. The same doubleness is inherent in many of Wordsworth's poems simply because they are poems of memory or return; in other poems ordinary human beings seem to be supernatural, like the leechgatherer who seemed "like a man from some far region sent" and the "phantom of delight" who was "A Spirit, yet a Woman too!" (*PW*, II: 213). Mirror imagery would seem to be not just an appropriate but almost an inevitable way for Wordsworth, who himself resembles "A Borderer dwelling betwixt and death / A Living Statue or a Statued Life,"[7] to express the doubleness he perceived in the world.[8]

III

To Coleridge the mirror imagery of "There was a Boy" is an example of Wordsworth at his most idiosyncratic, as his well-known reaction to the lines, "Uncertain heaven received / Into the bosom of the steady lake," demonstrates: "had I met these lines running wild in the deserts of Arabia, I should instantly have screamed out 'Wordsworth!' "[9] But inevitably mirror imagery recalls its own traditions (even if only to dismiss them), and the language of "There was a Boy" is in fact an adaptation of the Picturesque formulas for the description of lakes, especially those of the English Lake District. And the Picturesque tradition is not isolated from Pope's Neoclassical tradition, although Wordsworth's distance from Pope is vast. Maynard Mack has shown how, in his "Aegerian Grott," "where *Thames'* translucent Wave / Shines a broad Mirrour thro' the shadowy Cave," Pope imagined himself Egeria playing host to modern Numas.[10] Wordsworth, remembering a scene of echoes and watery reflections, studiously avoids an overt reference to Echo and Narcissus.

The mirror imagery of "There was a Boy," in which the mirroring lake reflects the "scene" of "rocks," "woods," and sky, is to be found in one of the seminal documents of the Picturesque tradition, Dr. John Brown's letter of 1758 in which he describes Derwent Water, Keswick's lake: "in calm weather the whole scene becomes new: the lake is a perfect mirror; and the whole landscape in all its beauty, islands, fields, woods, rocks, and mountains, are seen inverted and floating on its surface."[11] Brown's letter was first published in 1767, and two years later Thomas Gray, in his famous journal letter for 3 October 1769, repeated Brown's praise of Derwent Water: "beneath you, & stretching far away to the right, the shining purity of the *Lake*, just ruffled by the breeze enough to shew it is alive, reflecting rocks, woods, fields, & inverted tops of mountains, with the white buildings of *Keswick, Crosthwait*-church, & *Skiddaw* for a back-ground at a distance."[12]

The context of both quotations is the tradition of Picturesque travel, and what both Brown and Gray are pointing out is that Derwent Water is an example of Picturesque beauty. Both descriptions exemplify the Picturesque at its most obvious: the lake itself, which is small and round, is a picture made by Nature. The frame, of course, is the margin of the lake, and the subject is the landscape which the mirror-water paints so perfectly.[13]

The mirroring picture-lake was connected with another Picturesque mirror, the Claude glass, a convex mirror in which the tourist could view the landscape composed into a perfect landscape picture; and because the glass was tinted a color approximating the finish of Claude Lorrain's paintings, the landscape reflected on the Claude glass was indeed a miniature Claude.[14] Thomas Gilpin, one of the chief theoreticians of the Picturesque, argued that the main virtue of the Claude glass is that it presents a large scene on a small surface (generally small lakes were preferred by the connoisseur of the Picturesque), so that both the general and the particular might be seen together, whereas in nature the observer must concentrate on one or the other, but not both. Gilpin's discussion shows that the context of the Picturesque is almost always exclusively aesthetic, as do his visually imaginative comments about one possible use of the Claude glass, which incidentally reveals that the moving picture was preceded by the moving Picturesque: "In a chaise particularly the exhibitions of the convex-mirror are amusing. We are rapidly carried from one object to another. A succession of high-coloured pictures is continually gliding before the eye. They are like visions of the imagination or the brilliant landscapes of a dream. Forms, and colours, in a brightest array, fleet before us; and if the transient glance of a good composition happen to unite with them, we should give any price to fix, and appropriate the scene."[15] The true Woman of Taste did not even need a Claude glass in order to view the moving Picturesque; Mrs. Ann Radcliffe, with a vocabulary almost entirely drawn from the fine arts, provides the following sketch of a walk under the cliffs along Derwent Water: "These, with every woody promontory and mountain, were perfectly reflected on its surface. Not a path-way, not a crag, or scar, that sculptured their bold fronts, but was copied and distinctly seen even from the opposite shore in the smooth water, which, as it gave back the painted sides and gleaming sail, displayed a moving picture."[16]

As in "There was a Boy" descriptions of mirroring water were frequently accompanied by testimonials about the echoing ability of the landscape. In the English Lake District it was a common amusement to row out to the middle of a calm lake and listen to the echoes of horns or guns which were sounded for the gratification of the tourists who demanded *son* with their *lumière*. In *An Excursion to the Lakes in Westmorland and Cumberland* (1776), William Hutchinson establishes himself as a lover of the Picturesque by his minute rendering of the coloring of the prospect: "The beauties of this scene were increased by the reflection of the water, where the deep green hue was seen to mix with the olive and grey of the adjoining objects; whilst the background seemed to decline in faintest purple, variegated with the deep crimson streaks of an evening sky" (p. 72). After he has appreciated Nature's use of the palette, he praises her musical genius: "We lay upon our oars some time, reluctant to quit this prospect, and enjoyed the music of the horns;—the exquisite softness and harmony which the echoes here produced, were not to be described; the muse seemed to issue from some resounding temple, which stood concealed behind the mountains, where the most solemn and delicate symphony was heard" (p. 72). And William was not the only Wordsworth whose eyes and ears were trained by the Picturesque; Dorothy's *Grasmere Journals* contain at least sixteen references to the mirroring surfaces of lakes; her July 1800 entry, in which she recounts an excursion to view Rydal lake, presents the typical Picturesque description of painted lake-mirror and echoes (the caws of the raven take the place of the hoots of the Boy of Winander's owls):

> The lake was now most still and reflected the beautiful yellow and blue and purple and grey colours of the sky. We heard a strange sound in the Bainriggs Wood as we were floating on the water it *seemed* in the wood, but it must have been above it, for presently we saw a raven very high above us—it called out and the Dome of the sky seemed to echo the sound—it called again and again as it flew outwards, and the mountains gave back the sound, seeming as if from their center a musical bell-like answering to the bird's hoarse voice. We heard both the call of the bird and the echo after we could see him no longer.[17]

From these examples it is clear that the significance of the Picturesque's handling of reflections and echoes for a poet like Wordsworth is that, except for the inevitable association of reflecting water with reflective calm, most of the traditional associations of those images are refused: Picturesque reflection imagery is significant because of its omissions. Reflecting waters are not seen as dark shadows of heaven; here are no deceitful crystal floods waiting to snare self-loving Narcissi; here are no souls tempted by their reflections on the sea of hyle (as Blake Neoplatonically interpreted Gray's "Ode on the Death of a Favourite Cat, Drowned in a Tub of Gold Fishes"); here are no emblems of *vanitas*, like Belinda's mirror-altar; here are no analogues of the mind reflecting the Archetypes. Only rarely does the analogy of the mirror with the reflective mind emerge, as it does implicitly when Gilpin compares the continually changing pictures in his Claude glass as he rides along to "visions of the imagination or the brilliant landscape of a dream"; and the explicit use of the analogy by Cowper, as he describes the "pleasure in poetic pains" in *The Task* (ll, 290–93), is still controlled by the picture-drawing metaphor that is the heart of the Picturesque:

> To arrest the fleeting images that fill
> The mirror of the mind, and hold them fast,
> And force them sit, till he has pencilled off
> A faithful likeness of the forms he views.

What is present in Picturesque reflection imagery, and what makes its adaptation so natural for Wordsworth, is an attempt to see the world in purely aesthetic terms, without the mediation of traditional associations. Originally the Picturesque was an integral part of the Enlightenment's attempt to see the world without the distorting mirrors of Romance, Religion, or Superstition. The categories generated to account for the landscape—Sublime, Beautiful, Picturesque, Romantic—were intended to have something of the status of other categorizations of natural phenomena. Reflections on lakes, from the beginning of the Picturesque tradition, were important examples of the Beautiful or the Picturesque (the application of the correct label in any specific case was mainly a function of the theorizer),[18] just as the reflection of the sky on the ocean was an example of the Sublime. The goal of the cultured man, as he stood gazing at the landscape, was to see the world in a new way, so that the associations of the past would not disturb his purely aesthetic intercourse with the scene. The logical conclusion of the Picturesque quest was what Martin Price has called "the picturesque moment": "that phase of speculation . . . where the aesthetic categories are self-sufficient."[19]

The Picturesque, therefore, may be seen as part of the Enlightenment's drift towards the unmediated vision, but it may also be seen as proof of the counter-proposition that an unmediated vision is impossible. No sooner had the eye been freed from the bondage of tradition by the aestheticism of the Picturesque than it became a prisoner of the Picturesque itself: it became impossible to view the landscape except through a Claude glass. Inevitably the Picturesque became a subject for satire for William Combe (*The Tour of Doctor Syntax in Search of the Picturesque*, 1809), for Jane Austen, and for Thomas Love Peacock (whose *Headlong Hall* parodies the Uvedale Price/Richard Payne Knight controversy, one of the centerpieces of the Picturesque). And by 1814 watery reflections had become so banal that Scott could count on his readers seeing the kind and degree of young Waverley's naiveté by simply displaying his hero's trite effusion, "Mirkwood Mere," whose first stanza is an assemblage of Picturesque reflection clichés:

Late, when the Autumn evening fell
On Mirkwood-Mere's romantic dell,
The lake returned, in chastened gleam,
The purple cloud, the golden beam:
Reflected in the crystal pool,
Headland and bank lay fair and cool;
The weather-tinted rock and tower,
Each drooping tree, each fairy flower,
So soft, so true, the mirror gave,
As if there lay beneath the wave,
Secure from trouble, toil and care,
A world than earthly world more fair.
                                        (Chap. 5)

But the failure of the Picturesque was crucial for Wordsworth, whose main problem may be seen as one of vision.

IV

Wordsworth commemorated his Alpine tour of 1790 in search of the Sublime and the Picturesque with two major memorials: his letters to Dorothy on 6 and 16 September 1790 and *Descriptive Sketches* (1793). Both documents show Wordsworth fully committed to the Picturesque mode. In the letters, which are extremely carefully composed compositions, he announces the rationale behind all travels: "It is the end of travelling by communicating Ideas to enlarge the mind" (*EY*, 32). While at this time Wordsworth specialized in the Sublime, he also appreciated the Picturesque. He was then, he confesses, "a perfect Enthusiast in my admiration of Nature in all her various forms" (*EY*, 35). After his famous Sublime intercourse with the Simplon Pass, Wordsworth proceeded to the Picturesque charms of the lake of Como. As he describes the lake he brings the often latent Picturesque analogy, that the landscape is a painting, to the surface. After describing the "new picture" which appears at every turn in his path, he comes to the crowning Picturesque beauty, the mirroring lake which is a perfect landscape painting: "Nor was the surface of the lake less interesting than its shores; part of it glowing with the richest green and gold the reflexion of the illuminated woods and part shaded with a soft blue tint. The picture was still further diversified by the number of sails which stole lazily by us, as we paused in the woods above them" (*EY*, 34).

No response could be more commonplace. But Wordsworth has put the Picturesque to his own personal purposes, even if his language is contained by its formulas. He has used the scene to wean him back to earth and man. The self-containment of the lake, its easily felt analogy with a painting (a purely human creation)—these aspects of the Picturesque landscape are used by him in order to combat the supra-human mind expansion engendered by the Sublime Alps: "At the lake of Como my mind ran thro a thousand dreams of happiness which might be enjoyed upon its banks, if heightened by conversation and the exercise of the social affections. Among the more awful scene of the Alps, I had not a thought of man, or a single created being; my whole soul was turned to him who produced the terrible majesty before me" (*EY*, 34).[20] While the taming function of the Picturesque is clear here, it seems that the Sublime, because it too is a category created by man in order to comprehend the external world, might also be credited (or blamed) for the circumscription of the Imagination.

By the time of the writing of *The Prelude* Wordsworth was convinced that he had conquered the hold that the aesthetics of categorization had on him. The central passage about his fight with the Picturesque occurs in Book XI of the 1805 version where, following a discussion about the lesser kind of Reason (the logical and analytical power), which unfortunately had dominated his mind for some time, Wordsworth illustrates its deleterious effect upon him by showing how he wronged Nature by seeing it through the eyes of a typical product of the lesser Reason, the aesthetics of the Picturesque, which he now understands to be merely "rules of mimic art transferr'd / To things above all art" (XI: 154–55). The time when Wordsworth was a devotee of the Picturesque was a time in which the sights of the world blinded him to real insight, but the domination of the eye was always doomed in Wordsworth by powers within himself and within Nature. Even as a child he had come into contact with his own imagination, a power that would strip away the monkish, life-denying "habit" of the Picturesque vision:

> I had felt
> Too forcibly, too early in my life,
> Visitings of imaginative power
> For this to last: I shook the habit off
> Entirely and for ever, and again
> In Nature's presence stood, as I stand now,
> A sensitive, and a creative Soul.
>   (XI: 251–57)

Curiously, Nature also works against the Picturesque. The eye, which learns to see Nature (and all of reality, for that matter) through the rules and paradigms of tradition and convention, must finally fail in its attempt to control external reality because Nature itself has means which it "studiously employs to thwart / This tyranny" (XI: 179–80).

Wordsworth's emancipation from the tyranny of the Picturesque allowed him to see "things above all art," and those things were most specifically visitings of the transcendent in the most mundane circumstances. In order to express the natural supernaturalism, the doubleness of reality he found miraculously embodied in water reflections, he had to avoid two pitfalls. Even though he was attracted to the Picturesque, he had to be careful not to let aestheticism become his exclusive focus; and as sympathetic as he was to the religious emotion expressed by Christian and Platonic mirror symbolism, he could not accept any transcendentalism that did not give nature as much value as the divine.

We can witness his success by examining the first important reflection imagery in *The Prelude*, the wonderful ice-skating scene from book I:

> Not seldom from the uproar I retired
> Into a silent bay, or sportively
> Glanced sideway, leaving the tumultuous throng,
> To cut across the image of a star
> That gleam'd upon the ice: and oftentimes
> When we had given our bodies to the wind,
> And all the shadowy banks, on either side,
> Came sweeping through the darkness, spinning still
> The rapid line of motion; then at once
> Have I, reclining back upon my heels,
> Stopp'd short, yet still the solitary Cliffs
> Wheeled by me, even as if the earth had roll'd
> With visible motion her diurnal round;
> Behind me did they stretch in solemn train
> Feebler and feebler, and I stood and watch'd
> Till all was tranquil as a dreamless sleep.
>
> (I:474–89)

The star, reflected on the ice, is of course an example of the heavenly revealed on earth, and the young Wordsworth found himself magically drawn to its gleam. Wordsworth intends us to see that as a child he possessed a special sensitivity that naturally drew him into isolation and self-communion. But the hint that he has a special destiny, that the star is his genius to which he is inevitably attracted—that kind of suggestion is perfectly contained by the complete naturalness of the action. After all, the scene is also just an illustration of any child's fascination with a glittering object. The whole passage demonstrates Wordsworth's amazing tact when he is at his best; the endless possibilities for theologizing the imagery by recalling its potential Platonic-Christian significances are carefully restrained; and the other danger, to trivialize the imagery by reducing it to a Picturesque beauty, is averted with equal finesse. The same is true of the rest of the ice-skating scene, especially when the boy enters into a vertiginous trance after playing crack the whip. Like the Boy of Winander the boy Wordsworth enters a semi-mystic state of detachment, but at a time when he is most profoundly being ministered to by Nature herself.

The union of the mind and the world that occurs during such privileged moments is the result of spontaneous reflection: just as a lake needs only a clear and calm day to mirror the sky, so the boy needs only a lucky combination of a moment of silence and an externally induced "gentle shock" for his mind to perfectly mirror the external world. But such moments are not "wise passiveness"; in fact, the boy has no wisdom. Only the reflective poet, the mature Wordsworth, can reflect upon his past and transform the isolated, privileged moments into the fabric of his life. In the fourth book of *The Prelude* Wordsworth describes his active pursuit of reflection as a mature man; the mirror imagery is complicated here because the reflecting surface is not the calm water of a lake or the infinite expanse of the ocean: the poet pursues the reflection on the surface of the ever-moving river of life:

> As one who hangs down-bending from the side
> Of a slow-moving Boat, upon the breast
> Of a still water, solacing himself
> With such discoveries as his eye can make,
> Beneath him, in the bottom of the deeps,
> Sees many beauteous sights, weeds, fishes, flowers,
> Grots, pebbles, roots of trees, and fancies more;
> Yet often is perplex'd, and cannot part
> The shadow from the substance, rocks and sky,
> Mountains and clouds, from that which is indeed
> The region, and the things which there abide
> In their true dwelling; now is cross'd by gleam
> Of his own image, by a sunbeam now,
> And motions that are sent he knows not whence,
> Impediments that make his task more sweet;
> —Such pleasant office have we long pursued
> Incumbent o'er the surface of past time
> With like success . . .
>
> (IV: 247–64)

The consciousness presented here is complex but not fragmented, multifaceted but not discontinuous. Readers have noticed that the passage repeats Wordsworth's confessed inability to distinguish what he called in book III "naked recollection" from "after meditation" (III: 646, 648);[21] and when that confusion is added to the fluid nature of memory implicit in the relativistic simile in which both the object perceived (the reflection and the objects in the moving river) and the perceiver (because the boat with the perceiver in it always moves) are constantly changing, it is plausible to suggest that Wordsworth

must be disoriented. But Wordsworth manages to avoid the uncom-
fortable implications of his simile; for one thing he does not pursue
its logic, but most importantly he means the reader to respond to
the confusions as examples of blendings. On the literal level the fact
that the reflections mix with the real objects suggests an interpenetration of past and present. Wordsworth's own evaluation of the
scene, that "Impediments" make the act of memory "more sweet,"
as well as the beautifully achieved calm slowness of the lines, assure
us that the exploration of his past is indeed to him a "pleasant office."

The traditional associations of reflection imagery are, so to speak,
closer to the surface here than in "The Boy of Winander" or in the
ice-skating scene. But again Wordsworth effectively suppresses the
threat that they might intrude too far. The theme of narcissistic self-
delusion is raised when Wordsworth points out that what his memory
might reveal is really his "own image"; but, paradoxically, because
he can recognize his own image he is therefore able to recognize
what is not himself: he acknowledges the alterity of other reflections.
His most obvious flirtation with traditional mirror imagery arises when
he invokes the formulaic distinction between "shadow" and "substance." Usually implicit in that distinction is the notion that reality
is divided into two related but well-defined levels, a primary one
with greater ontological status and a secondary one that is merely a
shadow of the first. But again, Wordsworth refuses to make the
traditional distinction and rests satisfied with a reality in which
"shadow" and "substance" remain inextricable.

Home at Grasmere is the culmination of the quest described in
The Prelude.[22] For Wordsworth Grasmere is a recovered Eden, and
so the return there constitutes the completion of a naturalized version
of the Christian journey, including the recognition that the expulsion
was actually the result of a *felix culpa*. As might be expected in a
poem with so many biblical echoes, the mirror imagery in *Home at
Grasmere* comes very close to being traditionally Christian. While
Wordsworth insists that his natural home is sufficient, the pull of the
transcendental is evident throughout. His position is revealed in a
marvellous passage describing birds torn between the sun and their
reflections on the ice and the water below:

> They tempt the sun to sport among their plumes;
> They tempt the smooth water, or the gleaming ice,
> To shew them a fair image,—'tis themselves,
> Their own fair forms, upon the glittering plain
> Painted more soft and fair as they descend,
> Almost to touch;—then up again aloft,
> Up with a sally, and a flash of speed,
> As if they scorned both resting-place and rest!
>
> (II: 219–29)

The birds, traditional symbols of the soul, are enacting the drama going on inside Wordsworth; like him they are torn between the desire to fly into the sun (to return to the "burning fountain") and their love for this naturally supernatural earth. Another traditional mirror motif present here is the theme of Narcissus: it may be dangerous to dedicate yourself to the "fair image" reflected on the ice and water because that image is, after all, only yourself. Iconographically the passage has a long heritage, too; as D. W. Robertson, Jr. points out in his discussion of the *Roman de la rose*, the well of Narcissus was conventionally thought of as "a bird-snare where *illicita delectatio* or 'the desire for pleasure' catches its victims."[23] Wordsworth's birds, like his soul, are not trapped by the watery reflections of their own beauty, but, again like Wordsworth, they restlessly occupy the space between the heavens and the water, vacillating between the impulse to soar above the earth and the desire to plunge into the water. The Picturesque is present also; the "fair forms" are pictures, "Painted more soft and fair" as the birds get closer to the water. The implication seems clear: the aesthetic appeal of the earthly image is dangerously seductive, and the closer you come to paying attention exclusively to earthly beauty the closer you come to being drowned in the pleasure of this world.

The final reflection passage in *Home at Grasmere* counteracts the restlessness and vacillation Wordsworth reveals in the passage just examined. His ability to create images of blending finds its full power in this description of a perfect union of reflection and reality in a boundless mirrorscape:

> while all the distant grove
> That rises to the summit of the steep
> Shows like a mountain built of silver light.
> See yonder the same pageant, and again
> Behold the universal imagery
> Inverted, all its sun-bright features touched
> As with the varnish, and the gloss of dreams;
> Dreamlike the blending also of the whole
> Harmonious landscape; all along the shore
> The boundary lost, the line invisible
> That parts the image from reality;
> And the clear hills, as high they ascent
> Heavenward, so piercing deep the lake below.
> (II: 567–79)

The key phrase here is "The boundary lost," indicating that Wordsworth has found his home. The upward thrust of the hills, like Wordsworth's aspirations for the divine, are perfectly counterbalanced by the downward thrust of the hills' reflection in the earthly element, the water. As usual when Wordsworth is comfortable with his subject, his blank verse is effortlessly expressive. In this passage his control of enjambment is particularly effective, especially in the phrase "dreamlike the blending also of the whole / Harmonious landscape." Because the previous lines are a mixture of enjambment and end-stopping, the reader must pause slightly at the last word, "whole," and by doing so "whole" is first interpreted as a noun, releasing its ability to embody the theme of wholeness that underlies the entire passage. Only after the reader moves to the next line is it clear that "whole" is part of the compound adjective, "whole / Harmonious," that modifies "landscape." The word "landscape," of course, reintroduces the Picturesque dimension of the scene that was first hinted at with the mention of coloring ("silver light") and then fully developed by the painterly phrasing in the clause "all its sunbright features touched / As with the varnish, and the gloss of dreams." The finish of the Claude glass has been brushed over a painting of the imagination. However, once more Wordsworth has made the Picturesque function within the framework of his overarching theme: the blended coloring created by the mixture of the silver mountains bathed in sunlight and the tint lent the reflected picture by the water prepares the way for the even more spectacular blending of image and reality caused by the lack of a boundary line and the climactic interpenetration of earth and heaven in the last two lines.

As the examples from *Home at Grasmere* indicate, Wordsworth's resolve to restrain his impulse to elevate and theologize his reflection imagery became increasingly tenuous. Gradually natural supernaturalism gave way to what was more or less exclusively supernaturalism. A passage which occurs first in one of the *Prelude* manuscripts that de Selincourt dates from about 1804 and that finally found its way into the last book of *The Excursion* illustrates the transition. The *Prelude* version recounts an encounter of the young Wordsworth with a white ram whose reflection in a calm mountain stream created a mysterious image of doubleness:

> at a glance I saw
> A twofold image; on the grassy bank
> A snow-white ram, and in the peaceful flood
> Another and the same; most beautiful
> Beneath him, was his shadowy counterpart;
> Each had his [glowing] mountains, each his sky,
> [And each seem'd centre of his own] fair world.[24]

At this point in the 1804 manuscript Wordsworth introduced three lines that recall "Nutting" and episodes in *The Prelude* like the famous boat-stealing and bird-snare robbing scenes; the instinctual destructive nature of the boy Wordsworth contrasts with the harmony of nature:

> A stray temptation seiz'd me to dissolve
> The vision,—but I could not, and the stone,
> Snatch'd up for that intent, dropp'd from my hand.

These quietly dramatic lines were replaced by three rather redundant and pompous lines in *The Excursion:*

> Antipodes unconscious of each other,
> Yet, in partition, with their several spheres,
> Blended in perfect stillness, to our sight!
> (IX: 449–51, *PW*, V, 300)

In both versions the doubled white ram is still a naturally supernatural image, like the white doe of Rylstone, whose allegiance is neither to earth nor heaven; but the tide is shifting towards an openly religious symbolism. Wordsworth's placement of the passage in the last book of *The Excursion* completes the shift from a vision retaining a tension between miracle and explanation to verbose religiosity. The description of the reflected ram comes after a long sermonic speech by the Wanderer, and its function is to serve as a proof of both his godliness and the truth of his principles. So that his intention is unmistakable to the reader, Wordsworth reports the words that the Pastor's wife whispers to him after the pious party has viewed the miraculous scene. In her gloss on the image she praises the Wanderer's mind by picturing it (using the vocabulary of the Picturesque) as a *speculum sine macula:*

> 'How pure his spirit! in what vivid hues
> His mind gives back the various forms of things,
> Caught in their fairest, happiest attitude!'
> (IX: 462–64, *PW*, V, 301)

In the rest of her speech the reflection image is cited as an example of the transience of natural and moral beauty; there is no longer any attempt to suggest the sufficiency of nature:

> 'While he is speaking, I have power to see
> Even as he sees; but when his voice hath ceased,
> Then, with a sigh, sometimes I feel, as now,
> That combinations so serene and bright
> Cannot be lasting in a world like ours,
> Whose highest beauty, beautiful as it is,
> Like that reflected in yon quiet pool,
> Seems but a fleeting sunbeam's gift, whose peace
> The sufferance only of a breath of air!'
> (IX: 465–73, *PW*, V, 301)

In slightly later poems like the "Epistle to Sir George Howland Beaumont" (1811) and the "Effusion, in the Pleasure-Ground on the Banks of the Bran, near Dunkeld" (1814), we can see Wordsworth's

ever increasing willingness to combine Picturesque mirror imagery
with the moralizing aesthetics of eighteenth-century nature poetry.
His popular tourist book, *A Guide through the District of the Lakes
in the North of England,* however, is the most important example of
his reversion to the Picturesque mode, despite the claims of those
Wordsworthians who would place it in a category by itself. In the
Guide Wordsworth repeatedly resorts to the formulas of the Picturesque (perhaps partly to satisfy the expectations of the typical tourist),
directing the visitor to enjoy Windermere where the sunset is painting
such a lovely picture: "The surface of the lake will reflect before
the eye correspondent colours through every variety of beauty, and
through all degrees of splendour" (p. 174), or advising the novice
Lake District tourist who plans to walk through a valley in the morning
that "if the horizon in the east be low, the western side may be
taken for the sake of the reflections, upon the water, of light from
the rising sun" (p. 230).

At such times Wordsworth speaks only as a conventional guide,
but in the most extended reflection passage in the *Guide* the Claude
glass is set aside, and the authentic Wordsworthian voice emerges.
The description of the reflecting lake becomes a metaphor enabling
Wordsworth to trace the journey of his imagination descending to
an underworld where it can learn the relationship of life to death
and where it momentarily achieves a poised reflectiveness that is
emotionally its home. This movement begins dramatically: "While
looking on the unruffled waters . . . the imagination, by their aid,
is carried into recesses of feeling otherwise inpenetrable" (192). In
the next sentence "heavens" and "bosom of the earth" are substituted
for "imagination" and "recesses of feeling" ("brought down into"
replaces "carried into"), and so the imagination's journey home is a
return to the maternal breast: "The reason of this is, that the heavens
are not only brought down into the bosom of the earth, but that the
earth is mainly looked at, and thought of, through the medium of a
purer element" (p. 192).

The rest of the passage describes the perfect setting to reflect
upon the newly discovered emotion in "tranquility," and reveals what
Wordsworth gains when he returns home. In autumn, after the storms
have departed, except for "a few shattered boughs,"

> all else speaks tranquility;—not a breath of air, no restlessness of
> insects, and not a moving object perceptible—except the clouds
> gliding in the depths of the lake, or the traveller passing along, an
> inverted image, whose motion seems governed by the quiet of a
> time, to which its archetype, the living person, is, perhaps, insen-
> sible:—or it may happen, that the figure of one of the larger birds,
> a raven or a heron, is crossing silently among the reflected clouds
> while the voice of the real bird, from the element aloft, gently

awakens in the spectator the recollection of appetites and instincts, pursuits and occupations, that deform and agitate the world—, yet have no power to prevent nature from putting on an aspect capable of satisfying the most intense cravings for the tranquil, the lovely, and the perfect, to which man, the noblest of her creatures, is subject. (p. 192)

Here one of Wordsworth's favorite themes, the concurrence of stillness and movement, finds expression. The lake, whose surface is so still that it does not in fact have any motion, mirrors the moving objects above it—the heavens, the clouds, the traveller, the birds. The scene in the water then, is both still and moving. The balance needed to remain in such an attitude has been described by J. Hillis Miller: "This poise, when it appears in Wordsworth, indicates that the poet has entered into full awareness of the powers and dangers of the human imagination. It involves always the copresence of motion and stillness as essential components of human time."[25] The passage can only be read fully when it is perceived that Wordsworth, as Miller finds in "Composed upon Westminster Bridge," "is both there and not there, as if he were his own ghost" (p. 307). That is, Wordsworth, by realizing his death in the "inverted image" in the still water, views himself, the moving "traveller," from the point of view of the dead Wordsworth. While such a text can be related to all the themes reflecting waters figure in, most obviously the "another world" topos (as in *Paradise Lost* IV: 451–91, Traherne's "Shadows in the Water," and Shelley's Jane poems, "The Invitation" and "The Recollection") and the doppelgänger, the passage reflects unmistakably Wordsworth's peculiar power, which so often surprises the reader, to conjure up, with a skill Freud uncovers in Hoffmann and then reveals in himself, that realm of the simultaneously strange and familiar—the uncanny.

V

This essay has been limited to a study of Wordsworth's mirror imagery in its most immediate context, the Picturesque tradition of reflection description. Other contexts, such as Neoplatonic and Christian mirror iconography, could have been explored at greater length, but their relation to Wordsworth is generally tenuous. One context, however, the psychoanalytic interpretation of narcissism and mirrors, does hold real promise, even though to establish its precise importance for Wordsworth would require great tact.[26] In order briefly to suggest what is at stake here, it will serve to return to "There was a Boy" and to recall its conclusion, omitted when first quoted:

This boy was taken from his mates, and died
In childhood, ere he was full twelve years old.
Pre-eminent in beauty is the vale
Where he was born and bred: the churchyard hangs
Upon a slope above the village-school;
And through that churchyard when my way has led
On summer-evenings, I believe that there
A long half-hour together I have stood
Mute—looking at the grave in which he lies!

That the entire poem invokes Ovid's story of Narcissus is attested to by the fact that its constituent elements are Echo (the owls), Narcissus (the Boy), a beautiful watery mirror (the lake's "bosom"), and the death of Narcissus (the Boy's death). As noted, Wordsworth's intention is to present a series of relations of the Boy to Nature that increase in closeness, depth, and profundity, until the Boy is one with Mother Nature: in Freudian terms he incorporates her (he drinks in the scene of the bosom—it "enters" his "mind"), and she incorporates him (the scene is "receiv'd" into her "bosom"). The first major shift occurs when the lesser harmony of echoing owl and Boy gives way to the greater narcissistic mirroring of landscape, heavens, water, and Boy.[27] The final mirror union, the dream of perfect interpenetration until all boundaries are lost as Self and Other dissolve into One, inevitably brings to mind Freud's description of primary narcissism and the "oceanic" feeling, a Wordsworthian theme noted by Lionel Trilling in his famous essay on the Immortality Ode.[28] Wordsworth's imagery (and not only his mirror imagery, of course, as the "Blest Babe" passage of Book II of *The Prelude* proves), suggests that he would certainly not have been surprised at psychoanalytic interpretations of narcissism and mirroring in which the mother's breasts and eyes are the original narcissistic mirrors in which the infant first drinks in his sense of wholeness, boundlessness, power, and entitlement.[29] But more uncanny is Wordsworth's knowledge and acceptance of the wages of a return to the state of primary narcissism—death. The Boy of Winander–Wordsworth, like Lucy, achieves a perfect identification with Mother only by acting out the compulsion to repeat, and so return to death.

Finally, to give Wordsworth his due, it must be recognized that he could record his own momentary rejection of the image that lured him so powerfully and fatally. That the Xanadu of narcissism is an illusion over an abyss of infinite need, feelings of incompleteness, and fantasies of fragmentation is never revealed directly, but in passages like the one in which he records his "stray temptation" to splinter the "twofold image," the dark side of narcissism is momentarily glimpsed.

The problems raised by a psychoanalytic interpretation of Wordsworth's mirror imagery reopen the split in Wordsworth criticism that is so sharp that at times the critical mirror seems to reflect two Poets, one an inversion of the other: the Poet of wholeness, recovery, and health (the image Wordsworth wanted to project—the Friend offered to Coleridge as a model of successful self-analysis), and the Poet of chronically troubled self-consciousness whose self-proclaimed Joy fails to cover up an essential dis-ease. And like all other aspects of Wordsworth's poetry, his mirror imagery can successfully be read as the record of either Poet.

Notes

1. Some of this is discussed by Masao Miyoshi in *The Divided Self* (New York: New York Univ. Press, 1969). Most pertinent is his brief mention of double mirror imagery in *Dorian Gray* and *À Rebours* in Chap. 6, "Masks in the Mirror: The Eighteen-Nineties."

2. For example, ll. 1864–65, 2008–09 in the *Poetical Works of William Wordsworth*, eds. Ernest de Selincourt and Helen Darbishire, 5 vols. (Oxford, 1940–49), I, 202, 208. Hereafter cited as *PW*.

3. *The Prose Works of William Wordsworth*, eds. W. J. B. Owen and J. W. Symser, 3 vols. (Oxford: Clarendon Press, 1974), II, 231. Hereafter cited as *Prose Works*. This edition is of special importance to studies of the Picturesque because it contains the fragmentary essay, "The Sublime and the Beautiful" (ll, 349–60). Page numbers after quotations from the *Guide* refer to this edition.

4. As early as 1712 Addison had associated large bodies of water with Greatness, by which he meant the Sublime (*The Spectator*, eds. Gregory Smith and Peter Smithers, 4 vols. [New York: Dutton, 1958], III, 279); but the ocean's place in the Picturesque tradition was permanently established in 1757 by Edmund Burke in his *Enquiry* (ed. J. T. Boulton [New York: Columbia Univ. Press, 1958], pp. 57–58), in which he credits the ocean's immensity with the creation of sublime terror. The Romantic poets were interested in the ocean's terror also, but they were more attracted to its infiniteness and especially to its ability to mirror the heavens. For example, in Keats's "Hymn to Pan" in *Endymion*, the god is asked to "Be still a symbol of immensity / A firmament reflected in a sea" (I: 299–300). Other instances of the same imagery occur in *Childe Harold* (IV: 1639–44) and *Prometheus Unbound* (IV: 382–87).

5. *Wordsworth's Poetry 1787–1814* (New Haven and London: Yale Univ. Press, 1964; rev. 1971), pp. 37–48. Wordsworth's closest approximation of sublime sea/sky mirror imagery is his vision from Mt. Snowdon in book XIII of the 1805 *Prelude*, esp. ll. 39–84.

6. In American literature, the most important scene of echoes and a watery mirror is in *Walden*, ed. J. Lyndon Stanley (Princeton: Princeton Univ. Press, 1971), pp. 176, 188. Thoreau's debt to the Picturesque tradition is too complex a matter to be entertained here.

7. These lines come after the Mt. Snowdon episode in an 1804 manuscript of *The Prelude* printed in *The Prelude or the Growth of a Poet's Mind*, ed. Ernest de Selincourt, 2nd ed. rev. Helen Darbishire (Oxford, 1959), p. 624. Cited hereafter as de Selincourt-Darbishire edition. Unless noted all quotations from *The Prelude* are from the 1805 version presented in this text.

8. Hartman calls such images "boundary images" (p. 198).

9. *Collected Letters of Samuel Taylor Coleridge,* ed. Earl Leslie Griggs, 6 vols. (Oxford, 1956–71), I, 453.

10. *The Garden and the City: Retirement and Politics in the Later Poetry of Pope, 1731–1743* (Toronto: Univ. of Toronto Press, 1969), pp. 69–76.

11. Dr. Brown's letter was frequently reprinted. My text is taken from the reprint of the letter in Thomas West's *A Guide to the Lakes in Cumberland, Westmorland, and Lancashire,* 7th ed. (1799), p. 196. In every edition of his *Guide* (including the first edition, 1810), Wordsworth quoted the echo-reflection passage from "The Boy of Winander" (ll. 21–25) to illustrate the charms of Derwent Water. In the *Guide* Wordsworth frequently cites West.

12. *Correspondence of Thomas Gray,* ed. Paget Toynbee and Leonard Whibley, 3 vols. (Oxford, 1935), III, 1079–80.

13. Some indication of the mania for Picturesque water-mirror imagery might be indicated by the following list of reflection passages: William Chambers, *A Dissertation on Oriental Gardening* (1772), p. 64; Uvedale Price, *A Dialogue on the Distinct Character of the Picturesque and the Beautiful* (1801), pp. 170–72 (on the Claude glass), 214–21; Uvedale Price, *A Letter to H. Repton, Esq.* (1798), pp. 158–60, 162; Joseph Palmer, *A Fortnight's Ramble to the Lakes,* 2nd ed. (1795), pp. 144–47 (Palmer, whose real name was Joseph Budworth, included his poem "To the Lakes" in which he praises the echoes and reflection of Windermere in heroic couplets: "The trees, the crags, and the high-tufted steep, / Reflect their beauties on the MIRROIR deep. / The azure softness of a cloudless sky / Tints on the surface—a celestial dye," [p. 145]); Thomas West, *A Guide to the Lakes,* 7th ed. (1799), in the Picturesque tradition charted by Elizabeth Manwaring, compares the reflections on the lakes to the paintings of the great landscapists: "The change of scenes is from what is pleasing, to what is surprising; from the delicate touches of Claude, verified on Coniston lake, to the noble scenes of Poussin, exhibited on Windermere-water; and, from these, to the stupendous, romantic ideas of Salvator Rosa, realized on the lake of Derwent" (p. 10). West recites the standard praise of Derwent Water's reflections repeatedly (pp. 86, 99, 113–14); Harriet Martineau, in *The English Lakes,* 2nd ed. (1858), maintained the tradition for the Victorians with her description of Derwent: "Its waters are singularly clear, and its surface often unruffled as a mirror then reflects the surrounding shores with marvellous beauty of effect" (p. 73); Picturesque water-reflection imagery was also standard in the sentimental novel; for example, in Charlotte Smith's *Ethelinde; or the Recluse of the Lake,* 5 vols. (London: T. Cadell, 1789), the heroine, who carries about "that volume of the works of Gray, in which he, with the clearest simplicity, describes the small lake," stands before Grasmere and exclaims: "How calm, how beautiful is its surface, spangled with stars, and deeply contrasted by those dark tufts of evergreen which crowd over it" (I, 58, 49); and Mary Shelley used the calmness of Picturesque reflections as a contrast to the violence of sublime Gothic emotion and scenery in *Frankenstein* (New York: New American Library), pp. 147, 153, 156, 185.

14. Gray's place in the pantheon of Picturesque tourists was assured by the dedication he showed his Claude glass even in a moment of personal danger: "fell down on my back across a dirty lane with my glasses open in one hand, but broke only my knuckles" (*Correspondence,* III, 1079). In a letter of 29 July 1805 Wordsworth mentions a more serious version of the same kind of accident: "The Body, or more properly speaking Bones of a poor Fellow were yesterday found . . . in the rocks at the head of Red Tarn. . . . His name appears to have been Charles Gough, several things were found in his pockets; fishing Tackle, Memorandums, a Gold Watch, Silver Pencil, Claude Lorraine Glasses & c" (*The Letters of William and Dorothy Wordsworth: The Early Years,* ed. Ernest de Selincourt, rev. ed. Chester L. Shaver [Oxford, 1967], p. 612. Cited hereafter as *EY*).

15. *Remarks on Forest Scenery*, 2 vols. (1791), II, 225. (Stendhal's epigraph for Chapter 13, Book I of *Le Rouge et le Noir*, "un roman: c'est un miroir qu'on promène le long du chemin," proves that the moving Picturesque is a near relative of the moving Picaresque.) Gilpin attempted to classify water reflections with an almost scientific precision in *Observations on Several Parts of England*, 3rd ed., 2 vols. (1808), I, 104–09, 132–33. While Gilpin sees some drawbacks in the reflected image on the Claude glass and the mirror-lake, his remarks show that his habit (esp. *Remarks on Forest Scenery*, II, 224 ff.) and the tendency of users of the Picturesque generally, is to see the reflected image in the water as an instance of *la belle nature*, an aesthetic version of the purifying mirror, standing between the *speculum sine macula* of the Christian tradition and the epipsyche of Romanticism. The *speculum sine macula* is discussed by Heinrich Schwartz, "The Mirror in Art," *Art Quarterly*, 15 (1952), 97–103, and by Sister Ritamary Bradley, "Backgrounds of the Title *Speculum* in Medieval Literature," *Speculum*, 29 (1954), 100–15. The connection between the mirror and *la belle nature* is discussed by Jean Hagstrum in *The Sister Arts* (Chicago and London: Univ. of Chicago Press, 1958), pp. 134–43.

16. *A Journey Made in the Summer of 1794*, 2nd ed., 2 vols. (1795), II, 345–48. The description of Windermere in *A Tour from London to the Lakes: Containing Natural, Oeconomical, and Literary Observations, Made in the Summer of 1791. By a Gentleman* (1792) illustrates that the mirroring lake and the Claude glass came to possess equivalent functions for the Picturesque tourist: "Not a breath of wind troubled the Lake this day; it was consequently a mirrour, and doubled every beauty, while my convex mirror brought every scene within the compass of a picture" (p. 64).

17. *Journals of Dorothy Wordsworth*, ed. Mary Moorman (Oxford, 1971), p. 31.

18. Dorothy Wordsworth's account of Coleridge's conversation with a fellow tourist at the waterfall Cora Linn is a homely example of the difficult pseudo-science of classification: "C., who is always good-natured enough to enter into conversation with anybody whom he meets in his way, began to talk with the gentleman, who observed that it was a *'majestic* waterfall.' Coleridge was delighted with the accuracy of the epithet, particularly as he had been settling in his own mind the precise meaning of the words grand, majestic, sublime, etc., and had discussed the subject with Wm. at some length the day before. 'Yes sir,' says Coleridge, 'it *is* a majestic waterfall.' 'Sublime and Beautiful,' replied his friend. Poor C. could make no answer, and, not very desirous to continue the conversation, came to us and related the story, laughing heartily" (*Journals of Dorothy Wordsworth*, ed. Ernest de Selincourt, 2 vols. [London: Macmillan, 1959], I, 223–24).

19. "The Picturesque Moment," in *From Sensibility to Romanticism: Essays Presented to Frederick A. Pottle*, ed. Frederick W. Hilles and Harold Bloom (New York: Oxford Univ. Press, 1965), p. 262.

20. In *Descriptive Sketches* (ll. 53–105), Wordsworth repeats his praise of the domesticating power of Como's Picturesque mirror-lake.

21. For example, Jack Stillinger, ed. *William Wordsworth: Selected Poems and Prefaces* (Boston: Houghton Mifflin, 1965), p. 549, and M. H. Abrams, *Natural Supernaturalism*, p. 75. For a less successful rendering on the mirroring surface of the river of life see *The Excursion*, III: 967–91.

22. *Home at Grasmere* is printed in *PW*, V, 813–39 as Appendix A.

23. *A Preface to Chaucer: Studies in Medieval Perspective* (Princeton: Princeton Univ. Press, 1962), p. 94.

24. De Selincourt-Darbishire edition, p. 581. The note there reads: "The words enclosed in brackets, which are illegible in the ms., have been supplied from the corresponding lines in the *Excursion*" (p. 581).

25. "The Still Heart: Poetic Form in Wordsworth," *New Literary History*, 2 (1971), p. 309.

26. The most important psychoanalytic interpretation of Wordsworth is Richard Onorato's *The Character of the Poet: Wordsworth in "The Prelude"* (Princeton: Princeton Univ. Press, 1971). Onorato's argument generally swerves away from a full discussion of narcissism because he is interested especially in Wordsworth's Oedipal conflicts. Leon Waldoff, in his review of Onorato (*Journal of English and Germanic Philology*, 72 [1973], 144–47), makes the point that Onorato undervalues the significance of Wordsworth's narcissism. For a French Freudian view of Onorato's handling of narcissism, see Jeffrey Mehlman's review and Onorato's reply in *Wordsworth Circle*, 4 (1973), 206–10.

27. Paul de Man rightly notes the foreboding of the verb "to hang" in "There was a Boy," in "Wordsworth und Hölderlin," *Schweizer Monatshefte*, 12 (1966), 1146.

28. "Wordsworth's 'Ode: Intimations of Immortality,' " in *English Institute Annual* (New York: Columbia Univ. Press, 1942).

29. In addition to Freud's many writings on narcissism, the following psychoanalytic interpretations of narcissism and mirrors are helpful: Otto Fenichel, "The Scoptophilic Instinct and Identification," in *The Collected Papers of Otto Fenichel* (New York: Norton, 1953), pp. 373–97; Paula Elkisch, "The Psychological Significance of the Mirror," *Journal of the American Psychoanalytic Association*, 5 (1957), 235–44; D. W. Winnicott, "Mirror-role of Mother and Family in Child Development," in *Playing and Reality* (New York: Basic Books, 1971), pp. 111–18; Heinz Kohut, *The Analysis of the Self* (New York: International Universities Press, 1971); Leonard Shengold, "The Metaphor of the Mirror," *JAPA*, 22 (1974), 97–115; and Jacques Lacan, "Le stade du miroir comme formateur de la fonction du Je," trans. as "The Mirror-phase as formative of the Function of the I," in *New Left Review*, 51 (1968), 71–77. For the way that Lacan's theory complicates Freud's primary narcissism, see the entries headed "Mirror Stage" and "Narcissism" by Jean Laplanche and J. B. Pontalis in *Yale French Studies*, 48 (1972), 192–97.

In Wordsworth's English Gardens

George H. Gilpin[*]

> The art in seeing Nature is a thing almost as much to be acquired as the art of reading the Egyptian hieroglyphics.
>
> —John Constable[1]

As a practical guide for touring, Wordsworth's *A Guide Through the District of the Lakes in the North of England* would never suffice: it lacks the details—point to point, landmark by landmark, scene after scene—to direct the traveler. Rather than guiding the eye, the *Guide* addresses the "*Minds* of Persons of taste,"[2] as Wordsworth demonstrates by recalling a topographical model that he once saw:

[*] This essay was written specifically for this volume and is published here for the first time by permission of the author.

At Lucerne, in Switzerland, is shewn a Model of the Alpine country which encompasses the Lake of the four Cantons. The Spectator ascends a little platform, and sees mountains, lakes, glaciers, rivers, woods, waterfalls, and vallies, with their cottages, and every other object contained in them, lying at his feet; all things being represented in their appropriate colours. It may be easily conceived that this exhibition affords an exquisite delight to the imagination, tempting it to wander at will from valley to valley, from mountain to mountain, through the deepest recesses of the Alps. But it supplies also a more substantial pleasure: for the sublime and beautiful region, with all its hidden treasures, and their bearings and relations to each other, is thereby comprehended and understood at once.

The kind of overview afforded by the Alpine model, with its revelation of the "bearings and relations" of individual aspects of the scenery to the whole landscape, becomes the example that orients the reader to Wordsworth's avoidance of description of beautiful or sublime details:

Something of this kind, without touching upon minute details and individualities which would only confuse and embarrass, will here be attempted, in respect to the Lakes in the north of England, and the vales and mountains enclosing and surrounding them. The delineation, if tolerably executed, will, in some instances, communicate to the traveller, who has already seen the objects, new information; and will assist in giving to his recollections a more orderly arrangement than his own opportunities of observing may have permitted him to make; while it will be still more useful to the future traveller, by directing his attention at once to distinctions in things which, without such previous aid, a length of time only could enable him to discover.[3]

For specific directions and information, the traveler would have to consult a guide to the Lakes like Thomas West's A Guide to the Lakes (1778), which maps a tour based on fashionable eighteenth-century principles: "The change of scenes is from what is pleasing, to what is surprising, from the delicate and elegant touches of Claude to the noble scenes of Poussin, and from these to the stupendous romantic ideas of Salvator Rosa."[4] In contrast, the Romantic Wordsworth assists the reader not in actual traveling but, as the Guide insists, in "recollections," or in anticipations that will bring an appreciation of the natural order implied by the subtitle of the first section, "View of the Country as Formed by Nature." Wordsworth presents a "guide" to the order in the landscape that cannot be perceived by touring, but only by imagining in tranquility. He invites the reader not physically to climb high mountains but mentally to fly above them, "to place himself with me, in imagination," not just on top of Great Gavel or Scawfell, but "suppose our station to be a cloud hanging midway between those two mountains."[5] The reader is invited to a realm above the tour of the picturesque and even beyond the sublimity of the highest mountains; the reader is invited to experience a vision of Nature from the very heavens. This vision represents the perspective of angels, one that in Milton is beyond the ken of fallen mortals; for Wordsworth's readers, it becomes accessible through the imagination.

Wordsworth had been aspiring to such a perspective since *Lines Composed a Few Miles Above Tintern Abbey* (1798), in which he is already eschewing any interest in "minute details and individualities" that provoke picturesque feelings. He chooses, instead, to focus on the process of "recollection" prompted by revisiting a place. He is already asserting a sublimity of mind over a sublimity of nature,[6] and to permit this focus aesthetic distance from the real landscape is upheld assiduously in the poem to stifle demands for details from readers with the prevailing eighteenth-century taste for picturesque effects. Establishing the necessary aesthetic distance begins with the convoluted title, which places the point of view of the speaker at some distance "above" the landmark abbey (not, as in Wordsworth's *Guide*, as high as the clouds above the mountains, but certainly at the level of the sky, for a bird's-eye view down the length of the valley) and announces the subject to be an act of "revisiting"; distance, both temporal and spatial, is maintained in the opening passage describing the scene (lines 1–22)[7] both by sentimental rhetoric (the opening exclamation, "Five years have past . . . with the length / Of five long winters!" as well as the repeatedly interjected "again" and "once again") and by emphasis on presenting a carefully considered whole, the sense of unity created by the merging and blurring of details and the dominant green hue. The sense of distance and unity imposed on the reader by Wordsworth's rhetoric is greater than that experienced by looking at scenery in a Claude glass, that tool of painters recommended to travelers in eighteenth-century guides like West's *Guide to the Lakes*. (A Claude glass was a mirror of convex shape that consolidated and framed landscape objects for picturesque effect and had a greenish-blue tint to give the reflection the hue of fashionable Italianate paintings.) Indeed, the sense of distance created by Wordsworth's opening lines is more like that achieved by the artist who paints a landscape in his studio relying on sketches and his recollection to recreate the scenery: the outcome is a picture coherent in composition and unified in color to be appreciated as a whole rather than admired for the beauty of its parts.[8] Nature so composed becomes orderly, accessible, and, most of all, enduring.[9]

Wordsworth does more, however, than just establish aesthetic distance between the perspective of the poem and an actual view of the Wye valley. At the verse-paragraph (line 22), he effects a transition from the landscape seen again with an artist's eye in the present to the idea of it that has remained with him in memory since he first saw it. Addressed as "These beauteous forms," the scene is transformed into a sentimental subject for recollection that has sustained the emotional life of the speaker during the preceding five years when he was faced with the adversity of living in "lonely rooms, and 'mid the din / Of towns and cities" (lines 25–26).[10] This version of the landscape, conceived as a kind of Platonic ideal retained in memory, has given him gifts of physical rejuvenation and charitable feelings (lines 27–35) and has offered even more, "another gift, / Of aspect more sublime" (lines 36–37). This ultimate sensation not only uplifts him emotionally,

> that blessed mood,
> In which the burthen of the mystery,
> In which the heavy and the weary weight
> Of all this unintelligible world,
> Is lightened,

it provides dreamlike, almost mystical, vision:

> Until, the breath of this corporeal frame
> And even the motion of our human blood
> Almost suspended, we are laid asleep
> In body, and become a living soul:
> While with an eye made quiet by the power
> Of harmony, and the deep power of joy,
> We see into the life of things.
>   (lines 37–41, 43–49)

This perception of the vitality of Creation within himself is quite beyond the reach of ordinary sight; that vitality can be *seen* only by being *felt* intensely. Its apprehension is neither direct nor immediate; it can only be known indirectly as an ideal experience of the mind. It can be described poetically only at the greatest possible aesthetic distance from the reader: in abstract terms as an experience of silence and tranquility associated with the poet's memory of the past. Philosophically, Wordsworth is merging the empiricism of John Locke's emphasis on the sensibility and the senses—which in the eighteenth century had engendered principles of the beautiful, the sublime, and the picturesque to explain feelings in response to scenery—with the idealism of his friend Coleridge's transcendental psychology of the Imagination.

The result is lyric ode becoming Romantic sermon. Wordsworth describes his role as that of a "worshipper of Nature" (line 152) preaching its blessings rather than being merely a guide to the sensations it creates. Coleridge's "Conversation Poems," composed prior to Wordsworth's ode, are the immediate source of this view of the speaker as a priest of Nature. To *Reflections on Having Left a Place of Retirement,* composed and first published in 1796, Coleridge in 1797 added the Horatian motto, *"Sermoni propriora."* In *Frost at Midnight,* composed in 1798 (before *Tintern Abbey* was written), Coleridge, addressing his infant son who is asleep in a moment of quiet midnight calm, promises him a spiritual experience of Nature conceived as Logos:

> so shalt thou see and hear
> The lovely shapes and sounds intelligible
> Of that eternal language, which thy God
> Utters, who from eternity doth teach
> Himself in all things, and all things in himself.
> (lines 58–62)[11]

He concludes his ode with a prayer bestowing the blessings of Nature on his son. Wordsworth expands Coleridge's prayer into a sermon, the tripartite form of the ode easily accommodating the conventional order of a preacher's meditation: the reading of the text of the day and an abstract statement of its thesis; the meditation on the meaning of the text in personal, anecdotal terms; the closing prayer and benediction reiterating the significance of the text and asking for the blessing of its understanding on the listeners.[12]

Instead of the preacher's Biblical word of God cited by chapter and verse, Wordsworth's divinely inspired "text" is a landscape of God's Creation identified by place and time: a few miles above Tintern Abbey on the banks of the Wye, 13 July 1798. Composed poetically, like the Bible, Wordsworth's chosen text is divine word to be meditated upon; therefore, after his initial "reading" of the text and abstract statement describing the "gifts" that the scenery can bestow, the anecdotal meditation commences as the second part of the ode (lines 58–111). The poet traces his own discovery of the gifts of Nature, beginning with the sheer "physical"—and thoughtless—joys of his childhood romps "Wherever nature led" (line 70). In youth, he experienced the spiritual in pantheistic intimacy with Creation:

> The sounding cataract
> Haunted me like a passion: the tall rock,
> The mountain, and the deep and gloomy wood,
> Their colours and their forms, were then to me
> An appetite; a feeling and a love,
> That had no need of a remoter charm,
> By thought supplied.
> (lines 76–82)

In maturity, however, he finds that this spirituality must be maintained philosophically—indeed, "by thought supplied"; by the end of the meditation he is celebrating a divine vitalism that he discovers to be in his mind by the very act of conceiving that his mind, too, is part of Creation:

> And I have felt
> A presence that disturbs me with the joy
> Of elevated thoughts; a sense sublime
> Of something far more deeply interfused,
> Whose dwelling is the light of setting suns,
> And the round ocean and the living air,
> And the blue sky, and in the mind of man:
> A motion and a spirit, that impels
> All thinking things, all objects of all thought,
> And rolls through all things.
>
> (lines 93–102)

Completing the meditation and the middle portion of the ode is a passage paralleling Coleridge's promise to his son in *Frost at Midnight:* Wordsworth explains how he learned to read the texts of Nature in terms that could be used to describe the reading of Biblical revelation:

> Therefore am I still
> A lover of the meadows and the woods,
> And mountains; and of all that we behold
> From this green earth; of all the mighty world
> Of eye, and ear,—both what they half create,
> And what perceive; well pleased to recognise
> In nature and the language of the sense,
> The anchor of my purest thoughts, the nurse,
> The guide, the guardian of my heart, and soul
> Of all my moral being.
>
> (lines 102–111)

The final part of Wordsworth's ode and sermon is a closing prayer like Coleridge's. Wordsworth's audience is his sister Dorothy, in whose "wild eyes" (line 119) he sees the image of his own youth, and he prays that she, too, will learn from Nature, which can "so inform / The mind that is within us, so impress / With quietness and beauty, and so feed / With lofty thoughts" (lines 125–128).[13] Wordsworth's prayer, following Coleridge's example, assumes the incantatory rhetoric of a benediction; he promises to his sister the gifts that Nature in all her "beauteous forms" can bestow (as the preacher invokes the divine forms: Father, Son, and Holy Ghost) to sustain her, as they have the poet, through adversity in her future life:

> Therefore let the moon
> Shine on thee in thy solitary walk;
> And let the misty mountain-winds be free
> To blow against thee: and, in after years,
> When these wild ecstasies shall be matured

Into a sober pleasure; when thy mind
Shall be a mansion for all lovely forms,
Thy memory be as a dwelling-place
For all sweet sounds and harmonies.

(lines 134 142)

Like William, Dorothy will have "healing thoughts" (line 144) to comfort her; she will be made tranquil by the music of the spheres perceived in Creation. She is like the "future traveller" addressed by Wordsworth in his *Guide*, whose attention he directs "at once to distinctions in things which, without such previous aid, a length of time only could enable him to discover." This promise, then, is Wordsworth's gift as a "worshipper of Nature" who, "Unwearied in that service" (lines 152–153), is a preacher, the mediator of the Creator who, as Coleridge said, "doth teach / Himself in all things, and all things in himself."

Like the "Cold Pastoral" on Keats's Grecian urn, Wordsworth's scene is meant to be read aesthetically. But unlike the skeptical Keats, who attributes paradox to his subject, the religious Wordsworth finds meaning in his, the setting of his poem still being, as the reader knows, only "a few miles" from the sacred ruins of the abbey. This spatial displacement from the religious setting is reinforced by the temporal displacement between the ecstatic, present experiences in the poem and both the poet's memory of the past and his anticipation of his sister's future. In this, too, he follows Coleridge, who in his *"Sermoni propriora," Reflections on Having Left a Place of Retirement,* recalls climbing to the top of the highest mountain near his cottage and achieving there a sense of the divinity of Creation. As in Wordsworth's poem, there is a ruined abbey nearby; however, it is in plain sight to Coleridge. Its proximity, and Coleridge's metaphoric awareness of it, is reflected in rhetoric describing the mountain vision of Nature that is more conventionally religious than Wordsworth's language: "It seem'd like Omnipresence! God, methought, / Had built him there a Temple: the whole World / Seem'd *imag'd* in its vast circumference" (lines 38–40). Wordsworth's promise to his sister of the gifts that Nature can bestow in the future, which maintains the temporal displacement of speaker from intense experience to the end of his poem, is modeled on the end of *Frost at Midnight:* Coleridge's promise to his sleeping infant of revelatory experience in the future that the poet himself has never been able to attain. Coleridge's relationship to these moments of intense feeling in the "Conversation Poems" has been described both as vicarious—experiencing them through another person, usually a loved one or friend—and as playing the part of an "usher" showing others to places where they, rather than the speaker, can receive the blessings of Nature and perceive its divinity.[14]

Wordsworth's conflation of Coleridgean sources in his ode inevitably gives his descriptions of intense experience a similar appearance, at first glance. Like Coleridge, Wordsworth places the inspiring gifts of nature at a distance—in memories of the past, in anticipation of the future, or in the intense feelings of others not presently shared by the speaker. In contrast to Coleridge, however, who thinks that his schooling in London denied him intimacy with nature, Wordsworth believes that during his childhood in the Lake District he actually knew such moments of ecstasy and joy in the presence of the divine.[15] Wordsworth becomes the child of Nature in the middle of his own ode; he presents himself as still knowing through recollection the vitality of nature as perceived through the sensationalism of Lockean epistemology, as someone who feels the divinity of Creation through his senses. In *Ode: Intimations of Immortality from Recollections of Early Childhood*, begun in 1802 and completed in 1804, he will depend on memories of these experiences, retained as vague "intimations," to be the foundation of his "philosophic mind" with its "faith that looks through death" (lines 185–186); in *Lines Composed a Few Miles Above Tintern Abbey* Wordsworth, like his friend Coleridge, is already keeping feelings of ecstasy at a similar distance. The Wye valley lacks vitality perceived in the present; it has meaning only in "recollections" of past experience, elsewhere, or in anticipations for his sister, elsewhere—cold pastoral, indeed.

The role of worshiper and priest of Nature assumed in *Tintern Abbey* is an antidote and corrective for readers of *Lyrical Ballads* who would question the seriousness of its content. Even though the first edition of the volume began with an "Advertisement" warning readers that "the majority of the . . . poems are to be considered as experiments,"[16] the ode in Miltonic blank verse added at the end at least could be taken seriously in comparison with those poems preceding it in which readers encounter the innovative irony of Wordsworth and Coleridge, who confound, by their choice of subject and form, the conventions of neo-classical poetry. Eschewing the artifice and pretension of eighteenth-century style by using the simple poetic forms ranked at the bottom of the Virgilian hierarchy of genres (which viewed the epic as the highest form of expression, elegy and ode in the middle, and ballad and pastoral as the lowest), the poets mock the expectations of their contemporary readers. Pastoral dialogues advocating a simplistic Lockean epistemology, like *Expostulation and Reply* (" 'I sit upon this old grey stone, / And dream my time away' " [lines 31–32]) and *Tables Turned* (Give up reading Shakespeare in order to "Let Nature be your Teacher" [line 16]); or a mock epic with a hero who has the perfect tabula rasa of a mind,

The Idiot Boy, written from the perspective of a rambling Shandian narrator who has failed his literary apprenticeship and, disdained by the Muse, presents irregular stanzas and outrageous rhymes; ballads like *Lines Written in Early Spring* celebrating the sheer pleasures of children at play in nature and *Anecdote for Fathers* and *We Are Seven* advocating the wisdom of children's hearts at the expense of adult reason; a strange tale of superstition and guilt like Coleridge's *The Rime of the Ancient Mariner* thought to contain too little moral or "too much"[17]—poems like these were enough to disorient even the most discriminating readers of the late eighteenth century. Hence, a poem conventional in form—an ode in blank verse—and serious in argument—a sermon—was required at the end of *Lyrical Ballads* to mitigate what would appear to many readers to be the "extreme simplicity" in style and thought of the "experiments."

To better orient readers and to respond to critics, the role of the poet is defined in the Preface with which Wordsworth replaced the Advertisement in the second edition of *Lyrical Ballads* (1800) and expanded in the third (1802). Besides defending the diction and the form of the poems against prevailing taste, the Preface is concerned with deflecting the charge of simplicity by describing the characteristics of the poet and his role as a mediator between Nature and the reader. Good poetry is not just the "spontaneous overflow of powerful feelings," as some readers, following their misreading of the poems as being about simple Lockean sensation, would conclude. "Poems to which any value can be attached," Wordsworth immediately continues, "were never produced on any variety of subjects but by a man who, being possessed of more than usual organic sensibility, had also thought long and deeply."[18] Such a brief description of the poet's role, however, still seemed an inadequate response to critics, and, probably at Coleridge's urging, the Preface in the 1802 edition was emended to emphasize the superior characteristics of the poet:

> He is a man speaking to men: a man, it is true, endowed with more lively sensibility, more enthusiasm and tenderness, who has a greater knowledge of human nature, and a more comprehensive soul, than are supposed to be common among mankind; . . . To these qualities he has added a disposition to be affected more than other men by absent things as if they were present; an ability of conjuring up in himself passions, which are indeed far from being the same as those produced by real events . . . than anything which, from the motions of their own minds merely, other men are accustomed to feel in themselves:—whence, and from practice, he has acquired a greater readiness and power in expressing what he thinks and feels, and especially those thoughts and feelings which, by his own choice, or

from the structure of his own mind, arise in him without immediate external excitement.[19]

When Wordsworth revised the Preface, then, his conception of the poet had evolved beyond the figure of the "worshipper of Nature" described in *Tintern Abbey* to a figure of genius with unusual powers to learn and to teach. The "egotistical sublime" remarked by Keats had been born, with Coleridge in attendance, and any experience of Nature is seen as transformed by the uniqueness of the poet's understanding.

By the time that the third edition of *Lyrical Ballads* appeared in 1802, the change in Wordsworth's view of the importance of the poet was affecting his treatment of landscape: his poetic settings had become even less specific and more obviously allegorical. The four opening stanzas of the *Intimations* ode, composed in 1802, present a scene that is too vague to be identifiable; the sentimental idea of a place is clearly more significant than the actual presentation of it. Unlike *Tintern Abbey,* in which a particular scene is described overall in an orderly fashion, the *Intimations* ode offers a catalogue of details—meadow, grass, stream, rainbow, rose, birds, cataracts, echoes, winds, flowers, tree, field, pansy—that only by their juxtaposition constitute a May day: it is as if the scene is being refracted rather than reflected by a shattered Claude glass. The details are not assimilated into one composition, nor is a particular one clearly singled out to be an object for meditation, as in short lyrics of the period like *To a Butterfly* or *My heart leaps up,* from which the epigraph for the ode is taken. (The completed poem of 1804 could be conceived, however, as a meditation on the pansy that prompts the questions at the end of stanza 4 and to which, as "the meanest flower that blows" (line 201), Wordsworth returns at the end.) The opening stanzas convey no sense of natural order and no vision of a composed picture; indeed, there is a sense of incompleteness and a lack of clarity. While the speaker struggles to achieve a feeling of ecstasy by invoking the image of a child of nature in whose joy he might share—"Thou Child of Joy / Shout round me, let me hear thy shouts, thou happy Shepherd-boy!"—or by contemplating the happiness of the activities of a spring day in which he can participate—"My heart is at your festival, / My head hath its coronal, / The fulness of your bliss, I feel—I feel it all" (lines 34–35, 39–41)—he cannot sustain the effort. He is overtaken by dejection, expressed in questions— raised by seeing the pansy—about his experience of not being able to see evidence of a divine presence in the details of nature surrounding him: "Whither is fled the visionary gleam? / Where is it now, the glory and the dream?" (lines 56–57).

When, two years later, Wordsworth responded to these questions by completing the ode, his answer was entirely in terms of a myth upholding faith rather than vision. Philosophy, not sensibility, now sustained him, as he articulated, employing conventional metaphors derived from neo-Platonic myth, an allegory of the progress of the soul from preexistence in immortality through mortal life to its return to immortality. The myth both explained Wordsworth's personal feelings about his darkening vision of Creation and permitted him to continue to uphold his belief in childhood as a unique period of intimacy with Nature and its Creator. Hence, in the *Intimations* ode, there is no definable pastoral scene, not even a "cold" one, because the sense of artistic vision that composed it in *Tintern Abbey* has been superseded by myth to explain the "faith that looks through death, / In years that bring the philosophic mind" (lines 185–186). The pastoral scene has become mundane "earth," and its elements of merely "common sight" have become reflections of the poet's own feelings. Wordsworth's understanding of psychology has changed: the sense of reality formed by Lockean sensation has given way to allegory created by Coleridgean idealism. Emotion derived from within the mind, rather than sensations received from Nature, dominate: "The Clouds that gather round the setting sun / Do take a sober colouring from an eye / That hath kept watch o'er man's mortality" (lines 196–198).

In *Resolution and Independence*, also written in 1802, allegory is even more ascendant as Wordsworth again begins not by presenting a specific place or a sense of a whole but with an inventory of elements that add up to the general idea of a morning after a storm; then he moves to the account of the speaker, identified as a "Traveller then upon the moor" (line 15), encountering a leech gatherer, one of the poet's recurring wanderer figures, who in this instance appears like an allegorical character out of *Pilgrim's Progress:* "His body was bent double, feet and head / Coming together in life's pilgrimage" (lines 66–67). The traveler-speaker tries to see himself, in contrast, as a child of Nature "as happy as a boy" in a "pleasant season" (lines 18–19), "a happy Child of earth" (line 31); but he soon becomes dejected from "blind thoughts" (line 28) about human fate—"Solitude, pain of heart, distress, and poverty" (line 35)—and about the fate of poets: "We Poets in our youth begin in gladness; / But thereof come in the end despondency and madness" (lines 48–49). His meeting, in this sad state of mind, with the leech gatherer appears to the traveler to be more than coincidence; it is described as almost miraculous, even predestined:

> Now, whether it were by peculiar grace,
> A leading from above, a something given,
> Yet it befel, that, in this lonely place,

> When I with these untoward thoughts had striven,
> Beside a pool bare to the eye of heaven
> I saw a Man before me unawares:
> The oldest man he seemed that ever wore grey hairs.
>
> (lines 50–56)

In entering the realm of Bunyan, Wordsworth is responding to Coleridge's despairing verse-epistle to Sara Hutchinson, the first, quite personal, version of *Dejection: An Ode*, which is set during a thunderstorm at night and in terms of an encounter that recalls the meeting of the wedding guest and the mariner in *The Rime of the Ancient Mariner*. Instead of suffering the fate of Coleridge's haunted mariner, however, Wordsworth's leech gatherer, while also fated to wander, is like a preacher whose task is medicinal both physically and spiritually; his speech is described as being "Such as grave Livers do in Scotland use / Religious men, who give to God and man their dues" (lines 97–98). While the traveler initially responds with trepidation to meeting the leech gatherer—like the wedding guest encountering the mariner—he soon becomes reassured and comforted by the leech gatherer's perseverance and faith in "God's good help" (line 104). Like the speaker's sister who acquires "healing thoughts" in *Tintern Abbey*, the traveler, too, ends up receiving a sermon on life.

As Wordsworth's scenery becomes increasingly absorbed into abstract thoughts, his landscape becomes explicitly literary. *The Prelude* (commenced after the completion of *Lyrical Ballads* when viewed at a distance as if it were the Alpine model at Lucerne described by Wordsworth in his *Guide to the Lake District*, becomes an English garden landscaped by a poet-gardener on the principles of Spenser, Milton, and Bunyan; its scenery is metaphoric and its human encounters emblematic as the poet shapes his life into a meaningful account of the growth of a poet's mind. The strength of *The Prelude* is not in descriptions of scenery or in autobiographical detail or in the revelations of a *bildungsroman;* rather, it is in the superior qualities of artistic control achieved through generic design that shape the autobiographical materials into an accessible, unified fiction. As pastoral, the poem balances unnatural "residences" in the "vast city" unnamed at the beginning (from which the poet flees *in medias res*), in Cambridge, in London, and in France, against the "natural" hills and valleys of home, the English countryside to which the poet regularly and inevitably returns to seek his fate. As epic, the experiences selected from the poet's life are rearranged into the myth of an intellectual wandering hero who, as both the Odysseus and the Telemachus of his own mind, escapes—in adventures in the unnatural "residences"—first from the mental underworld fostered by a classical education in traditional Cambridge; then from the diverting sensations of awe-inspiring London; and finally from his battle against the temptation to take up revolutionary politics in France. Upholding his artistic calling, he finds his way home to assume his true identity as a poet. As allegory, the wandering "Pilgrim resolute" (I:91) finds salvation from the temptations of intellectual, sensual, and political "Vanity Fairs" in Cambridge, London, and France through morally uplifting encounters on the road—like the lesson in the charity of being a "good Samaritan" learned in assisting the discharged soldier (IV:369–471), which anticipates the central lesson of the pilgrimage stated as the title of Book VIII: "Love of Nature Leading to Love of Man," or through rare visions from the "Delectable Mountains" of England that show him the way to the "Celestial City" of art. These simultaneous journeys, in which the generic shapes the autobiographical, are set in a moral landscape that transforms the Miltonic levels of hell, paradise, and heaven into a topography of Wordsworth's own life lived in three settings: on the plains, in spectacular and awesome cities that threaten creativity; in tranquil English hills and valleys that engender creativity; and in mountain passages—crossing the Alps and climbing Mount Snowden—that encourage both transcendent vision and discovery of the profession of poet. Hence, *The Prelude* is not about actual places so much as about metaphoric landscape shaped into the personal literary garden of Wordsworth and composed according (and in tribute) to the formal organizing principles of his national forebears in the literary art of grand design. Being, then, the ultimate cultivation of poetic landscape, life transformed into literature, *The Prelude* becomes the appropriate antechapel in Wordsworth's plan for his magnum opus, *The Recluse*, proposed in its prospectus to be "On Man, on Nature, and on Human Life" (line 754). *The Excursion*, the only part of *The Recluse* published in the poet's lifetime, was immediately recognized for the fictional contrivance that it represented; William Hazlitt, trained in the way of eighteenth-century criticism to find and define literary genre, said in his review of 1814:

> The *Excursion* may be considered as a philosophical pastoral poem,— as a scholastic romance. It is less a poem on the country, than on the love of the country. It is not so much a description of natural objects, as of the feelings associated with them; not an account of the manners of rural life, but the result of the poet's reflections on it. . . . He may be said to create his own materials; his thoughts are his real subject. . . . He sees all things in himself. . . . The general and the permanent, like the Platonic ideas, are his only realities. All accidental varieties and individual contrasts are lost in an endless continuity of feeling, like drops of water in the ocean-stream! An intense intellectual egotism swallows up every thing.[20]

Hence, Wordsworth succeeded in placing himself, and being found to be, at the center of his own literary garden.

Wordsworth's artistic success paralleled his efforts—literally—to cultivate his own garden. He was fascinated with English landscape gardening throughout his life, proclaiming to the painter Sir George Beaumont, "Painters and Poets have had the credit of being reckoned the Fathers of English Gardening; they will also have hereafter the better praise of being fathers of a better taste."[21] Not only did Wordsworth read avidly on the subject and correspond with some of the principal theorists, he engaged in landscape gardening himself; he rehabilitated the little garden behind Dove Cottage, designed and supervised the creation of a winter garden for the Beaumonts at their Leicestershire home, Coleorton Hall, and, later in his life, created on the four and one-half acres surrounding his last home, Rydal Mount, a garden with little waterfalls, small pools, paths, fields, and a wide variety of plants and trees. The garden of Rydal became a composition in miniature, a living Claude glass, that imitated the grander landscape around it[22]—a fit residence for the established poet who would live to become poet laureate.

For Wordsworth, the Romantic poet who evolved into a Victorian gentleman, the act of cultivating his own garden to mirror its setting or of composing an epic that celebrated its creator is more than egotistical and literary; it is finally an expression of the poet's imagination in improving taste and in asserting nationalism. The concluding books of the *Poem on my own life* are about "Imagination and Taste, How Impaired and Restored"; in addressing the *"Minds* of Persons of taste" in his *Guide to the Lake District,* Wordsworth devotes a section to preserving the beauty of the region by addressing the issue of "Changes, and Rules of Taste for Preventing Their Bad Effects." Moreover, near the end of his *Guide,* Wordsworth returns to the subject of the Alps and a comparison of the scenery of the Lake District to them, his purpose being "to reconcile a Briton to the scenery of his own country."[23] He expresses the view that, save for the lack of pine forests, "the elements of the landscape would be the same—one country representing the other in miniature."[24] Conceived, like his own garden, to be a kind of scale model of a vast region, he suggests that the Lake District is superior in being more aesthetic to the eye and feelings of the beholder; because of lack of color and a "jagged outline," the Alps are "so ill suited to the pencil" that "the ancient masters [painters like Titian, the Poussins, and Claude] . . . have not left a single landscape, the materials of which are taken from the *peculiar* features of the Alps."[25] Like the model at Lucerne that helped the poet comprehend the beautiful and sublime form of the Alps, the Lake District through its manageable size and greater accessibility offers the traveler a similar opportunity to comprehend in miniature the high order of nature and, at the same time, to refine his taste. Wordsworth concludes his statement of nationalist enthusiasm for his own home and country by quoting the opinion of West—whose guide preceded his—that "they who intend to make the continental tour should begin here; as it will give, in miniature, an idea of what they are to meet with there, in traversing the Alps and Appenines. . . ."[26] Hence, just as Wordsworth's poetry evolves into literary garden and national epic, so, too, his *Guide* appealing for imagination and good taste becomes a celebration of home and England. The legacy of his way of seeing, so intellectual ultimately, and of his kind of landscape, so fictionalized finally, is the transformation, as Aldous Huxley recognized for our century, of a cultural sense of Nature into something that must be termed, indeed, Wordsworthian:

> For good Wordsworthians—and most serious-minded people are now Wordsworthians, either by direct inspiration or at second hand—a walk in the country is the equivalent of going to church, a tour through Westmorland is as good as a pilgrimage to Jerusalem. To commune with the fields and waters, the woodlands and the hills, is to commune, according to our modern and northern ideas, with the visible manifestations of the "Wisdom and Spirit of the Universe."[27]

Notes

1. Quoted by Russell Noyes, *Wordsworth and the Art of Landscape* (Bloomington: Indiana University Press, 1968), 251.

2. *The Prose Works of William Wordsworth*, eds. W. J. B. Owen and Jane Worthington Smyser, 3 vols. (Oxford: Clarendon Press, 1974), II: 155. The text quoted here is from the 1835 fifth and last edition revised by Wordsworth. Parts of the *Guide* appeared as early as 1810; it was revised extensively in 1820 and 1822. For the textual history, see *Prose Works*, II: 136–149.

3. Ibid., II: 170–171.

4. Quoted by Peter Bicknell, "Introduction" to *The Illustrated Wordsworth's Guide to the Lakes*, ed. Peter Bicknell (New York: Congdon and Weed, 1984). Wordsworth's undated prose draft [*The Sublime and the Beautiful*], thought to have been written in 1811–1812—the period immediately following his composition of the first version of the *Guide*—suggests that he may have attempted a similar approach to his subject; see *Prose Works*, II: 128–129, 349–360.

5. *Prose Works*, II: 171. In the prose draft [*The Sublime and the Beautiful*], Wordsworth writes of "the precipitous form of an individual cloud which a Child has been taught by tales & pictures to think of as sufficiently solid to support a substantial body, & upon which he finds it easy to conceive himself as seated, in imagination . . . (*Prose Works*, II: 353); the editors comment (*Prose Works*, II: 454) that the image may have come from the introductory poem to William Blake's *Songs of Innocence* ("On a cloud I saw a child, / And he laughing said to me"), from which some poems,

though not the Introduction, had been copied into Wordsworth's commonplace book, dated January 1800.

6. For detailed discussion of the context of aesthetic theory in which Wordsworth wrote the poem, see Carl Woodring, "The New Sublimity in *Tintern Abbey*," reprinted in this collection.

7. Short references are to *Selected Poems and Prefaces by William Wordsworth*, ed. Jack Stillinger (Boston: Houghton Mifflin, 1965).

8. Noyes, *Wordsworth and the Art of Landscape*, 62, quotes a letter from Wordsworth to the Bishop of Lincoln: "The imagination is that intellectual lens through the medium of which the poetical observer sees the objects of his observation, modified both in form and colour." For detailed discussion of the Claude glass, see Stephen J. Spector, "Wordsworth's Mirror Imagery and the Picturesque Tradition," reprinted in this collection.

9. Wordsworth, contributing to the theories of his time, considered "duration" to be a characteristic of the sublime. See *A Guide Through the District of the Lakes in the North of England, Prose Works*, II: 223, 283; and the unpublished [*The Sublime and the Beautiful*], *Prose Works*, II: 351.

10. While Wordsworth is maintaining the conventional contrast between country and city of the pastoral mode, he does date his meditation on the eve of the ninth anniversary of the storming of the Bastille. In the interim, he had suffered political disillusionment with the French Revolution and the Terror, separation from Annette Vallon and his daughter because of the English declaration of war, and distress over the poverty and misery caused by the war.

11. All short references are to *The Complete Poetical Works of Samuel Taylor Coleridge*, ed. Ernest Hartley Coleridge (Oxford: Clarendon Press, 1912). John Beer reminds me that Coleridge's motto should read *sermoni propiora* and that Charles Lamb was apparently the source of the joke translation "properer for a sermon" since the word *sermo* actually means "conversation."

12. The "meditative tradition" in seventeenth-century poetry was a model for both Coleridge and Wordsworth; for an account of the tradition, see Louis L. Martz, *The Poetry of Meditation: A Study in English Religious Literature of the Seventeenth Century* (New Haven, Conn.: Yale University Press, 1954).

13. While Dorothy Wordsworth was only two years younger than her brother, he treats her in the poem as if she, like Coleridge's infant son in *Frost at Midnight*, were much younger; Wordsworth's tone combines the authority of a preacher with that of parent and teacher.

14. See Walter Jackson Bate, *Coleridge* (London: Weidenfeld and Nicolson, 1968), 48–51; and George H. Gilpin, "Coleridge and the Spiral of Poetic Thought," *Studies in English Literature* 12 (1972): 639–652.

15. This distinction between the formative experiences of the two poets is acknowledged and defined by Coleridge in *Frost at Midnight* when he describes his son as a child of Nature like those encountered in some of Wordsworth's ballads and like Wordsworth himself:

> For I was reared
> In the great city, pent 'mid cloisters dim,
> And saw nought lovely but the sky and stars.
> But *thou*, my babe! shalt wander like a breeze
> By lakes and sandy shores, beneath the crags
> Of ancient mountain, and beneath the clouds,

Which image in their bulk both lakes and shores
And mountain crags.

(lines 51–58)

Coleridge goes on to promise his son that he will know Nature with an intimacy that was denied to his father as a child.

16. *Prose Works*, I: 116.

17. Coleridge responded to Mrs. Barbauld's criticism that the poem "had no moral" as follows: ". . . as to the want of a moral, I told her that in my own judgement the poem had too much; and that the only, or chief fault, if I might say so, was the obtrusion of the moral sentiment so openly on the reader as a principle or cause of action in a work of such pure imagination" (quoted by Robert Penn Warren in "A Poem of Pure Imagination: An Experiment in Reading," in *Selected Essays* [Vintage Books, 1966], 199).

18. *Prose Works*, I: 127. Compare Coleridge's description of the specific symptoms of poetic power in *Biographia Literaria*, in *The Collected Works of Samuel Taylor Coleridge*, eds. James Engell and W. Jackson Bate, 16 vols. (Princeton, N.J.: Princeton University Press, 1983), VII: ii, 25–26: "The last character . . . is DEPTH, and ENERGY of THOUGHT. No man was ever yet a great poet, without being at the same time a profound philosopher."

19. *Prose Works*, I: 138.

20. "Observations on Mr. Wordsworth's Poem *The Excursion*," in *The Complete Works of William Hazlitt*, ed. P. P. Howe, 21 vols. (London and Toronto: J. M. Dent, 1930), IV: 112–113.

21. *The Letters of William and Dorothy Wordsworth: The Early Years, 1787–1805*, ed. Ernest de Selincourt; 2d ed. rev. Chester L. Shaver (Oxford: Clarendon Press, 1967), 624.

22. For a thorough description of Wordsworth's interest in landscape gardening, see Noyes, *Wordsworth and the Art of Landscape*.

23. *Prose Works*, II: 236.

24. Ibid., II: 232.

25. Ibid., II: 234.

26. Ibid., II: 239.

27. "Wordsworth in the Tropics," first published in 1929, reprinted in *The Oxford Anthology of English Literature* (New York: Oxford University Press, 1973), II: 2084.

WORDSWORTH THE MAN

Poetry of Familiarity: Wordsworth, Dorothy, and Mary Hutchinson

Donald H. Reiman*

In 1954 F. W. Bateson created a minor scandal in the then-staid precincts of Wordsworth scholarship by declaring in *Wordsworth: A Re-Interpretation* that much of Wordsworth's best poetry arose directly from the Sturm and Drang not only of his love affair with Annette Vallon in 1792 (as well as the guilt consequent on their separation) but also of his unacknowledged love for his sister Dorothy.[1] Bateson's thesis is, in fact, much broader. In his opening chapter, "The Two Voices," and in his conclusion, "The Critical Verdict," he tries to explain all of Wordsworth's poetry by examining the conflict between the poet's stated motive of providing "his readers with moral instruction," which, Bateson believed, underlay the poems in Wordsworth's "Augustan Voice," and the unconscious motivation behind his writing of such poems as "Tintern Abbey," the Lucy poems, and *The Prelude*, which exhibit Wordsworth's "Romantic Voice."

Bateson's basic approach to Wordsworth—using the poetry as well as biographical evidence to pinpoint problem areas in the poet's psyche and then reexamining individual poems with these conflicts in mind—has gained wide acceptance.[2] But—though many earlier statements by Ernest de Selincourt in his notes to the Oxford English Text Edition and by Mary Moorman in her later two-volume *William Wordsworth: A Biography* provide factual material tending to corroborate Bateson's view of the poet—there has been a militant resistance on the part of some Wordsworthians, particularly in Great Britain, to accepting two possibilities: first, that William Wordsworth felt a stronger emotional tie to his sister Dorothy during their years of living together at Windy Brow, Racedown, Alfoxden, Germany, and Grasmere (1794–1802) than he did to Mary Hutchinson, whom he married in 1802; and, second, that the Lucy poems and several

* Reprinted from *Romantic Texts and Contexts*, by permission of the University of Missouri Press. © 1987 by the Curators of the University of Missouri. First published in *The Evidence of the Imagination: Studies of Interactions Between Life and Art in English Romantic Literature*, eds. Donald H. Reiman, Michael C. Jaye, and Betty T. Bennett (New York: New York University Press, 1978).

other poems owe their inception to the conflict deep within Wordsworth between his strong feelings for his sister and his fear of the
possibly dangerous consequences of their mutual love.

The strength of this resistance, which some of us believed to be
dying out, was illustrated in 1970 in Mary Moorman's lecture to the
Royal Society of Literature in which, by simplistic paraphrasing, she
reduced Bateson's complex argument to this conception: "All the
poems addressed to Dorothy, directly or indirectly, are considered
to be out-and-out love poems, and on this evidence, and this alone—
for there is no other—he based his 'reinterpretation' of Wordsworth."[3] Mary Moorman, provoked by Kenneth Clark's equally simplistic account of Wordsworth and Dorothy in his lectures on *Civ-
ilisation,* attempted to discredit what she termed "crude and insensitive
writing about" William and Dorothy (p. 93). In her lecture she brings
together much useful information about the history of Wordsworth's
relationship with his sister, providing for example (as Helen Darbishire
had earlier in the fine edition of *Journals of Dorothy Wordsworth*
that bears both scholars' names)[4] a clear account of the history of
Dorothy's later physical and mental deterioration. But she overlooks
the tone of the many poems Wordsworth wrote to or about Dorothy
(and Mary Hutchinson). Sometimes—even in the generally judicious
account of Dorothy's health—she identifies superficial causes for
reactions that, from the tone of both Dorothy's letters and journals
and William's poetry, may well have had deeper psychological roots.
For example, she mentions the many "headaches and internal upsets"
that Dorothy and William suffered during their years of living alone
and then attributes the "great improvement in her health" after
William's marriage partly to the fact that "the care of her brother
was now shared with Mary" (pp. 92–93). But the psychosomatic
effects of conflicts between sexual desire and social taboos had been
recognized at least as early as the biblical account of Amnon, who
"was so tormented that he made himself ill because of his sister
Tamar" (2 Samuel 13:2). Dorothy's minor illnesses and her later
improvement in health cannot be definitely related to William's marriage, but Moorman's explanation of the possible relation is patently
inadequate.

During a subsequent exchange in the letters column of *TLS,*
initiated by Alethea Hayter's contention that Moorman's lecture should
have "refuted once for all" the "allegation of incest against William
and Dorothy Wordsworth," I maintained the position that, while we
could never know what exactly went on between William and Dorothy
Wordsworth during their years together, several of Wordsworth's
poems seem to reflect an emotional struggle to define his feelings
toward Dorothy within a socially acceptable context.[5]

While I acknowledge my debt to *Wordsworth: A Re-Interpretation,*

it will be clear that I reject a number of Bateson's detailed conclusions.[6] I believe that Wordsworth's great original contribution to
English poetry lies in those poems that grew out of his own various
psychological turmoils (which I do not regard, however, as ending
with his marriage) and that his decline as a poet can be traced directly
to the resolution, one by one, of the conflicts within him—one of
the strongest of which arose from the mixed feelings of fraternal
affection, passion, and guilt toward his sister Dorothy. Thus, though
the following pages concentrate on some of the less frequently examined poetry relating to Wordsworth's feelings for his sister and
his wife, the discussion should be seen as part of a larger view of
Wordsworth's art relevant to all of his poems that evidently resulted
from the series of internal conflicts that began to surface soon after
his return to England from France in 1792. I do not attempt to trace
the origins of these conflicts to possible deeper roots in Wordsworth's
childhood, though I think that some suggestions made by Bateson
and Onorato are probably relevant here.[7] My central focus, at present,
is on the poetry arising directly out of the interactions of William,
Dorothy, and Mary Wordsworth.

I

On 4 October 1802, Mary Hutchinson married William Wordsworth. The emotional relationships among Mary, William, and his
sister Dorothy during the months leading up to that union are ad-
equately documented only by Dorothy, who in her *Journals* recorded
her feelings about the event in great detail—too great to include
here in full. After recounting with warmth and affection her last
weeks alone together with William at Dove Cottage, Grasmere, and
their departure from it on 9 July 1802, Dorothy describes their
journey to see the Hutchinsons at Gallow Hill, where they arrived
on Thursday evening, 15 July. Within this account of the week in
transit, we find Dorothy and William, who were riding atop the coach,
protecting themselves from the rain: "we buttoned ourselves up, both
together in the Guard's coat and we liked the hills and the Rain the
better for bringing [us] so close to one another—I never rode more
snugly."[8] After a brief stay with the Hutchinsons at Gallow Hill,
William and Dorothy traveled to London (where they arrived on 29
July) and thence via Dover to Calais (1 August) where they met
Annette Vallon and William's natural daughter Caroline. They spent
exactly four weeks at Calais, living in lodgings and seeing Annette
and Caroline, or Caroline alone, daily. The Wordsworths returned to
England on 30 August, having settled financial arrangements with
Annette and having had an opportunity to become well acquainted
with William's daughter.[9] After remaining in London from 31 August

till 22 September, Dorothy and William returned to Gallow Hill on 24 September. Dorothy's account of the wedding day (even those crucial sentences omitted from earlier printed texts) is too well known to quote in full. Dorothy did not attend her brother's wedding, though she had worn the wedding ring the night before it; she lay on her bed in emotional shock during the time the wedding party was gone and pulled herself together to greet the groom (and bride) only at the insistence of Sara Hutchinson; Dorothy writes at the end of her account, perhaps projecting her feelings into Mary Hutchinson Wordsworth: "Poor Mary was much agitated when she parted from her Brothers and Sisters and her home."[10]

William Wordsworth's marriage, no matter how much Dorothy liked Mary Hutchinson, was a turning point in Dorothy's life, leaving her ever after half an outsider in the household that she and William had kept together for seven years. Dorothy's feelings are more than explicable: they are inescapable. William selected a mate who, as one of Dorothy's closest friends, would accept her as a continuing member of the family (beginning with their honeymoon), but even though his choice was itself an act of kindness and love, Dorothy was displaced as William's closest companion.

It was natural that at age thirty-two, seeing ahead the means to meet the responsibility of supporting a wife and children, William Wordsworth—a virile man of exceptional sexual magnetism, if we are to trust Coleridge[11]—should desire to marry. It was natural also that he should want to do so in a way compatible not only with his own needs, but also with those of Dorothy, whom he repeatedly acknowledged to be the person dearest to him throughout the years since his return from France. In those few allusions to Mary Hutchinson in William's surviving early letters there is, on the contrary, no evidence of warmth, passion, or love that was more than brotherly. Perhaps the most striking allusion occurs in a letter Wordsworth wrote to Coleridge from Grasmere on Christmas Eve 1799, five days after he and Dorothy had moved into Dove Cottage. After he and Coleridge had visited Grasmere to select the house, Coleridge had preceded him to Sockburn, Yorkshire, where Dorothy was staying with Mary and Sara Hutchinson and *their* brother Tom. William writes: "I arrived at Sockburn the day after you quitted it . . . I was sadly disappointed in not finding Dorothy; Mary was a solitary housekeeper and overjoyed to see me. D[orothy] is now sitting beside me racked with the tooth-ache" (*Early Letters*, p. 274). William's disappointment at finding himself alone with Mary Hutchinson may be either genuine or feigned (Dorothy is sitting at his side). In neither case is it the sentiment a lover would express to his closest friend. The most charitable interpretation, and the one that fits best with the other evidence, is that William had no deep romantic feelings for Mary at this date, that Mary was (as the other surviving correspondence suggests) a closer friend of Dorothy's than of William's.

When William and Dorothy settled at Dove Cottage, Grasmere, neither of them apparently thought of marrying or of ever changing their household. For example, on 8 November 1799, a few weeks before the letter I have quoted, Wordsworth and Coleridge wrote a joint letter from Keswick in which William remarks to Dorothy: "C[oleridge] was much struck with Grasmere and its neighbourhood and I have much to say to you, you will think my plan a mad one, but I have thought of building a house there by the Lake side." He goes on to discuss the cost and financing, mentioning that "a Devonshire gentleman has built a Cottage there which cost a £130 which would exactly suit us every way, but the size of the bedrooms we shall talk of this." He closes his part of the letter by mentioning Dove Cottage as an alternative: "There is a small house at Grasmere empty which perhaps we may take, and purchase furniture but of this we will speak. But I shall write again when I know more on this subject" (*Early Letters*, p. 272). In suggesting they borrow money to buy land and build a cottage suitable to the needs of the two of them, Wordsworth at the end of 1799 envisioned their joint household to be a permanent arrangement. Early in 1799 Dorothy had complained in letters from Goslar, Germany, that they could not afford to enter into German society: "a man travelling alone may do very well, but, if his wife or sister goes with him, he must give entertainments," for "*a man and woman*" were there "considered as a sort of family" (*Early Letters*, pp. 247, 244). Clearly throughout their time of living together since September 1795—first at Racedown with Basil Montagu's young son, then at Alfoxden, then in Germany—Dorothy and William had considered themselves a viable family.

Dorothy's own attitude toward spending a lifetime keeping house for her brother is mirrored interestingly in her letter from Sockburn in April 1795 to her childhood friend Jane Pollard. Dorothy writes:

> You must recollect my friends the Hutchinsons, my sole companions at Penrith, . . . whose company in the absence of my brothers was the only agreeable Variety which Penrith afforded. They are settled at Sockburn—six miles from Darlington *perfectly to their satisfaction,* they are quite independent and *have not a wish ungratified,* very different indeed is their present situation from what it was formerly when we compared grievances and lamented the misfortune of losing our parents at an early age and being thrown upon the mercy of ill-natured and illiberal relations. Their brother has a farm, of about 200£ a year, and they keep his house; *he is* a very amiable young man, *uncommonly fond of his sisters,* and in short, *every thing that they can desire.* (*Early Letters*, pp. 141–42, italics added)

In the pre-Freudian culture, Dorothy's emphasis on how the Hutchinson sisters' life with their brother *satisfied* their every *desire* did not, of course, carry the nuances that the same language would bear today. Rather, it suggested the limits of Dorothy's aspirations for her own life. She does not speak about either marriage (and children) or a separate life with some personal career as a situation more desirable than that of keeping house for one's brother.

Presumably, even in a pre-Freudian culture young women experienced sexual longings and needs, but their psychic and social censors must have been more militant, often preventing them from viewing consciously their needs in this direction. Ellen Moers, in a perceptive article in the *New York Review of Books*, after pointing to certain Gothic elements in the imaginations of Emily Brontë and Christina Rossetti, writes:

> both women grew up in a family of four siblings, male and female, bound together in a closed circle by affection and by imaginative genius, as well as by remoteness from the social norm. . . . Quentin Bell's recent biography of Virginia Stephen, a girl in another family of like-minded sisters and brothers, allows us at least to speculate openly on the sexual drama of the Victorian nursery. (Though Mr. Bell does not . . . settle the question of the fantasy component in Virginia Woolf's memories of fraternal incest, to the reality of the incest fantasy he brings important evidence, if evidence is needed.) . . . to Victorian women the sister-brother relationship seems to have had . . . perhaps greater significance—especially to those women, so commonplace in the intellectual middle class, who in a sexual sense never grew to full maturity. The rough-and-tumble sexuality of the nursery loomed large for sisters: it was the *only* heterosexual world the Victorian literary spinsters were ever freely and physically to explore.[12]

Without speculating as to the specific nature of Dorothy Wordsworth's sexual development, it seems quite clear that her affection for her brothers—especially William and John—satisfied her and that she usually demanded no more sexually fulfilling relationship.[13]

II

As one would expect from a poet, William Wordsworth recorded his emotions during the months just before his marriage chiefly in his verse, embodying them in a group of poems he wrote at Grasmere in a prolific burst of inspiration from mid-March 1802 until the very day of his wedding, 4 October of the same year. Some of these poems center on the experience of others and many draw upon the past, exemplifying the doctrine of the 1800 Preface by taking their "origin from emotion recollected in tranquillity" that generates "an emotion, kindred to" it and spontaneously overflows into expressions of "powerful feelings." Such are four poems of 11–17 March: "The Sailor's Mother," "Alice Fell; or Poverty," "Beggars," and "The Emigrant Mother."[14] But a large number of the poems of March through May of this year treat specifically and with great warmth and affection incidents in the long relationship between William and Dorothy Wordsworth. On 14 March he wrote "To a Butterfly" ("Stay near me—do not take thy flight!"), a poem recalling,

> Oh! pleasant, pleasant were the days,
> The time, when, in our childish plays,
> My sister Emmeline and I
> Together chased the butterfly!
>   (*PW*, 1:226)[15]

On 12 April, William wrote the poem later called "The Glow-worm," beginning,

> Among all lovely things my Love had been;
> Had noted well the stars, all flowers that grew
> About her home; but she had never seen
> A Glow-worm, never one, and this I knew.

The twenty-line poem ends: "I led my Lucy to the spot, 'Look here!' / Oh! joy it was for her, and joy for me!" (*PW*, 2:466). Mary E. Burton mentions a transcription by Sara Hutchinson "with the name of Mary where the printed versions use 'Lucy' and 'Emma.' "[16] That must have seemed right to the Hutchinson sisters when Dorothy transcribed the poem in a letter to Mary Hutchinson on 16 April 1802: who else could be addressed as "my Love" by William on that date? But as Wordsworth explained to Coleridge, in his letter of the same day where he transcribed the same poem (using "Emma" instead of "Lucy" for his beloved's name), "The incident of this Poem took place about seven years ago between Dorothy and me" (*Early Letters*, p. 348). Dorothy, not Mary, is the "Emma" or "Lucy" of the poem, which like "To a Butterfly" describes the siblings' appreciation of the minor elements of nature.[17] On 20 April, he wrote another poem "To a Butterfly" (beginning, "I've watched you now a full half-hour, / Self-poised upon that yellow flower"). The second stanza of this poem is significant for our theme:

> This plot of orchard-ground is ours;
> My trees they are, my Sister's flowers;
> . . . .
> Sit near us on the bough!
> We'll talk of sunshine and of song,
> And summer days, when we were young;

> Sweet childish days, that were as long
> As twenty days are now.
>
> *(PW,* 2:22–23)

The interaction between the Grasmere family—"we"—Dorothy and William—continues in the poems that follow, as Mary Moorman's edition of Dorothy's journal of the period, containing the texts of the appropriate poems, makes clear. The poems written early in 1802 about the smaller living forms of nature—the daisy, the cuckoo, the green linnet, the robin, the skylark, and the sparrow's nest—derived their imaginative force, as Wordsworth himself tells us in *The Prelude* (XIV:232–66), from his associations with Dorothy.[18] The chief emotional catalyst to Wordsworth's imagination during the unusual poetic activity early in 1802 was not Coleridge nor pleasurable excitement about his forthcoming marriage to Mary Hutchinson: rather, that imaginative stimulus was his struggle to take the step that would inevitably create an irrevocable psychic barrier between himself and his beloved sister. Wordsworth's regrets about breaking up his happy "Home at Grasmere"[19] are epitomized in a poem that Dorothy, in her journals, called "his poem on Going for Mary,"[20] which exhibits in almost painful detail the emotional struggle William faced. Though I cannot quote the entire poem here, three of its eight stanzas should illustrate my point:

> Farewell, thou little Nook of mountain-ground,
> Thou rocky corner of the lowest stair
> Of that magnificent temple which doth bound
> One side of our whole vale with grandeur rare;
> Sweet garden-orchard, eminently fair,
> The loveliest spot that man hath ever found,
> Farewell!—we leave thee to Heaven's peaceful care,
> Thee, and the Cottage which thou dost surround.
>
> . . . .
>
> We go for One to whom ye will be dear;
> And she will prize this Bower, this Indian shed,
> Our own contrivance, Building without peer!
> —A gentle Maid, whose heart is lowly bred,
> Whose pleasures are in wild fields gathered,
> With joyousness, and with a thoughtful cheer,
> Will come to you; to you herself will wed;
> And love the blessed life that we lead here.
>
> . . . .
>
> Help us to tell Her tales of years gone by,
> And this sweet spring, the best beloved and best;
> Joy will be flown in its mortality;
> Something must stay to tell us of the rest.
> Here, thronged with primroses, the steep rock's breast

Glittered at evening like a starry sky;
And in this bush our sparrow built her nest,
Of which I sang one song that will not die.

William and Dorothy are the "we" into whose garden Mary, the "gentle Maid" with "lowly bred" heart, will come and "wed" the garden as she learns its history. He and Dorothy will tell her tales of "this sweet spring, the best beloved and best," though "Joy" will have "flown" with the "mortality" of the season. This poem is, in part surely, a poem about the mortality of the moment, about "Joy, whose hand is ever at his lips, / Bidding adieu," but it is something more. It is more than merely a poem of solidarity with Dorothy, assuring her that her brother will always love and value her and that the home they have loved together will always be theirs, no matter who else enters its magic garden. The poem is a farewell to an Eden that, as the tone clearly indicates, can never be recaptured, no matter how wide the world of choice that lies before them.

III

As we have seen, from March through May 1802, while he and Dorothy at Grasmere contemplated the end of their private Eden, many of Wordsworth's poems deal with the relationship of childhood experiences to the poet's adult attitudes. In the first poem "To a Butterfly," the poet says that the creature brings "a solemn image to my heart, / My father's family! . . . The time, when, in our childish plays, / My sister Emmeline and I / Together chased the butterfly!" When he listens "To the Cuckoo," Wordsworth can recall his "school-boy days"—"till I do beget / That golden time again" (*PW*, 2:207–8). There is no question that the famous poem beginning "My heart leaps up when I behold / A rainbow in the sky," written on 26 March 1802, in the midst of these poems associated with Dorothy, also derives from the same inspiration. Wordsworth's greatest earlier assertion of the continuity of past and present, "Lines composed a Few Miles Above Tintern Abbey," had also been written (1798) with Dorothy present, and it contains an address to her in the final lines.[21] The same is true of another poem in which the poet moves from an experience in his boyhood and relates it to his present state of mind— this on a theme of crucial importance to my argument.

In "Nutting," written in Germany late in 1798 when William and Dorothy were living alone at Goslar, Wordsworth recounts how, while he was a boy at Hawkshead School, he went out one day with his "nutting-crook in hand": "O'er path-less rocks, / Through . . . tangled thickets, / Forcing my way, I came to one dear nook / Unvisited, where . . . hazels rose / Tall and erect, with tempting clusters hung, / A virgin scene!—'' The poet recalls his reaction thus:

> A little while I stood,
> Breathing with such suppression of the heart
> As joy delights in; and with wise restraint
> Voluptuous, fearless of a rival, eyed
> The banquet;—or beneath the trees I sate
> Among the flowers, and with the flowers I played;
> A temper known to those who, after long
> And weary expectation, have been blest
> With sudden happiness beyond all hope.
> . . . .
>   . . . Then up I rose,
> And dragged to earth both branch and bough, with crash
> And merciless ravage: and the shady nook
> Of hazels, and the green and mossy bower,
> Deformed and sullied, patiently gave up
> Their quiet being: and, unless I now
> Confound my present feelings with the past,
> Ere from the mutilated bower I turned
> Exulting, rich beyond the wealth of kings,
> I felt a sense of pain when I beheld
> The silent trees, and saw the intruding sky.—

The version of the poem Wordsworth published in 1800 concludes with three lines addressed to Dorothy, urging her, in the manner of the conclusion to "Tintern Abbey," to learn the same lesson William believed he had learned from his earlier experience:

> Then, dearest Maiden, move along these shades
> In gentleness of heart; with gentle hand
> Touch—for there is a spirit in the woods.
>   (PW, 2:211–12)

But in a long manuscript fragment published by de Selincourt in *Poetical Works* (2:504–6) there is another, much longer conclusion, which begins:

> Ah! what a crash was that! with gentle hand
> Touch these fair hazels—My beloved Friend!
> Though 'tis a sight invisible to thee
> From such rude intercourse the woods all shrink
> As at the blowing of Astolpho's horn.
> Thou, Lucy, art a maiden "inland bred"
> And thou hast known "some nurture"; but in truth
> If I had met thee here with that keen look
> Half cruel in its eagerness, those cheeks
> Thus [ ] flushed with a tempestuous bloom,
> I might have almost deem'd that I had pass'd

A houseless being in a human shape,
An enemy of nature, hither sent
From regions far beyond the Indian hills—

Here William chides Dorothy for her almost unnatural "half cruel
. . . eagerness" to ravage the hazel trees of a more recent day. And
he calls Dorothy "Lucy," as he later referred to her in the manuscript
of "The Glow-worm."

"Nutting," as has been recognized by recent critics, is filled with
language of sexual ravishment. It describes, in fact, the rape of "a
virgin scene" of Nature. The boy "voluptuous, fearless of a rival,"
toys with and fondles the secluded nook and then lets himself go in
an act of "merciless ravage," leaving the "mossy bower, / Deformed
and sullied." In the published poem, William cautions the "dearest
Maiden" against making his mistake; in the manuscript version, he
accuses her of having done so. All is expressed in terms of two hazel
groves, one of the distant past and the other in the present.

Soon after William addressed these lines to Dorothy as "Lucy,"
asking her not to exhibit so much "tempestuous bloom" of the kind
that he recalled as his own "voluptuous" state of being, he wrote
the first versions of two of the five poems now called the "Lucy
poems." Two of these poems, now identified by their first lines as
"She dwelt among the untrodden ways" and "Strange fits of passion
have I known," have their first surviving texts in a letter that William
and Dorothy wrote to Coleridge on 14 or 21 December 1798 (*Early
Letters*, pp. 236–38).

1
My hope was one, from cities far,
Nursed on a lonesome heath;
Her lips were red as roses are,
Her hair a woodbine wreath.

2
She lived among the untrodden ways
Beside the springs of Dove,
A maid whom there were none to praise,
And very few to love;

3
A violet by a mossy stone
Half-hidden from the eye!
Fair as a star when only one
Is shining in the sky!

4
And she was graceful as the broom
That flowers by Carron's side;
But slow distemper checked her bloom,
And on the Heath she died.

5
Long time before her head lay low
Dead to the world was she:
But now she's in the grave, and Oh!
The difference to me!

Wordsworth later revised the poem essentially by compression, elim-
inating its original first and fourth stanzas and rephrasing the first
two lines of the final stanza (*PW*, 2:30). But the discarded stanzas
cast considerable light on the poem, if only in the reference to
"Carron's side": Carron is the name of a river and a lake in Ross
and Cromarty County in the Highlands of Scotland, an area that
Wordsworth had not visited by this date. Like "the bonny braes of
Yarrow," it apparently came to him through his reading of eighteenth-
century ballads (in this case "Owen of Carron" by John Langhorne).
Since Wordsworth is attempting a ballad of an idealized sort, the
equally arbitrary "springs of Dove" allusion cannot be used to
identify—or eliminate—the personal origins or thematic content of
the lyric. As de Selincourt observes, "Wordsworth knew a river Dove
in Derbyshire, in Yorkshire, and in Westmoreland; and it is impossible
to say of which he was thinking" (*PW*, 2:472).

The early text of "Strange fits of passion" begins and ends quite
differently than does the later, more familiar one:

1
Once, when my love was strong and gay,
And like a rose in June,
I to her cottage bent my way,
Beneath the evening Moon.

. . . .

6
Strange are the fancies that will slide
Into a lover's head.
"O mercy" to myself I cried
"If Lucy should be dead!"

7
I told her this; her laughter light
Is ringing in my ears;
And when I think upon that night
My eyes are dim with tears.

This poem—"a favorite of mine," Dorothy writes to Coleridge
before copying it—certainly refers to Dorothy as Lucy, as de Selincourt observes. And, as he notes in connection with "She dwelt
among the untrodden ways," "If Coleridge is right in saying that 'A
slumber did my spirit seal' was written to suggest what W[ordsworth]
would have felt on the death of his sister, this poem had probably

a similar source."[22] From the last stanza of the version in the letter to Coleridge, we see not only the origin of the poem in Wordsworth's fearful premonition of Dorothy's death, but Dorothy's own reaction of "laughter light." There can be no doubt, I believe, that the five so-called "Lucy poems" were written about the same imagined death of Dorothy, as Wordsworth writes of his own imagined death in "There was a Boy."[23] As I have argued elsewhere, another poem beginning " 'Tis said that some have died for love" (written at Grasmere in 1800) is also about Dorothy's imagined death and William's imagined reaction to it.[24]

Most of the poems I have named as being inspired by William's affection for Dorothy are among his best, and the five "Lucy poems" are among the best short lyrics in English. "Tintern Abbey," whatever its structural difficulties, contains some of Wordsworth's finest language as well as his most elevated thoughts. Many of the lyrics on birds and flowers written at Grasmere are among Wordsworth's most characteristic and successful shorter poems. And one quality they convey is shared with Dorothy Wordsworth's journals: deep, spontaneous emotional commitment. The emotional force of the seven-quatrain lyric about Dorothy's death was undoubtedly what moved William to add the stanza that gives it both its name and its categorization as a love poem:

> Strange fits of passion have I known:
> And I will dare to tell,
> But in the Lover's ear alone
> What once to me befell.
>
> (PW, 2:29)

Only a lover, says Wordsworth, can really appreciate this poem. Why? Because it is essentially a *passionate poem* about *true love*—not necessarily about passionate love, but about deeply felt, romantic love.

There has been considerable discussion about the question of Lucy's age. In one of the poems she is represented as dying very young, soon after "her virgin bosom" began to "swell."[25] But this aspect of the poems—a mystery if they are thought to have been associated with an actual lover of Wordsworth—becomes clear in the light of William's recurring emotional association of Dorothy with his own childhood and growth. The ambiguity of tone remains in the poems (though the text itself can be shown to speak in terms of a mature woman rather than a child) because Wordsworth loved "Lucy" as his sister from childhood as well as the helpmate of his adult years. William continually alludes to his childhood associations with Dorothy. William and Dorothy, though siblings, had been separated upon the death of their mother in 1778, when William was nine and Dorothy seven years old. There is no evidence that they so much as saw each other again until 1787, when William was seventeen and Dorothy fifteen years old. For sociological, if not genealogical purposes, they were (like Byron and his half-sister Augusta) not siblings but a boy and a girl of similar backgrounds and sympathetic aspirations meeting at a highly impressionable stage in their maturation.[26] The only surviving evidence[27] of William's feelings for his newly found sister emerges from his poems, in which he repeatedly ties his adult relationship with her to their childish play as siblings. Perhaps he needed constantly to reinforce this sense of kinship with Dorothy, reminding himself (probably subconsciously) that Dorothy was an unacceptable object for a romantic or sexual attachment.

If I am correct in discerning this tendency in the pattern of William's poems, then the origin—not of the writing of the "Lucy poems" themselves, but of the dream or premonition of Dorothy's death that provided their emotional impact—may lie in William's subconscious struggle to avoid focusing his obviously strong sexual drive on the sister he lived with for seven years.[28] It would also suggest why, in such poems as "Strange fits of passion" and "The Glow-worm," Wordsworth would shift his imaginative stance from brother to lover. Because he had, for the most part, successfully repressed his desire for Dorothy in his dreams—which end in her death rather than in their forbidden union—he was free at the conscious level to revise them, fully utilizing their emotional energy by casting them as love poems.

IV

Having surveyed the emotional interaction between Dorothy and William, let us glance briefly at the much smaller body of poems William wrote to and about Mary Hutchinson. Here one crucial document is, obviously, "She was a Phantom of delight," a poem written in 1804 that is usually pointed to as embodying Wordsworth's strong love for his wife. The poem begins, ostensibly, with an impression of Mary as she appeared to William on their first encounter:

> She was a Phantom of delight
> When first she gleamed upon my sight;
> A lovely Apparition, sent
> To be a moment's ornament. . . .
>
> (PW, 2:213)

But in his talks with Isabella Fenwick, Wordsworth explained the origin of these lines and of the poem: "The germ of this poem was four lines composed as a part of the verses on the Highland Girl. Though beginning in this way, it was written from my heart, as is sufficiently obvious" (*PW*, 2:506). If the first four lines were inspired by an unknown Highland girl seen on the six-week Scottish tour that William, Dorothy, and Coleridge took in 1803 (while Mary remained behind, caring for her first child), we must eliminate the first stanza from serious consideration as being about Mary—for the subsequent lines of that stanza merely elaborate the first abstractions in which Mary is called a "machine" and "A Being breathing thoughtful breath, / A Traveller between life and death." The remaining stanza reads:

> I saw her upon nearer view,
> A Spirit, yet a Woman too!
> Her household motions light and free,
> And steps of virgin-liberty;
> A countenance in which did meet
> Sweet records, promises as sweet;
> A Creature not too bright or good
> For human nature's daily food;
> For transient sorrows, simple wiles,
> Praise, blame, love, kisses, tears, and smiles.

Here, I submit, is the true measure of William's feelings for Mary, articulated about two years after their wedding but referring to the feelings that determined his decision to marry her. He was attracted by her "household motions," her "virgin-liberty," a countenance combining "sweet records" with "promises as sweet," and he was glad that she was a "Woman" "not too bright or good / For human nature's daily food." The "daily food" image is fundamental to William's conception of Mary, as is evident from his poem "To M. H.," written late in December 1799, soon after he and Dorothy had taken up their residence at Dove Cottage.

> Our walk was far among the ancient trees:
> There was no road, nor any woodman's path;
> But a thick umbrage . . .
>   . . . of itself had made
> A track, that brought us to a slip of lawn,
> And a small bed of water in the woods.
> . . . .
> The spot was made by Nature for herself;
> The travellers know it not, and 'twill remain
> Unknown to them; but it is beautiful;
> And if a man should plant his cottage near,
> Should sleep beneath the shelter of its trees,
> And blend its waters with his daily meal,
> He would so love it, that in his death-hour
> Its image would survive among his thoughts:

> And therefore, my sweet MARY, this still Nook,
> With all its beeches, we have named for You!
> (PW, 2:118)

It should be obvious that William here uses the place as a metaphor for Mary and that he is the "man" who may "plant his cottage" in this "still Nook" and "blend its waters with his *daily meal*," just as in "A Farewell" he speaks of Mary as "A gentle maid" who will come to the "little Nook of mountain-ground" at Dove Cottage and to it "herself will wed" (PW, 2:23–24). And, for those to whom these two "nooks" recall that other isolated, "virgin bower" in "Nutting," it may be equally clear that I shall suggest that all this "blending" and "daily food" are metaphors for sexual union. If, in "Nutting," Wordsworth recalled with regret his ravage of "one dear nook . . . a virgin scene" to convey to Dorothy during their dangerous isolated proximity at Goslar the perils of excessive passionate license, it is equally clear that Mary provided the proper and acceptable substitute object for those strong passions that were chained within William. She was acceptable to William as a "virgin" at "liberty," with graceful "household motions" and the promise of sweet "daily food" (PW, 2:213).

One of the most striking corroborations of this judgment is to be found in two sonnets, the first composed by Wordsworth on the day of his marriage as he, Mary, and Dorothy traveled toward Grasmere. At sunset among the clouds and light "in the western sky, we saw shapes of Castles, Ruins among groves, . . . a minster with its tower unusually distinct, minarets in another quarter, and a round Grecian Temple also (*Journals*, p. 156). The sonnet, beginning "Dark and more dark the shades of evening fell," describes the scene faithfully as Dorothy records it before concluding: "but we felt the while / We should forget them; they are of the sky, / And from our earthly memory fade away" (PW, 3:25–26). The second sonnet, written sometime before March 1804, carries further the message that the poet must (regretfully) renounce the sky-castles in favor of the more mundane pleasures:

> Those words were uttered as in pensive mood
> We turned, departing from that solemn sight:
> A contrast and reproach to *gross delight*,
> And life's unspiritual pleasures *daily wooed!*
> But now upon this thought I cannot brood;
> It is unstable as a dream of night;
> Nor will I praise a cloud, however bright,
> Disparaging Man's gifts, and *proper food.*

. . . .

> The immortal Mind craves objects that endure:
> These cleave to it; from these it cannot roam,
> Nor they from it: their fellowship is secure.
>   (*PW*, 3:26; italics added)

"Wordsworth is by nature incapable of being in Love," wrote Coleridge to Henry Crabb Robinson in 1811, "tho' no man more tenderly attached—hence he ridicules the existence of any other passion, than a compound of Lust with Esteem & Friendship, confined to one Object, first by accidents of Association, and permanently, by the force of Habit & a sense of Duty. Now this will do very well—it will suffice to make a good Husband—. . . but still it is not *Love*."[29] So, at least, Wordsworth's feelings for Mary, several years after marriage, appeared to Coleridge (whose own romantic attachment had much greater proportions of both fantasy and impossibility). And however much one discredits Coleridge, there remain Wordsworth's poems written to and about Mary that invariably stress the habitual and the practical, the "compound of Lust with Esteem & Friendship," and there remains the clear tone of his "poem on going for Mary" and the two sonnets written about the day he got her, saying he had knowingly sacrificed a romantic joy to cleave to "secure fellowship" and Man's "proper food."

Aside from the ambiguity of his own feelings, there was only one obstacle to William's union with Mary, and this was the known— and perhaps declared—affection of his brother John for her. We must assume that Mary had made clear to the younger brother her preference for William, but John's farewell letter, written "when he has returned from a voyage to receive her announcement of her plan to marry shows," the editor of Mary's letters writes, "much deeper emotion": "I have been reading your letter over and over again, My dearest Mary, till tears have come into my eyes and I know not how to express myself—Thou art a kind and dear Creature.—But whatever fate Befal me I shall love thee to the last, and bear thy memory with me to the grave."[30] "John, (who is to be the sailor,) has a most excellent heart," Dorothy had written to Jane Pollard in July 1787, and of the Wordsworth children's inheritance, she added: "John poor fellow! says that . . . two hundred pounds will be enough to fit him out, and he should wish Wm to have the rest for his education . . ." (*Early Letters*, pp. 3–4). Thus William, who began by sharing part of John's inheritance for his education, ended by appropriating John's beloved for his "daily food." And, though I do not intend to pursue this topic, William's resultant naggings of guilt had important consequences for another group of his greatest poems.[31]

V

Another subject there is no space to pursue here in detail is the large group of Wordsworth's early poems centering on the theme of "Guilt and Sorrow" (which is the ultimate title of one of them). Aside from the ballads and lyrics that derive from his feelings for Dorothy and for Mary Hutchinson, poems on this theme constitute almost all the poems about romantic love written before 1807. Included are such excellent works as "The Ruined Cottage" (later incorporated into the first book of *The Excursion*), "The Thorn," and "Ruth." In each of these poems, a loving, trusting woman marries or is seduced by a weak or thoughtless or undisciplined young man and is then abandoned with a child or two that she is unable to care for. These poems—which relate thematically to Wordsworth's many early poems and passages on such topics as poor, vagrant women or the abandoned Indian woman—clearly embody Wordsworth's feelings of guilt and sorrow for his own abandonment of Annette Vallon. All these are, in their published versions, rather long narratives, usually filtered through the consciousness of an objective observer (such as the Pedlar in *The Excursion,* or the curious retired sea captain in "The Thorn") whose presence is clearly intended to mitigate the pain generated by the tale itself.[32] After William and Dorothy visited Annette and Caroline at Calais in 1802, the only further poem on this theme is "Vaudracour and Julia," at one time destined for *The Prelude*. That retrospective, official account of the romance seems finally to have exorcized the demon of guilt and sorrow that had driven Wordsworth to so much of his best early poetry.

Likewise, after William's marriage to Mary in October 1802, there are no more passionate lyrics like the "Lucy poems." Instead, in 1802, Wordsworth, who had earlier written few sonnets that he thought worth preserving,[33] suddenly composed eighteen sonnets—some good, some excellent—most of them during his trip to see Annette and Caroline. As Carl Woodring observes, "His sonnet-writing began, then, in a period of great agitation. He probably had this private agitation much in mind when he wrote the sonnet beginning, 'Nuns fret not at their convent's narrow room.' "[34] The emotional force of his visits with Caroline on the beach at Calais and of his love for England in its confrontation with France is shaped into fourteen-line jewels. After this date Wordsworth never published a new volume of poetry without including one or more sonnets.[35] The control that the sonnet form provided for his intense emotions of 1802 was later supplanted by the support it gave to his flagging imagination in such sequences as *The River Duddon, Ecclesiastical Sketches*, and "Sonnets on the Punishment of Death." This complete reversal of the needs of both his psyche and his poetry is epitomized in one of the few important poems that is not a sonnet and that he began after 1808. " 'Laodamia,' " Wordsworth told Isabella Fenwick, "cost me more trouble than almost anything of equal length I have ever written" (*PW*, 2:519). Why this should be so provides the focus of my final speculative look into the workings of Wordsworth's imagination.

"Laodamia" is based on a classical legend treated by Euripides, Virgil, and Ovid. Laodamia was the wife of Protesilaus, the first Greek to be killed by the Trojans. In her bereavement, as Wordsworth relates the tale, Laodamia prays to Jove to restore her husband to her. When the god grants her request and the shade of Protesilaus joins her for a three-hour visit, she is delighted and suggests that they go to bed:

> "No Spectre greets me,—no vain Shadow this;
> Come, blooming Hero, place thee by my side!
> Give, on this well-known couch, one nuptial kiss
> To me, this day, a second time thy bride!"

But at this proposal, "Jove frowned in heaven" and her husband admonished Laodamia for her light and irreverent thoughts:

> ". . . Earth destroys
> Those raptures duly—Erebus disdains:
> Calm pleasures there abide—majestic pains.
>
> "Be taught, O faithful Consort, to control
> Rebellious passion: for the Gods approve
> The depth, and not the tumult of the soul;
> A fervent, not ungovernable, love."
>> (*PW*, 2:269; lines 70–76)
>
> "And Thou, though strong in love, art all too weak
> In reason, in self-government too slow;
> . . . .
> Learn, by a mortal yearning, to ascend—
> Seeking a higher object. Love was given,
> Encouraged, sanctioned, chiefly for that end; . . . ."
>> (*PW*, 2:271; lines 139–40, 145–47)

Laodamia, however, refuses to accept her husband's advice, and when "Hermes reappears" to carry off the shade of Protesilaus, she shrieks, and—anticipating the ending of Keats's *Lamia*—"on the palace-floor a lifeless corse She lay."

The poem's final regular six-line stanza, in which the poet passes judgment on Laodamia, was repeatedly revised during Wordsworth's lifetime, with the severity of the judgment increased dramatically. The first version, published in 1815 and 1820, reads:

> Ah, judge her gently who so deeply loved!
> Her, who, in reason's spite, yet without crime,
> Was in a trance of passion thus removed;
> Delivered from the galling yoke of time
> And these frail elements—to gather flowers
> Of blissful quiet 'mid unfading bowers.

But the final version (1845) is much harsher:

> Thus, all in vain exhorted and reproved,
> She perished; and, as for a wilful crime,
> By the just Gods whom no weak pity moved,
> Was doomed to wear out her appointed time,
> Apart from happy Ghosts, that gather flowers
> Of blissful quiet 'mid unfading bowers.
>   (lines 158–63)

The poem concludes with eleven irregularly rhymed lines that, Wordsworth said, had provided the germ of his poem. They describe "a knot of spiry trees" which grew "for ages" along the Hellespont; whenever they grew tall enough to see the walls of Troy, "the trees' tall summits withered at the sight; / A constant interchange of growth and blight!"

If Wordsworth wrote the poem simply, as he told Isabella Fenwick, because "the incident of the trees growing and withering put the subject into my thoughts, and I wrote with the hope of giving it a loftier tone than . . . has been given it by any of the Ancients" (PW, 2:518), then his numerous revisions of the poem between manuscript and print, in proof in 1815, and during the next thirty years may simply indicate how slowly and intermittently his stream of inspiration flowed after the great years 1797–1808. But close examination of the text of the poem, as it evolved in proofs in 1815 and as Wordsworth revised it, suggests other possible reasons for his having written a moving poem on the theme of withering treetops and the need for a woman to control her passions.

Two of Wordsworth's children died in 1812, four-year-old Catharine in June and six-year-old Thomas late in November. Wordsworth tried to bear the deaths with Christian stoicism. Mary reacted more openly, especially to the death of Catharine. William wrote to his brother Christopher: "I have but a poor account to give of Mary. . . . she is yet little recovered from the deplorable dejection in which I found her. Her health has suffered: but I clearly see that neither thought nor religion nor the endeavours of friends, can at once quiet a heart that has been disturbed by such an affliction."[36] When Thomas died, however, Wordsworth depicted Mary as stronger in meeting their common suffering:

My Wife bears the loss of her Child with striking fortitude. . . .
Miss Hutchinson also supports her sorrow as ought to be done. For
myself dear Southey I dare not say in what state of mind I am; I
loved the Boy with the utmost love of which my soul is capable,
and he is taken from me—yet in the agony of my spirit in surren-
dering such a treasure I feel a thousand times richer than if I had
never possessed it. God comfort and save you and all our friends
and us all from a repetition of such trials—O Southey feel for me!
(2 December 1818; *MY*, 2:51).

In January 1813 William began drafting additional lines for Book II
and Book III of *The Excursion*, adding to the story of the Solitary,
as the chief cause of that man's disillusionment, the deaths of a young
son and daughter and the consequent alienation and (ultimately) the
death of his beloved wife. De Selincourt was convinced by these
additions that Wordsworth "was led to imagine personal bereavement
as a leading contributory cause of his [the Solitary's] despondency
by his own passionate grief at the loss of his two children" (*PW*,
5:419), but no one has, I believe, commented upon the significance
of lines like these about the Solitary's marriage to his "Anna" (which
again support the theme of the earlier sections of this paper):

> "To my heart's wish, my tender Mate became
> The thankful captive of maternal bonds;
>
> . . . .
>
> Her whose submissive spirit was to me
> Rule and restraint—my guardian—shall I say
> That earthly Providence, whose guiding love
> Within a port of rest had lodged me safe;
> Safe from temptation. . . ."
>   (III:554–55, 563–67; *PW*, 5:94)

Or these lines, about the aftermath of the bereavement of the Solitary
and his wife:

> "Calm as a frozen lake when ruthless winds
> Blow fiercely, agitating earth and sky,
> The Mother now remained. . . .
>
> . . . .
>
> This second visitation had no power
> To shake; but only to bind up and seal;
> And to establish thankfulness of heart
> In Heaven's determinations, ever just.
> The eminence whereon her spirit stood,
> Mine was unable to attain. Immense
> The space that severed us! . . ."
>   (III:650ff.; *PW*, 5:98–99)

From Dorothy's letter to Catherine Clarkson in January 1813, we learn how the family could not separate their sadness from their locale in the Rectory, Grasmere:

> . . . in spite of all we could do, the very air of the place—the stillness—the occasional sounds, and above all the view of that school, our darling's pride and joy—that church-yard his playground—all oppressed us and do continue to oppress us with unutterable sadness—(*MY*, 2:60)

And in this letter Dorothy tells of their determination to move to Rydal Mount. On 1 May the family removed to their new home. In a letter to Francis Wrangham on 28 August 1813, Wordsworth speaks briefly of his children's deaths as a subject almost too painful to face. On 28 April 1814, he writes to Thomas Poole of the "heavy affliction" of the deaths and suggests that he has been unable to compose poetry. Later, in November 1814, Wordsworth writes to his brother Christopher that William, his second surviving son, is very ill. Between these two dates Wordsworth wrote his poem about the need to control passions, deriving it from a myth about how the very trees withered when they viewed the place that had been the cause of two lovers' deaths.

The story of Laodamia centers on a grief of bereavement, but Protesilaus's admonition is directed against misuse of the sexual passion. Is Wordsworth here using a metaphor to strengthen himself and his family in their Christian stoicism? Just as we have seen him use food as a metaphor for sex, we have seen him employ a sexual metaphor for a psychic problem of another nature in "Nutting" and we have seen him turn his fears about his sister's death back into love poems. But, as we have also seen, the conscious use of the sexual metaphor seems, in Wordsworth's case, to have released in a disguised form something otherwise trapped below his consciousness. Thus, when in the first published version of "Laodamia" he uses a highly charged sexual word in an unusual way and then entirely revises the line in the next edition, we can speculate on two possible reasons for the original choice and the revision. In 1815, the lines finally designated 74–76 read:

> Be taught, O faithful Consort, to control
> Rebellious passion: for the Gods approve
> The depth, and not the tumult of the soul;
> The fervour—not the impotence of love.[37]

In 1820, he revised the fourth line of the stanza to read: "A fervent, not ungovernable, love." Wordsworth's use of "impotence" conforms with *OED* definition 3, "Lack of self-restraint, violent passion." This usage, now obsolete, finds its latest *OED* examples in Milton's *Paradise Lost* (II:156) and Pope's translation of *The Iliad* (XXIV:53).[38] With such precedents, Wordsworth may well have included the word for its archaic precision. In this case, his revision is explicable as an attempt to make the line more immediately comprehensible and to avoid suggesting irrelevant meanings, such as *impotence* in its most usual modern meaning: *OED* 2b, "Complete absence of sexual power; usually said of the male." To a student of Shelley, however, who has traced from the letters of Shelley and *his* Mary through the complexities of the maniac's speeches in *Julian and Maddalo* the effect of the deaths of two children within one year into the dim world of *their* marriage bed,[39] it seems more than possible that the unusual diction in line 76 of "Laodamia" may point to another kind of withering in the wake of the Wordsworth's bereavement.

In her January 1813 letter to Catherine Clarkson, Dorothy had described Mary Wordsworth as being "as thin as it is possible to be except when the body is worn out by slow disease" (*MY*, 2:60), suggesting the state of Mary's health to be such as William in *The Excursion* pictures the Solitary's wife Anna, who "fell / Into a gulf obscure of silent grief," and, wasting away in his arms, "left me, on this earth, disconsolate!" (*PW*, 5:99). Sara Hutchinson's letters throughout 1813, even after the move to Rydal Mount, give evidence that, though life in the household had returned to normal at the surface, Mary's spirits remained precarious. On 23 June she wrote to Thomas Monkhouse: "We have had abundance of other visitors; I think we have scarcely been one day unengaged for the last month."[40] In the next surviving letter to Mary Monkhouse Hutchinson, Sara writes of her sister Mary: "Her spirits have I think been better—at least in company—and except when in bed she has never been out of it [i.e., company] for many weeks" (SH, *Letters*, p. 58). Forced to keep up her spirits in public because of the stream of summer visitors to Rydal Mount, Mary Wordsworth may well have had only one place to vent her true emotions—when she retired to bed. And if the emotional distance that Wordsworth describes coming between the Solitary and his wife after their children's deaths reflects, in part, an emotional distancing in Wordsworth's own marriage (a relationship Coleridge had described in 1811 as "a compound of Lust with Esteem & Friendship"), one element may have passed out of Wordsworth's feelings for Mary, never to return.

A year later, on 18 July 1814, William, Mary, and Sara Hutchinson set out on a tour of Scotland. By 3 August 1814, Sara could write to Mrs. Thomas Hutchinson: "dearest Mary is much improved by her journey; she truly enjoys herself; & William is happy that the journey has accomplished this his chief aim" (SH, *Letters*, p. 77). By October 1814, Mary Wordsworth had, by all the available evidence, resumed her accustomed equanimity. At the same time,[41] Wordsworth was composing "Laodamia," suggested by a story of trees that repeatedly wither when confronted by a scene of former anguish, and including both an unusual use of the phrase "impotence of love" and stern admonitions to a woman to control her passions in the presence of a bodily lover who was yet only the ghost of his former self.

The possible inference is complicated further when we read in one of Mary Wordsworth's letters to Dorothy on 29 October 1814: "Poor William's right hand is crippled—the speck which he was examining thru the microscope last Saturday has proved another plaguy boil. It is situated between the thumb and forefinger of his right hand and carries the inflammation in a red line all the way to the arm-pit. I hope it may not be so tedious as his last was . . . but for this he meant to have written to you. . . ."[42] Here we have impotence of yet another kind and definition, a series of boils that incapacitate Wordsworth from writing. Is there a causal relationship among these phenomena that seem to coalesce in the various meanings of a single word? Does the progressively harsher judgment on Laodamia in late editions of the poem suggest that Wordsworth felt increasingly threatened by both conjugal and literary expectations that he was incapable of fulfilling?

These hints and complexities do not yield themselves to certainties. But I hope that my agnostic speculations about some of the possible motive forces behind "Laodamia," added to the somewhat more complete evidence surrounding the poems of 1797–1808, will contribute to the understanding of the kinds of circumstances that drove Wordsworth to produce great poetry. Like most artists, he seems to have had psychic wounds—feelings of guilt and isolation; hidden fears of incestuous passion and equally hidden guilt for dreaming Dorothy's death; guilt concerning his brother's sacrifices; sorrow at the deaths of loved ones; and quite possibly, resentment toward his wife for his own feelings of sexual and creative inadequacy. And when these wounds are seen as the source of Wordsworth's poems that we all acknowledge to be great, the most obvious answer to those who ponder the later decline of Wordsworth's powers is that, one by one, the ghosts that haunted the poet's psyche were exorcized either by the march of events or by the transmutation of emotion into poetry.

Wordsworth's greatest poems—those nuggets of gold washed down the stream of time—derive from a massif that on its surface stonily resisted the winds of guilt, self-doubt, and despair. Whereas Coleridge was like a tree whipped, buffeted, and twisted by his fears, doubts, guilt, and sense of isolation, William Wordsworth flung back each blast of life's emotional storm in "an echo and a light unto eternity." Here again, his sister Dorothy knew him best, and he himself became her voice, speaking to us of William's sublime egoism, poetically triumphant over circumstance:

There is an Eminence,—of these our hills
The last that parleys with the setting sun;
. . . .
                              . . . this Peak, so high
Above us, and so distant in its height,
Is visible; and often seems to send
Its own deep quiet to restore our hearts.
. . . .
                              . . . 'Tis in truth
The loneliest place we have among the clouds.
And She who dwells with me, whom I have loved
With such communion, that no place on earth
Can ever be a solitude to me,
Hath to this lonely Summit given my Name.[43]

Author's Note

The text and footnotes of this paper provide the reader with the proximate cause of my entry into the exploration of Wordsworth's sexuality, as that may be evidenced in his poetry. Though there was a certain amount of open hostility in TLS and New York Review to my letters to TLS that initially raised these questions, since the publication of this full treatment of it, the subject seems no longer to be a forbidden one. In May 1975, I delivered a short form of my argument as the DeCoursey Fales Memorial Lecture at New York University and then gave an expanded version, containing the discussion of "Laodamia," in July 1975 at the Wordsworth-Coleridge Conference at Ambleside, England, under the title "Wordsworth, Dorothy, and Mary Hutchinson: The Evidence of the Imagination." Members of both audiences—the second of which included several leading Wordsworthians—countered with alternative readings of the evidence, but because I was taking Wordsworth seriously as a poet and a human being struggling with issues that relate him to central concerns of other human beings, rather than pursuing a prurient interest in his sex life, others were able to consider the argument without extreme prejudice. It may have been important to Lord Clark or to Mary Moorman whether or not Wordsworth and his sister misbehaved, or were tempted to misbehave; at least each made a moral judgment upon what each seemed to consider a matter that had been factually established. I was—and am—agnostic about the specific expressions of feeling by the poet and his family, except as the feelings are embodied in poems exhibiting an exceptional emotional power that helped to reopen the wells of feeling in English society in the early nineteenth century. "Poetry of Familiarity" is, in fact, a companion study to my earlier "Shelley's 'The Triumph of Life': The Biographical Problem," in which

I use similar biographical and textual evidence to refute an equally strong assertion that Shelley's final poem resulted simply from his sexually oriented feelings and actions. In both papers, I try to undercut biographical simplifications and dogmatisms that are unwarranted by the available evidence and to redirect the discussion to larger issues of the poet's psychological orientation and values and to the interplay between the original emotional poetic impulse and the traditional and technical constraints of the literary form, thereby suggesting some of the complexities of that interrelationship.

Great poetry results when the seams that mark the poet's struggle for self-expression within the constraints of language, genre, and versification do not show at all to the casual observer, but are turned under the fabric, to be inferred only by other "tailors" (poets) or by those who find the pattern and scraps in an old bin (the scholars who look through the drafts and various published revisions and who study the surviving biographical evidence). Almost axiomatically then, there can be no certainty about the genetics of a great poem, unless the evidence of the various stages of its creation is unusually complete. In Wordworth's case, the evidence, though voluminous, is still incomplete. My explorations are, therefore, meant to suggest possibilities and to stimulate thinking on the part of others who bring to the questions different experiences and knowledge. The very attempt to follow these winding paths within the labyrinthine human psyche should help to banish the dogmatic air that oversimplifiers bring to their biographical analyses. As I answered a critic who accused me of holding a simpleminded view of Wordsworth's Lucy poems, the truly simpleminded biographical view of them is this: "Wordsworth loved a maiden who lived beside the springs of Dove; she died, and it made a great difference to him."

Since the publication of "Poetry of Familiarity" in 1978, the publication of the full texts of The Love Letters of William and Mary Wordsworth, *edited by Beth Darlington (Ithaca: Cornell University Press, 1981), brought into public view important new evidence on the relations between William and Mary Wordsworth. Though when I published "Poetry of Familiarity" I was aware of the existence and tone of this correspondence through excerpts quoted in the Sotheby's auction catalogue (see note 27 below), those excerpts seemed to me and my friends to suggest a forced insincerity on William Wordsworth's part. The letters in their full panoply proved to be more impressive, though they clearly represented a new phase of the relations between William and Mary Wordsworth. Had I discussed the years in which those letters were written, I should have to revise a number of my inferences and conclusions. As it is, I still hold to my basic view of the psychological sources of the poems of 1798–1802, 1804, and 1813–1815.*

At the 1984 MLA convention in Washington, a scholar alluded to my argument while asserting that Wordsworth's real problem was that he was too prudish to discuss his sexuality in his poetry, thereby weakening his impact as a psychological poet. I do not find Wordsworth at all prudish by the standards of his time. Our candor in these matters, though probably beneficial in our lives, seems not to have generated any poetry of such great emotional power as arose when such feelings and the expression of them had to be displaced into less graphic language. Part of my point in exploring the unprovable was to suggest how rich and strange this reincarnation of sexually allied feelings might be in situations—and cultures—where an artist was not as free as were Hemingway, Henry Miller, and Auden to describe in letters to friends or in creative writings every aspect of sexual desire or the emotional life as soon as it developed.

Notes

1. I have used the 1963 impression of the second edition (London: Longmans, 1956), hereafter cited as "Bateson." In this edition, while maintaining his thesis, Bateson softened the language in various places. (See his "Preface to the Second Edition.") For a sidelight on Bateson's early differences with the Dove Cottage Trustees, see his letter to *Times Literary Supplement*, 9 April 1976, p. 430.

2. The most ambitious attempts thus far to interpret Wordsworth's poetry in relation to his psychology are Wallace W. Douglas's *Wordsworth: The Construction of a Personality* (Kent, Ohio: Kent State University Press, 1968) and Richard J. Onorato's *The Character of the Poet: Wordsworth in "The Prelude"* (Princeton: Princeton University Press, 1971). Though I have consulted both books, I have related my argument to the latter, hereafter cited as "Onorato."

3. "William and Dorothy Wordsworth," in *Essays by Divers Hands, Being the Transactions of the Royal Society of Literature*, NS 55 (London: Oxford University Press, 1972): 75–97.

4. *Journals of Dorothy Wordsworth*, ed. Mary Moorman, with an Introduction by Helen Darbishire (London: Oxford University Press, 1971; corrected 1973, 1974), hereafter cited as *Journals*.

5. The correspondence, most of it published under the heading "Brothers and Sisters," appeared in *Times Literary Supplement* in 1974 on 9 August (p. 859), 23 August (p. 906), 13 September (pp. 979–80), 4 October (pp. 1078–79), 1 November (p. 1231), 8 November (p. 1261), 15 November (p. 1288), 22 November (p. 1317), and 27 December (p. 1464). My contributions appeared on 13 September, 1 November, and 27 December.

6. Among them, his contention that "after the Lucy poems, . . . there was no place for [Dorothy] in the organs of Wordsworth's poetic imagination, and she was cut out like so much decayed tissue" (Bateson, p. 202). As will become clear, I believe that William's feelings for Dorothy remained a vital force in his poetry up to the very day of his wedding (see pp. 204–5) and beyond.

7. Both Bateson (pp. 41–56) and Onorato (pp. 24–25 et passim) rightly emphasize, for example, the effect upon the Wordsworth siblings of the early deaths of their mother and father and their unhappy childhood among unloving kinsmen. Onorato sees Wordsworth's repression of his sorrow at his early bereavement as determinative for his later attitude toward Nature.

8. *Journals*, pp. 147–48.

9. William and Dorothy had carried on a regular correspondence with Annette and Caroline that has disappeared. See *The Letters of William and Dorothy Wordsworth*, ed. Ernest de Selincourt, vol. 1, *The Early Years: 1787–1805*, 2nd ed., revised by Chester L. Shaver (Oxford: Clarendon Press, 1967), p. 282 (hereafter cited as *Early Letters*).

10. *Journals*, p. 154.

11. See, for example, Coleridge's frequent references to his jealousy of Wordsworth in relation to Sara Hutchinson. In *The Notebooks of Samuel Taylor Coleridge*, ed. Kathleen Coburn, vol. 2 (New York: Pantheon Books, 1961), entries 2001n, 2055n, 2975n, 2998 and n, 3148 and n (and others) show that Coleridge imagined that on Saturday, 26 December 1806, in the Queen's Head Inn, Stringston, Wordsworth had gone to bed with Sara Hutchinson, his sister-in-law and Coleridge's beloved. (Coleridge later accused his imagination of playing tricks on him in this instance.) Bateson (p. 44) quotes Thomas De Quincey, who wrote (in part): "Wordsworth's intellectual passions were fervent and strong: but they rested upon a basis of preternatural animal sensibility diffused through *all* the animal passions (or appetites). . . ."

12. "Female Gothic: Monsters, Goblins, Freaks," *New York Review of Books* 21 (14 April 1974): 36–37.

13. Many have surmised Dorothy's interest in Coleridge from 1797, and John E. Jordan presents some evidence to support Malcolm Elwin's speculation that Dorothy at age thirty-eight may have been infatuated with young Thomas De Quincey during his early years in the Lake District. See *De Quincey to Wordsworth: A Biography of a Relationship* (Berkeley: University of California Press, 1962), pp. 228–30. I should add, also, in fairness to Dorothy and her modern admirers who would object to a description of her as a case of arrested sexual development, that a number of readers of the evidence are more willing than I to suggest the occurrence of actual physical incest between William and Dorothy. See, for example, Rachel Mayer Brownstein's excellent essay "The Private Life: Dorothy Wordsworth's Journals," *Modern Language Quarterly* 34 (1973): 48–63, especially 51–52.

14. Unless otherwise indicated, Wordsworth's poems and their titles are quoted from *The Poetical Works of William Wordsworth*, ed. Ernest de Selincourt and Helen Darbishire, Oxford English Text Edition, 5 vols. (Oxford: Clarendon Press, 1940–1954), vols. 1–3 being the second editions (hereafter cited as *PW*). The reader will often have to consult the notes and variant readings to reconstruct the earliest texts.

15. Additional information may eventually be forthcoming from a previously unknown manuscript, sold at Sotheby's in London (6 July 1977, lot 405), which contains nine lines apparently intended as an addition to this poem, copied by Dorothy Wordsworth. This addition can be dated (from the contents of a fragmentary letter by Dorothy on the verso) before June 1802. This and other new letters and manuscripts by Wordsworth, Coleridge, and their circle, sold at the same time, are now in the Dove Cottage Library.

16. *The Letters of Mary Wordsworth, 1800–1805* (Oxford: Clarendon Press, 1958), p. xxiv.

17. In *William Wordsworth: A Biography* (Oxford: Clarendon Press, 1957; corrected 1967), Mary Moorman, always scrupulous both in handling facts and in acknowledging the force of William's affection for Dorothy, writes of "The Glow-worm": "It was written in the spring of 1802, when William was riding back to Dorothy after a visit to Mary Hutchinson, with whom he had just completed the arrangements for their wedding. His first and immediate thought even in that hour was for Dorothy, and [Mrs. Moorman adds by way of interpreting these facts] he speaks as if to reassure her that the communion between them could never be changed" (vol. 1, pp. 319–20).

18. See, for example, Dorothy's account of the composition of "Children Gathering Flowers" ("Foresight") (*Journals*, pp. 116–17) and her allusion on 15 April to the flower that, two weeks later, Wordsworth immortalized in two poems "To the Small Celandine" (pp. 109, 118–19).

19. William's exceptionally blissful reaction to the residence that he and Dorothy chose at Town End, Grasmere (the cottage now known as Dove Cottage), has been widely, if not universally, acknowledged. See, for example, Karl Kroeber, " 'Home at Grasmere': Ecological Holiness," *PMLA* 89 (1974): 132–41. For a reading of "Home at Grasmere" involving Wordsworth's possible ambiguous feelings in the period, see Kenneth R. Johnston, " 'Home at Grasmere': Reclusive Song," *Studies in Romanticism* 14 (1975): 1–28. Johnston and those who see underlying tensions in all parts of "Home at Grasmere" emphasize the poet's recognition that the idyllic situation is necessarily mortal and, therefore, temporary. One necessary cause of the transitory nature of the poet's bliss was, I submit, the instability of the situation involving the cohabitation of a brother and sister who could never fulfill each other's sexual longings without guilt. For the dating of various portions of this poem and Wordsworth's revisions, which gradually removed most of the references to Dorothy and cast the poem into a far less personal form, see Beth Darlington's edition of *Home at Grasmere: Part First, Book First of "The Recluse"* in the Cornell Wordsworth Series (Ithaca: Cornell University Press, 1978).

20. In the Appendix to *Journals* the poem is titled "Our Departure" (p. 217); when published in 1815 it was titled "A Farewell" (*PW*, 2:23–24).

21. Stephen Parrish reveals in his Cornell Wordsworth edition of *The Prelude, 1798–1799* (Ithaca: Cornell University Press, 1977) that in "the earliest state of *The Prelude*," found in MS JJ, "where a listener is identified at the close, it seems, as in *Tintern Abbey*, to be the poet's sister" (p. 8).

22. *PW*, 2:472. See, in confirmation of this judgment, Moorman, *William Wordsworth*, 1:318–19.

23. The confirming evidence of the origin of this poem is found in MS JJ, where "my" appears in the place of "his" (see Onorato, p. 196).

24. *Times Literary Supplement*, 13 September 1974, pp. 979–80.

25. "Three years she grew in sun and shower" (*PW*, 2:214–16). Some commentators have (mistakenly) interpreted the poem as referring to the death of a three-year-old child; but see lines 31–33. Frances C. Ferguson, whose essay "The Lucy Poems: Wordsworth's Quest for a Poetic Object" (*ELH* 40 [1973]: 532–48) takes rigidly anti-biographical analysis of the poems about as far as it can go, argues that "through the course of these poems, Lucy is repeatedly and ever more decisively traced out of existence," and she goes on to assert that "the chief difficulty in talking about these poems lies in our uncertainty about what the name 'Lucy' refers to" (p. 533). Many of the difficulties that Professor Ferguson explores disappear, however, if one recognizes that "Lucy" derives from Wordsworth's conflicting feelings about his sister Dorothy and that the ambiguities in "Lucy's" nature (as well as her eventual disappearance) evolve naturally from Wordsworth's symbolic, externalized resolution of his psychic dilemma.

26. Dorothy's first surviving letter, to Jane Pollard in July 1787, describes her brothers—especially William and John—with deep affection, but conveys no hint of romantic attachment. She clearly looked to her brothers to provide her the stable home that she had lacked since the death of their mother (*Early Letters*, pp. 4–5).

27. One of the nagging difficulties that haunts Wordsworth studies is the absence or mutilation of crucial manuscripts that might have cast light on some of the questions raised here. Dorothy's Alfoxden Journal has disappeared since 1897, and there are erasures and cancellations in the surviving journals by someone other than Dorothy

(see Moorman in *Journals*, p. viii). What must have been numerous letters exchanged by the Wordsworths and Annette Vallon are not to be found, and we know that some references to Annette and Caroline in surviving letters were destroyed by Gordon Graham Wordsworth (see *Early Letters*, p. 282 and n). No letters at all of Mary Hutchinson Wordsworth or Sara Hutchinson survive from the crucial years 1801–1804, and we have none of their letters to each other until 1811. In short, many important questions that may once have been answered in manuscripts that survived the principals cannot be answered, perhaps because the evidence has been destroyed or mutilated by those responsible for safeguarding the manuscripts for posterity. The emergence of previously unknown letters between Wordsworth, Mary, and Dorothy at the Sotheby sale of 6 July 1977 not only provides new evidence for the questions explored in this essay, but also offers some hope that further documents may ultimately come to light.

28. Here are relevant, I suggest, the headaches and tensions that Dorothy's journals record as afflicting William and her during the years of their life together.

29. *Collected Letters of Samuel Taylor Coleridge*, ed. Earl Leslie Griggs, vol. 3 (Oxford: Clarendon Press, 1959), p. 305. It may be significant that Wordsworth composed "Yarrow Unvisited," which celebrates the free play of the visionary imagination, as a result of his Scottish tour with Coleridge and Dorothy in 1803, whereas he wrote "Yarrow Visited," a derivative poem that tells how the poet's loss of his "waking dream" was mitigated by a fine (though inferior) reality, in September 1814 while touring with Mary and Sara Hutchinson (*PW*, 3:83–85, 106–8).

30. *The Letters of Mary Wordsworth*, p. xxiii. The full text of this letter is to be found in *The Letters of John Wordsworth*, ed. Carl H. Ketcham (Ithaca: Cornell University Press, 1969), pp. 125–26.

31. I have not presumed to encroach upon the area of the relations between William and John Wordsworth in 1802 because Irene Tayler has stated the case so well in "By Peculiar Grace: Wordsworth in 1802," in *The Evidence of the Imagination*, pp. 119–41.

32. A variant of this theme appears in "Michael," which—though partially based on the objective story associated with the sheepfold in Green-head Ghyll—generates much of its emotional force from the failure of Luke to vindicate his tutelage by Nature and the trust placed in him by his parents. Like the other poems on the "guilt and sorrow" theme, the story of Michael and Luke is told by a narrator who centers on the reactions of the betrayed party. Like the Youth who seduces Ruth and like the wayward husband in "The Ruined Cottage," Luke seeks "a hiding-place beyond the seas." The emotional power of this poem derives, I suggest, from Wordsworth's own passionate feelings about his failure to carry out his responsibility toward Annette Vallon, though by 1800 he was able to give his feelings further aesthetic distance through the story of Michael's devotion to his fathers' land and through the poet-narrator's own quest for a different kind of permanence—his desire for the immortality of poetry through which to relate the homely history "For the delight of a few natural hearts / And . . . for the sake / Of *youthful Poets, who* among these hills / *Will be my second self when I am gone*" (*PW*, 2:81; italics added).

33. The sonnet "Written in Very Early Youth" ("Calm is all nature as a resting wheel"; *PW*, 1:3), which de Selincourt dates in its present form ca. 1795–1797, but which Wordsworth retrieved and first published in the *Morning Post* on 13 February 1802, is one. On the questionable "Sonnet on Seeing Miss Helen Maria Williams Weep at a Tale of Distress," see Carl Woodring, *Politics in English Romantic Poetry* (Cambridge: Harvard University Press, 1970), p. 339n. Mark Reed, in *Wordsworth: The Chronology of the Early Years, 1770–1799* (Cambridge: Harvard University Press, 1967), lists also "Sonnet Written by Mr.——Immediately after the Death of His Wife" (p. 19) and two unpublished sonnets preserved in manuscripts (pp. 22, 23).

34. *Wordsworth,* corrected ed. (Cambridge: Harvard University Press, 1968), p. 157.

35. I base this assertion on my personal conviction, held since 1963 and expressed at a number of conferences but not yet argued in print, that Wordsworth restructured *The Prelude* from thirteen to fourteen books to give it the form of the Italian sonnet, with the books now forming natural groupings of four/four/three/three, with the strongest break occurring between the first eight books and the last six.

36. *The Letters of William and Dorothy Wordsworth,* ed. Ernest de Selincourt, *The Middle Years,* revised by Mary Moorman and Alan G. Hill, 2 vols. (Oxford: Clarendon Press, 1969–1970), Part II, 26. Though there may be some confusion (since Parts I and II of *The Middle Years* are also numbered as volumes 2 and 3 of *The Letters*), I shall follow the established practice of Wordsworthians in citing these two volumes as *MY1* and *MY2* (plus the page references).

37. Wordsworth's *Poems, including Lyrical Ballads and the Miscellaneous Pieces of the Author, . . . in Two Volumes* (London: Longman, Hurst, Rees, Orme, and Brown, 1815), 1:228.

38. The words *impotence* and *impotent* occur eight times in the texts analyzed in Lane Cooper's *Concordance to the Poems of William Wordsworth* (London: Smith, Elder, 1911). In every instance, the context shows that the meaning intended is either *OED* 1 ("utter inability or weakness; helplessness") or 2a ("Want of physical power; feebleness") for the noun and either 1 ("powerless, helpless; ineffective") or 2a ("Physically weak; . . . decrepit") for the adjective.

39. See Donald H. Reiman, *Shelley and his Circle,* vol. 6 (Cambridge: Harvard University Press, 1973), pp. 857–65.

40. *The Letters of Sara Hutchinson from 1800 to 1835,* ed. Kathleen Coburn (London: Routledge & Kegan Paul, 1954), pp. 55–56 (hereafter cited as SH, *Letters*).

41. Mark L. Reed in *Wordsworth: The Chronology of the Middle Years, 1800–1815* (Cambridge: Harvard University Press, 1975) dates the composition of the 130-line original version of "Laodamia" as ca. mid-October to 27 October (pp. 53, 580) and that of lines 115–20 ca. early February, "certainly by 5 Feb" (pp. 580, 590).

42. *The Letters of Mary Wordsworth,* pp. 22–23. Mark L. Reed suggests that Mary began this letter on 27 October.

43. "Poems on the Naming of Places," III (*PW,* 2:115), written and published in 1800.

Wordsworth's Lucy Poems in Psychobiographical Context   Richard E. Matlak[*]

> I hear that the Two Noble Englishmen have parted no sooner than they set foot on German earth, but I have not heard the reason— possibly, to give novelists an handle to exclaim, "Ah me! what things are perfect?"
>
> —(Charles Lamb to Robert Southey)

Wordsworth's experience at Goslar, that "melancholy dream" the poet endured in isolation with Dorothy, bereft of Coleridge's pres-

[*] Reprinted by permission of the Modern Language Association of America from *PMLA* 93 (1978).

ence, provides an illuminating context for the composition of the Lucy poems. Critics usually ignore or treat the circumstances of the Lucy poems' composition perfunctorily, despite the convention of analyzing Wordsworth's poetry with full biographical apparatus in hand. This critical anomaly is probably due in part to an assumption that identifying Lucy is the synecdochic equivalent of reconstructing Wordsworth's Goslar experience. Rather than become entangled again in the morass of biographical speculation over Lucy's real-life counterpart,[1] critics have profitably shifted their interest either to the poet/narrator's developing consciousness or to the language and imagery of the cycle. Consequently, one hesitates to ask, "Who was Lucy?" because, as one critic has stated, "there is no answer to this question except to say that it is irrelevant."[2]

The charge of irrelevance cannot be made categorically, however; issues are relevant or irrelevant with respect to contexts of preoccupation, not a priori. The goal of this study is to provide a comprehensive psychological and biographical ambience for the Lucy poems that will dispel the mystery of their genesis and account for their intriguing peculiarities; and to reach this objective, an important assumption must be made about the identity of Lucy. Ultimately, I concur with F. W. Bateson that Wordsworth's relationship with Dorothy is the emotional foundation of the Lucy poems, but, far from being incestuously inclined, as Bateson argues,[3] Wordsworth's relationship with Dorothy was probably stifling and inhibitive at the time of the Lucy poems' composition. Why this should be so is a part of the more important and general issue of Wordsworth's vocational anxiety, which at Goslar is best understood in terms of his sense of self-worth.

During this extremely intense and concentrated period (October 1798–February 1799), when Wordsworth was writing so much of importance in addition to the Lucy poems—the Matthew poems, "Lucy Gray," most of Part I of The Prelude, 1798–99, together with its associated passages, "Nutting" and "There Was a Boy"—the poet's relationships with Dorothy and Coleridge figured prominently in the psychobiographical context of his work. Wordsworth was depressed at Goslar, mainly because he was separated from Coleridge and was growing uneasy about the constancy of Coleridge's friendship and devotion. Not only was Coleridge becoming increasingly concerned about his own career, rather than about Wordsworth's, as he had been in the bloom of the poets' relationship, but he was also beginning to recognize that Thomas Poole, rather than Wordsworth, was the sole anchor of his affections. Dorothy could hardly be of comfort in this situation because it was the added cost of keeping her that prevented Wordsworth from joining Coleridge, first in Ratzeburg and later in the expensive university town of Göttingen. The consequence of Wordsworth's depression for his work was the fantasy of Dorothy's death in the Lucy poems. Wordsworth both loved Dorothy and wished to be rid of her, because of the serious inconvenience of her presence, and the Lucy poems formed as an expression of this ambivalence. Lucy became not so much an exact equivalent of Dorothy as an amorphous, and thus safe, object for the hostilities Dorothy aroused. This psychobiographical context also has ramifications for the remainder of the poetry written at Goslar, but the emotional line of the Lucy poems is sufficiently distinct to restrict this discussion almost exclusively to their development.[4]

The composition of the Lucy poems occurred in three phases, demarcated by circumstantial and emotional vicissitudes in Wordsworth's relationships with Dorothy and Coleridge: the first, and most important, phase, during which "Strange Fits of Passion," "She Lived among the Untrodden Ways," and "A Slumber Did My Spirit Seal" were written, occurred within a three-month period following the Wordsworths' separation from Coleridge in Germany; the second phase, during which "Three Years She Grew in Sun and Shower" was composed, occurred before Wordsworth's reunion with Coleridge after their winter-long separation; the third phase, which saw the composition of "I Travelled among Unknown Men," occurred in England about two years later in response to another threatened separation from Coleridge, and thus functions as an important thematic and emotional conclusion to the Lucy cycle.[5] During this period of separation, reunion, and anticipation of perhaps permanent separation from Coleridge, the curve of Wordsworth's ambivalence toward Dorothy is manifested in the Lucy lyrics.

Wordsworth's mental and physical condition during the first phase is detailed in his letter of 14 or 21 December 1798 to Coleridge in Ratzeberg:

> As I have had no books I have been obliged to write in self-defence. I should have written five times as much as I have done but that I am prevented by an uneasiness at my stomach and side, with a dull pain about my heart. I have used the word pain, but uneasiness and heat are words which more accurately express my feeling. At all events it renders writing unpleasant. Reading is now become a kind of luxury to me. When I do not read I am absolutely consumed by thinking and feeling and bodily exertions of voice or of limbs, the consequence of those feelings.[6]

It is commonly understood that anxiety is a result of uncertainty vis-à-vis an object of endearment—a loved one, an ideal, a sense of self-esteem, or, according to recent theory most appropriate to this case, an "affective state of well-being," as it were, an environment of safety and love for nurturing the self.[7] The cause of Wordsworth's anxiety is no mystery if we consider the recent disruption he suffered and the risk it betokened, that is, the end of his blissful residence with Coleridge at Alfoxden and the likelihood that the creative experience of that year might never again be attained.

The Prelude records Wordsworth's deep love for the *annus mirabilis* (July 1797 to June 1798) at Alfoxden, singling it out as an experience that justifies the poem's unparalleled attention to the growth of an individual mind. Addressing Coleridge, Wordsworth writes:

> When, looking back, thou seest in clearer view
> Than any sweetest sight of yesterday
> That summer when on Quantock's grassy Hills
> Far ranging, and among the sylvan Coombs,
> Thou in delicious words, with happy heart,
> Didst speak the Vision of that Ancient Man,
> The bright-eyed Mariner, and rueful woes
> Didst utter of the Lady Christabel;
> And I, associate with such labour, walk'd
> Murmuring of him who, joyous hap! was
>   found,
> After the perils of his moonlight ride
> Near the loud Waterfall; or her who sate
> In misery near the miserable Thorn;
> When thou dost to that summer turn thy
>   thoughts,
> And hast before thee all which then we were,
> To thee, in memory of that happiness
> It will be known, by thee at least, my Friend,
> Felt, that the history of a Poet's mind
> Is labour not unworthy of regard:
> To thee the work shall justify itself.[8]

What was the essence of this period, if not Wordsworth's discovery of his own self-worth?

Until meeting Coleridge, Wordsworth had experienced disappointment or failure through most of his adult life: he had almost suffered breakdown over the failure of the French Revolution; he had abandoned Annette Vallon in France with their child; he was in penury and estranged from his family; and he and Dorothy were without the permanent home they needed and desired. Above all, in the matter of vocation, as Wallace W. Douglas has emphasized,[9] Wordsworth was without purpose, hope, or direction. Wordsworth wrote to his friend Mathews, "I am doomed to be an idler thro[ughou]t my whole life" (*EY*, p. 62), and as late as 1796, in his twenty-seventh year, the prediction was still holding; life with Dorothy at Racedown was dull and unpromising. Wordsworth wrote of their present life as "utterly barren of such events as merit even the shortlived chronicle of an accidental letter" and, after commenting that he plants cabbages with Dorothy, mused that "if retirement, in its full perfection, be as powerful in working transformations as one of Ovid's Gods, you may perhaps suspect that into cabbages we shall be transformed." Under these conditions of vegetative torpor, "writing . . . [was] out of the question" (*EY*, p. 169). Like a whirlwind, Coleridge entered this scene of sedentary retirement to arouse Wordsworth's genius, chiefly through a transformation of his self-image. In no time at all, the "idler" became the successor to Milton.

After the briefest association with Coleridge in the early spring of 1797, Wordsworth at last began to write—"Lines Left upon a Seat in a Yew-Tree," "The Old Cumberland Beggar," and the first part of *The Ruined Cottage* being gatherings of this early poetic harvest. When Coleridge heard Wordsworth recite *The Ruined Cottage*, he recognized greatness and persistently endeavored to make it known. "Wordsworth is a very great man," he wrote to Southey, "the only man, to whom *at all times* & in *all modes of excellence* I feel myself inferior. . . ."[10] To Cottle, his publisher friend, he wrote, "The Giant Wordsworth—God love him!—even when I speak in the terms of admiration due to his intellect, I fear lest tho[se] terms should keep out of sight the amiableness of his manners . . ." (Griggs, I, 391). Spreading the notice of Wordsworth's abilities and character even wider, Coleridge wrote to John Prior Estlin, the Unitarian minister at Bristol, "I have now known him a year & some months, and my admiration, I might say, my awe of his intellectual powers has increased even to this hour—& (what is of more importance) he is a tried good man" (Griggs, I, 410). Wordsworth became prolific as a result of Coleridge's enthusiam. Writing from Alfoxden, where the Wordsworths moved to be nearer Coleridge, Dorothy describes William's burgeoning industry: "His faculties seem to expand every day, he composes with much more facility than he did . . . and his ideas flow faster than he can express them" (*EY*, p. 200). Coleridge hoped that Wordsworth would assume a station in line after Milton, but he realized that Wordsworth would have to write a major long poem. Out of this challenge, as a culmination and symbol of Coleridge's expectations—and, indeed, of Wordsworth's growing self-expectations as well—arose Coleridge's plan for *The Recluse*, which would be "the *first* and *only* true Phil. Poem in existence" (Griggs, IV, 574).

A year or so earlier, Wordsworth had been in early retirement, sullenly composing imitations of Juvenal; now he was beginning a work that would ensure his poetic immortality. The difference was Coleridge, who was bold enough to believe that "since Milton no man has *manifested* himself equal to him" (Griggs, I, 582), except Wordsworth. After the unrelieved mediocrity, if not failure, of his life to that point, Wordsworth was wholly committed to fulfilling Coleridge's expectations, for, thereby, he could ensure Coleridge's continued adulation, or so he thought.

Wordsworth allotted himself eighteen months to complete *The Recluse* (*EY*, p. 212), and, indeed, he had composed 1,300 lines of blank verse, 900 lines of which were *The Ruined Cottage*, with such facility that eighteen months might have seemed a conservative estimate, even for completing a masterwork on "Nature, Man, and Society." Coleridge had praised the lines as "blank verse, superior . . . to any thing in our language which any way resembles it" (Griggs, I, 391), and at this point Wordsworth's belief in himself, in his vocation, reached an apex of confidence. He described his new project to James Tobin: "I have written 1300 lines of a poem in which I contrive to convey most of the knowledge of which I am possessed. My object is to give pictures of Nature, Man, and Society. Indeed I know not any thing which will not come within the scope of my plan" (*EY*, p. 212). He informed James Losh of the same large ambitions, as if to say, I am now to be taken seriously: "I have written 1300 lines of a poem which I hope to make of considerable utility; its title will be *The Recluse or Views of Nature, Man, and Society*" (*EY*, p. 214). In fact, we know that the Pedlar's character in *The Ruined Cottage* was now becoming Wordsworth's thematic fixation (*EY*, p. 199), and we may conclude that Coleridge had been so successful in convincing Wordsworth of his greatness that he now found it permissible to think and to write on his own life, albeit behind the thin fiction of a wanderer's boyhood.

Unfortunately, however, Wordsworth's "state of well-being" was abruptly disturbed when the lease on Alfoxden expired, forcing a move. The time must have seemed propitious to Coleridge for convincing Wordsworth that a German sojourn was in their mutual interest. Actually, as Walter Jackson Bate has perceptively argued, Coleridge was beginning to suffer from "floating anxiety"; he had received the Wedgwood annuity to do something significant with his life and almost a year had passed without his establishing a direction for his own energies.[11] Surely, the Wedgwoods would not consider his dedication to Wordsworth a satisfactory return for their beneficence. Hence, in a vocational quandary, and, truly, not finding in Wordsworth's friendship reciprocal concern, support, or guidance, Coleridge determined, hoped, that several years in Germany, the fomenting center of knowledge in natural science and philosophy, would provide the foundation for a vocation of his own. He could not be explicit on what his specific goal would be, but he deemed that study in Germany would be "of high importance to [his] intellectual utility; and . . . to [his] moral happiness" (Griggs, I, 414). Wordsworth required some rationalization for following Coleridge, and his declared intention was the desire to learn German sufficiently to earn an income as a translator of German literature, which was enjoying a vogue in England. But while recognizing that it is often necessary to bow for one's bread, one cannot really take Wordsworth's modest ambition seriously or justify its necessity. It was certainly a far cry from the exalted aspirations bound up in *The Recluse,* as Wordsworth was shortly to discover when he found himself settled in Germany, without Coleridge, without the energy to continue with *The Recluse,* and without the desire to learn German. In September 1798, the Wordsworths, Coleridge, and one of Coleridge's ardent admirers, John Chester, embarked for Germany.

After a brief stay in Hamburg, the friends parted company, although they had originally planned to stay together in an inexpensive town near Hamburg until they had mastered the language sufficiently to take advantage of the preferred, but more expensive, environment of a university town (*EY,* pp. 213, 221). Hence, they had arrived in Hamburg with a goal but without certain destinations. In a "state of doubt and oscillation" about where they should go next, the friends were happy to receive some direction from the brother of the poet Klopstock; Ratzeburg was a beautiful town, not far from Hamburg, they were told, and Klopstock's brother could provide them with a letter of introduction to the *Amtmann,* or "perpetual Mayor" (Griggs, I, 446, 448). Coleridge was appointed the "Missioner" and set out alone to reconnoiter the area. After several days, he returned to report the town enchanting but expensive. Excited about the prospect of living in such a beautiful, socially active town, however, Coleridge had arranged board and lodging for Chester and himself,[12] but the Wordsworths, now preoccupied with expenses and feeling beset by German avarice,[13] "determined," according to Coleridge, "to go on, & seek, lower down, obscurer & cheaper Lodgings without boarding—" (*STCNB,* I, 346). Whether or not the Wordsworths desired obscurer lodging to avoid the active social life of Ratzeburg, it is certain that they could not afford it. Two could not live as cheaply as one. Coleridge would be incurring a bill of eighteen marks per week for himself; Wordsworth's bill would be thirty-six. How the Wordsworths came to choose Goslar as their destination is not known, but several reasons might be suggested: the town was affordable; being in the Harz mountain region, Goslar was similar geographically to their beloved home environment; but, of most importance perhaps, it was only fifty miles from Göttingen, where Wordsworth may have known that Coleridge intended to settle after a preparatory stay at Ratzeburg. Possibly the Wordsworths could visit Coleridge or even join him there if they could live frugally enough in the interim. But still there was to be the long winter wait.

When Wordsworth writes to Coleridge, then, of his having to write in "self-defence," of the "uneasiness and heat" afflicting his heart, and of the absolute consumption absorbing his being, we can appreciate something of the loss that unnerved him. Only a few months earlier, he and Dorothy had been in Coleridge's constant company, enjoying his conversation "teem[ing] with soul, mind, and spirit" (EY, p. 188); Wordsworth was bathing in the light of Coleridge's wonderful enthusiasm; and he was aglow with a major ambition. Now, he was alone with Dorothy again. It must have seemed like the vegetable existence of Racedown redivivus, except that this time it was worse being alone with Dorothy, because, having experienced the excitement of Coleridge's presence, Wordsworth could hardly do without it.

And if we consider further the cause of Wordsworth's separation from Coleridge, the added expense of keeping his dear sister, we begin to develop a sense of the transmogrification Wordsworth's love for Dorothy was undergoing. It must have been painfully clear to Wordsworth that, without Dorothy, he could have afforded to be with Coleridge. A check of their German expenditures reveals that Wordsworth and Coleridge both drew upon Josiah Wedgwood for almost the same amount of money for almost the same period of time, a little over a hundred pounds each for about half a year.[14] The great difference in their life-styles in Germany[15] and the necessity for their separation were mostly due to Wordsworth's having another to support.

This financial issue becomes quite poignant when one reads time and again in the letters of the inconvenience of Dorothy's presence, most often emphasized by Dorothy herself. In writing to her brother Christopher, for example, Dorothy says that she and William cannot afford to be received into society because they would be expected, "being considered as a sort of family, to give entertainments in return for what they receive" (EY, p. 244). Coleridge, Dorothy points out, is "all in high life, among Barons counts and countesses. . . . It would have been impossible for us to have lived as he does," Dorothy continues, "we should have been ruined" (EY, p. 245). In another letter, Dorothy more directly confesses her hindrance to her brother. "Here in Germany," she emphasizes, clearly implying a negative contrast to England, where she felt she was always an asset, "a man travelling alone may do very well, but, if his wife or sister goes with him, he must give entertainments" (EY, p. 247). Wordsworth himself complains at one point of being "compelled to be together alone at meal-times &c, &c" (EY, p. 249) and, writing later to Coleridge, reveals a little envy of those "more favored sojourners," obviously

referring to Coleridge and Chester, who are "chattering and chatter'd
to, through the whole day" (*EY*, p. 254). The obvious implication of
these statements is made explicit by Coleridge, who, in writing to
his wife, describes the awkwardness, the seeming impropriety, of
Wordsworth's situation: "His taking his Sister with him was a wrong
Step," he writes; "it is next to impossible for any but married women
or in the suit of married women to be introduced to any company
in Germany. Sister [here] is considered as only a name for Mistress"
(Griggs, I, 459). In short, without Dorothy, Wordsworth would have
been enjoying both favored circumstances and Coleridge's company,
rather than the boredom, melancholy, and pain that were now his
lot, and it seems that they were all aware of it.

This biographical reconstruction does not seek to dismiss Wordsworth's need—indeed his love—for Dorothy. It would be foolish to
deny that Dorothy's love and faultless dedication provided an emotional center to Wordsworth's life during all periods of their relationship. Recollecting her saving grace at Racedown, for example,
Wordsworth writes in *The Prelude*, 1805:

> then it was
> That the belovèd Woman in whose sight
> Those days were pass'd, . . .
> . . . .
> Maintain'd for me a saving intercourse
> With my true self; . . .
> . . . .
> She, in the midst of all, preserv'd me still
> A Poet, made me seek beneath that name
> My office upon earth, and nowhere
>   else, . . .
>   (X:908–21)

Even at Goslar, as contradictory as it may seem, Wordsworth was to
find physical and emotional warmth in Dorothy. Musing on the fate
of a solitary fly in their frigid apartment, Wordsworth contrasts his
circumstances favorably with those of the unfortunate insect, because
of Dorothy's presence:

> No brother, no mate has he near him—while I
> Can draw warmth from the cheek of my Love;
> As blest and as glad, in this desolate gloom,
> As if green summer grass were the floor of my
>   room,
> And woodbines were hanging above.[16]

But these testaments of love and affection surely do not imply that
the relationship of William and Dorothy was exempt from normal
strains. One ought to expect them to tire of each other at times,

especially under such circumstances as they endured at Goslar, where, as Bateson reminds us (*Wordsworth*, p. 149), for the first time in their lives together they were alone for more than six months. If Dorothy's saving grace at Racedown "preserv'd [Wordsworth] still / A Poet," it was yet true that their torpid existence did not inspire much writing; if Wordsworth felt himself "blest and . . . glad, in [the] desolate gloom" at Goslar because of Dorothy's presence, his complaint that they were "compelled to be together alone at mealtimes &c, &c" just as surely indicates that his patience with the monotony of their existence was wearing thin. One hesitates to state that the letters contradict the poetry, because each may represent emotional conditions held simultaneously—that is, both love and the frustration due largely to that love.

Thus, we might expect that Wordsworth struggled to ward off feelings of hostility toward his sister, especially early in his separation from Coleridge, when pangs of separation anxiety would have been acute. Perhaps he attempted to show her more affection in atonement for the amorphous ill will welling within him. But there was no way out: he both needed and resented her, and I think that the Lucy lyrics began to form as an outlet for Wordsworth's ambivalence and frustration.

II

As unpopular as Bateson's incest theory has always been, it has the obvious advantage of bringing theory and fact into harmony: here are love poems aroused by a love that had to be curtailed, only because forbidden in its excess. In contrast, the theory I am proposing may seem untenable because it accounts for these love poems as manifestations of ambivalence. It is not that one would deny the possibility of an ambivalent love; it is rather that these poems have not struck readers as expressions of ambivalence. Surely, this is a serious objection to a literary hypothesis—that generations of sensitive readers have failed to notice something a new reader considers of paramount importance. It is one thing to acknowledge the plausibility of a biographical reconstruction but quite another to relate poems to an emotional milieu that does not seem to be operative in their form and content. Needless to say, healthy skepticism causes one to be wary, but, in the final analysis, the case must rest on the critical enlightenment offered by a hypothesis: How much does it account for? What does it better account for? As I hope to show, the ambivalence theory accounts for many of the crucial issues that have been raised—Lucy's evanescence, her sexlessness and unexplained death, the irony and understatement of the poems—and several issues that have not yet been raised—the peculiar behavior of the lover in

"Strange Fits," the declension of grief in the cycle, and the relationship between biography and composition, especially in accounting for the continuance of the cycle in three phases. A theory promising such interpretive power cannot be ignored.

"Strange Fits of Passion," which was probably the first Lucy poem composed, introduces the radical fantasy of Lucy's death through a psychic event analogous to a nightmare. The schizoid structure of the poem reflects the inherent ambivalence of this mental experience, often referred to, somewhat innocuously, as a premonition. Until the disappearance of the moon in stanza 6 (final text), two lines of each stanza depict the narrator's changing perspective of the moon and two lines indicate either his physical motion, his location, or his progress of mind, with these functional pairs divided by an emphatic stop. This stanzaic discontinuity of narrative pattern makes it structurally possible to interject the poem's reversal and psychologically possible to "slide" the strange "fancy" into the narrator's shifting consciousness, which moves from self, to position, to perspective, to nascent awareness. Following are the final version of the poem and its original text, which appears in the December letter to Coleridge prefaced by Dorothy's comment, "the next poem is a favorite of mine—i.e. of me Dorothy—" (*EY*, p. 237).

1798 Text
(*EY*, pp. 237–38)

1

Once, when my love was strong and gay,
    And like a rose in June,
I to her cottage bent my way,
    Beneath the evening Moon.

2

Upon the moon I fixed my eye
    All over the wide lea:
My horse trudg'd on, and we drew nigh
    Those paths so dear [to] me.

3

And now I've reached the orchard-plot,
    And as we climbed the hill,
Towards the roof of Lucy's cot
    The moon descended still.

4

In one of those sweet dreams I slept,
    Kind nature's gentlest boon,
And all the while my eyes I kept
    On the descending moon.

5

My horse moved on; hoof after hoof
    He raised and never stopped,
When down behind the cottage roof
    At once the planet dropp'd.

6

Strange are the fancies that will slide
    Into a lover's head,
"O mercy" to myself I cried
    "If Lucy should be dead!"

7

I told her this; her laughter light
    Is ringing in my ears;
And when I think upon that night
    My eyes are dim with tears.

Final Text
(PW, II, 29)

Strange Fits of passion have I known:
    And I will dare to tell,
But in the Lover's ear alone,
    What once to me befell.

When she I loved looked every day
    Fresh as a rose in June,
I to her cottage bent my way,
    Beneath an evening-moon.

Upon the moon I fixed my eye,
    All over the wide lea;
With quickening pace my horse drew nigh
    Those paths so dear to me.

And now we reached the orchard-plot;
    And, as we climbed the hill,
The sinking moon to Lucy's cot
    Came near, and nearer still.

In one of those sweet dreams I slept,
    Kind Nature's gentlest boon!
And all the while my eyes I kept
    On the descending moon.

My horse moved on; hoof after hoof
    He raised, and never stopped:
When down behind the cottage roof,
    At once, the bright moon dropped.

> What fond and wayward thoughts will slide
> Into a Lover's head!
> "O Mercy!" to myself I cried,
> "If Lucy should be dead!"

Clearly the poem was esthetically and psychologically sharpened by the revisions made over the course of its textual history. The most significant alteration of the final text is the precise definition of audience we find in the first stanza; the poet will tell his tale "in the lover's ear alone." Presumably, those not under love's sweet spell cannot understand the strange association of the moon's declension with the death of the beloved. Spencer Hall has nicely described the lover as one who "represents a type of specifically and uncompromisingly *human* involvement in the world of process and change" because he "has only one all-too-human being as the object of his passion. That being once dead, his loss is as total as it is definitively human." It is this "fragile kind of humanism" that the figure of the lover suggests, contributing to the poignancy of the Lucy cycle.[17] Another significant alteration is the omission of stanza 7 in the final text. Thematically, it became unnecessary after the other poems of the cycle completed the story, whereas, if "Strange Fits" were the only Lucy poem, the last stanza implying Lucy's death would still be essential to complete the narrative. Psychologically, ending the poem with the premonition arouses anticipation, binding "Strange Fits" to the poems that follow in a strangely causal way. There is the queasy suspicion that the premonition somehow causes Lucy's death, but, again, only those sensitive to love's strange ways would understand. One wonders, however, who, in fact, would be excluded from the select and precisely defined audience of lovers if all who ever dreamed of the death of a loved one were included? The poem is essentially based upon a death dream, and thus its audience is universal, and we, that audience living in the wake of Freudian psychology, can hardly find such experience baffling.

Given the somnambulistic state, the dream, and the sudden eruption of what is analogous to a nightmare, it is hardly possible, in considering Lucy's demise, to ignore the Freudian thesis that dreams are wish-fulfillments. More precisely, in considering the process of mind that culminates in the fantasy of Lucy's death, there are two psychological phenomena that must be considered. One, of course, is the identification of Lucy with the optical illusion of the falling moon. The second phenomenon, the lover's somnambulistic state, has never yet been considered unusual, and yet it is surely no less important than the identification and no less strange than the fit itself. The point is that one does not expect a lover to fall asleep when nearing the dwelling of his beloved. Why does he drift off, instead of becoming increasingly excited at the prospect of seeing Lucy, as one might expect? And how does this behavior lead to the fatal symbol of the moon's declension?

The strangeness of the lover's behavior becomes especially apparent when contrasted with an alternative response to a similar circumstance, such as the following from *Anna Karenina* (trans. Rosemary Edmonds [Harmondsworth, Eng.: Penguin, 1954]), where Tolstoy describes Levin's awakening love for Kitty on the approach to their home: "He rode home thinking only of her, of her love, of his own happiness, and the nearer he came to the house the warmer grew his tenderness for her." According to libido theory, the application of which helps to conceptualize states of love, Levin's arousal is related to the flow of libido outward. Later, his excitation reaches its height in Kitty's presence, where Levin feels that his consciousness has blended with hers: "he was not simply close to her, . . . he could not tell where he ended and she began." By extension of the libido theory, we come to understand that the identification Levin experiences is a dissolution of ego boundaries resulting from a depletion of self-love; all of his libido has been submitted to Kitty, including that normally reserved for the self.

On the other hand, the lover's reaction in "Strange Fits" is separative, owing to an equally unconscious, yet opposite, movement of libido. His welcoming of the state of sleep can be interpreted as a desire to withdraw from Lucy, because sleep is brought on by the withdrawal of libido, or concern, from the external world so that one may rest.[18] Thus, as he nears Lucy's cottage, his libido is returning to the self, with the result that he is unconsciously, but assuredly, increasing his emotional distance from Lucy with each beat of his horse's hoofs. Textual evidence supports this insight as well. In the 1798 text, the narrator comments, "My horse trudg'd on"; in the final text, this belabored movement is amended to read, "With quickening pace my horse drew nigh." But while this emendation may have effaced the semantic indication of the lover's lack of eagerness, ignored was the almost preternatural slowing of time effected by the rhythm of "My horse moved on; hoof after hoof / He raised and never stopped," which even more strongly suggests the lover's reluctance to reach his destination.

In the lover's state of increasing torpor, then, he becomes increasingly vulnerable to the fantasies of the unconscious, and the quiescent withdrawal he seeks to reach through sleep ("Kind Nature's gentlest boon!") is disrupted by the "fit." As Freud once remarked, because we do not expect to wish our loved ones out of existence, the censorship faculty of the mind completely relaxes with respect to such fantasies, and, consequently, the desires of the unconscious are pristinely revealed.[19] With the ego and superego at rest, the

unconscious seizes the moment to reveal its wish for Lucy's death—
of course, much to the lover's shock:

> Strange are the fancies that will slide
> Into a lover's head.
> "O mercy!" to myself I cried,
> "If Lucy should be dead!"

In the unconscious, where wishes are omnipotent, fate is decided by
a suggestion, and, as we know, Lucy soon ceased to be. The final
stanza of the 1798 text implies her death and suggests that the lover's
memory of the premonition occurs with some frequency to renew
his sense of loss, perhaps to atone for his guilt ("And when I think
upon that night / My eyes are dim with tears").

Mary Moorman suggests that "Strange Fits of Passion" is probably
based upon a memory of Racedown,[20] and this may be why it was a
favorite of Dorothy's. "A Night-Piece" corroborates that Wordsworth
and Dorothy were wont to observe the lunar sky closely, and thus
it may not be too speculative to suggest that Wordsworth experienced
something akin to the optical illusion described in "Strange Fits"
and, possibly, discussed its dreaded fantasy with Dorothy. If so, we
are faced with an interesting parallel. We have noted the similar
circumstances of Racedown and Goslar—the boredom, difficulty of
composition, the frustration, and the isolation. It seems now that in
both cases Wordsworth may have held Dorothy responsible for his
plight. In other words, his ambivalence toward her at Goslar was a
recurring feeling and, because the circumstances of Racedown and
Goslar were painfully similar, an experience of Racedown is recalled
at Goslar to effect the same psychic release.

If the expression of his unconscious hostility toward Dorothy in
"Strange Fits" afforded Wordsworth relief from the oppression of
her love, the poet dwelt upon the fantasy of Lucy/Dorothy's death
in succeeding Lucy poems to give full vent to that unconscious
impulse. But this is never a simple matter of opening the mind's
windows for aeration, because, as the abhorrent wish is being gratified
through fantasy, guilt for permitting the fantasy becomes unbearable
unless other mental strategies are simultaneously employed to relieve
the guilt. The role of the mourning lover becomes apparent in this
connection; his grief atones for the poet's guilt. In fact, the lover
persona goes through an entire process of mourning parallel to the
intensity of the poet's desire to be rid of his sister. He mourns most
when the poet's feelings of ambivalence are strongest; his grief dissipates as the poet moves further from his fantasy, until, finally, both
grief and ambivalence are spent in the last poem of the cycle, "I
Travelled among Unknown Men." Allied to this mixed expression of
grief and underlying hostility is an important strategy of denial that

the poet employs to efface Lucy's relationship with Dorothy. As a result, Lucy is virtually absent, physically and mentally, from the poems devoted to her memory.

Guilt, with its attendant grief and denial, is strongest in the Lucy poems of the first phase—in other words, immediately after the fantasy's emergence. "She Dwelt among the Untrodden Ways," which was also transcribed in the mid-December letter to Coleridge, seeks to rid the poet of responsibility for the fantasy of Lucy's death by accounting for her death metaphorically, as a bloom smitten by disease.

1798 Text
(*EY*, pp. 236–37)

1

My hope was one, from cities far,
Nursed on a lonesome heath;
Her lips were red as roses are,
Her hair a woodbine wreath.

2

She lived among the untrodden ways
Beside the springs of Dove,
A maid whom there were none to praise,
And very few to love;

3

A violet by a mossy stone
Half-hidden from the eye!
Fair as a star when only one
Is shining in the sky!

4

And she was graceful as the broom
That flowers by Carron's side;
But slow distemper checked her bloom,
And on the Heath she died.

5

Long time before her head lay low
Dead to the world was she:
But now she's in her grave, and Oh!
The difference to me!

Final Text
(*PW*, II, 30)

She dwelt among the untrodden ways
Beside the springs of Dove,
A Maid whom there were none to praise
And very few to love:

> A violet by a mossy stone
> Half hidden from the eye!
> —Fair as a star, when only one
> Is shining in the sky.
>
> She lived unknown, and few could know
> When Lucy ceased to be;
> But she is in her grave, and, oh,
> The difference to me!

Most conspicuous in the early text is Wordsworth's exaggerated attempt to establish Lucy's metaphorical equivalence to a flower. The rose, the woodbine, the violet, the broom—all compose the bouquet that is Lucy. This plethora of imagery seeks to create a presence where the real object cannot be permitted. In effect, Lucy is a signifier for a signified that cannot be admitted into consciousness; consequently, there is an absence of reality that the poet seeks to fill with the stock of his trade, his figures and myth. One could say that Wordsworth, for once, could not keep his eye on an object of his poetry.[21] Of course, if "Strange Fits" is based on a memory of Racedown, then the poet's consciousness of Lucy as surrogate for Dorothy is certain. But "Strange Fits" is primarily a poem of anticipation. Fulfilling the premonition, in the poems devoted to Lucy's death, required a massive denial of Lucy's relationship to Dorothy, lest Wordsworth have to confront the inevitable question, Why am I writing of my sister's death? And so, at this early stage in the development of the Lucy cycle, we find the poet stumbling, not yet knowing how to develop Lucy or how to account for her demise. Not until the second phase of composition, in the myth of Lucy's osmotic development in "Three Years She Grew in Sun and Shower," will the poet discover how to manage his fantasy so as to represent Lucy suitably as well as to transfer his guilt for her death to an outside agency. In the final text of "She Dwelt," the poet prunes the floral excess wisely, leaving but one floral image to set in equipoise with the stellar image that was overwhelmed in the earlier text:

> A violet by a mossy stone
> Half hidden from the eye!
> —Fair as a star, when only one
> Is shining in the sky.

Lost in the later text is the desire to create a Lucy; here it is sufficient to assume she existed and to capture her unique and solitary beauty with a pair of objective correlatives. Not only does the excision of imagery from the 1798 text purify our vision of the brilliant and delicate images that remain, it also allows the expression of grief to achieve some weight in the poem. Not until the final text do we feel the power of grief in the dramatic understatement, "But now she's in her grave, and Oh! / The difference to me!"

The nature of the lover's grief for Lucy is best explored in "A Slumber Did My Spirit Seal," the last poem of the first phase, where grief is restrained as understatement to such an extreme degree that the poet's motivation becomes suspect. In fact, we grant intense grief to "A Slumber" without the poem's textual support. Once we are aware that Wordsworth was probably composing the Lucy poems out of ambivalence, we have to read "A Slumber" with a more complex set of expectations than usual, because we can no longer assume the poet's unmitigated grief.

"A Slumber" was also included in a letter to Coleridge while the friends were in Germany, but the letter has been lost. The first text of the poem is thus a letter Coleridge sent to Thomas Poole (Griggs, I, 480). Referring to "A Slumber" as a "most sublime Epitaph," Coleridge makes a comment relevant to our discussion: "whether it had any reality, I cannot say.—Most probably, in some gloomier moment he [Wordsworth] had fancied the moment in which his Sister might die" (Griggs, I, 479). The poem begins with the lover's candid admission of naïveté, which recalls several images from "Strange Fits of Passion":

> A Slumber did my spirit seal,
>   I had no human fears:
> She seem'd a Thing, that could not feel
>   The touch of earthly years.

The literal slumber of "Strange Fits" here becomes a symbol of the lover's casualness toward mortality, but the relationship between experience and symbol is suggestively inaccurate. If it was during his hypnagogic state in "Strange Fits" that the lover was exposed to his radical fantasy of Lucy's death, then a slumber did *not* his spirit seal; in fact, a slumber did his spirit release from the bondage of his love. Also, Lucy's early and unexpected death cannot be related to the implication of her aging in the phrase "touch of earthly years." Of course, one could argue that this is a separate poem requiring analysis independent of even related poems; but, within the psychobiographical framework we have established, this poem is linked to the other Lucy poems not only thematically but also emotionally. Consequently, one way of accounting for the apparent inconsistencies between these two poems is to posit an attempt at denial. There is the unconscious need to deny what "Strange Fits" makes the poet responsible for—the fantasy of Lucy's death and, much deeper, the desire for her death. "A Slumber" claims that he was naïve, that he was unconcerned and casual about the mortality of his beloved. But to admit this is to confess to a lesser wrong; it is an evasion. He is guilty of wishing Lucy dead, and she dies by fiat of his premonition in "Strange Fits."

It is the second stanza, however, that more intriguingly displays the complex nature of the poem's emotion:

> No motion has she now, no force;
>   She neither hears nor sees,
> Mov'd° round in Earth's diurnal course
>   With rocks, & stones, and trees!

°*Roll'd* in 1800 text

This statement of bald naturalism is usually read to support the contention of "the unsentimental sources of the grief's extraordinary power."[22] But does not the text really have it two ways? In its absolute avoidance of stated affect, it is shockingly void of natural sentiment. Lucy "seem'd a Thing" in stanza 1, and stanza 2 perceives her as that thing literally become one with "rocks, & stones, and trees!" This perspective would be insufferable were it not that we grant the poet an undue measure of sorrow. The text is clearly naturalistic, while the implied emotion is usually presumed to be greater for being suppressed. The poet cannot lose; he can treat Lucy with guarded hostility and have it interpreted as magnificent management of grief. It must be allowed that, consciously, Wordsworth undoubtedly intended sorrow, just as the reader expects sorrow (and amplifies it when it is not there), but the unconscious, to achieve its purposes, works within the scope of the conscious intention. Through a complex interaction of text with emotion, Wordsworth's intense ambivalence is perfectly expressed and the strategy of grief is consummately managed. The tone of understatement becomes the vehicle of the poet's released hostility.

The Lucy lyrics of the first phase of composition, then, introduce the fantasy of Lucy's death and provide several responses influenced by the causative ambivalence. But, after this initial period of symbolic relief, Wordsworth's hostility declined. The poems arose when antagonism toward Dorothy was acute, because, having just separated from Coleridge, Wordsworth was not yet adjusted to his absence. Wordsworth then settled down to make the best of his situation and to write on his own life. His depression did not wane, nor did his hostility entirely subside, but, in keeping with the psychological mechanics of depressive anxiety, his hostility became inner-directed.[23] The posture of self-reproach manifest in the earliest manuscript of *The Prelude* and also prominent in the two-part *Prelude* (1798–99) is evidence of this inward turning.[24] However, when the prospect of rejoining Coleridge arose at the close of that dreadful winter, Wordsworth returned to the Lucy theme, with new insight but with the same desire to be rid of Dorothy. Again, Wordsworth perceived Dorothy as a ball and chain to his freedom. Dorothy, of course, would not prevent Wordsworth's visit; she also missed Coleridge and wanted to see him. But Dorothy and Wordsworth had been alone for too long not to want a change in companionship, and Wordsworth wanted to be alone with Coleridge. He thus returned to the fantasy of Dorothy's death, but the grief and shock were gone. Lucy was not dying; rather, recalling her death served a purpose. Furthermore, judging from the low-keyed expression of sorrow in the poem, we might conclude that guilt for the fantasy was correspondingly reduced. Wordsworth now had a suitable myth to account for Lucy's development and death, a myth related to the idealized account of his nurturing by a purposeful nature.

In "Three Years She Grew in Sun and Shower," the Lucy poem of the second phase, a causal connection between Lucy's form and development replaces the metaphorical equivalence of "She Dwelt among the Untrodden Ways." If Lucy moves as lightly as the clouds, it is because the "floating clouds their state" have lent her; if she is as lithe as the willow, it is because the willows bend for her and she assimilates their grace. Nature continues describing the osmotic influence he maintains over Lucy's life and, concomitantly, developing the justification for his claim to Lucy:

> Nor shall she fail to see
> Even in the motions of the Storm
> Grace that shall mould the Maiden's form
> By silent sympathy.
>
> "The stars of midnight shall be dear
> To her; and she shall lean her ear
> In many a secret place
> Where rivulets dance their wayward round,
> And beauty born of murmuring sound
> Shall pass into her face.
>
> "And vital feelings of delight
> Shall rear her form to stately height,
> Her virgin bosom swell;
> Such thoughts to Lucy I will give
> While she and I together live
> Here in this happy dell."
>
> (PW, II, 215)

Irene H. Chayes suggests that "Three Years" offers a variation of the Demeter myth, that is, a personified nature claiming a virgin for his own.[25] Undoubtedly, Lucy and nature do resemble figures from classical myth, but it is more likely that both are indigenous to the poetical and psychological milieu of Goslar.

In MS. JJ, Wordsworth seeks to follow the course of his consciousness *ab ovo:*

> was it for this
> That one, the fairest of all rivers, loved
> To blend his murmurs with my nurse's song
> And from his alder shades and rocky falls
> And from his fords and shallows sent a voice
> To intertwine my dreams, for this didst thou
> O Derwent—travelling over the green plains
> Near my sweet birthplace didst thou beauteous
>   stream
> Give ceaseless music to the night & day
> Which with its steady cadence tempering
> Our human waywardness compose[d] my
>   thought
> To more than infant softness giving me
> Amid the fretful tenements of man
> A knowledge, a dim earnest of the calm
> That Nature breathes among her woodland
>   h[aunts?]
>   (MS. JJ, II. 22–36, pp. 123–24)

Wordsworth likewise recalls holding, while still a boy,

> unconscious intercourse
> With the eternal beauty drinking in
> A pure organic pleasure from the lines
> Of curling mist or from the smooth expanse
> Of waters coloured by the cloudless moon.
>   (MS. JJ, II. 147–51, p. 127)

And so it goes throughout the manuscript, the poet emphasizing both the unconscious and conscious influence natural forms held over his early development. The "unconscious intercourse" Lucy holds with the clouds, the springs, and the stars is essentially the same tale, but with one essential difference in MS. JJ and later forms of *The Prelude:* nature is developing the poet's mind, but nature's concern for Lucy is exclusively emotional and physical. External motions will "mould the Maiden's form / By silent sympathy"; "beauty born of murmuring sound" will "pass into her face"; "feelings of delight" will "rear her form to stately height, / Her virgin bosom swell." Her emotional development is equally controlled, as nature makes clear:

> "Myself will to my darling be
> Both law and impulse: and with me
> The Girl, in rock and plain,

> In earth and heaven, in glade and bower,
> Shall feel an overseeing power
> To kindle or restrain.
>
> "She shall be sportive as the fawn
> That wild with glee across the lawn
> Or up the mountain springs;
> And her's shall be the breathing balm,
> And her's the silence and the calm
> Of mute insensate things.

Geoffrey H. Hartman makes the valid point that Lucy "seems to jump over the crisis of self-consciousness . . . by dying into nature,"[26] although it could just as readily be argued that Lucy is devoid of any consciousness at all. She simply has no more mental presence than she has specifically physical presence, and both aspects of her void can be attributed to the function of denial. As a victim of Wordsworth's fantasy about Dorothy, Lucy could not bear any semblance to Dorothy at all; Lucy was never more explicit than Wordsworth could safely manage. In "Three Years She Grew," however, Wordsworth could transfer guilt for wishing her death to the logic of his myth: it was intended that Lucy should die young, just as it was intended that Wordsworth should be a poet; therefore, wishes directed against her could not be at fault. It was not her human lover who was responsible for her death; it was nature. Not unexpectedly, her lover acquiesces, responding to her loss with more nostalgia than sorrow:

> She died, and left to me
> This heath, this calm, and quiet scene;
> The memory of what has been,
> And never more will be.

Although the grief of the early Lucy poems is blended with hostility, it remains intense; after the development of the mythical rationalization for Lucy's death in "Three Years," her death is, as the lover admits, a memory, an acknowledged event, indicating that the crisis of his mourning period has passed.

It probably seemed to Wordsworth that his personal crisis was now at an end as well, for the passing of time not only alleviated his hostility toward Dorothy but also brought him closer to rejoining Coleridge. But there followed an experience with Coleridge that exacerbated Wordsworth's anxiety, eventually leaving him bedridden until Coleridge returned to him at Sockburn-on-Tees. Coleridge had moved to Göttingen and the Wordsworths wasted no time in visiting him. The inevitable topic arose: Would he join them in the North of England after his return? Would he rescue Wordsworth again by reviving the glorious experience of Alfoxden? His answer was no. While separated from both Wordsworth and Poole, Coleridge came to realize that Poole was more essential to his emotional weal.[27] In the following letter to Poole, Coleridge describes the painful encounter with an air of emotional certitude that reduces Wordsworth's reaction to, as Sandor Rado has defined melancholia, "a great despairing cry for love" (Mendelson, p. 115). Coleridge writes:

> Wordsworth & his Sister passed thro' here. . . . I walked on with them 5 english miles, & spent a day with them. They were melancholy & hypp'd—W. was affected to tears at the thought of not being near me, wished me, of course, to live in the North of England. . . . I told him plainly, that *you* had been the man in whom *first* and in whom alone, I had felt an *anchor*! With all my other Connections I felt a dim sense of insecurity & uncertainty, terribly uncomfortable / —W. was affected to tears, very much affected; . . . (Griggs, I, 490–91)[28]

We might imagine Wordsworth's emotions toward Coleridge turning "round / As with the might of waters." The whole winter Wordsworth had been anticipating this moment with the hope that Coleridge would feel equally committed to their living together again. Now it seemed that the dream was dissolved. What had happened to his concern for Wordsworth's poetic greatness? What had happened to his love?

Departing Germany shortly thereafter with the disheartening belief that their friendship with Coleridge was in eclipse, the Wordsworths, penniless and homeless, took up residence with the Hutchinsons at Sockburn-on-Tees in April 1799. The homecoming was not so joyful as it might have been; even the spring's return could not distract Wordsworth from his financial, vocational, domestic, and emotional woes. Richard Wordsworth, the poet's brother, had been left in charge of financial matters, which Wordsworth had hoped would include repayment of a loan he had made to Basil Montagu, but nothing had come of it, as Montagu was still as poor as ever. The Bristol publisher Cottle had ignored Wordsworth's request to transfer his copyright to *Lyrical Ballads* to Wordsworth's former publisher Johnson, so that the edition could have readier access to the London Market. A combined blow to finances and reputation was struck by Southey, who gave *Lyrical Ballads* a mixed review in the *Critical Review* for October 1798. But undoubtedly the most important cause of Wordsworth's tribulation was the Göttingen meeting with Coleridge and Coleridge's subsequent silence. During a period from early May until his return to England in July 1799, Coleridge wrote eight letters, but not one to Wordsworth. In fact, the Wordsworths heard nothing from him until the middle of September and did not see him until the end of October.

A letter Coleridge sent to Wordsworth circa 10 September 1799 provoked an interesting reaction from Wordsworth that indicates how desperately intent Wordsworth was to please him and, in truth, to win him back from Poole. The topic was *The Recluse*, the project that had bound the poets' dreams and aspirations together at Alfoxden. Coleridge writes:

> I am anxiously eager to have you steadily employed on 'The Recluse.' . . . My dear friend, I do entreat you go on with 'The Recluse;' and I wish you would write a poem, in blank verse, addressed to those, who, in consequence of the complete failure of the French Revolution, have thrown up all hopes of the amelioration of mankind, and are sinking into an almost epicurean selfishness, disguising the same under the soft titles of domestic attachment and contempt for visionary *philosophes*. It would do great good, and might form a part of 'The Recluse,' for in my present mood I am wholly against the publication of any small poems. (Griggs, I, 527).

Wordsworth had been working on Part II of the *Prelude*, 1798–99, and, in obedient response to Coleridge's wishes, he translated the gist and even the very words of Coleridge's injunction into the text of his autobiography.[29] At the close of Part II, Wordsworth writes:

> if in these times of fear,
> This melancholy waste of hopes o'erthrown,
> If, 'mid indifference and apathy
> And wicked exultation, when good men
> On every side fall off we know not how
> To selfishness disguised in gentle names
> Of peace, and quiet, and domestic love,
> Yet mingled, not unwillingly, with sneers
> On visionary minds, if in this time
> Of dereliction and dismay I yet
> Despair not of our nature, but retain
> A more than Roman confidence, a faith
> That fails not, in all sorrow my support,
> The blessing of my life, the gift is yours,
> Ye Mountains! thine, O Nature!
> (II. 478–92, p. 66)

Wordsworth also decided to address the poem to Coleridge, and in mid-October Coleridge replied joyfully to his friend's compliment:

> I long to see what you have been doing. O let it be the tail-piece of 'The Recluse!' for of nothing but 'The Recluse' can I hear patiently. That it is to be addressed to me makes me more desirous that it should not be a poem of itself. To be addressed, as a beloved man, by a thinker, at the close of such a poem as 'The Recluse,' . . . is

the only event, . . . capable of inciting in me an hour's vanity—vanity, nay, it is too good a feeling to be so called; it would indeed be a self-elevation produced *ab extra.* (Griggs, I, 538)

Wordsworth's strategy for drawing Coleridge back seemed appropriate, but despite this offering Coleridge still made no move to visit Wordsworth. In the meantime, Wordsworth's frustration was rising, and his health was growing proportionately worse. Dorothy wrote of his being "sadly troubled with a pain in his side" (*EY*, p. 270); the symptoms Wordsworth had described to Coleridge at Goslar were intensifying as his melancholia deepened. At last, in October, Coleridge was sufficiently alarmed by reports of Wordsworth's health to make the trip to Sockburn (Griggs, I, 545). He traveled there with Cottle, who had been meaning to accept Wordsworth's open invitation to visit. They reached Sockburn on 26 October, and the very next day an incredible and revealing event occurred: Wordsworth was suddenly well enough to set out on a walking tour of the Lake Country! It would have been impossible for Cottle not to feel his intrusion on the renewed intimacy of Wordsworth and Coleridge, and within a short while he dropped out of the tour. As Moorman says, "It was a tactful departure. Wordsworth and Coleridge wanted to be by themselves" (*Early Years*, p. 447). Wordsworth's love and health had returned, and the emotional period that had inspired the sublime lyrics of a lover's lost love was over.

III

Wordsworth eventually won the tug of war for Coleridge's presence against Poole, when, after a brief but hectic stint in London as a political journalist for the *Morning Post*, Coleridge felt a need to retire and to begin the great work he had conceived in Germany, his *Life of Lessing*. Although Coleridge had been promising Poole that he would move to Stowey, at last he decided on the North of England because, as he claimed, too many inconveniences at Stowey would interfere with his work. The only houses Poole could find were too small; Mrs. Coleridge's relatives at Bristol would be too close; lately, Poole had turned his head when his brother's widow insulted Mrs. Coleridge; and Poole himself might be leaving Stowey for a year or two to travel about the Continent "in case of a Peace & his Mother's Death." Keswick, on the other hand, offered space, retirement, and beauty that Coleridge never tired of extolling to his correspondents: "The room in which I sit, commands from one window the Basenthwaite Lake, Woods, & Mountains, from the opposite the Derwentwater & fantastic mountains of Borrowdale—straight before me is a wilderness of mountains, catching & streaming lights or shadows at all times . . . (Griggs, I, 609–10). And beyond all of this natural grandeur was the poetic grandeur of Wordsworth.

The period from his settlement at Grasmere in December of 1799 to the composition of "I Travelled among Unknown Men" in April of 1801 was a good one for Wordsworth. A new volume of *Lyrical Ballads* was completed in 1800, the second edition was in the press, and Coleridge was nearby, assiduously promoting him again. It would almost seem a continuation of Alfoxden, but it was not turning out nearly so wonderful. Coleridge was ill much of the time, the dampness of the North seeming to aggravate every weakness in his constitution. Consequently, the friends saw little of each other— once a month, according to Coleridge—and Coleridge's ill health was affecting his position vis-à-vis Wordsworth in a most adverse way. Instead of being the brilliant, inspiring, directive mentor again, himself a poet, Coleridge was, as Poole claimed, in a position of "prostration in regard to Wordsworth" (Griggs, I, 584). Coleridge protested, but Poole was right. At one point in the correspondence, we find Coleridge writing to Godwin that he is unworthy to unloosen the latch of Wordsworth's shoe, and he repeatedly belittles his own genius in writing to friends (Griggs, I, 620, 623, 656, 658). Finally, about a month before the composition of "I Travelled," we have Coleridge writing pathetically to Godwin, "The Poet is dead in me. . . . If I die, and the Booksellers will give you any thing for my Life, be sure to say—'Wordsworth descended on him, like the Γνῶθι σεαυτόν [Know Thyself] from Heaven; by shewing to him what true Poetry was, he made him know, that he himself was no Poet' " (Griggs, II, 714). It was sickness that held Coleridge down, in bed, looking up at Wordsworth, who was finally realizing the potential that Coleridge had anticipated at Alfoxden; but the frustration and self-revulsion provoked in Coleridge by his illness were far more devastating than the pain now wracking his body. It is out of this context of Wordsworth's growing strength and acceptance as a poet and Coleridge's debilitation as a man that the third phase of composition emerges.[30]

In desperation, especially over ill health that blighted the opportunity to achieve, Coleridge began restlessly speculating on locations where he might live cheaply and healthily. The South of France, America, and the Azores are all considered at one time or another in the correspondence as possibilities of escape, and, from the start of even the most casual speculation, Coleridge anticipates Wordsworth's accompaniment. If we now examine the correspondence shortly before the composition of "I Travelled" in April of 1801, we will understand the relationship of the poem to the contemporary situation and to the dismal past of Germany.

On 18 April, the day before the Wordsworths arrived at Keswick for a nine-day visit, at the conclusion of which Wordsworth composed

"I Travelled," Coleridge writes to Poole, despairing of his declining health. Of course, we know that Coleridge lived far beyond this, his twenty-ninth year, but it is important to appreciate that Coleridge felt, probably rightly, that he was close to death:

> I have written a long Letter & said nothing of myself. In simple verity, I am disgusted with that subject. For the last ten days I have kept my Bed, exceedingly ill. I feel and am certain, that 'I to the Grave go down.'—My complaint I can scarcely describe / it is a species of irregular Gout which I have not strength of constitution sufficient to ripen into a fair Paroxysm—it flies about me in unsightly swellings of my knees, & dismal affections of my stomach & head. What I suffer in mere *pain* is almost incredible; but that is a trifle compared with the gloom of my Circumstances.—I feel the transition of the Weather even in my bed—at present, the Disease has seized the whole Region of my Back, so that I scream mechanically on the least motion.—If the fine Weather continue, I shall revive—& look round me—& before the Fall of the Year make up my mind to the important Question—Is it better to die or to quit my native Country, & live among Strangers?—Another Winter in England would *do for me.* (Griggs, II, 721–22)

Within a week after the Wordsworths had departed Keswick, Coleridge was writing wistfully to the chemist Humphry Davy of plans that were apparently discussed during Wordsworth's visit:

> But that this long long Illness has impoverished me, I should immediately go to St Miguel's, one of the Azores—the Baths & the delicious Climate might restore me—and if it were possible, I would afterwards send over for my Wife & children, & settle there for a few years—it being exceedingly cheap.—On this supposition Wordsworth & his Sister have with generous Friendship offered to settle there with me. . . . (Griggs, II, 726)

Clearly, there had been some discussion of leaving England with Coleridge, and Coleridge's detail about Wordsworth's interest in the low cost of living convinces one that the subject of a journey to the Azores was discussed forthrightly. Yet, in their letter to Mary Hutchinson, written immediately after returning from Keswick, the Wordsworths mention nothing of a possible sojourn. In fact, Dorothy simply refers in passing to the necessity of Coleridge's removing himself to "Lisbon in the South of France or at one of the Western Isles," but then the subject is dropped (*EY*, p. 330). Was she not in on the conversation? Wordsworth's portion of the letter leads one to believe that he had discussed such a move with Coleridge, but, if Wordsworth had consented to go along, he was now to renounce his agreement in a most interesting way. Wordsworth writes, "We had a melancholy visit at Coleridges," remarks plaintively, "Adieu," and transcribes "I Travelled among Unknown Men":

> I travell'd among unknown men,
>   In lands beyond the sea;
> Nor, England did I know till then
>   What love I bore to thee.
>
> 'Tis past—that melancholy dream!
>   Nor will I quit thy shore
> A second time; for still I seem
>   To love thee more and more.
>
> Among thy mountains did I feel
>   The gladness of desire
> And she I cherish'd turn'd her wheel
>   Beside an English fire.
>
> Thy mornings show'd, thy nights conceal'd,
>   The bowers where Lucy play'd;
> And thine is too the last green field
>   Which Lucy's eyes survey'd.
>
> (EY, p. 333)

That Wordsworth should return to the Lucy theme after two years, again under a cloud of separation from Coleridge, indicates how closely his feelings at this time were related to those of the Goslar experience. But the poem reveals an important transition toward independence both from the anxiety over the fantasy about Dorothy's death and from the anxiety over losing Coleridge.

The final working out of the death wish is related to the narrator's emission of grief throughout the cycle, which we can now view as comparable to the normal course of emotions in an actual period of bereavement. Grief burns intensely at the onset of loss, wanes with time, lingers as memory, to be finally extinguished when love has been transferred to another. The psychology of mourning defines this process as the effort and achievement of withdrawing libido from the loved one who has died.[31] Applied to our case, Lucy died upon the Wordsworths' arrival at Goslar, and several poems were composed in reaction, just as an actual mourner will begin his recollection of experiences shared with the loved one, for the purpose of withdrawing his love at the behest of reality; Lucy was recalled several months later, just after the Wordsworths departed Goslar to meet with Coleridge, and the decline in the lover's expression of sorrow is evident; finally, Lucy is remembered only to be associated with the narrator's growing love for England two years later, and this indicates that the process of his mourning has been completed and his ego is now free to transfer its love to England, the new object of its choice.

One realizes with some surprise that "I Travelled" contains the strongest expression of love in the entire Lucy cycle, and the love it expresses most strongly is not even for Lucy, but rather for England. The second stanza is notably effective in representing the lover's passionate avowal that he will never quit England's shores again ("for still I seem / To love thee more and more"), its enjambment intensifying the mixture of passion and relief felt upon recalling his emergence from the "melancholy dream" of Goslar and Germany. The central metaphor of the Lucy cycle, the sleep and its dream, now transcends the thematic boundary of the poems to include the circumstances of composition, casting the entire Goslar experience as a distortion of emotional reality. All had been perfect for Wordsworth in his relationships with Dorothy and Coleridge before the three departed for Germany. But then everything fell apart. Coleridge was untrue; Dorothy's presence became unavoidably distressing; and the heightened self-confidence fostered by Coleridge at Alfoxden collapsed. The effect on Wordsworth's consciousness was strange and unmanageable, like the progression of a dream; Dorothy became victimized.

But now they were back, located in the landscape Wordsworth rediscovered at Goslar as the one secure attachment of his life, and, though it had taken a while, life had reassembled itself satisfactorily. Coleridge had returned to him, and Dorothy became valued again. The fact that Lucy finally appears in one of her poems in human form—"And she I cherished turned her wheel / Beside an English fire"—indicates that the death fantasy about Dorothy had spent itself; thus, denial was no longer necessary. But still there had been a change, as "I Travelled" implies in its transferral of love from Lucy to England. The certain firmness of England's soil and the abiding associations related to his life there, in other words, the matter of the two-part *Prelude*, 1798–99, Wordsworth now held dearer than his closest human relationships, fraught with all their vicissitudes. Not that Wordsworth would break relationships with loved ones; rather, he would now subordinate them to place and nature. Wordsworth had learned that place is the catalyst to love and relationship; thus, he could not follow Coleridge again, although he recognized that something must be done for him.[32] It did matter that Lucy sat beside an *English* fire, and, through the composition of the Lucy cycle, Wordsworth came to understand that it was wiser, safer, necessary, and certainly more comfortable to remain with her there.

Notes

1. As early as 1934 the list of possible originals for Lucy had grown embarrassingly large; she had been identified as Dorothy, Mary Hutchinson (Wordsworth's future wife), Annette Vallon (Wordsworth's estranged lover), some ideal maiden, an adopted

gypsy child, an early love, Hartley Coleridge, and a conventionalized heroine arising from the poet's experiments with popular ballads. See Herbert Hartman, "Wordsworth's Lucy Poems," *PMLA*, 49 (1934), 134–42, for a fuller accounting.

2. Geoffrey Durrant, *William Wordsworth* (London: Cambridge Univ. Press, 1969), p. 60.

3. *Wordsworth: A Re-Interpretation* (London: Longmans, Green, 1954), pp. 151–54.

4. In " 'That Melancholy Dream': Wordsworth's Goslar Experience and Poetry" (Diss., Indiana Univ. 1976), I analyze the Matthew poems, the Lucy poems, and the two-part *Prelude* (1798–99) in the light of the psychobiographical context offered here.

5. I am primarily dependent upon Mark L. Reed, *Wordsworth: The Chronology of the Early Years 1770–1799* (Cambridge: Harvard Univ. Press, 1967), and *Wordsworth: The Chronology of the Middle Years 1800–1815* (Cambridge: Harvard Univ. Press, 1975), for the dating of the Lucy lyrics.

6. *The Letters of William and Dorothy Wordsworth, I, The Early Years, 1787–1805*, ed. Ernest de Selincourt, 2nd ed., rev. Chester L. Shaver (Oxford: Clarendon, 1967), p. 236. Hereafter cited as *EY*. The relationship of Wordsworth's health to his composing is a matter still requiring investigation. Violent headaches and pain in the side troubled Wordsworth at least from his college days (*EY*, p. 7), but it is not until Goslar that the Wordsworths write of the pain attendant upon composition. Later we learn that Wordsworth's pain was most severe when revising, rather than when composing anew (*EY*, p. 332). At one point, Dorothy writes that "we have put aside all the manuscript poems and it is agreed between us that I am not to give them up to him even if he asks for them" (*EY*, p. 335). At Goslar, of course, it was new composition that was affecting Wordsworth, and the passage discussed in the text is the most explicit and detailed description we have of Wordsworth's psychosomatic distress. In arguing for the influence of Coleridge, or rather Coleridge's absence, on Wordsworth's emotional and physical condition at Goslar, it is relevant to note that this particular bout with anxiety and ill health was foreshadowed at Alfoxden between late February and early March, just about the time the Wordsworths learned that they might have to part with Coleridge because of their losing the lease on Alfoxden and because of the unlikelihood that they would be granted another, due to their great unpopularity in the neighborhood. Dorothy writes: "It is decided that we quit Allfoxden—The house is lett. It is most probable that we shall go back again to Racedown, as there is little chance of our getting a place in this neighbourhood. We have no other very strong inducement to stay but Coleridge's society, but that is so important an object that we have it much at heart. . . . William was very unwell last week, oppressed with languor, and weakness. He is better now" (*EY*, pp. 199–200). Wordsworth's recovery was probably due to the fact that Poole, the day preceding this letter, gave the Wordsworths "great hopes that we shall get a very pleasant house a quarter of a mile from [Alfoxden] with furniture &c" (*EY*, p. 209); but then plans for the German venture intervened, and Poole's action on Wordsworth's behalf was most likely discontinued.

7. Meyer Mendelson, M.D., *Psychoanalytic Concepts of Depression*, 2nd ed. (New York: Spectrum, 1974), esp. pp. 95–100.

8. *The Prelude: Or, Growth of a Poet's Mind*, ed. Ernest de Selincourt, 2nd ed., rev. Helen Darbishire (Oxford: Clarendon, 1959), 1805 text, XIII:391–410.

9. *Wordsworth: The Construction of a Personality* (Kent, Ohio: Kent State Univ. Press, 1968), pp. 27, 37–39.

10. *Collected Letters of Samuel Taylor Coleridge*, ed. Earl Leslie Griggs (Oxford: Clarendon, 1956–71), I, 334. Hereafter cited as Griggs.

11. *Coleridge* (1968; New York: Collier Books, 1973), pp. 87–88.

12. *The Notebooks of Samuel Taylor Coleridge,* ed. Kathleen Coburn (New York: Pantheon, 1957–), I, 344. Hereafter cited in the text as *STCNB.*

13. Hardly a day went by without Dorothy recording in her journal that one of the party had been cheated or harassed by German shopkeepers, innkeepers, and even porters. See *Journals of Dorothy Wordsworth,* ed. Ernest de Salincourt (New York: Macmillan, 1941), I, 26–28.

14. In the period October 1798–April 1799, Wordsworth drew on Wedgwood for £110/13/-. See Reed, *Chronology of the Early Years,* p. 266, No. 25. In a letter to Wedgwood dated 21 May 1799, Coleridge estimates that he will have drawn on Wedgwood for £103 for Göttingen bills, transportation, etc., through May 1799 (Griggs, I, 519).

15. Wordsworth to Josiah Wedgwood:

[Goslar] was once the residence of Emperors, and it is now the residence of Grocers and Linen-drapers who are, I say it with a feeling of sorrow, a wretched race; the flesh, blood, and bone of their minds being nothing but knavery and low falshood [sic]. We have met with one dear and kind creature, but he is so miserably deaf that we could only play with him games of cross-purposes, and he likewise labours under a common German infirmity, the loss of teeth, so that with bad German, bad English, bad French, bad hearing, and bad utterance you will imagine we have had very pretty dialogues. . . . (*EY,* p. 249)

Coleridge to Thomas Poole:

Every one pays me the most assiduous attentions—I have attended some Conversations at the Houses of the Nobility—stupid things enough.—It was quite a new thing to me to have Counts & Land-dr[osten] bowing & scraping to me—& Countesses, old & young, complimenting & amusing me.—But to be an Englishman is in Germany to be an Angel—they almost worship you. (Griggs, I, 435)

16. From "Written in Germany," *The Poetical Works of William Wordsworth,* ed. Ernest de Selincourt and Helen Darbishire (Oxford: Clarendon, 1940–49), IV, 65. Hereafter cited as *PW.*

17. "Wordsworth's 'Lucy' Poems: Context and Meaning," *Studies in Romanticism,* 10 (1971), 160–61.

18. *The Standard Edition of the Complete Psychological Works of Sigmund Freud,* ed. James Strachey (London: Hogarth Press, 1953–), XVI, 417. Hereafter cited as *CPW.*

19. See "Dreams of the Death of Persons of Whom the Dreamer Is Fond," *CPW,* IV, 248–71, p. 250–55, where Freud considers dreams of the death of brothers and sisters.

20. *William Wordsworth: A Biography: The Early Years, 1770–1803* (1957: London: Oxford Univ. Press, 1968), p. 423. Hereafter cited as *Early Years.*

21. "I do not know how without being culpably particular I can give my Reader a more exact notion of the style in which I wished these poems to be written than by informing him that I have at all times endeavoured to look steadily at my subject, . . ." Preface to *Lyrical Ballads, with Other Poems (1800),* in *Literary Criticism of William Wordsworth,* ed. Paul M. Zall (Lincoln: Univ. of Nebraska Press, 1966), p. 22.

22. David Ferry, *The Limits of Mortality* (Middletown, Conn.: Wesleyan Univ. Press, 1959), p. 77.

23. In "Mourning and Melancholia," Freud identifies self-reproach as depression's distinguishing symptom (*CPW*, XIV, 244).

24. In MS. JJ, the earliest manuscript of *The Prelude*, composed at Goslar, Wordsworth repeatedly poses the question, "Was it for this . . .," i.e., for wasting my time and talent at Goslar, that nature fostered my development with a watchful eye? And in MS. JJ and subsequent forms of the first book of *The Prelude*, Wordsworth casts the shadow of reproach over his entire childhood. The sounds of "undistinguishable motion" that pursued him through the dark wood after his poaching escapades, the cliff that rose monstrously above him in the stolen boat on Ullswater Lake, even his kite rebuffed by the storm—all emphasize a guilt-oriented relationship with the world. The guilt reaches its thematic and formal climax in the two-part *Prelude*, Pt. I, in Wordsworth's presentation of his father's death as a punishment from God, which, he says, "appeared / A chastisement" for certain unstated desires (*The Prelude, 1798–1799, by William Wordsworth*, ed. Stephen Parrish [Ithaca, N.Y.: Cornell Univ. Press, 1977], p. 51). It can be argued then that the self-reproach we find as such a strong thematic influence in Wordsworth's recounting of his early life and as such a forceful spur to his present inertia (*The Prelude*, 1798–99, I:450–53) is related to his melancholic depression at Goslar. All references to MS. JJ and to *The Prelude*, 1798–99, are taken from the edition by Parrish cited in this note.

25. "Little Girls Lost: Problems of a Romantic Archetype," *Bulletin of the New York Public Library*, 67 (1963), 579–92; rpt. in *Blake: A Collection of Critical Essays*, ed. Northrop Frye (Englewood Cliffs, N.J.: Prentice-Hall, 1966), p. 76.

26. *Wordsworth's Poetry, 1787–1814* (New Haven, Conn: Yale Univ. Press, 1964), p. 158.

27. Coleridge's love for Poole makes his feelings for Wordsworth seem pale in contrast, as we see in these tender testaments of his love. Before leaving for Germany, Coleridge writes to Poole: "I am on the point of leaving my native country for the first time—a country, which, God Almighty knows, is dear to me above all things for the love I bear to you.—Of many friends, whom I love and esteem, my head & heart have ever chosen you as the Friend—as the one being, in whom is involved the full & whole meaning of that sacred Title" (Griggs, I, 415). After departing England, Coleridge writes again: "The Ocean is between us & I feel how much I love you! . . . Go to my house and kiss my dear babies for me—my Friend, my best Friend, my Brother, my Beloved—the tears run down my face—God love you" (Griggs, I, 418, 420). After a month on foreign soil, Coleridge finds it impossible to control his emotions when writing to his "best and dearest Friend": "My spirit is more feminine than your's—I cannot write to you without tears / and I know that when you read my letters, and when you talk of me, *you* must often 'compound with misty eyes'—" (Griggs, I, 430). By the following springtime, Coleridge is overwhelmed with the desire to see Poole again: "O my God! how I long to be at home—My *whole Being* so yearns after you, that when I think of the moment of our meeting, I catch the fashion of German Joy, rush into your arms, and embrace you. . . . Now the Spring comes, the vital sap of my affections rises, as in a tree!" (Griggs, I, 490).

28. Clement Carylon, an English medical student at Göttingen during Coleridge's residence there, provides an interesting comment on Wordsworth's visit to Coleridge: "Soon after Coleridge's arrival at Göttingen, Mr. Wordsworth and his sister came from Goslar to pay him a visit, and I have been informed, by one well acquainted with the fact, that the two philosophers rambled away together for a day or two (leaving Miss Wordsworth at Göttingen)" (quoted in George McLean Harper, *William Wordsworth: His Life, Works, and Influence*, 2nd ed. [New York: Scribners, 1923], I, 370, from Carylon's *Early Years and Late Reflections*). Although neither the Wordsworths nor Coleridge mentions such an excursion, it does seem plausible in the light of the theory of Dorothy's unwanted presence offered in this article.

29. Noted by Sybil Shepard Eakin, "The Composition of *The Prelude* 1794–1804: A Critical History," Diss. Harvard, 1972, p. 96.

30. Coleridge's addiction to opium probably begins at this time as well. See Bate, *Coleridge*, p. 101.

31. It almost sounds too mechanical, but surely it is metaphorically sound, to depict this process as Freud does: "Each single one of the memories and expectations in which the libido is bound to the object is brought up and hyper-cathected, and detachment of the libido is accomplished in respect of it. Why this compromise by which the command of reality is carried out piecemeal should be so extraordinarily painful is not at all easy to explain in terms of economics. It is remarkable that this painful unpleasure is taken as a matter of course by us. The fact is, however, that when the work of mourning is completed the ego becomes free and uninhibited again" (*CPW, XIV, 245*).

32. Wordsworth wrote to Poole on Coleridge's behalf, requesting that he lend Coleridge the amount necessary for the Azores trip, at least £50, "unshackled by any conditions, but that he should repay it when he shall be able." Wordsworth then continues with an entreaty that one would think would be unnecessary among friends. "If he dies, if he should be unwilling that any debt of his should devolve on his Brothers," Wordsworth writes, "then let the debt be cancelled" (*EY*, p. 340). Perhaps still smarting from Coleridge's rejection of Stowey and his company, Poole replied, to Coleridge rather than to Wordsworth, that he could not lend any more than £20, that Coleridge might ask his brothers for assistance, and then—the coup de grace— that the £37 that Coleridge supposed he owed him in his last letter was in error; it was actually £52 (Griggs, II, 755, headnote).

William Wordsworth: "Relationship and Love"   Jean H. Hagstrum[*]

To be at one with the otherness of nature is the arching complement to that other impulse, to be at one with the otherness of people. The erotic life of nature, like that of other people, is both warming and chastening to contemplate.

—Christopher Ricks, *Keats and Embarrassment* (1974), 210

The poet, trusting to primary instincts, luxuriates among the felicities of love and wine, . . . nor does he shrink from the company of the passion of love though immoderate—.

—Wordsworth, "A Letter to a Friend of Robert Burns" (1816),
Prose, III, 124

> From love, for here
> Do we begin and end, all grandeur comes,
> All truth and beauty—from pervading love—
> That gone, we are as dust.
> —Wordsworth, *The Prelude* (1805), XIII: 149–52

Having proclaimed in the *Prelude* of 1805 that love was the Alpha and Omega of his song and the source of all value in life, Wordsworth proceeds to distinguish its four kinds. The first, the organic vitality of all nature, manifested especially in the spring season, is followed by the heart-touching, "tender ways" of the "lamb / And the lamb's mother" (*Prel.*, 1805: XIII: 154–56, *Prel.*, 466).[1] Since the poet is erecting a scale of ascending values, even higher is the "green bower" of uxorial happiness, where with the "one who is [our] choice of all the world" we "linger, lulled, and lost, and rapt away" (lines 156–60)—words surely bearing considerable sexual meaning. But highest of all is "a love that comes into the heart / With awe and a diffusive sentiment" (lines 162–63). This highest love, about which Wordsworth can be eloquent but certainly can also be prolix and vague, is not my essential theme. I shall be concerned rather with the human bower of love where man is "not alone" (line 157) but can be "lulled, and lost, and rapt away."

Why should so many of Wordsworth's commentators have failed to see such a central pre-occupation of the poet's best work? Hazlitt said, "One would suppose, from the tenor of his subjects, that on this earth there was neither marrying nor giving in marriage," and M. H. Abrams, who more luminously than any one else, has displayed the image of passionate marriage that is at the heart of the poet's high argument, nevertheless calls him an "ascetic" poet.[2] Dr. Leavis has observed that "sex . . . is virtually absent from Wordsworth's poetry,"[3] and Carl Woodring thinks that "sexual passion has little space in his poetic canon; it is observed at some distance . . . it receives no open tribute."[4] The weight of such authority is heavy, and it does indeed make it impossible to assert that Wordsworth was overtly, directly, or continuously a sexual poet.

WORDSWORTH THE MAN AND LITERARY THEORY

> Is not the co-adunation of Feeling & Sensation the specific character of the sexual Pleasure: and that which renders this particular mode of bodily intercourse the apt outward Sign, Symbol & sensuous Language of the union desired & commenced by the Souls of sincere Lovers?—
> —Coleridge, *Notebooks*, no. 3605, *f* 118

That the greatest of the Romantic poets was in fact sometimes a highly obsessed and more frequently a highly successful poet of physically based love, it is the purpose of this chapter to assert, and I am curious as to why the opinions cited above have become so pervasive, though they are by no means unanimous. They may go back to Shelley in this sense, that Wordsworth in personal manner and often in literary style seems to invite the charge that he was "a solemn and unsexual man," "a kind of moral eunuch," who "touched the hem of Nature's shift, / Felt faint—and never dared uplift / The closest, all-concealing tunic."[5] No one but an unsympathetic satirist would have imagined Wordsworth engaged in so unseemly an act as Shelley describes, though, with considerable help from Wordsworth himself, we are tempted to be impish in some such way. Yet it is only fair to say that the few who knew him best in the days of his vigor as man and artist ever conceived of him as a male prude. That shrewd man of the world, Samuel Rogers, a writer not given to overstatement, remarked, "Few men knew *how* Wordsworth loves his friends"[6]—the word *much* being clearly implied after *how*. Dorothy his sister was one of the few who knew, and she said that he had "a sort of violence of Affections . . . which demonstrates itself every moment of the Day when the objects of his affection are present with him" (*Letters Early*, 83). Coleridge said that "Wordsworth has the least femineity in his mind. He is *all* man"[7]—a virility his tortured friend was capable of envying, sometimes morbidly and mischievously. And De Quincey, who deplored the absence of sexuality from the poetry, thus described the poet's face, traditionally considered the *index mentis*.

> The nose, a little arched, and large; which, by the way . . . has always been accounted an unequivocal expression of animal appetites organically strong. And that expressed the simple truth: Wordsworth's intellectual passions were fervent and strong: but they rested upon a basis of preternatural animal sensibility diffused through *all* the animal passions (or appetites); and something of that will be found to hold of all poets who have been great by original force and power. . . .[8]

De Quincey's last generalization may be as suspect as his "science" of physiognomy; but this is a verbal portrait drawn from the first-hand observation of a skillful writer, and its bluff and honest perception of sensuality must be trusted.

The strong animal appetites De Quincey saw mirrored in the poet's face are of course a natural endowment, and nature, traditionally thought to be Wordsworth's supreme subject, can scarcely be thought of as in itself ascetic or puritanical. But the most influential Wordsworthian critic of our day, Geoffrey Hartman, believes that Nature herself "weans" the poet's mind from "its early dependence on immediate sensuous stimuli," converting "the immediate or external into the quietly mediate, which then unfolds a new, less exhaustible source of life."[9] It is the central view of this book, particularly of this chapter, that natural and bodily energy inspires and shapes the poetry of both tender familial affection and transcendental vision and that when it does not, the reason is not that nature is *exhaustible* but that the poet is *exhausted*. Wordsworth's own criticism, I believe, refutes Professor Hartman's thesis. If we consider carefully the famous statement, in the 1800 Preface to *Lyrical Ballads*, that poetry presents "emotion recollected in tranquility," we discover that what happens as we keep on recalling the original experience is not that the emotion but that the tranquility disappears and that an emotion kindred to the original stimulus "does itself actually exist in the mind" (*Prose*, I, 148).

Wordsworth's discursive writings on society and literature reveal the persisting presence not only of nature broadly conceived but of specifically sexual nature. His political philosophy, even as his conservatism grew upon him, rested firmly on the notion that the nation is, as he says in *The Convention of Cintra* of 1809, "a machine, or a vital organized body" (*Prose*, I, 225)—we shall later observe that in an important poem he calls his wife's attractive body a "machine" in this sense. The philosophy of society also rests on a belief in "the efficacy of principles and *passions* which are the *natural* birth-right of man" (*Prose*, I, 303, emphasis added). By passions Wordsworth says he means "the soul of sensibility in the heart of man," and he insists that such sensibility respects "the dignity and intensity of human desires" (*Prose*, I, 339). Both the dignity and the intensity— and we must take careful note of the point being made if we are to understand Wordsworthian transcendence—include the very lowest of the passions: "The higher mode of being does not exclude, but necessarily includes, the lower; the intellectual does not exclude, but necessarily includes, the sentient; the sentient, the animal; and the animal, the vital—to its lowest degrees" (*Prose*, I, 340). The lowest rung of this gradation we might call, in the words of "I grievéd for Buonaparté," "the stalk / True Power doth grow on" (*PW*, III, 111).

Such a continuum is even more necessary to literary criticism, as we see in the famous Preface to *Lyrical Ballads* (1800), where the metaphors of the aroused senses keep animating the more abstract logocentrism. The real language of men is most available to poetry when it is in "a state of vivid *sensation*" (*Prose*, I, 118). The thinker-poet also possesses "a more than usual *organic* sensibility" (126). We associate ideas in "a state of *excitement*" (122, 124), and "the end of Poetry is to produce excitement in coexistence with an overbalance of *pleasure*" (146). The literary virtue called *pathos*, which goes back at least as far as Aristotle, Wordsworth brings into vital conjunction with his own comprehensive and realistic view of the animated world:

our passions are "connected" with both "our moral feelings and *animal* sensations" (142), and "the pathetic participates of an *animal* sensation" (1815: *Prose*, III, 82). Can there be any doubt, if we concede power as well as meaning to discursive language, that the critic has actual human sexuality in mind and not merely the sense-data basic to empirical or associative psychology—a much-studied subject? Wordsworth himself seems to dispel doubt when he confronts "the pleasure which the mind derives from the perception of simi-litude in dissimilitude." He says:

> From this principle the direction of the *sexual* appetite, and all the *passions* connected with it take their origin: It is the life of our ordinary conversation; and upon the accuracy with which similitude in dissimilitude, and dissimilitude in similitude are perceived, depend our taste and our moral feelings. (*Prose*, I, 148: here and above, emphasis added)

This is the same continuum, including the lower appetites, that we observed as being functional in the political writings. Here the "accuracy" for which the critic pleads forces us to note that sexual appetites, however basic, are not themselves primary. What then is? Clearly, human differentiation, specifically sexual dissimilitude. This fact, as we have said earlier, clearly distinguishes Wordsworth, in theory at least, not from Coleridge and Keats but certainly from the pre-Romantic and Romantic love of delicate and only slightly differ-entiated bodies revealed in Canova's *Cupid and Psyche* and in Shelley's *The Witch of Atlas*, with its Hermaphroditus. Wordsworth may indeed be closely related to the earlier and more robust eighteenth-century traditions, expressed briefly and pungently by one of its leading medical men, George Cheyne, who in *An Essay of Health and Long Life* expressed the view that poets, writers, and artists—that *genus irritabile vatum*—possess livelier sensations than most and "generally excel in the *Animal* Faculty of Imagination."[10]

To see the source of the pervasive pleasure Wordsworth finds in sexual differentiation and attraction does not, however, do full justice to what he is claiming here in these enlarging utterances. On one level he is asserting the importance of what Dylan Thomas called "the force that through the green fuse drives the flower"—a sexual force that pulsates in nature as energy and that continues to structure mental reality once the energetically sensuous details have become imaginative. But we must also see what the presence of sexuality has to do with the end-product itself, for Wordsworth is here speaking as a critic of poetry. If we translate Wordsworth's concern with difference in similarity and its obverse back to the ancient Latin formulae, *concordia discors* and *discordia concors*, and if we remember Samuel Johnson's brilliant uses of these terms,[11] it becomes clear that

Wordsworth is relating the union of sexual opposites in love to metaphor, simile, allegory, symbol, and variants of these—to the *wit* of good conversation and to the tropic structures of good literary ordering. Wordsworth, like Johnson before him, is transferring the ancient oxymorons, originally applied to the ultimately unifying struggles of love and chaos in the creation of nature, to the antithetical unions of wit and the imagination. We should note the impressive fact that Coleridge, who made the fusion of opposites the very essence of symbol, used that typically uncouth verbal construction of his, *coadunation*, for both the metaphoric structures of language and the union of "Feeling & Sensation" in "sexual Pleasure" (*Notebooks*, no. 3605, f118). Here I emphasize the unmistakably sexual parallel to the purely imaginative fusion:

> I cannot conceive of any thing more lovely, more divine, more deserving of our admiration, than that identification or co-adunation of the two lovers, Amatus Amata, in which each retains its individualizing contra-distinguishing qualities, and yet *eminenter*, in a certain transcendent mode, acquires the virtues of the other—the rich tenderness, the woman elevation &c—the Sublime & the Beautiful—.
>
> (*Notebooks*, no. 4158)

Wordsworth, as we shall see at the very end of this chapter, was not comfortable with such Coleridgean fusion at its most transcendental, but his criticism shows him to be fully committed to a deep coincidence between sexual union and the creative reconciliations of imagination and art.

Sexuality is deeply pervasive in the thought of Wordsworth and his circle. What about his life and poetic practice?

ANNETTE VALLON: WORDSWORTH'S "DELIRIOUS HOUR"

> Farewell! those forms that, in thy noon-tide shade,
> Rest, near their little plots of wheaten glade;
> Those stedfast eyes, that beating breasts inspire
> To throw the "sultry ray" of young Desire;
> Those lips, whose tides of fragrance come, and go,
> Accordant to the cheek's unquiet glow;
> Those shadowy breasts in love's soft light array'd,
> And rising, by the moon of passion sway'd.
> —Thy fragrant gales and lute-resounding streams,
> Breathe o'er the failing soul voluptuous dreams.
> —Wordsworth, *Descriptive Sketches* (1793),
> lines 149–57, *PW*, I, 50, 52

Tell all the Truth but tell it slant—
Success in Circuit lies.
—Emily Dickinson, *Complete Poems* (1963), no. 1129

What if we do discover that the greatness of poetry is grounded in animal passions? What if we do discover that the basis of all art is a certain measure of sensuality?
—Herbert Read, *Wordsworth* (1930), 17

The ideas to be discussed in the remainder of this chapter are grouped around the three women in Wordsworth's life, his French mistress, his English wife, and his sister; but no one should conclude from this arrangement that I assume a simple equation between the life and the poetry. We shall soon see how complex that relationship is, how deeply sexuality can sometimes be buried, how skillfully disguised: as Herbert Read has said of Wordsworth, "By apostrophizing the mind, he hoped to conceal the significance of the body."[12] The very complexities make it even more necessary for the critic to respect the ultimate source of Wordsworth's inspiration in nature and self and to disclose the currents flowing from the poet to his poetry.

In Wordsworth's poetic beginnings he sometimes strikingly anticipates himself and so reveals the essential integrity of his being. His early and energetic verses in *An Evening Walk*, published in 1793, about the rooster, in which I sense an undertow of sexuality, could be seen as a foreshadowing of Wordsworth in his own ménage with Dorothy, Mary, Sara:

> Sweetly ferocious, round his native walks,
> Gaz'd by his sister-wives, the monarch stalks; . . .
> Bright sparks his black and haggard eyeball hurls
> Afar, his tail he closes and unfurls.
> (lines 129–30, 133–34, *PW*, I, 16)

Sometimes early Wordsworth even anticipates the voluptuousness of early Keats: "Beating breasts" inspire the " 'sultry ray' of young Desire"—

> Those shadowy breasts in love's soft light array'd,
> And rising, by the moon of passion sway'd.
> (*Descriptive Sketches*, 1793, lines 154–55, *PW*, I, 50)

Wordsworth's walking tour of Switzerland in 1790 inspired these verses, but he actually wrote them in 1792, perhaps not much before his departure for England after his affair with Annette Vallon and some months before the birth of his natural daughter, Caroline. He was then in the firm grip of revolutionary sympathy, and, as was true of so many others in this period, political passion was accompanied by sexual ardor. Indeed, the late F. W. Bateson believed that "Words-worth would probably not have become an active political revolutionary, if the barriers of his passivity had not been previously overthrown by sexual passion. Beaupuy [the young French officer who had guided Wordsworth into radical thought] was only an effect, the cause was Annette."[13]

The love of the French girl, four years his senior (he being twenty-one), was known to Wordsworth's sister, wife, family—to his most intimate circle, where it caused neither grief nor jealousy, though it was buried by his heirs deep in family secrecy until twentieth-century scholarship disclosed it. The facts are now well known and need not be rehearsed here, but a few summary observations need to be made to younger students of the poetry. The passion between the young lovers was strong and the desertion of the mother and child (owing to the outbreak of a long war) constituted a deep ravage of the poet's heart, from which, however, he recovered without becoming embittered or morbid about sexual experience.

It is undoubtedly true, as Emile Legouis saw, that Wordsworth's distress over leaving a mother and his own child in revolutionary, war-torn France, now an enemy state, bore poetic fruit in the many "affecting stories of seduced maidens, forsaken wives, or simply of wretched women whose lives have been wrecked by the war."[14] Every now and then in the later poetry, even as late as Book VIII of the 1805 *Prelude*, there remain pathetic moments that seem to recall desertion, with the details of course altered. For example, a lone man comes out with a child to enjoy the sun and air; but then, as if to shield the child from these very elements, he bends over it: "He eyed it with unutterable love" (line 859, *Prel.*, 310). Does Caroline lurk behind the deeply loved child or Wordsworth's own paternal feeling behind the "unutterable love" the man is thought to display? But we are chiefly concerned with love between the sexes, not so much with the general psychological crisis that certainly affected the poetry of 1797 and 1798 and even later; and we must therefore inquire further into the poet's literary response to the passion that produced the child.

Much of that was buried on the Salisbury Plain, a wild and haunted setting. The poem, first named after the place and much later given the title *Guilt and Sorrow* (the title words must epitomize Wordsworth's own post-Annette melancholy), exists in three versions. The first (dating from 1793–94), within a year or so of his French experience, describes a Female Vagrant before she tells her sad story of desertion by her husband. (The true setting, is, I believe, France, but the poet sets the scene on Derwent water, psychologically as well as physically a place much nearer to his own heart):

> Like swans, twin swans, that when on the sweet brink
> Of Derwent's stream the south winds hardly blow,
> 'Mid Derwent's water-lillies swell and sink
> In union rose her sister breasts of snow,
> (Fair emblem of two lovers' hearts that know
> No separate impulse).
> > (lines 208–13, *Salisbury Plain*, 27–28)

The breasts here are sexually alluring,[15] but they are not always so in Wordsworth, who in the intense, almost hysterical cries of "Her eyes are wild," has a mad girl say of her own abandoned breasts that they are now fiercely sucked by a hungry child as "fiendish faces, one, two, three, / Hung at my breast and pulled at me" (*PW*, II, 108). But on Derwent water we have only the sweet sexual rise and fall of snowy breasts, those Keatsian delights, showing the wide range of his response to sexuality in this period. Even here, however, the sensual delights are followed by despair at the fleeting quality of love:

> And are ye spread ye glittering dews of youth
> For this,—that Frost may gall the tender flower
> In Joy's fair breast with more untimely tooth?
> > (lines 217–19, *Salisbury Plain*, 28)

Finally Wordsworth turns to the plangent tale of the Vagrant's miserable life, heart-rending in its pathos.

Paradoxically, the passion in France that led to the sadness and pain associated with the Salisbury Plain had to await for more direct poetic telling until the Ninth Book of the 1805 *Prelude*, where in the relative calm of distance the "tragic tale" of Vaudracour and Julia, which Wordsworth heard in France, both resurrects and veils the story of Wordsworth and Annette. With some justification, though with considerable exaggeration, Matthew Arnold called this the very worst of Wordsworth's poetry. The story is indeed ineptly told and the plot is insufficiently motivated, but it has two moments worth observing by students of Wordsworthian love, one of grim intensity and one analytical of the very climax of the passion, of what Wordsworth calls the "delirious hour." As the story concludes—to confront the grimness first—Vaudracour ceases to be a manly, mature, hopeful lover and regresses to childhood. Julia thus has in effect two children, the infant offspring of the passion and the paternal wreck of that same passion. At one breast the child is suckled, while upon the other rests the "pale and melancholy face" (line 812, *Prel.*, 352) of the father. Whatever the causes in real life of the once passionate Vaudracour's regression to helpless abjectness—a hostile father, a hostile society, sexual guilt—Wordsworth's treatment of it could scarcely be less Keatsian; indeed, the scene could be viewed as a parody of "Bright Star," as a hideous inversion of dreaming forever upon love's fair ripening breast, to feel forever its soft fall and swell. Wordsworth would surely have penetrated to the potentially dangerous and illusory quality of Keats's poetic love in this utterance; but the evidence from the poetry before us is that he regarded Vaudracour's regression as more deeply dangerous and ignoble. Wordsworth's ultimate health in love did not come automatically or easily.

The analytical passage must be quoted in full, for it reveals Wordsworth contemplating a passionate moment surely like the one that produced his French daughter and presenting some ten years later the alternative he himself may then have faced:

> whether through effect
> Of some delirious hour, or that the youth,
> Seeing so many bars betwixt himself
> And the dear haven where he wished to be
> In honorable wedlock with his love,
> Without a certain knowledge of his own
> Was inwardly prepared to turn aside
> From law and custom and entrust himself
> To Nature for a happy end of all,
> And thus abated of that pure reserve
> Congenial to his loyal heart, with which
> It would have pleased him to attend the steps
> Of maiden so divinely beautiful,
> I know not—but reluctantly must add
> That Julia, yet without the name of wife,
> Carried about her for a secret grief,
> The promise of a mother.
>   (lines 596–612, *Prel.*, 342)

Wordsworth may be giving us a rare glimpse, though in fairly cool, structured, and not particularly inspired language, into his own ravished heart as he sees it from a decade's distance. The youth is naturally reserved and loyal, regarding himself as serving a divinely beautiful maiden; but the role strikes us as not a fully authentic one for the writer. He loved romance, as we shall see, and his eroticism is not untouched by Spenser. But can we take seriously his imagining himself, in revolutionary France with a pregnant and unwed mistress, as a *cavaliere servente*, as a gallant knight in a courtly tableau? But when he longs for "honorable wedlock," no one can doubt that the pull of that "dear haven" even the fervent young liberal felt as the very bias of his nature to the true magnetic North. Still, we must observe that he is not the least bit afraid to admit that the child came as a result of "delirious" passion, which he does not condemn. He even considers as a possible alternative rejecting law and custom and undertaking an entirely natural relationship. It is an eloquent fact that the poet of 1805, with his fully developed doctrine of nature, should imagine his own earlier self in crisis as being fully willing to abandon convention, throw himself upon nature for "a happy end," and put his deeds where his words are, trusting fully to the belief that "Nature never did betray / The heart that loved her" (*Tintern Abbey*, lines 122–23; *PW*, II, 262). It is almost as exciting a moment as when Alexander Pope has his Eloisa passionately long for a life that is free, lawless, and unconfined. For our purposes now, the importance of the passage is that it shows that Wordsworthian nature unmistakably sanctions sexual passion and love and that to such shared vitality a man disappointed in the structures both of romance and of law and custom might gladly commit himself.

But however historically important or intellectually interesting, the passage does not come close to realizing—nor does anything else in the Wordsworthian *corpus*—what the poet calls distantly "the raptures of the pair" (IX:635, *Prel.*, 344). Such emotions Wordsworth brushes aside as having been treated by more skillful poets than he. Why has he done such scant justice to the passionate ravage of his own heart's deep core? At first he *could* not fully confront it—the guilt and sorrow were too deep for measured words—and his poetic outlet came in the kindred subjects of desertion and suffering. He could apparently handle the results of passion but not the passion itself. And once his mind was healed, he turned to the healer, Dorothy, to neighborhood, to English nature loved since childhood. Treating such subjects in his own special way of indirect suggestiveness he restored the sensuous—and the sexual too—to his poetic personality.

It is about the persistence of sexual love that many critics and scholars need the correction that the balance of this chapter proposes to provide. Herbert Read, who deserves credit for seeing the enormous psychic importance of the affair with Annette, in which "animal passions, personal love, self-devotion—all had been engaged to their fullest degree,"[16] is nevertheless mistaken in believing that serenity was won only by the slow starvation of all such passion. If passion did not die, and I believe firmly that it did not, certainly guilt did; and F. R. Leavis is right when he says he finds in the poetry "no signs of morbid repression."[17] H. J. C. Grierson has calculated that in the writings the ratio of the word *love* to *nature* is thirteen to eight.[18] Where love is, sex in some form is sure to lurk, and Wordsworth could hardly have devoted so much poetic space to love and do so with such notable success and evident joy had his state been one of guilty fear. We must sharply distinguish his spirit from that of Felicia Hemans, whose works he owned and marked and who after early sexual disappointment apparently "drank in *soul!*" and indulged in a kind of "spirit-love" within the recesses of her "long-shut heart."[19] Now no one can deny that there is evidence of suppression in Wordsworth's work. It could not have been accidental that, by William Empson's count, there are no examples in the 1805 *Prelude* of *sense* meaning sensuality, one of the commonest eighteenth-century meanings of that term. But *sup*pression—for reasons of modesty, taste, one's assessment of public preference, one's concern about one's friends or family or one's own personal image—is not to be confused with *re*pression. If Empson is right—and I think he is—that in Wordsworth "Sensation and Imagination interlock,"[20] it then must follow that sexuality remains an ever-present force even in transcendental moments, for there is simply no intellectually honest way of excluding it from so comprehensive a sensationism as Wordsworth's own literary and political criticism establishes.

Wordsworth was by his own admission moved by both conscious and unconscious pleasure. He also had experienced "the Nightmare Conscience" (*Borderers*, line 866, *PW*, I, 162; the word *conscience* is of course closely related to *conscious*), and he was fully aware that the soul might sometimes receive "a shock of awful consciousness" (*Excursion*, IV:1157, *PW*, V, 145). In assessing the state of Wordsworth's mind, we can easily be misled by Freud and the moderns, who tend to be too fatalistic in making trauma permanent and who are not always historically just in understanding older vocabulary. From deep woundings Wordsworth seems always to have recovered,[21] and by *unconscious* he seems to have referred not to guilty but rather to guiltless, worry-free, healing monitions. For one of the chief eighteenth-century and classical meanings of *conscious* and *conscius* was precisely guilty or criminal.[22] And *unconscious* was therefore most likely to mean exactly the obverse.

When we come to the most fertile periods of Wordsworth's genius, sensuousness sparkles and crackles everywhere but sexuality is only implicitly present. Why such finding out of direction by indirection? In the words of Emily Dickinson, the poet may of course have wanted to

> Tell all the Truth but tell it slant—
> Success in Circuit lies.
> (*Complete Poems*, no. 1129)

If so, the reasons may lie in his own conscious choices, one of them undoubtedly the desire to be artistically effective. If there are other reasons for reserve and even chastity of utterance, these may emerge out of the contexts provided by his wife Mary and his sister Dorothy.

MARY HUTCHINSON WORDSWORTH:
THE POET'S "DEAR HAVEN . . . IN HONORABLE WEDLOCK"

Wisdom doth live with children round her knees.
—Wordsworth, "I Grievéd for Buonaparté," *PW*, III, 111

Life, I repeat, is energy of love
Divine or human.
—Wordsworth, *The Excursion*, V:1012–13, *PW*, V, 185

I am giddy at the thought of seeing thee. . . .
—Wordsworth to Mary, 19 August 1810,
Love Letters, 90

Because what we may call the "Dorothy period" (from 1797 to 1802, the date of Wordsworth's marriage to the friend of his boyhood, Mary Hutchinson) was the most prolific in producing intense love-poetry and since I wish to reserve discussion of that verse to the climax of this chapter, I break chronology to consider now the poetry written during the early married life of the poet up to 1815, the year in which *Laodamia* was published. I do not analyze the very latest poetry because I take the usual path and regard it as being in such sad decline as to silence a commentator, particularly on the subject of love. I find that the mentality of the poet has now hardened into conventional stereotypes incapable of producing the fresh insights or utterances that invite contemplation. Declarations about love continue to be made, but they seem not to arise from the depths of the poet's being and strike one as utterly devoid of sexual energy. But that energy does continue to animate the poet and the poetry when as a husband he was enjoying and portraying "the gentle and domestic virtues of an affectionate heart."[23]

We have seen how voluptuously Keats treated the legend of Cupid and Psyche. Wordsworth's response to it has hitherto been confined to a report of the painter Haydon, who believed that the poet was characterized by an "utter insensibility to . . . the beautiful frailties of passion,"[24] an indifference that seemingly became hostility when the two dropped in at Christie's one day and saw a statue of Cupid and Psyche: "Wordsworth's face reddened; he showed his teeth, and then said in a loud voice, 'THE DEV-V-VILS!' "[25] It is unlikely that Wordsworth in 1820 was only feigning or mocking an emotion of sexual shock; but we now know that such an outburst was not characteristic of the period in his life we are now considering. On 7–9 May 1812, writing to Mary a love letter only recently published, the poet described at length Washington Allston's now lost painting of the mythic pair (*Love Letters*, 136–37). Though he found a little fault with the use of light in the execution, his pleasure was obviously intense. He dwelt upon the sensuality portrayed: he described without the least hint of disapproval the luminous naked flesh, the expression of enthusiastic love on the faces and in the attitudes of the subjects. In fact, given the context of sexual longing that these love letters provide, it is not impossible that he identified himself and Mary with the amorous couple on the canvas.

There was emotional, even physical, intensity at the heart of the intimate Wordsworth circle, what Thomas McFarland calls "the significant group."[26] To some that small circle has seemed like a confinement. Keats, who admired its inmates, made this comment when the Wordsworths on one occasion departed from London: "I cant help thinking he has returned to his Shell—with his beautiful Wife and his enchanting Sister—" (LK, I, 251). Surely to others the bland coziness of the ménage has been unattractive—with its provinciality, its self-flattering sense of safety and repose. It is true that union with Mary came during a time when Wordsworth was growing conservative in a truly English and rural manner so unlike the revolutionary, humanitarian, dawn-like enthusiasm for political change that accompanied the passion for Annette Vallon. But however much we may see repose in the Dove Cottage retreat, it will not do to look on it as sexless or passionless, the home of a frustrated man never able to recapture the first fine careless rapture of his Continental love.

Crabb Robinson once observed to Charles Lamb in 1816 (some fourteen years after Wordsworth's marriage) that "he never saw a man so happy in three wives as Mr. Wordsworth is"[27]—the three being of course Mary, her sister Sara, beloved of Coleridge, and Dorothy, beloved of all. One is reminded of Samuel Richardson and his circle, which has been called a "harem," while the novelist's fantasies have been called polygamous.[28] A closer parallel than the actual Richardson ménage is the situation of Sir Charles Grandison in Richardson's last novel, a parallel that suggests that there may be something in the English character, at least during the eighteenth century, that loved to multiply domestic presences, as though they were in a hall of mirrors. Sir Charles was passionately loved by at least four women. The one he finally married, Harriet Byron, a girl who possessed, besides the very highest principles, a fresh country skin, was not unlike Wordsworth's wife—also English, beautiful, radiant, kindly, gracious. Annette can perhaps be loosely assimilated to the Italian Catholic beauty, the Lady Clementina, who—and this is unlike anything we know about Annette—for a while lapsed into a serious love-melancholy. The fierce-tempered Olivia, a raven-haired beauty from Florence, and the fourteen-year-old ingénue Emily have no parallels at Grasmere or Rydal Mount. But the lively high-spirited, devoted sister Charlotte certainly does—in Dorothy, even though Charlotte married and Dorothy remained single all her life. The parallel is worth making because there is that in the domestic loves of the Wordsworths which looks very much like the culmination of the liberal, bourgeois, secular trend that Lawrence Stone has called "Affective Individualism"[29] and to which I have applied the phrase "sex and sensibility." Coleridge, who saw limitations in Wordsworth's conception of love which I shall refer to at the end of this chapter, did concede that it "will do very well—it will suffice to make a good Husband—it may be even desirable (if the largest sum of easy & pleasurable sensations in this life be the right aim & end of human Wisdom) that we should have this, & no more—. . ." (Coll. Letters, III, 305).

Irvin Ehrenpreis has discriminated two contrasting views of familiarity in Wordsworth's own time.[30] One is Sir Walter Scott's, that familiarity deadens sexual or romantic passion; the other, Jane Austen's, that neighborhood and close acquaintance quicken it. Wordsworth is decidedly a Janeite in this respect, for he believed that the poet, like the good and happy man he should also strive to be, must bring relationship and love into the very essence of being. As a civil man with a social conscience he hoped that by sending Michael and The Brothers to Charles James Fox he would alert the statesman and his Parliamentary colleagues to the threat that the spread of manufacturing and the new workhouses posed to what had been one of the great glories of the small independent proprietorship of English land—the domestic affections.[31]

How they loved, these friends, neighbors, and relatives in the Lake Country! When, for example, Coleridge heard of the loss of Wordsworth's beloved son Thomas not long after the loss of a daughter, he wrote a letter (7 Dec. 1812) that ended: "Dear Mary! dear Dorothy! dearest Sara! . . . Again and again my dearest Wordsworth!!!" (Coll. Letters, III, 425). Such love in the extended group might not have existed had there not been at the very core of the nest a passionate, sexually fulfilling love between the husband and the wife. That kind of love did indeed exist, as we now know from the love letters of William and Mary, which came to light in 1977, which were kept a secret even from the significant group, but which the poet wanted preserved for posterity to see, all thirty-one, as a monument to his love.

These letters, written by both husband and wife after their first decade of marriage, yet possessing all the tender freshness of first love, must be among the most moving epistles of deep marital affection in English. Admittedly the genre is rare. One thinks back to the letters of Steele, but these of William and Mary totally lack the soft side that Dick expressed and also the contrasting hard, practical side provided by Prue. Here there is perfect frankness, trust, mutuality— and friendship. (The word is used more than once and the substance is unmistakably there.) An even higher perspective on the love is provided by the lovers themselves and conveyed by the repeated application by both of the word *blessed* to their relationship. Mary, like her namesake, bursts out in a Magnificat periodically: she has breathed William's name again and again to her children in his absence to give them some knowledge, conscious and unconscious, "how blessed, yea blessed above all human blessedness is their Mother.—" (*Love Letters*, 50).

Was there also passion? Indubitably, though it is expressed in the modest vocabulary characteristic of Wordsworth and his friends. Confessedly, some of the excitement arises from the fact that the passion is being written down. These letters bear out Foucault's point that language about sexual love may be even more important than the action itself, or Barthes' insight that the dialogue of lovers is more important than the very love, which of course could not have subsisted without articulation.[32] Mary says it was "so new a thing to see the breathing of thy inmost heart upon paper that I was quite overpowered" (*Love Letters*, 46). She responds in kind: "now that I sit down to answer thee in the loneliness & depth of that love which unites us & which cannot be felt but by ourselves, I am so agitated & my eyes are so bedimmed that I scarcely know how to proceed—" (ibid.) I have already quoted William's emphatically sexual description of a Cupid and Psyche painting. He also imagines an earlier scene when he and she might have been "fondly locked in each others arms" never to part (ibid., 61–62), and he confesses himself "giddy" (90) at the thought of seeing her. He calls Mary in almost Shelleyan terms his "love of loves" (59), he stresses the ardor of the love as much as its tenderness, he calls it a "passion" (62) which is "lively, gushing, thought-employing, spirit-stirring" (60). Such phrases, which Wordsworth might have used of nature or of his own poetry, recall not only Shelley but Keats, who also saw sexual love as employing the thought and stirring the spirit.

The mention of Keats reminds us of that poet's use of antecedent art to help produce as well as to reflect sensuality. Literary, though not pictorial, romance is also present in Wordsworth's love of woman; and he and Mary, like Keats and Fanny Brawne, together entered "the realm of Faery" (*Peter Bell*, line 101; *PW*, II, 335) and "the hemisphere of magic fiction" (1805 *Prelude*, VI, 102–103; *Prel.*, 190), particularly "Spenser's Lay" (Dedication to *White Doe*, 1.5, *PW*, III, 281). The beautiful but marmoreal poem, *The White Doe of Rylstone*, set in the chivalric past, is born in the bosom of Wordsworth's uxorial love. It now and then blushes a faint roseate hue but for the most part it is chastely and whitely cool. And one River Duddon sonnet, going back to "some far-distant time" (Number XXII, called "Tradition," *PW* III, 255), though it is suffused with passion, warns in exquisite verse of the dangers that can attend the climax of sexual ravishment. *Laodamia*, a good if not great poem, is one of the substantial achievements of the Mary period. Wordsworth once compared himself to Mary, who was also "Nature's inmate" (1805 *Prelude*, XI: 213, *Prel.*, 426) and who had the gift of love. Like her, he said "I loved whate'er I saw, nor lightly loved / But fervently—" (ibid., lines 225–26; *Prel.*, 428). We are permitted to ask why in the poems just mentioned, the products of his love of Mary and with Mary of his love of Spenser and chivalry, he did not achieve fervency or even strive to cultivate passion. It is more than likely that the stoical control he prayed for after the shattering grief over the loss of his brother John in 1805 extended its restraints to "Tradition" and to the *White Doe*; and *Laodamia* will also have to be considered in connection with harrowing loss.

But first its story, a revision of one of Ovid's heroic epistles,[33] product of what has been regarded as Wordsworth's period of discipline derived from the ancient Latin classics. Laodamia, a widow of the Trojan war, prays to Jupiter to restore her slain lord, her bosom heaving in "impassioned" and "fervent love" as she prays. She is vouchsafed Protesilaus' return for three hours, and she then longs, "a second time" his bride, for "one nuptial kiss" on their "well-known couch" (lines 7, 11, 25, 63, 64, *PW*, II, 267–69). At this rapturous desire, Jove frowns; and her husband, whose mead is now a spiritual love that is "equable and pure" (line 98, *PW*, II, 270), rebukes her carnal passion, chiding her for not being strong in reason and self-government. In all versions of the poem Wordsworth seems to share Jove's and Protesilaus' and also the Parcae's preference for virtuous, disciplined, transcarnal affection.

What shall we make of such stoicism after the warm love letters? Surely Herbert Read is wrong either in condemning the poet for "manifest hypocrisy" in this poem or in seeing it as a late rebound from Wordsworth's own violent passion for Annette Vallon.[34] From those flames Wordsworth had indeed emerged wounded, but he had been healed years ago. Can it be, as Donald H. Reiman has suggested, that after the loss of their two young children in the early summer and late autumn of 1812 something died in his feelings for Mary never to return and that the rebuke of the wife in the poem arises from his own sexual withering.[35] In that interpretation the ghost in the poem admonishes Mary "to control her passion in the presence of a bodily lover who was yet only the ghost of his former self."[36] This analysis is surely right in calling attention to the grief, for it was profound; but the suggestion of impotence, brilliantly ingenious though it is, strikes one as melodramatic and unproven, indeed unprovable.[37] Let no one, however, underestimate the suffering caused by the loss of the two sweet innocents (*Letters Middle*, 24, 32, 51),

as Dorothy and also William called the children—first the loss of
little Catherine and a few months later of Tom, the darling of Wordsworth's affection and his hope for the future, intellectually his most
promising child. Families tied together in such intense affection have
indeed given hostages to fortune! After the girl's death Mary remained
in the deepest depression; after "my sweet little Thomas [was] no
more" (50), William was once more "oppressed with sorrow and
distracted with anxiety" (53); and one suspects that Wordsworth's
language reveals only the tip of the iceberg. In fact, he wrote almost
a month later: "we have suffered as much anguish as it is possible
to undergo in a like case" (56); and a few weeks later still he referred
to "my present depression of mind" (66). He was said by Dorothy
to have aged ten years in a few weeks, while Mary remained "greatly
shattered" (85) for months, and there was even some despair over
her recovery. The grief of both husband and wife bordered on impiety
as well as madness, for Wordsworth seemed to have felt an inability
to pray. So the ghost who warns in *Laodamia* against "rebellious
passion" and "the tumult of the soul" and who recommends that
human beings "meekly mourn" in "fervent, not ungovernable, love,"
in "transports moderate," may have found fit audience in *both* the
poet himself and his wife (lines 74–77, *PW*, II, 269).

It is surely not sexual love per se that is rebuked in *Laodamia*.
We must remember that the embraces the husband now discourages
are between a living human being and a ghost. Laodamia is tragically
deluded when she cries out, "No Spectre greets me," for that is
exactly what she encounters—a "vain Shadow," now "no blooming
Hero" (lines 61, 62, *PW*, II, 269). She has mistaken the dead for
the living in a mischievously misplaced affection that has, to be sure,
arisen from recollections of physical bliss and deep love but that
should by no means be necessarily identified with sexuality in and
of itself. Laodamia's sin is therefore far from what Defoe called
"conjugal lewdness"[38] or from the excessive passion in the married
state that the present Pope, following a long tradition, has recently
so sternly condemned. Her sin lies in mistaking the dead for the
living, in a refusal to accept the limits of mortality, in a failure to
acquiesce in the inescapable law that death follows life.

Portions of that overly long, occasionally pompous or flaccid, but
often majestic poem, *The Excursion*, come from the very experiences
we have seen to underlie *Laodamia*. Some passages in its first book,
going back as far as 1797, do breathe the kind of passion that seared
Wordsworth's soul in the Annette period. There are some stirrings
of the animal spirits of the great Dorothy period we have not yet
analyzed: consider the oxymoronic juxtapositions (steadiness and excess) present in Margaret's love in the first book, in which she is
presented as "a Woman of a steady mind, / Tender and deep in her

excess of love" (I:513–14, *PW*, V, 26). But the spirit of the later
books is recognizable as that of the married Wordsworth meditating
on life, love, and loss, on aspects of his own personality and being,
from the usually unruffled state of domesticity. Into that uxorial peace
the body thrusts itself again and again. Sometimes Wordsworth keeps
the body present from earlier inspirations. Margaret, for example,
that finely realized figure of pathos, makes poignantly clear the
importance to happiness of the flesh as it suffers progressive loss:
with loss of husband comes loss of bodily pleasure and Wordsworth
makes it a piercing pity. "Her body was subdued. . . . / . . . no
motion of the breast was seen, / No heaving of the heart" (I:795,
800–801; *PW*, V, 35). When the Solitary appears, the man with "an
intense and glowing mind" (II:274; *PW*, V, 52), surely in part a
Wordsworthian avatar, whose gloomy skepticism, however, is badly
in need of correction, the text introduces materials about married
life closely parallel to the poet's own. Wordsworthian love, like so
much human love, brings anxiety, and the lover imagines the death
of the beloved; and indeed the wife does die soon, a woman of "bright
form" (III:481, *PW*, V, 89), "silver voice" (482), and "mild radiance"
(503). These phrases might easily have been directly applied to Mary,
as indeed could the following procession of adjectives, not perhaps
calculated to stir a modern heart but at the very heart of the poet's
sensibility: she was "Young, modest, meek, and beautiful" (III:514,
PW, V, 91). With her husband this "blooming Lady—a Conspicuous
flower" (187) enjoyed walks in nature and was animated by "full
. . . joy" and "free . . . love" (196) (uncensored feelings, bubbling
up naturally?); and when the children (a girl and a boy) came, she
presided over a nuclear family, isolated and blissful in a new Eden
sufficient unto itself. But when the children died, "heirs of our united
love; / Graced mutually by difference of sex" (590–91), first the girl
and then the boy, as in Wordsworth's own grievous loss, the mother
became "Calm as a frozen lake" (650) and melted in his arms shortly
thereafter when death released her spirit. Before tragedy had struck
it had been a beautiful conjugal scene, the kind so rarely portrayed
in Western literature, on which the sun was wont to shine.

What happened when the echoing green was darkened? It is
clear, whatever denials the Solitary now imposes upon himself, that
Wordsworth ultimately retained his belief in "fostering nature" (809)
and in the importance of the body and its energies.

> Oh! what a joy it were, in vigorous health,
> To have a body (this our vital frame) . . .
>   what a joy to roam
> An equal among mightiest energies.
>   (IV:508–509, 531–32, *PW*, V, 125)

A personal Providence is clearer now than in the earlier Wordsworth, but purely natural joys continue, loving, fruitful, fructifying, under "the great sun, earth's universal lord." There is

> participation of delight
> And a strict love of fellowship, combined.
> What other spirit can it be that prompts
> The gilded summer flies to mix and weave
> Their sports together in the solar beam
> Or in the gloom of twilight hum their joy?—
> (IV:443–48, *PW*, V, 122)

a celebration of sexuality in creation comparable to Keat's *To Autumn* and close in intellectual content to Samuel Johnson's perceiving the basis of all benevolence in the instinctual, sexual attractions of natural life which were implanted by Providence (*Rambler*, no. 99, par. 1).

The shortest and most beautiful expression of the love that sustained Wordsworth's domestic life, which we can regard as a concentrated essence of the love letters, is appropriately the poem addressed to Mary, "She was a Phantom of Delight" (*PW*, II, 213–14). In it the husband salutes his wife as "a perfect Woman, nobly planned," but unfortunately for a modern reader he also calls her a "machine," by which of course he means merely her body, as Hamlet did when he used the same word for his own fleshly mansion (II, ii. 124). Frank McConnell has seen that the term also refers to the "whole complex process of the poet's perception" of her body.[39]

Herbert Read's outline of the poem has the merit of clarity and completeness: Wordsworth moves in each successive stanza from sight to acquaintance to intimacy—that is, from astonishment to courtship to marriage.[40] We can get beyond such institutional progression—and beyond too the general praise of the wife—by concentrating on the central paradoxes of the vision—for so indeed it is: Mary is a "Phantom," a "lovely Apparition," a "Spirit," mediating "something of angelic light." But she also treads a household floor, bestows "love, kisses, . . . and smiles." She demonstrates powers of leadership and possession of "a reason firm" and of a "temperate will." (Protesilaus of *Laodamia* would have nothing to complain of in this wife!) And she also has the power "To haunt, to startle, and way-lay," that last word *way-lay*, put like the others into a verbal infinitive, without boundaries, with no temporal limitations, is peculiarly delicious. It is not merely the delicate suggestions of sexual playfulness and of the protected pleasures of domestic seduction that endear the word but also the hint of solidity and permanence provided by the context. Domestic happiness is not usually rewarded with such complex poetic patterning.

Love of the intensest kind animated the Mary period, a love that was, however, controlled by stoical reason, by dedication to what Irving Babbitt called the classical *frein vital*. Controls are not usually applied to natural timidity, to bloodless placidity, and Wordsworth prayed for the reproving rod precisely because he was a Wordsworth Agonistes, a man driven to potential excess in grief and love. But the stern daughter of the Voice of God is no enemy per se of "the genial sense of youth," of love, joy, and sexuality. She wears a benignant smile, and "Flowers laugh before [her] on their beds" ("Ode to Duty," *PW*, IV, 83–86). The delicate balance achieved in this poem between discipline and delight is the key that unlocks the amorousness of this period of domestic felicity. The married state, milder, less intense, though sexually fulfilling, was an uninterrupted extension of the pleasures of life with Dorothy, which we consider next.

DOROTHY: THE "ONE DEAR STATE OF BLISS" AND WORDSWORTH'S "HIGH CALLING"

> Witness thou
> The dear companion of my lonely walk,
> My hope, my joy, my sister, and my friend,
> Or something dearer still, if reason knows
> A dearer thought, or in the heart of love
> There be a dearer name.
> —Wordsworth, in *Dorothy's Journals*, *PW*, V, 347

> There is creation in the eye,
> Nor less in all the other senses; powers
> They are that colour, model, and combine
> The things perceived with such an absolute
> Essential energy that we may say
> That those most godlike faculties of ours
> At one and the same moment are the mind
> And the mind's ministers.
> —Wordsworth, Notebook fragment, *PW*, V, 343

From the "substantial world" of antecedent literature in which can grow tendrils "strong as flesh and blood," Wordsworth chose the following for especial emphasis:

> Two shall be named, pre-eminently dear,—
> The gentle Lady married to the Moor;
> And heavenly Una with her milk-white Lamb.
> ("Personal Talk," lines 40–42, *PW*, IV, 74)

If we were to assimilate these to the women in Wordsworth's own life, Spenser's Una, from the first book of the *Faerie Queene*, would have to be associated with his wife Mary, an association, indeed,

made, though indirectly, by the poet himself. In Shakespeare's Des-
demona, if the speculation is not too bold, may be seen the lineaments
of the deserted Annette, against whom, in a few profound ways that
did not involve jealousy, Wordsworth played a passionate and ultimately cruel Othello-role. To select a literary parallel for Dorothy
we must go outside the three lines just quoted, to Milton, over whose
portrayal of the expulsion from the garden in the eleventh book of
Paradise Lost the brother and sister "melted into tears" (*Journals*,
106). For it was Milton who gave unrivaled embodiment to the Edenic
bower, which the home and life in Grasmere frequently recalled. But
perhaps after all the best locus for Dorothy is not a book but nature,
for the poetry dedicated to her and inspired by her partakes of the
impulses that seemed to "roll" through her, to use a favorite Wordsworthian verb for the movement of natural energy. Wordsworth's
personification of nature as woman does not invoke the age-old topos
of the alma mater nor is it, I believe, instinct with memories of his
own mother lost in childhood. It is, rather, Dorothy—child, girl, and
woman, muse and friend—who is the chief begetter and sustainer of
the great Wordsworthian persona, Nature. It is she who blends with
daffodils and sounding cataracts and with "natural" people too, like
the Highland lass whom the poet addresses:

> I would have
> Some claim upon thee, if I could, . . .
> Thy elder Brother I would be,
> Thy Father—anything to thee!
> ("To a Highland Girl," lines 56–57, 60–61, *PW*, III, 74)

Over the Wordsworthian landscape move, not stately matrons or the
nymphs of Titian and Claude, whom Keats loved, but fresh young
country girls, nubile, blooming, flower-like.

Of the problems that this insinuation of Dorothy into nature and
of nature into her raises about the brother-sister relationship I shall
have something to say presently. Now it is important to emphasize
that the sexual energies that the poet seems to find in nature must
of course have been imposed by him, by that virile, strongly sensual
person we confronted at the outset. And these energies must have
first entered his emotional transactions with nature without any em-
barrassing or otherwise impeding awareness, for they were largely
compounded of glad animal movements and unconscious desires.
Later, as we have seen, the underlying sexuality could enter the
critical sentences of discursive prose, and some of the poetry deliberately cultivates an imagistic significance that is quite explicitly
sexual. But the synthesis, the coalescing of imagination and appetite
(when "deep feelings had impressed / Great objects on his mind"
and when he was being prepared to receive "the lesson deep of

love" [*The Ruined Cottage*, lines 81–82, 116; *PW*, V, 381, 382]),
must have begun on a level well below that of conscious construction.

The great synthesis of psychological subject and natural object
that underlies the earlier versions of the *Prelude*—present in passages
that arc often allowed to remain in even the 1850 edition—is frequently expressed in language whose sexual resonance has seldom
been acknowledged. It would be unnatural of nature to be ascetic;
it would be perverse if "the bond of union betwixt love and joy"
(1799 *Prelude*, I:390; *Prel.*, II) were free of physical cathexis. The
imagery always seems to point overtly away from the obvious coupling
of desiring bodies. But how often such unions and the bodily passions
are indirectly suggested by trope, descriptive word, rhythm, and
incident! The boy with panting heart and beating bosom is overpowered by "strong desire / Resistless" as he reaches up to steal a
captive bird belonging to another, whereupon "Low breathings"
among the solitary hills pursue him (lines 42–43, 47). The stealing
of a boat is presented as "an act of stealth / And troubled pleasure"—
suggestions enforced by the boat "heaving through the water like a
swan," a bird image that we have seen and shall again see associated
with the sexual (lines 90–91, 106). The "intercourse of touch" (1799
Prelude, II:312) extends far beyond the child at the breast; in his
seventeenth year the boy reacts to nature "with bliss ineffable," as
earlier he had lain on the "genial pillow of the earth, . . . soothed
by a sense of touch" (1805 *Prelude*, II:419, I:88–89; *Prel.*, 86, 32).
He strayed "voluptuously through fields and rural walks" for "it was
a time of rapture" and of "giddy bliss" that "like a tempest works
along the blood" (I:253, 457, 611–12). Such language has all the
marks of the libidinal about it and could scarcely be conceived as
produced by a eunuch. It is extended to the coming of poetry, as
the author

> kindled with the stir,
> The fermentation and the vernal heat
> Of poesy, affecting private shades
> Like a sick lover.
> (IV:93–96)

Erotic feeling beats insistently even if it cannot be said to boil or
seethe beneath the blank verse of the *Prelude*. Examples could be
multiplied: it will suffice here to notice that the crucial moment
during the first vacation from Cambridge when the poet feels himself
"a dedicated spirit" follows a night of dancing and prattle:

> Slight shocks of young love-liking interspersed
> That mounted up like joy into the head,
> And tingled through the veins.
> (IV:325–27)

Wordsworthian joy should never be totally separated from such tinglings. The sexual basis of poetic art, however dreamlike, is deeply if obscurely sensed. The "beauteous pictures" arising in "harmonious imagery"

> left
> Obscurely mingled with their passing forms
> A consciousness of animal delight,
> A self-possession felt in every pause
> And every gentle movement of my frame.
> (IV:395–99)

Such vital and kinaesthetic energy, "dumb yearnings, hidden appetites" (V:530), never deserted the best poetry of this master. From the placid orthodoxies of the later laureate, to be sure, they seem to be absent, though a turn of phrase or thought can now and then recall them as from a great distance.

If such staminal powers as these animate the vision of nature, some kind of clashing crisis is inevitable. *Rapture* and *rapt*, words used obsessively by Wordsworth about natural joys, are related to *rape;* and *Nutting* (*PW*, II, 211–12), probably composed in late 1798, is a powerful, even a shocking and disturbing poem, to which such words are applicable. Accoutred quaintly in cast-off clothes, the poet as a boy comes to an untouched bower, a kind of Eden, "one dear nook / Unvisited." As poet recounting the experience, he insists at once on a sexual metaphor (the trees stand "Tall and erect, with tempting clusters hung, / A virgin scene!"), and he presents himself as "Voluptuous, fearless of a rival" as he "eyed / The banquet." For a brief moment he has refuge in romance—he plays with the flowers and hears the murmur of "fairy water-breaks"—a strategy typical of both the erotic Keats and the erotic Wordsworth in vacant and voluptuous moods. But then comes a spasm of sexual violence:

> up I rose,
> And dragged to earth both branch and bough, with crash
> And merciless ravage,

leaving the nook "mutilated," "Deformed and sullied," the last word reminding us, though perhaps not Wordsworth, of the "too, too sullied flesh" of Hamlet.

Literary context of sorts is provided by the attack on the trees of the forest by the love-crazed Orlando of Ariosto's epic, but the differences outweigh the similarities. The true context for *Nutting* is provided by Wordsworth himself, by the nature he knew, and by Dorothy, who is deeply involved in this recollection. After reporting the violation of nature's virginity he has inflicted, he turns to her and bids her "move along these shades / In gentleness of heart; with

gentle hand / Touch—for there is a spirit in the woods." These lines
do more than enforce a cautionary moral that urges us to be gentle,
and Wordsworth is far from turning away from all sexual contact,
which it is one purpose of his verse to show can be decent and
tender. "Touch," he tells his sister; "with gentle hand," of course;
but "touch," Dorothy, "touch!"

Dorothy is even more deeply involved in another version of the
scene, one not sent on to Coleridge and not a part of the publication
of *Nutting* in 1800 (*PW*, II, 504–506). In this version the girl is
imagined, at least fleetingly, as the ravisher; and the exhorter to calm
and gentleness is the poet himself, speaking without the sexual metaphors prominent in the final version. But he is disturbed by this
vision of his sister

> with that keen look
> Half cruel in its eagerness, those cheeks
> Thus flushed with a tempestuous bloom,
> I might have almost deem'd that I had pass'd
> A houseless being in a human shape,
> An enemy of nature.
> (lines 8–13)

The two versions show that even in this recollection of sexually troped
violence toward nature William is mingling or even exchanging identities with Dorothy; and it is fair to say that it was not always true,
as he said of her in the *Prelude*, that

> thy breath,
> Dear sister, was a kind of gentler spring
> That went before my steps.
> (1805 *Prelude*, XIII:244–46)

The night before his wedding (a ceremony that Dorothy was
emotionally incapable of attending, though she was nearby) Wordsworth gave her the wedding ring to keep until the morning. She
wore it on her forefinger, and the next day she gave it back to him
with what she called "how deep a blessing." He then "slipped it
again onto my finger and blessed me fervently." Wordsworth's best
biographer, who quotes these words, calls this private ceremony "a
sacramental renewal of an unbreakable fidelity."[41] It was followed
by a lifetime in the home of the Wordsworths passed, in unclouded
friendship and love, with Mary and her children. It was preceded by
a period of unmatched creativity, when the poet produced some of
the tenderest love poetry in our language, all addressed to Dorothy
or inspired by her.

All of the above and more—in addition to the fact that there
seemed to have been something in current and immediately ante-

cedent culture that was tolerant toward brother-sister incest (Shelley called it "like many other *incorrect* things a very poetical circumstance")[42]—has laid suspicion on the relations of the poet to his sister. The late Lord Kenneth Clark, in a popular television series on Romantic art, seemed to take abnormality between the Wordsworths for granted and drew what I regard as a tasteless and unwarranted parallel between them and Lord Byron and his sister Augusta. The imputation of overt incest has been called ludicrous, lurid, inappropriate, mischievous; to this list of angry words I would add *difficult*, if not *impossible*, to conceive. Dorothy's journals show that the deep love Wordsworth revealed in his life, letters, and poetry was fully reciprocated. Their life together before Wordsworth's marriage was one of devotion, tenderness, and intimacy, with scenes of some physical contact like caressing and kissing and of tender proximities at not inappropriate moments. And when there was excess of feeling—as there certainly was when Dorothy could not find it in herself to throw into the fire the remainder of an apple into which her brother had bitten (*Journals*, 119)—the excess is sentimental and mawkish, not sensual and morbid. Moreover, the house was a bustle of activity: neighbors and friends from far and near came in and out, sometimes staying for long periods. Dove Cottage was a place of incessant, strenuous, symptom-producing work for the poet, who just before his marriage went through one of his most fertile and exacting poetic periods. The taboo was still too strong in the Romantic period in England to have been challenged by such friendly, hospitable, rural, relaxed, and, on one level, conventional people. When they did not reveal the qualities I have just listed, the Wordsworths were either overworked or suffering from very common ailments like aches in the head or stomach.

And yet the love was fervent indeed. If the thesis of this chapter has validity—that physicality was an essential ingredient of Wordsworthian nature and entered almost every emotion that touched the poet's psyche—then we must expect that sexual attraction of some kind found a place here too, mostly natural and unaware but capable of coming to the surface of the poet's mind.

I may have overstressed the conventionality of the circle in order to obviate what inevitably gets in the way of a discussion of Wordsworthian love, the charge or hint of overt incest. But I have to concede that guilt and potential danger did lurk in the relationship: we have already seen Dorothy imaginatively implicated in the aggressively sexual poem *Nutting*. In *Tintern Abbey* the sister, with her "wild eyes," is associated with the period of "dizzy raptures" and "wild ecstasies" in the love of nature (lines 85, 119, 138, *PW*, II, 261–63). Although many poems to Emma or Emmeline, poetic names for Dorothy, the dear person he also called his "sweet friend" (1805

Prelude, XIII:227), are simple, sensuous, and sincere in their expressions of tender love, many are darkly disturbed with the thought of death. Such are the justly admired Lucy poems, products of the early Dorothy period in Wordsworth's creative life.

In the alternative version of *Nutting* the poet addresses his sister as Lucy (line 6, *PW*, II, 505), and I have come to agree with those who see Dorothy behind the shadowy figure who, in the short but multi-layered, severe but mysterious lyrics, haunts the borders between rural reality and a dream. In these poems Lucy is imagined as dying, but I cannot agree with the late F. W. Bateson that Wordsworth now solved the threatening relationship with his sister "by killing her off symbolically."[43] To *kill off* strikes me as unnecessarily sensational and blunt, and Donald Reiman's subtler approach is surely closer to the truth.[44] He believes that Lucy is allowed to die so that she cannot be united in a forbidden relationship and that the author shifts his imaginative stance from brother to lover to avoid focusing his sexual drive on a sister. Such a view has the merit of showing the psychic complexity that underlies the verse and of providing a basis for the rich mythography inscribed in these short lyrics.

Though sexuality comes in soon enough, it should not provide the first perspective. As we have seen, Wordsworth sometimes imagined, though often very indirectly, the death of those he loved the most intensely—perhaps Mary, even himself, and Mary and himself together:

> O sacred marriage-bed of death,
> > That keeps them side by side
> In bond of peace, in bond of love,
> > That may not be untied!
> > > ("George and Sarah Green," 1808, *PW*, IV, 376)

Dorothy—we must say particularly Dorothy—was not exempted from these intimations of mortality. That profound little poem, " 'Tis said, that some have died for love," portrays a strong man brought so low by suffering over the death of his "pretty Barbara" that beholding the eglantine once loved together "Disturbs me till the sight is more than I can bear." Wordsworth makes a quiet identification of himself with the sufferer, fearing a like fate for himself; and then turning to his sister he exclaims in pain,

> Ah gentle love! if ever thought was thine
> To store up kindred hours for me, thy face
> Turn from me, gentle Love! nor let me walk
> Within the sound of Emma's voice, nor know
> Such happiness as I have known to-day.
> > (lines 48–52, *PW*, II, 34)

But if indeed Emma-Dorothy should die, what consolations then? The answer lies in the Lucy poems, which begin in "strange fits of passion" and end in the girl's death into nature, with the following paradoxically different results imagined. (1) She may become a part of "earth's diurnal round"—

> No motion has she now, no force;
> She neither hears nor sees—
> ("A slumber did my spirit seal," PW, II, 216)

in which case she has achieved a state directly antithetical to the poet's earthly passion, which may have been so feverish as to require an insensate termination. (2) Or she may, more complexly and paradoxically, have become at once calm and wild, capable of being "sportive as the fawn" but also wrapped in "the silence . . . of mute insensate things." Climactically, the dead but imaginatively resurrected girl becomes a mature sexual being,

> 'And vital feelings of delight
> Shall rear her form to stately height,
> Her virgin bosom swell.'
> ("Three years she grew," lines 31–33, PW, II, 215)

Nature speaks here; and when she says, "Such, *thoughts* to Lucy I will give" (line 34, emphasis added), she invokes the poetic process. Lucy's death is thus swallowed up in victory through the myth of a sexually vital nature. Dorothy has not been "killed off." In one sense she has not even died. Her stately height and virgin bosom have now become available as a muse is available to the creating mind—more precisely, as an imaginatively created myth can turn back to its creator and renew his energy. Such energy is released when the *données* of reality become imaginative data living on in the mind. That is the high fate of the sexual Dorothy.

The Lucy poems were composed away from England, in Goslar, Germany, in late 1798 or early 1799. Lucy-Dorothy is thought of not as a little child but as a girl three-years grown into a love-relationship who then dies. In the first surviving portion of Wordsworth's great unfinished poem, *The Recluse*, dating from the first spring in Grasmere, 1800, the beloved is a woman, for all intents and purposes a wife, the occupant of a shared nest, a place described in the 1805 *Prelude* as providing "one dear state of bliss," the "dear delight" that surpasses all other human joy and that stands at the very top of Wordsworth's hierarchy of conscious pleasure—his chief intensity, as it were:

> The bliss of walking daily in life's prime
> Through field or forest with the maid we love

> While yet our hearts are young, while yet we breathe
> Nothing but happiness, living in some place,
> Deep vale, or anywhere the home of both
> From which it would be misery to stir.
> (XII:127, 129–34, 136; *Prel.* 444)

These lines from the *Prelude* could, I suppose, be taken to refer to life with Mary, but their youthful glow, the sense of isolation, the untroubled happiness, and the presence of only two seem to point primarily to the period we are now concerned with. They join the lines from the *Home at Grasmere* (the part written in 1800) now to be analyzed to celebrate life in the vale of Grasmere with Dorothy. Did we not know from history both the dwelling-place and the blood-kinship of the inhabitants, the poetry itself would lead us to exclaim: here the nuclear family has found its poetic celebrant at last!

Wordsworth certainly speaks of the beloved spot as a proprietor would:

> The unappropriated bliss hath found
> An owner, and that owner I am he.
> The Lord of this enjoyment is on Earth
> And in my breast. What wonder if I speak
> With fervour, am exalted with the thought
> Of my possessions?
> (*Home at Grasmere*, MS. B, lines 85–90; p. 42)

Wordsworth is himself the small owner of a rural plot, the kind of life he saw as the best preserver of the domestic affections. But he is also Adam—more precisely a new Adam, a second Adam, to use Pauline language. Originally, among "the bowers / Of blissful Eden," there was not, he says, the "possession of the good," the realized imagination, or the fulfilled "ancient thought" that he now owns in "highest measure" (*Home*, lines 122–28, p. 44). Why is Wordsworth's the higher boon, "absolute," of "surpassing grace" (ibid.), higher even than the prelapsarian? Not, I believe, for Christian reasons, for Christ never enters this picture. *Grace* is, however, not unimportant, for the poet is not a primal innocent; he has known loss and grief, suffering and sin, from which he has been mercifully rescued. But still the Edenic parallel remains cogent. Even though we are later made aware that the couple are not alone and that "Society is here: / The true community," he nevertheless regards himself as "peacefully embowered" (*Home*, lines 76, p. 43; and 818–19, p. 90). And his partner, whom he describes with historical accuracy as

> A younger orphan of a Home extinct,
> The only Daughter of my Parents,
> (*Home*, MS. D, lines 78=79, p. 43)

must be regarded as his beloved Eve. The very language that follows recalls *Paradise Lost:* the poet says he never lingered over "a lovely object"

> But either She whom now I have, who now
> Divides with me this loved abode, was there
> Or not far off. Where'er my footsteps turned,
> Her Voice was like a hidden Bird that sang;
> The thought of her was like a flash of light
> Or an unseen companionship, a breath
> Of fragrance independent of the wind.
>   (*Home*, MS. B, lines 107–13, p. 44)

I have mentioned *Paradise Lost,* but this Eve does not wish to wander off for a bit of separate but equal gardening nor does this Eden seem in any way threatened by a Fall.

The question forces itself upon us—can we avoid bringing to mind the lovely sexual dalliance of the Miltonic Eden? Since Wordsworth has confessed without embarrassment or strain to proper, though intense, sororal relations with his Eve, here called by Dorothy's poetic name "my Emma," any sexual allusion would have to be exquisitely indirect. But present it seems indeed to be.[45] In poetry of a very high order Wordsworth evokes bird-imagery and bird-calls in describing the pair, and we remember that such imagery was beautifully applied to Vaudracour and Julia, made by the poet the poetic equivalents of Wordsworth and Annette Vallon. Here the poetry is even tenderer—and better:

> Long is it since we met to part no more,
> Since I and Emma heard each other's call
> And were Companions once again, like Birds
> Which by the intruding Fowler had been scared,
> Two of a scattered brood that could not bear
> To live in loneliness.
>   (*Home*, lines 171–76, p. 48)

Wordsworth also compares himself and Dorothy to two "milk-white Swans" who failed one Spring to appear at their usual retreat in the center of the lake, even though they had come daily during two months of "unrelenting storm." The birds are especially dear because "their state so much resembled ours":

> They also having chosen this abode,
> They strangers, and we strangers; they a pair,
> And we a solitary pair like them.
> They should not have departed.
>   (*Home*, MS. B, lines 323, 330, 338, 339–42, p. 58)

The tenderness of that last sentence is piercing—in his heart of hearts the poet does not want the orphan brother and sister ever to leave their retreat.

Could swan-imagery for Wordsworth be entirely free of uxorial if not sexual content? Keats used swans in his poetry with overt sexual meaning—a poetic habit sanctioned by Jove who turned himself into one to woo Leda, and by Spenser, who introduced them into his *Prothalamion*, where their satin whiteness and bright beauty shone "Against [a] Brydale day, which was not long." Wordsworth in the *Salisbury Plain* poem quoted earlier had made his swans erotic, with heaving bosoms "soft and white." Guilt and sorrow over Annette may have entered those earlier lines; but there is no trace of morbidity here or even of present or past grief. There is, however, a touch of self-consciousness in applying the swan imagery to the siblings at Dove Cottage. In an early draft these birds seem to have been male and female, husband and wife, for they are called "partners"; and when one is imagined to have been killed, the other lives "in its widowhood." In a heavy cancellation that leaves these lines still readable, Wordsworth removes the distinction of sex, and the two become "Companions, brethren, consecrated friends." In the final version these companions "Inseparable" in "constant love" are no longer even "brethren" but only "consecrated friends, Faithful Companions."[46] Such changes could not help being deliberate, and we thus know that at least once the conscious mind of Wordsworth revised away sexually suggestive language that he had applied to his relations with Dorothy, though he did so with the full knowledge of his copyists, Mary and Dorothy.

John Beer sees Grasmere with Dorothy alone as a prelude to Grasmere with Dorothy and Mary, the intense love continuing from the smaller to the slightly larger community, "where the quiet work of the mature human heart, anchored in a deeply physical love, could contain, and find a place for, more intense and extreme attachments."[47] The comment on the physical anchor of sentimental love is admirably just, but could there be anything more spiritually intense or extreme than the poet's attachment to his sister, and was there ever again so rich an outpouring of immortal verse as during the Dorothy years?

It is appropriate to conclude with an apocalypse. The vision on Mount Snowdon has been much studied but has never, I believe, been regarded as a climactic expression of the poet's encounter with earthly love. The episode begins physically enough, with language that evokes a strongly kinetic sense: "Thus did we breast the ascent":

> With forehead bent,
> Earthward, as if in opposition set

> Against an enemy, I panted up
> With eager pace.
> (1805 *Prelude*, XIII:20, 29–32; *Prel.*, 458)

Here the earth is felt to be a foe, but the language establishes it as a real presence before its transcendence is contemplated. The vision may be said to begin when a light "Fell like a flash" upon the turf. At once re-establishing his own presence, the poet writes,

> I looked about, and lo,
> The moon stood naked in the heavens, at height
> Immense above my head,
>
> (XIII:40–42),

and we have entered the first phase of the experience. The moon is not alone the subject of contemplation, for at the poet's feet the mist rests like a sea, while hundreds of hills, like waves in that sea, upheave "their dusky backs" (line 45). So both mist and hill are not just vaguely organic but are giant bodies, appropriately accompanying the immensity overhead. There is no doubt who dominates: "the moon looked down upon this shew / In single glory" (lines 52–53).

The moon of the Romantics' delight has emerged in much great poetry and painting, and Wordsworth himself had often personified the lesser light as a woman, loved in childhood, associated with passion and the death of a beloved girl in the Lucy poems, and contemplated languidly as she hung between the hills of home "as if she knew / No other region but belonged to thee, / Yea, appertained by a peculiar right / To thee and thy grey huts, my darling vale" (1805 *Prelude*, II: 199–202; *Prel.*, 74, 76). And we recall Keats's "Queen-Moon . . . on her throne / Cluster'd around by all her starry Fays" in the *Nightingale* ode (lines 36–37). Blake, in a beautiful water-color illustration to *Il Penseroso*, portrays a lovely moon-maiden above the melancholy poet's head—she long-haired, delicate-featured, full-breasted, bare-footed but not nude, for she wears a gauzy gown and trencher. But neither Keats, nor Blake, nor the Wordsworth of the other passages cited rivals in power the arresting, solitary, nude female figure who dominates the night sky on Snowdon. How can she fail to be an overpowering sexual presence? "I looked about, and lo, / The Moon stood naked in the heavens at height / Immense above my head" (XIII:40–41).[48]

The other even more astounding image in this vision is the breach in the mist, in which the poet places the presence of God. If I have been right so far about the physical, even the kinaesthetic, realities of the scene, we must regard this great opening as also being palpably sensed: a third of a mile away (observe how typically exact Wordsworth's measurements are even here!)

Was a blue chasm, a fracture in the vapour,
A deep and gloomy breathing-place, through which
Mounted the roar of waters, torrents, streams,
Innumerable, roaring, with one voice. . . .
                    in that breach
Through which the homeless voice of waters rose,
That dark deep thoroughfare, had Nature lodged
The soul, the imagination of the whole.
                    (lines 56–59, 62–65)

The senses primarily appealed to are the eye and the ear, though it should be pointed out that the roar of many waters could easily penetrate to the poet's ear through the vapors and that he must have wanted a clearly *visible* breach for its power of suggestiveness. What does it suggest? All the words used to describe it are strong—and unusual in Wordsworth: chasm, fracture, breathing-place, thoroughfare.[49] There is an Alpine scene in one of Wordsworth's very earliest poems, *Descriptive Sketches*, that anticipates the Snowdon sea of mists and its corridor of sound—"a single chasm, a gulf of gloomy blue"[50] that gaped in the center of that earlier vapory sea, through which a roaring sound of innumerable streams arose. The image of a skyey chasm had thus been in Wordsworth's mind from an early date, and De Quincey has somewhere testified that it was a characteristic feature of cloud and mist in the Lake District sky. Wordsworth much later, writing rather blandly about sin, said that "Pain entered through a ghastly breach."[51] We human beings enter life through a canal and then a breach; and it is difficult not to feel—so powerful is Wordsworth's juxtaposition of images here—that the fracture and the breach[52] in the mists, seen as being below the nude woman of the night sky, are somehow related to her large and inescapable body. Since grotesque visualizing could easily take over, I wish to be as indirect and purely suggestive as Wordsworth is, without missing his meaning or losing the immense power of the description.

Even if we only half believe in the poet's literalness here, we must surely feel that he is suggesting that sexuality, birth, the body itself, and its orifices, somehow support, accommodate, or even produce ultimately "the soul, the imagination of the whole" (line 65). Soon after describing this vision Wordsworth speaks directly, without imagery, about the location in man of primal vitality:

The prime and vital principle is thine
In the recesses of thy nature, far
From any reach of outward fellowship,
Else 'tis not thine at all.
                    (XIII:194–97, *Prel.*, 470)

It would be a mistake to make the *recesses* of this passage refer only to quietistic, spiritual inwardness. It suggests rather the internalization of basic sexual instinct, and something like that seems to be what the poet requires of us in contemplating the chasm on Snowdon.

When meditation on this marvelous scene arose in Wordsworth's own mind later that night, considerable eloquence remains, as in the passage just quoted; but much poetic power is lost in abstraction and mere assertion. The "dim or vast" (lines 72–73) tends to take over, and the poet seems to revert to the view, expressed occasionally elsewhere, that the light of sense must go out before we can become spirits dedicated to the One Life, to intellectual love—that the higher love is no longer "human merely" (line 164) but takes on a supra-mundane reality, in which the body dies so that soul can clap her hands and sing. But the central propulsive force in Wordsworth's thought during his greatest years is that man is a "creature / Sensuous and intellectual," "A Two-fold frame of body and of mind," that "This love more intellectual cannot be / Without imagination" (lines 166–67)—in other words, that imagination cannot stand without sense and that sense is meaningless and powerless without the libido. A sexless nature is a contradiction in terms, and we remember that Wordsworth even as a conservative political thinker said that "the higher mode of being necessarily includes the lower"—right down through the sentient to the animal in us.[53] That kind of reality I have found in Wordsworth's intensest apocalypse, nobly refined but insistently present. I do not always find it in Wordsworth's grandiose rhetorical or philosophical utterances, where abstraction sometimes dulls the lineaments of desire. But on Snowdon, Wordsworth is at his most vibrant, and universal meaning is imagistically conceived as a mighty extension of energetic physical being.

Geoffrey Hartman's exciting insight into the importance to Wordsworth of the "spot-syndrome," the *omphalos,* the navel, the narrowed opening, I embrace with admiration.[54] But I do not, like Professor Hartman, see in it an "astonishing avoidance of apocalypse," nor do I locate Wordsworth's failures in his constant return to natural fact in which he ignores the inevitable need in apocalypse of rebirth and purgation. It is true that Wordsworth rarely introduced the Christian paradox of ravishment leading to wholeness, of the death of a corn of wheat that must precede the Spring quickening. He may not have been the kind of thinker who even understood such paradoxes, to say nothing of glorying in them, as did Donne or Lancelot Andrewes. It was his greatness to mythologize the fructifying energies of nature, including the sexual, and to make them tender and human in a society that relates us to one another. Inheritor of a powerful empirical strain and also of the eighteenth-century fusion of sex and sensibility, he dismayed Coleridge—and himself too—by not being able to realize the staggering Kantian demands his friend made upon him—to write a poem that would demonstrate that the senses were essentially growths of the mind and spirit and not the other way around. Indeed, Wordsworth may have clung to the more congenial Lockean notion that the mind was formed by the senses and by reflection upon the senses, however much he modified it.

Coleridge was equally dismayed by his friend's conception of love:

> Wordsworth is by nature incapable of being in Love, tho' no man is more tenderly attached—hence he ridicules the existence of other passion, than a compound of Lust with esteem & Friendship, confined to one Object (*Coll. Letters*, III, 305)

Substitute sexuality for *lust* (a tendentious word) and you have the great eighteenth-century ideal of esteem enlivened by desire. But what has Wordsworth missed? What does Coleridge want him to see? "Universal affinity" (what Freud criticized in *Civilization and Its Discontents* as the "oceanic" feeling); "a long & finely graduated Scale of elective Attractions" (*Coll. Letters*, III, 305)—a concept not unlike the great Chain of Being but clearly beginning in the family; ultimately, transcendental religious love that dissolves ego-love and in human relationships effects a union of opposites that permits a *tertium quid* to appear, in which the sublimity assumes beauty, masculinity assumes femininity, and vice versa. When such deep fusion occurs, when completely new qualities emerge, then indeed the highest poetry, the product of the secondary imagination, becomes a true analogy of man and woman in love. A musically profound example of such Romantic fusion occurs in the duets of the second act of Wagner's *Tristan und Isolde*, where the lovers achieve an eternal unity of consciousness,

> Ohne Nennen, . . .
> endlos ewig
> ein—bewuszt.

Just before this *höchste Liebeslust* each lover assumes the other's identity. Tristan sings to Isolde,

> Tristan du
> ich Isolde
> nicht mehr Tristan!

And Isolde sings to Tristan,

> Du Isolde
> Tristan ich
> nicht mehr Isolde.

Such abandonment of individual identity was outside the ken of Wordsworth's vision; had it not been, he may have found the very thought repellent. Nevertheless, some notion of appropriating the beloved's essential qualities is present in Wordsworth's thought. He was aware that Dorothy had "soften[ed] down" his own "over-stern-ness" (1805 *Prelude*, XIII:226–27; *Prel.*, 470) and given him a portion of her nature. But there was that within Wordsworth's genius that would not allow the boundaries of his own or others' being to be obliterated, and what he wanted in love was complementarity, not fusion into oneness.

Keeping the sexes separate and distinct, however complementary, does, as we know all too well today, risk aggression and violence, and not many of our own twentieth-century theorists of love leave much room for tenderness between sexes regarded as opposite. Words-worth did indeed confront violence and contrast in nature and in love, as our analysis of *Nutting* has shown. And however we interpret the realities of his sororal relationship—did they ever or never con-stitute a carnal imagination or temptation?—they should not be al-lowed to tame his notions of love down to the delicateness we have seen associated with pre-Romantic or Shelleyan love of similitude. But it was his greatest achievement, in loving collaboration with Dorothy, to subdue aggression to tenderness and ultimately to be inspired by the gentlest and kindliest muse of any great poet in English. The love he celebrated arose from sexual soil, but it fell back upon the earth as a gentle rain from heaven. This poet of the primary instincts came to see that love, as well as being a passionate giving, is the receiving of a blessing in passiveness, and that it can insinuate itself like a perfume into our vital air. Dorothy too perceived that love is not primarily a task, ritual, duty, or law but the vital air of our being, which we breathe in and breathe out. It is not inap-propriate that the begetter and refiner of so much that is natural, joyous, and beautiful in Wordsworthian love be given the last word. She wrote to her friend of many years, who was soon to become her sister-in-law for many, many more:

> Oh Mary my dear Sister, be quiet and happy. Study the flowers, the birds, and all the common things that are about you. Do not make loving us your business, but let your love of us make up the business you have.[55]

Notes

1. The following editions are cited in the text: *The Poetical Works of William Wordsworth*, 5 vols., ed. Ernest de Selincourt and Helen Darbishire (Oxford: Clarendon Press, 1940–54); *The Prelude 1799, 1805, 1850*, ed. Jonathan Wordsworth, M. H. Abrams, Stephen G. Gill (New York: Norton, 1979); *The Salisbury Plain Poems of William Wordsworth*, ed. Stephen Gill (Ithaca: Cornell University Press, 1975); *Home*

at Grasmere, Part First, Book First of The Recluse, ed. Beth Darlington (Ithaca: Cornell University Press, 1977); *The Prose Works of William Wordsworth,* ed. W. J. B. Owen and Jane Worthington Smyser, 3 vols. (Oxford: Clarendon Press, 1974); *The Letters of William and Dorothy Wordsworth: The Early Years,* ed. Ernest de Selincourt, 2nd ed., revised by Chester Shaver (Oxford: Clarendon Press, 1970); *Letters: Middle Years, Part II,* ed. de Selincourt, rev. Mary Moorman and Alan G. Hill, 2nd ed. (Oxford: Clarendon Press, 1970); *The Love Letters of William and Mary Wordsworth,* ed. Beth Darlington (Ithaca: Cornell University Press, 1981); *The Journal of Dorothy Wordsworth,* ed. Ernest de Selincourt (London: Macmillan, 1959).

2. M. H. Abrams, *Natural Supernaturalism,* (New York: Norton, 1971), 143. Abrams quotes Hazlitt.

3. F. R. Leavis, *Revaluation: Tradition and Development in English Poetry* (London: Chatto and Windus, 1936), 169.

4. Carl Woodring, *Wordsworth* (Cambridge, Mass.: Harvard Univ. Press, 1968), 77.

5. Shelley, *Peter Bell the Third,* IV, xi; VI, xix; *Shelley: Poetical Works,* ed. Thomas Hutchinson (London: Oxford University Press, 1967).

6. Quoted by Ernest de Selincourt, "Wordsworth and His Daughter's Marriage," *Wordsworth and Coleridge: Studies in Honor of George McLean Harper,* ed. Earl Leslie Griggs (1939; rpt. New York: Russell & Russell, 1962), 79.

7. Quoted by Derek Stanford in "Coleridge as Poet and Philosopher of Love," *English* 13 (Spring 1970):4. See Coleridge's often tortured comments implying or involving Wordsworth's sexuality, in the *Notebooks,* nos. 2998, 3146, and esp. 3148. *The Notebooks of Samuel Taylor Coleridge,* ed. Kathleen Coburn, vols. I and II (New York: Pantheon Books, 1957, 1961) and vol. III (Princeton: Princeton University Press, 1973).

8. *The Works of Thomas De Quincey,* 3rd ed., 16 vols. (Edinburgh, 1871), II, 144.

9. Geoffrey Hartman, "A Poet's Progress: Wordsworth and the *Via Naturaliter Negativa,*" reprinted from *Modern Philology* in the Norton Critical Edition of *The Prelude* (*Prel.,* 599, 604).

10. George Cheyne, *An Essay of Health and Long Life,* 2nd ed. (London, 1725), 159.

11. See Jean Hagstrum, "Johnson and the *Concordia Discors* of Human Relationships," in *The Unknown Samuel Johnson,* ed. John J. Burke and Donald Kay (Madison: Univ. of Wisconsin Press, 1983), 39–53.

12. Herbert Read, *Wordsworth* (London: Jonathan Cape, 1930), 13.

13. F. W. Bateson, *Wordsworth: A Reinterpretation* (1954; rpt. London: Longmans, 1965), 88.

14. Emile Legouis, *William Wordsworth and Annette Vallon* (London: J. M. Dent & Sons, 1922), 59. Legouis adds that the poet's heart was "tormented by remembrance and remorse" (ibid.). Paul Sheats has said, justly, that Annette's influence was "intimately incorporated with that of the Revolution itself and . . . each liaison amplified and reinforced the other." *The Making of Wordsworth's Poetry,* 1785–1798 (Cambridge, Mass.: Harvard Univ. Press, 1973), 75. Sheats also finds that Annette was "a contributory cause of the psychological crisis that did shape the poetry of 1797 and 1798." Ibid., 273, n.10.

15. Kenneth R. Johnston recognizes "sexual and romantic undertones" in the tale of the Female Vagrant in the early version of *Salisbury Plain.* But is it necessary to believe that this sexual element in response to suffering is an example of a journalistic streak in Wordsworth, reacting to contemporary examples? The sexual had been in

his sensibility from the beginning, as we have seen, and was peculiarly associated with suffering in his affair with Annette. See *Wordsworth and "The Recluse"* (New Haven: Yale Univ. Press, 1984), 44–45.

16. Read, *Wordsworth*, 117.

17. Leavis, *Revaluation*, 169.

18. Cited by Abrams, *Natural Supernaturalism*, 295.

19. The phrases from Felicia Hemans come from Wordsworth's copy in the Huntington Library of her *Songs of the Affections* (Edinburgh and London, 1830), 3, 15, 17.

20. William Empson, *The Structure of Complex Words* (London: Chatto & Windus, 1964), 299; see also 293.

21. For illuminating discussions of how Wordsworth's poems heal and restore the mind after mourning and loss, see Geoffrey H. Hartman, "A Touching Compulsion: Wordsworth and the Problem of Representation," *Georgia Review* 31 (Spring 1983):345–61, and Peter J. Manning, "Reading Wordsworth's Revisions: Othello and the Drowned Man," *Studies in Romanticism* 22 (Spring 1983):3–28. Manning, however, also shows how the poetry sometimes embodies the conflict which it tries to calm.

22. See Jean H. Hagstrum, "Toward a Profile of the Word *Conscious* in Eighteenth-Century Literature," forthcoming in a collection of essays on literature and psychology, ed. Christopher Fox. For examples of *unconscious* in Wordsworth, see 1805 *Prelude*, I:589; VI, 122; and 1850 version, XIII:455 (*Prel.*, 58, 192, 299).

23. These words are used to describe the Lake Poets by John Taylor Coleridge reviewing his uncle's *Remorse* in *The Quarterly Review* II (April 1814):182. See Donald H. Reiman, ed., *The Romantics Reviewed* (New York: Garland, 1972), part A, vol. II, 818, 821.

24. Cited by Ian Jack, *Keats and the Mirror of Art* (Oxford: Clarendon Press, 1967), 281, n.41.

25. Ibid. See also 213.

26. Thomas McFarland, *Romanticism and the Forms of Ruin* (Princeton: Princeton University Press, 1981), 148. For an illuminating discussion, see the entire third chapter.

27. Quoted by George Whalley in *Coleridge and Sara Hutchinson and the Asra Poems* (London: Routledge & Kegan Paul, 1955), 150.

28. Morris Golden, *Richardson's Characters* (Ann Arbor: Univ. of Michigan Press, 1963), 21, 22.

29. Lawrence Stone, *The Family, Sex and Marriage in England 1500–1800* (New York: Harper & Row, 1977), 4 and passim.

30. Irvin Ehrenpreis, *Acts of Implication* (Berkeley: Univ. of California Press, 1980), 136–37.

31. See the discussion by Karl Kroeber, "Constable: Millais/Wordsworth: Tennyson," in *Articulate Images: The Sister Arts from Hogarth to Tennyson*, ed. Richard Wendorf (Minneapolis: Univ. of Minnesota Press, 1983), 224–25.

32. See Foucault, *History of Sexuality* and Roland Barthes, *A Lover's Discourse: Fragments*, tr. Richard Howard (New York: Hill and Wang, 1978).

33. *Heroides*, no. XIII, "Laodamia to Protesilaus," is not an erotic poem which Wordsworth had to desexualize: far from being a Sappho, the ancient heroine is fairly close to what Wordsworth would want in a wife. On the other hand, the Romantic poet does not so much heighten as insert the stoicism, for there is none in the original.

34. Read, *Wordsworth*, 218.

35. Donald H. Reiman "Poetry of Familiarity: Wordsworth, Dorothy, and Mary

Hutchinson" in *The Evidence of the Imagination*, ed. Reiman, et al. (New York: New York Univ. Press, 1978), 168–70.

36. Ibid., 170.

37. We should note that there was worry about a pregnancy for Mary after her great grief, showing that sexual relations were thought to have continued at least until some time before 6 April 1813. See *Letters Middle*, III, 89.

38. See Jean H. Hagstrum, *Sex and Sensibility: Ideal and Erotic Love from Milton to Mozart* (Chicago: Chicago University Press, 1980), 102.

39. Frank McConnell, *The Confessional Imagination: A Reading of Wordsworth's Prelude* (Baltimore: Johns Hopkins Univ. Press, 1974), 182.

40. Summarized by Woodring, *Wordsworth*, 76.

41. Mary Moorman, "William and Dorothy Wordsworth," in *Essays by Divers Hands*, Transactions of the Royal Society of Literature, NS 37 (London: Oxford Univ. Press, 1972), 79.

42. Quoted by Frederick L. Beaty, *Light from Heaven: Love in British Romantic Literature* (DeKalb: Northern Illinois University Press, 1971), 140.

43. Bateson, *Wordsworth: A Reinterpretation*, 153.

44. Reiman, "Poetry of Familiarity," 158. Reiman sees the origin of the Lucy poems as lying in Wordsworth's unconscious attempt to avoid attaching his sexual drive to his sister. He shifts his stance from brother to lover, thus "fully utilizing their [the Lucy poems'] emotional energy by casting them as love poems."

45. See Bruce Clarke, "Wordsworth's Departed Swans: Sublimation and Sublimity in *Home at Grasmere*," *Studies in Romanticism* 19 (Fall 1980):355–74.

46. See *Home at Grasmere*, MS. A, line 347, p. 127 and cancellation after line 351, p. 129; MS. B, lines 336, 347, p. 58; MS. D, lines 250, 261–62, p. 59.

47. John Beer, *Wordsworth and the Human Heart* (London: Macmillan, 1978), 164. See also the important comment of Kenneth R. Johnston in *Wordsworth and "The Recluse"* that throughout the history of *The Recluse* "the image of a 'happy band' secure in a snug cottage" is "a symbolic contrast and partial resolution to dislocated lives and ruined cottages in the world at large. . . ." (8).

48. The 1850 revision of these lines reads: "The Moon hung naked in a firmament / Of azure without cloud," lines which lose the effectiveness of the earlier version. The conventional and classical "hung," which undoubtedly attracted Wordsworth as an intrinsically poetic verb, seems here to weaken the force of "stood" by making it impossible to visualize a hanging woman, and the placid "azure" removes the physicality of "height / Immense above my head" (1850 *Prelude*, XIV:40–41, *Prel.*, 461). Was the older Wordsworth too tame to tolerate a powerful sexual presence?

The word *naked* occurs frequently enough in Wordsworth to describe, mostly, rocks, stones, cliffs but also heaths, pools, walls, trees, the heavens. History, truth, the instincts can be naked, as is the soul (personified as female) in the presence of her God. Indians are more than once called naked. In the only clear instance of the application of the adjective to a single human being, it means unarmed. It therefore compels attention when Wordsworth calls a female personification standing large and alone "naked."

49. On the funerary as well as the birth implications of "dread chasm" in Wordsworth's sonnet, "To the Torrent at the Devil's Bridge, North Wales, 1824," see Geoffrey H. Hartman, "Blessing the Torrent: On Wordsworth's Later Style," *Publications of the Modern Language Association* 93 (March 1978):199.

50. I quote here from the revised version of 1849, line 413 (*PW*, I, 73). The 1793 version has merely "a gulf of gloomy blue" (line 498), which opens wide in a

"mighty waste of mist," a "solemn sea" (lines 495–96, *PW*, I, 72). I have been anticipated in drawing this parallel by Jonathan Wordsworth, with whose analysis I feel deeply sympathetic, though I go farther in drawing out physical and sexual meanings. J. Wordsworth wants to keep nature intact in this vision, finding the universe "humanized" and insisting that "the most noticeable feature of this landscape is that it is alive." "The Climbing of Snowdon," in *Bicentenary Wordsworth Studies in Memory of John Alban Finch*, ed. Jonathan Wordsworth (Ithaca: Cornell Univ. Press, 1970), 449–74, esp. 458, 461.

51. Wordsworth, "After-Thought" (1832, 1837), line 7, *PW*, III, 174.

52. Changed to *rift*, a more timid word, by the older Wordsworth in the 1850 *Prelude* (XIV, 56, *Prel.*, 461).

53. See earlier discussion, "Wordsworth the Man and Literary Theory."

54. See Hartman, *Wordsworth's Poetry*, 60–67, 122, 367, n.10. Hartman concedes hesitatingly that the vision on Snowdon possesses sexual energy and that the breach may have "sexual or birth-channel implications" (367, n.10).

55. Quoted by Moorman, "William and Dorothy Wordsworth," in *Essays by Divers Hands*, 82.

AFTERWORD: WORDSWORTH AND THE POLITICS OF CONSCIOUSNESS

Alan Grob[*]

For the Wordsworthians of my own generation, any reference to those political matters that in Wordsworth studies have traditionally come under the heading, "The Spirit of the Age," evokes a virtually conditioned reflex. A bell sounds, fragmentary phrases from Hazlitt and Abrams come floating to the surface of memory, and we find ourselves repeating the well-worn proposition that the major poetry of Wordsworth is in some significant sense the French Revolution by other means.[1] As a necessary preliminary, the familiar periodization is almost automatically spelled out: a phase before the major poetry when Wordsworth was an "active partisan" of the French Revolution; long years of apostasy afterwards, with intimations of that apostasy already appearing perhaps as early as the political sonnets of 1802; and often the years roughly between 1797 and 1801 singled out as that portion of the great period when a leveling muse is most in evidence. Admittedly by Wordsworth's own account a "time / Of dereliction and dismay" (*Prelude*, II: 456–57)[2] when even "good men / On every side fall off" (*Prelude*, II: 451–52), still, these years of deepening repression at home and a cynical Thermidorean and Napoleonic aftermath to "golden hours" in France were also a time when what was, at most, disenchantment had not yet turned into default, and when Wordsworth still professed "A more than Roman confidence, A faith / That fails not" (*Prelude*, II: 459–60) in what must surely in spirit be something not so very different from the democratic ideals and aims he had openly espoused only five years earlier.

But to utter a proposition that might at an earlier time appear so hackneyed as scarcely to bear reiteration is, at the present moment, a precarious undertaking. The claim that Wordsworth kept faith is currently one often put in question, most vigorously by the new historicism, one of whose leading practitioners describes it as "the

[*] This essay was written specifically for this volume and is published here for the first time by permission of the author.

trend in Wordsworth criticism today—and I do mean today"[3]—so that one risks not only error but imputations of datedness by reiterating such a claim. Concealed behind the interstices, absences, idealizations, and displacements of Wordsworth's poems, the new historicists invariably and predictably find the inexpungeable traces and residues of a self-betraying romantic ideology that the founding theoretician of the movement in romantic studies, Jerome J. McGann, has characterized as "supportive of established power."[4] Under new historicist scrutiny with its unflagging alertness to telltale signs of false consciousness and bad faith, our once crucial distinction between the beleaguered, troubled, but still persevering radicalism of Wordsworth in 1798—"a Jacobinism of doubt" E. P. Thompson calls it[5]—and the emerging conservatism of 1805 finds itself subsumed within the ideological uniformity of what McGann calls the revisionist phase of romanticism. Hence, *Peele Castle* and *Tintern Abbey*, McGann writes, "are only separated from each other, ideologically and stylistically, by a difference in emphasis."[6] Much of the energy of the new historicism in Wordsworth studies has, in fact, gone into just this enterprise of dissolving chronological distinctions and rolling back the date when an antirevolutionary conservatism sets in. So in an argument of the most consummate intricacy, James K. Chandler finds Wordsworth by 1798 already in ideological proximity to Burke,[7] and in a work of literary detection that long before publication obviously served as an audacious model for new historicist theory and practice, Marjorie Levinson discerns from the clue of the missing abbey the will of the poet of *Tintern Abbey* to accommodate himself to "dominant social structures,"[8] an act of ideological tampering with "the picture of the mind," allegedly as revealing in its own way as, let us say, the excision of the purged comrade from the widely reprinted group photo of the party leadership in Prague with which Milan Kundera begins *The Book of Laughter and Forgetting.* But the general suspicion that guides new historicist investigation of Wordsworth derives from yet more basic grounds for a presumption of ideological guilt: his participation in the beginnings of an almost by definition socially derelict turn to the subject, his key role in the founding of what McGann dismissively labels "the Consciousness Industry."[9]

Of course, with the hindsight acquired after almost two centuries of familiarity with the products of this industry, we are prone to believe that any turn to the subject is a kind of ideological malfeasance, a tacit acquiescence in the established social order that is almost tantamount to complicity with it. But I would submit that read historically, that is, from within the broad spectrum of feasible choices reasonably available to Wordsworth in the turbulent closing decade of the eighteenth century, the turn to consciousness in 1798 by this industry pioneer is not prima facie evidence of dereliction but merely

another form of adherence to that revolutionary faith in social betterment to which he even then held fast. Still attached to deeply
uniformitarian and necessitarian beliefs, facets of a socially committed
empiricism, Wordsworth at this time advanced a concept of consciousness that came to him already incorporated into that discourse
of virtue by which proponents of radical political and social change
on both sides of the channel gave expression to their political ideas,
expectations, and values. Self-representation, as Wordsworth then
engaged in it, was an activity empirically grounded, outwardly directed, implicitly progressive, and, at moments, clearly utopian. In
MS. 1 of the "Prospectus" to *The Recluse* Wordsworth in a key
passage proposes in just these terms the clearest possible rationale
for his subjective practice, for his having mingled "humbler matter,"
descriptions of "the mind and man / Contemplating" (lines 64–66)
with the visionary social matter of his great argument.[10] He has
written so much about "the little realties of life" (lines 68) of one
who is "In part a fellow citizen, in part / An outlaw, and a borderer
of his age" (lines 69–70). Wordsworth explains, in hopes that his life
may "Express the image of a better time / Desires more wise and
simpler manners" (lines 74–75). The turn to consciousness then is
not to be taken as a displacement and hence neglect of social re-
sponsibilities, covertly undermining the avowedly revolutionary aim
of the "Prospectus" of making "Paradise, and Groves / Elysian" (lines
35–36), long held to be only "A history, or but a dream" (line 38),
into a lived reality—indeed, "the growth of common day" (line 40)—
at some not very distant time. In his moral history, Wordsworth tells
us, he is to be regarded as a forerunner, a harbinger of the general
human betterment that awaits us, no doubt hoping that by rendering
those "better times" through the life that prefigures them he shall
hasten their realization. Framed in the image of one who still deemed
himself "in part / An outlaw and a borderer of his age," the social
arrangements of that future we would imagine are not just to be
amelioratively better but radically different from those of the present,
arrangements we can only infer that Wordsworth assumed would be
condemned as lawlessness in postrevolutionary Britain—the imagin-
ings of "An outlaw"—because they too closely resemble those first
promised by the "golden hours" of a republican France as yet un-
tarnished by an aftermath of Jacobin excess, Thermidorean compromise, and Napoleonic betrayal.

But what most distinctively identifies the politics of these lines
are the moral attributes he ascribes to himself and thus to those who
are to dwell in that anticipated future he now exemplifies. "Desires
more wise and simpler manners" are key terms and catchphrases in
that discourse of virtue by which radicalism everywhere declared
itself in the 1790s. We hear just such language, for example, with

a not uncustomary limiting adjective in Crabb Robinson's complaint that the radical John Thelwall still lacked "that republican simplicity of manners and ideas which I wish to see universally spread."[11] And in 1794 when the clamor for virtue was at its loudest, when France presented itself as a republic of virtue, literally making virtue the order of the day by proclamation in those days of rage, when even the terror was explained as "an emanation of virtue" by Robespierre the Incorruptible, the conception of public virtue took much of its character from moral notions like those put forward in the "Prospectus," from the example of Rousseau with his claims of naturalness and moral purity, and from the precedent of an imagined America that, in the words of R. R. Palmer, was conceived of by the revolutionary leadership in 1794 as "thirteen small republics of simple manners and exemplary virtue."[12] Though innocent-seeming in themselves as indicators of radical loyalty, wise desires and simple manners in those times of anger and retribution are not casually chosen moral attributes; they carry with them powerful oppositional resonances, signifying traces that recall despised traits that were on the verge of being supplanted, the paramount iniquities of the old regime, luxury and vice. So in the unpublished "Letter to the Bishop of Llandaff" of 1794, the most explicit and detailed statement by the young Wordsworth of his revolutionary principles, he clearly uncovers for us those antithetical roots, the radical social evils of display and depravity that, from Rousseau onwards, such formulations as the mild comparatives of "more wise desires and simpler manners" were called upon to remind us of and, beyond that, to help extirpate. Singled out in his general indictment are just those failings that the upper classes are most liable to and that have the most disastrous consequences for those below them: an appetite for luxury that leads the aristocracy "to snatch from the mouths of the poor to eke out the 'necessary splendor' of nobility,"[13] and a propensity to vice that produces "the prostitution which miserably deluges our streets," a social evil expressly attributed by Wordsworth to "aristocratical prejudices."[14]

Thus consciousness for Wordsworth in 1798 was a concept imbued with social purpose: to write about himself was to write of and for others. But it is not only by some imagined future community of the virtuous that Wordsworth assumes his mental and moral history will be reenacted. Even now, he tells us, there are certain contemporaries of his, kindred spirits—unnamed "philanthropists" as they were commonly designated by the radical discourse of the day— benefactors of humanity, whose course of development towards goodness, he believes, essentially parallels his own, so that in describing himself, he indirectly speaks of others. Throughout the whole of the "golden decade" one relative constant in Wordsworth's accounts of his mental history was a stated awareness that the various forms of intensity that occur in childhood, whether experienced as "glad animal movements" or as "celestial light," diminish and even disappear in later years. Though ominously regarded from 1802 onwards as evidence of spiritual decline, between 1797 and 1800 such loss was readily assimilated to Wordsworth's general social and psychological optimism and was taken as the regrettable but necessary by-product of a developmental process by which he had reached a tranquility that serves as a manifest psychological correlative to significant moral attainment, what he approvingly speaks of in the first book of *The Prelude* as "The calm existence that is mine when I / Am worthy of myself" (I: 360–61). Episodes in his mental life that Wordsworth might well have considered possessions exclusively his own and appropriated as testimony to the poet's uniqueness, are, in fact, almost axiomatically assumed to have their resembling counterparts in the lives of others, who by virtue of the moral accomplishment and social concern they share with the poet can be expected to share an essentially similar history as well. So when at the beginning of Book II of *The Prelude* Wordsworth nostalgically reflects upon childhood feelings now lost, it is an easy matter for him to conjure up the image of another like himself who has undergone the same process of development, becoming nothing less than "the wisest and the best / Of all mankind" (II: 22–23)—the philanthropist par excellence—and to wonder if he too, despite an obviously "abundant recompense," would still not wish to give "to duty and to truth / The eagerness of infantine desire" (II: 25–26). And after tracing his entry into the ethical life back to his childhood encounters with the old Cumberland beggar, Wordsworth is quick to assume that this has been no unique event, readily positing similar initiations for those whose moral advancement parallels his own: "lofty minds, / And meditative" (lines 106–7) who "from this solitary Being, / Or from like wanderer" (lines 110–11) have "found their kindred with a world / Where want and sorrow were" (lines 115–16).

Such forays into consciousness and memory clearly do not feed solipsistic tendencies nor instill feelings of alienation and estrangement. They are undertaken with the consciousness of other minds as a kind of reassuring surround and actually reinforce Wordsworth's sense of community and solidarity with the philanthropically inclined, "the wisest and the best," and "lofty minds, / And meditative." Moreover, though these representations of an idealized philanthropic community seem mere abstractions, the conventionalized products of the discourse of virtue, there is every reason to believe that for Wordsworth they meshed with real life and had roughly resembling counterparts among his own acquaintance. Even in 1798, what we might think of as the Wordsworth circle was comprised of those who would still be deemed and, more important, would still deem themselves philanthropists and hence radicals, those we know only as they appear in the letters or accounts of Wordsworth's early years, men like James Losh and Francis Wrangham and even the often maligned Basil Montagu. Some were friends from Wordsworth's Cambridge years who had been enthusiasts with him of the first phases of the French Revolution; others had joined him in 1795 in what must surely have been a risky association with philosophic radicalism and its most notorious proponent, William Godwin. And though in 1798 the combination of disillusionment with events abroad and the dangers posed by the severity of repression at home had made "good men, / On every side fall off," these members of the Wordsworth circle remained surprisingly and impressively steadfast in their dedication to revolutionary principles even then, and by that fidelity may well have conveyed to Wordsworth the sense that he dwelt among "lofty," even "visionary minds." And to that list of the steadfast, we must certainly add the name of a truly heroic champion of radical reform, John Thelwall, who was befriended and given refuge in 1797 by Wordsworth and Coleridge at considerable risk to themselves in an episode that must figure heavily in any assessment of Wordsworth's political allegiances during this period, and who, both by what he believed and what he endured, is not upon reflection an altogether implausible candidate for that conjectural "one" who might be considered "the wisest and the best / Of all mankind." In turning to poetry, declaring that to be his true vocation, Wordsworth did not really cast off old allegiances; he did not distance himself by a supposedly isolating withdrawal into consciousness from old allies with whom he had earlier shared a profoundly revolutionary faith. Indeed, speaking as a poet, Wordsworth clearly took for granted a fundamental identification with those whose interests were narrowly and specifically political, assuming that his inner history and theirs would be essentially alike, no doubt because he knew them to share common values that surely must have had similar antecedents. Because Wordsworth assumed his history and hopes to be so closely linked with those who had maintained the early revolutionary ideals, one of his stated purposes as a poet was to provide them with support, praising them as "lofty" and "visionary," wise and good, rallying them in a time of "dereliction and dismay," lending his voice to that joint enterprise that would culminate in the "better time" desired by every "outlaw of the present age." And that poetry and politics were so linked was tacitly understood by the politically minded as well. Nowhere is this linkage more strikingly indicated than in a passage found in the 1798 diary of James Losh, who surely must have had his friend Wordsworth in mind as one of those who could benefit from leaving Britain (as in fact Wordsworth did later that year): "Were there anyplace to go to emigration would be a prudent thing for literary men and the friends of freedom," he asserts, presumably assuming that both the "literary men" and "the friends of freedom" need to exercise prudence for the same reason, the implicitly illicit political beliefs they hold in common.[15]

It is in terms of these relationships—Wordsworth's sense, even as a poet, of affiliation and identification with the progressive and enlightened, and his continuing membership in the party of humanity, to use the language of the age—that we are best able to situate Wordsworth politically in 1798. To our current historicizing criticism, eager to dispel all claims that Wordsworth might be of that party and was thus a leveling poet after all, he remains the quintessential poetic solitary, *Spectator ab extra* as Coleridge disparagingly judged him, a judgment that an implacably hostile Marxist analysis has chosen to interpret as the manifest evidence and, indeed, the unassailable proof of Wordsworth's estrangement by virtue of irrevocably fixed class origins from those of inferior birth with whom he professes to sympathize. So Michael J. Friedman, after subjecting Coleridge's observation to just such analysis, is able to sum up Wordsworth's relations to those he writes about in these terms: "He was a gentleman. The shepherds and solitaries were not."[16] And David Aers, operating from similar presuppositions, condemns Wordsworth on much the same grounds as "someone whose social and economic assumptions and experiences had little in common with those in genuinely 'low estate' to whom he refers so knowingly."[17] For Marx himself, however, class is a more flexible and fluid category than this, so that accidents of birth need not be absolutely determining in the formation of class attitudes, especially as they emerge at those critical moments when society seems in "the process of dissolution." Indeed, at the "decisive hour" of revolutionary struggle, Marx tells us in an important passage from the "Communist Manifesto," we shall find—as he found himself in his study of the great revolution just concluded—"that a small section of the ruling class cuts itself adrift, and joins the revolutionary class, the class that holds the future in its hands."[18] Even on Marxist premises then, we cannot simply assume that by having been born a gentleman Wordsworth was rendered constitutionally incapable of truly feeling the sympathy he professed—nor incapable of a willingness to act on it—for those born to a station inferior to his own. The real issue to be settled is whether Wordsworth, who during most of the revolutionary decade had clearly cut himself adrift from the ruling class to which he belonged by birth, did not remain adrift in the early years of the period of his greatest poetry. At a time when the voice of dissenting political opinion in England had been effectively stilled, evidence that speaks to this matter is necessarily sparse: we can expect no manifestos or public pronouncements of radical allegiance from Wordsworth. But by these casual declarations of affiliation and identification with those who in the morally encoded political language of the day must surely be termed philanthropists, Wordsworth does send signals to those who would heed them that he still considers himself one of those who has cut himself adrift, "An outlaw of the present age" by his own admission. To be adrift, "An outlaw," is, however, to stand apart yet not alone, to work in concert with "the wisest and the best," the "lofty" and "visionary," those who in the vocabulary of a later revolutionary ideology would be thought of as a vanguard, moral and intellectual precursors who read the course of history rightly and choose future good over present ease and profit.

But the critics engaged in the current endeavor to prove Wordsworth, overtly or covertly, knowingly or unknowingly, a full-fledged conservative by 1798 are not all on the left. James Chandler is counted by Marjorie Levinson as one of those who does the serious and necessary work of the day—the true historicist being "at once materialist and deconstructive."[19] But in *Wordsworth's Second Nature*, despite its fashionable statement of purpose that would have us regard it as a treatment of "the ideologies of philosophy and power in Wordsworth's unfolding career,"[20] Chandler seems not at all a deconstructionist and scarcely more a materialist in method. It is not the absence of the names and approaches of key theoreticians like Marx and Althusser and Macherey that separates Chandler from what we normally think of as new historicist practice but rather a more basic principle of difference: if Wordsworth in 1798 was an adherent of Burke rather than Rousseau, a foe rather than friend of the French Revolution, if, in short, he was already by then a staunch reactionary, as Chandler certainly believes he was, then what would be grounds for condemnation of Wordsworth by McGann and Levinson is an ideological choice by the poet that plainly meets with Chandler's approval. Conservatism, which virtually everywhere else in the new historicism is a term of opprobrium, is to Chandler an unquestioned good.

For Chandler, Burke and Rousseau provide "the crucial intellectual axes"[21] by which we are to plot Wordsworth's relationships to conservatism and radicalism in the age of the French Revolution, and following Chandler's directions, we shall find Wordsworth's major work, "conservative from the start,"[22] a vehicle for giving "veiled expression to his Burkean views"[23] and of launching "(equally Burkean) attacks on Rousseauistic systems of (political) education."[24] As the term *veiled* suggests, Chandler's argument, like those of other new historicists, is teased out of the concealed and unapparent, "the silence or 'unspeakable' that inheres within the work"[25] in Levinson's phrase. But while these arguments are always subtle and intricate and often interesting, they are rarely compelling. A case in point is Chandler's analysis of *The Old Cumberland Beggar*, a work pivotal to his contention that in 1798 Wordsworth had absorbed, adopted, and was already giving "veiled expression" to the views of Burke. In a passage from the poem essential to Chandler's purposes, Wordsworth explains how acts of charity repeated over and over like those performed for the beggar by the villagers of the poet's childhood community play a key role in the formation of the fully achieved moral character through the workings of a principle he calls "habit":

> Where'er the aged Beggar takes his rounds
> The mild necessity of use compels
> To acts of love; and habit does the work
> Of reason; yet prepares that after-joy
> Which reason cherishes. And thus the soul,
> By that sweet taste of pleasure unpursued,
> Doth find herself insensibly disposed
> To virtue and true goodness. (lines 98–105)

The use of the word *habit* here, we are told, is the signal that should alert us, the lifting of the veil, a momentary but manifest acknowledgement of the influence of Burke that, according to Chandler, pervades and determines Wordsworth's thinking about political and social matters. Undeniably habit is a central concept in Burke: founded on prejudices whose wisdom is confirmed by the usage "of nations and of ages,"[26] habit is the key to those attachments to home and family, community and nation, those salutary prejudices on which a soundly functioning, indeed a good society rests. (Despite the piety with which Burke and later Chandler invest these concepts—habit and attachment and prejudice—Burke's many detractors then and now have been quick to point out that they were also the grounds for the mob's burning of Priestley's house in Birmingham in the name of church and king.)

But if we concede that the appearance in Wordsworth of a term as central to Burke's thought as *habit* should alert us to the possibility that Burke did, in fact, influence Wordsworth, we should not be lulled by the earnestness of Professor Chandler's predisposition to conviction into believing that this circumstance in itself constitutes proof of indebtedness. Two factors, indeed, militate against drawing such a conclusion: one is that the function of the term *habit* in Wordsworth's argument in *The Old Cumberland Beggar* bears little resemblance to the notion of habit as Burke conceives it; the other is that we can find the term *habit* used very much as Wordsworth uses it elsewhere, and most especially in the writings of another political philosopher antithetical to Burke in every respect, William Godwin. Closely examined, the passage in question does not, in fact, express the views of Burke but presents the most anti-Burkean views imaginable, for it describes nothing less than the making of a philanthropist, one who can act disinterestedly out of a truly rational benevolence in behalf of the interests of humankind in general, notions that for Burke not only run counter to our nature but are as injurious in their effects as they are experientially implausible. Here as elsewhere in the years between 1797 and 1800, Wordsworth adopted a characteristic strategy to answer the profoundly perplexing but critical question of how we can become and be philanthropists. Since we are not endowed at birth with a moral sense or any other innate propensity to benevolence, what then can the agent of transformation be that enables us to rise from self-centeredness, which, convinced by the example of his own experience, Wordsworth believed absolutely governs our conduct in our early years, to the pure disinterestedness that he intuitively perceived that he and a few gifted spirits had finally attained? In *The Old Cumberland Beggar* the agent that produces this transformation is very plainly identified: *habit* is the vehicle by which we are carried from selfishness to virtue. Even in our acts of charity, Wordsworth tells us, self-interest is originally the principal motive to welldoing. In the most gentle of hedonistic phrases, he explains how upon assisting the beggar we are rewarded by "the sweet taste of pleasure unpursued," a happiness that, felt upon and delighting the senses, induces in the giver the desire to give again, so that the remembered savor of "pleasure unpursued" becomes a subliminally enticing motive to charitable action. But through the wonderful economy at work not just in the external world but in our human nature too, the repetition of such acts—that is, habit—eventually converts what was initially the means to an end, charity for the sake of the pleasure it yielded, into an end in itself, and "the soul / Doth find herself insensibly disposed / To virtue and true goodness." At this point the work that habit had done in the service of reason is at last taken up by reason itself, and the soul "disposed / To virtue and true goodness" is ready to make its moral judgments on the basis of a fully rational benevolence.

That the passage in question should be read this way becomes most apparent when we view it together with the lines that immediately follow it, especially as these lines appear in the Alfoxden manuscript, where we can see just how completely reason has superseded habit in the exercise of the fully developed moral faculty.

> Some there are,
> By their good works exalted, lofty minds,
> And meditative, in which reason falls
> Like a strong radiance of the setting sun
> On each minutest feeling of the heart,
> Illuminates, and to their view brings forth

> In one harmonious prospect, minds like these
> In childhood, from this solitary Being,
> Or from like wanderer, haply have received
> (A thing more precious far than all that books
> Or the solicitudes of love can do!)
> That first mild touch of sympathy and thought,
> In which they found their kindred with a world
> Where want and sorrow were.
> (lines 105–16 Alfoxden MS.)

We need look no further than this to see how closely Wordsworth in 1798 still adhered to the radical principles he had at this time supposedly discarded: the perfectibilian assumption that men and women could act towards one another on the basis of a genuine benevolence, which had already been acquired by a scattered but special few and was thus the grounds of hope for a general human improvement; the emphasis on reason as the faculty preeminently involved in the highest form of moral choice; above all, a continuing fidelity to the great end for which, as Beaupuy had taught him, the French Revolution was being fought, the relief of "a hunger-bitten girl," an ideal carried forward into *The Old Cumberland Beggar* as the discovery by those "lofty minds / And meditative" through their childhood sympathy with the old Cumberland beggar of "their kindred with a world / Where want and sorrow were."

Habit then, as Wordsworth uses the term, is linked not to conservative doctrines of the salutary effects of prejudice but to radical ideas of benevolence, and rational benevolence at that. Though experience alone doubtlessly might account for Wordsworth's conception of habit, if we attribute that conception to a book we are obviously better advised to turn from Burke to Godwin in seeking it out; and in the third edition of *Political Justice* we do find a passage on the transition from self-interestedness to disinterestedness that presents the mediating function of habit in that transition in terms very much like those proposed by Wordsworth:

> A disposition to promote the benefit of another, my friend, my relation, or my fellow being, is one of the passions; understanding by the term passion, a permanent and habitual tendency toward a certain course of action. It is of the same general nature as avarice, or the love of fame. . . . But it is the nature of the passions, speedily to convert what at first were means, into ends. The avaricious man forgets the utility of money which at first incited him to pursue it, fixes his passion upon the money itself, and counts his gold, without having in his mind any idea but that of seeing it and handling it. Something of this sort happens very early in the history of every passion. The moment we become attached to a particular source of pleasure, beyond any idea we have of the rank it holds in the

catalogue of sources, it must be admitted that it is loved for its own sake. . . . If this be the case in the passion of avarice or the love of fame, it must also be true in the instance of beneficence, that, after having habituated ourselves to promote the happiness of our child, our family, our country or our species, we are at length brought to desire this happiness without retrospect to ourselves.[27]

Here, as in the passage from The Old Cumberland Beggar, we have an ostensibly descriptive account of moral improvement and change, one where *habit* at first "does the work / Of reason" and what was only the means to an end ultimately becomes an end in itself. But such descriptive summary readily turns into prescriptive instructions for the engendering of the person of genuine benevolence (and since these instructions come from Godwin we can trust such benevolence to be rational): "after having habituated ourselves to promoting the happiness" of others, "our child, our family, our country or our species," Godwin contends, the element of self-concern and even pleasurableness that leads us to wish to do this disappears as a motive, and instead we find we can and do behave with pure and unselfish concern for others, a disinterestedness that is fundamental to any ethic of benevolence.

On another matter too, the role of family attachment in our ethical development, Wordsworth is far more restrictive in what he is willing to count as behavior that might serve as a basis for benevolence than Chandler credits him with being. Not only does Wordsworth in The Old Cumberland Beggar differ sharply from Burke in his assessment of the value of the domestic sympathies but he also differs from Godwin, who regards love of family as sufficiently meritorious to serve as one of the types of beneficence in his list, one of those desires that, habitually enough acted on, we eventually pursue as an intrinsic good "without retrospect to ourselves." For Burke no fundamental conversion from self-interest to disinterestedness is even necessary: family feeling is the essential foundation for our larger attachments. "We begin our public affections in our families," Burke writes in what must surely have been one of the first of many conservative pronouncements of this sort.[28] But in The Old Cumberland Beggar, at any rate, Wordsworth will grant these primary affections no real part in the formation of the genuine moral character, but treats family feeling, in fact, as a distraction from and perhaps essentially inimical to the fostering of "virtue and true goodness." While the "Many" who are "not negligent / In acts of love to those with whom they dwell, / Their kindred, and the children of their blood" (lines 138–40) receive "Praise" from Wordsworth; it is a backhanded praise, since judged by a standard of genuine beneficence, these "acts of love" toward "kindred" and "children of their blood" amount to no more than "inevitable charities" (line 145) that lack

"Wherewith to satisfy the human soul" (line 146). Only by means of acts of pure charity in which we have no significant personal stake (and acts of kindness to the old Cumberland beggar perfectly suit such a category since he seems so devoid of any real interest for us that he well might stand for humanity in the abstract) can we ever hope to enter on a genuine moral course—that is, a rationally determined moral course—in which we act altruistically not from pleasure or habit but because "reason falls / Like a strong radiance of the setting sun / On each minutest feeling of the heart."

The second major element in Chandler's proof of Wordsworth's "veiled" conservatism in 1798, his opposition even then to Rousseau's educational theories, depends on even more tenuously connected threads of evidence and is therefore even less convincingly argued. For Chandler the principal ground for believing this is his ostensible demonstration that Rousseau was the object of Wordsworth's satire of education in a passage from Book V of *The Prelude*, a passage that, while not completed until 1804, plainly has its origin in lines written in 1798 or 1799 that appear in MS. 18A. The obvious objection to this claim, one acknowledged on occasion by Chandler himself, is that nothing could seem more unlike the intellectual force-feeding that "These mighty workmen of our later age" (V: 370) perform on Wordsworth's "prodigy" than the "negative education" proposed by Rousseau until Emile is about twelve. Nowhere is the common understanding of what Rousseau on education represents better summarized than in that notoriously anti-Rousseauistic educational tract, *Cultural Literacy* by E. D. Hirsch, Jr. For Hirsch, Rousseau is the archenemy of true cultural literacy, the thinker ultimately responsible for the "content-neutral curricula of our elementary schools,"[29] the first and foremost of those "who believe that we should encourage the natural development of young children and not impose adult ideas upon them before they can truly understand them,"[30] a principle that would seem to coincide with rather than run counter to those Wordsworth advocates in Book V of *The Prelude*. Surely the characteristic most in evidence in the account of the "prodigy"—"no Child, / But a dwarf Man" (V:294–95)—satirized by Wordsworth is an amazingly precocious cultural literacy:

> he can read
> The inside of the earth, and spell the stars;
> He knows the policies of foreign Lands
> Can string you names of districts, cities, towns,
> The whole world over, tight as beads of dew
> Upon a gossamer thread.   (V: 332–37)

But however culturally literate such a child may be, he is nothing like Emile, who in his purely "negative" preadolescent education will study no maps, learn no history, read virtually no books, which for children are "the instruments of their greatest misery."[31]

To meet what would seem to be virtually insurmountable objections to his contention, Chandler adopts two different strategies. One is to claim that what Wordsworth actually satirizes in *Emile* is Rousseau's theory of moral education, though it is never made clear why Wordsworth should choose to satirize a relatively secondary element of a work whose larger principles he must certainly have sympathized with, at least according to his own praise of the "negative education" of "A race of real children, not too wise, / Too learned, or too good" (V: 436–37). As narrow as this claim is, it remains unpersuasive, since Chandler simply identifies four passages of the utmost generality from the great length of *Emile* as those Wordsworth satirically alludes to, three of the four referring not to childhood, clearly the subject of the passages from *The Prelude,* but to Emile's adolescent education, which does not begin until Emile's childhood education of simplicity and freedom has ended.[32] Chandler's alternative strategy is to regard the passages from *The Prelude* not as satire upon the actual educational writings of Rousseau himself—for these do not appear to be in conflict with the views of Wordsworth— but as satire on the theories of Rousseau as they were put into practice in revolutionary France by the Committee on Public Instruction under the direction of the Ideologues, who in turn, according to Chandler, operated under "the aegis of Rousseau."[33] But in revolutionary France invoking the name of Rousseau was not as much an expression of his influence as it may, at first glance, appear to be. So great was the celebrity of the apotheosized Rousseau at the time of the French Revolution that in almost any dispute both sides could claim to be acting under his aegis, as, in fact, both prosecution and defense did at the trial of the king in 1792.[34] While the Committee on Public Instruction might invoke the name and prestige of Rousseau, their program actually bore little resemblance to the content-neutral curriculum devised for Emile. Though their students might have physical education and be instructed in a mechanical art, as Rousseau urged, they would also read books, study history, learn a science— this last, as Lakanal admitted, specifically contradicting the advice of Rousseau.[35] And in a study of the Ideologues that Chandler himself cites as the best in English, Charles H. Van Duzer points out that on the all-important issue of education for the masses there were two major and opposing points of view in eighteenth-century France. Rousseau was one of those who did not desire "a type of instruction which would make the masses more reflective and perhaps render them unsuited to their humble condition of life."[36] But, as Van Duzer explains, "D'Holbach, Helvetius, Turgot and others regarded education as an unqualified good, and championed the right of the people to be educated up to the full measure of their capacity." And, he adds, "it was the latter school which was to come into control during the years of the Revolution,"[37] a judgment that tellingly calls into question Chandler's contention that the educational programs of revolutionary France were essentially a putting into practice of the theories of Rousseau.

Though the Ideologues emerge as one of the principal antagonists in Chandler's account of how Wordsworth adopted a Burkean and thus essentially British conservatism in 1798, actually they provide a perfect perspective from which to comprehend the radical orientation of Wordsworth's conception of consciousness at that time. In a statement of the utmost tentativeness, Chandler admits that he is "aware" that "one might plausibly describe the French Ideologues as, say, 'empiricists,' "[38] a claim surprisingly qualified since that is the way historians of philosophy and historians of the Enlightenment have always described the leading theorists of the Ideologues, Condillac and Cabanis and Destutt de Tracy, and that is, in fact, what they surely were: empiricists, followers of Locke, sensationalists of the most committed and uncompromising sort. But even in acknowledging that the philosophy of the Ideologues might rest on concepts normally associated with Britain, Chandler—ever anxious to discriminate between British solidity and good sense and the shallow abstractness and fanaticism of the French—divides empiricism itself into two rival camps, the conservative empiricism associated with Hume that was in the ascendant in Britain at the end of the eighteenth century, and its great nemesis, the radical empiricism of the Ideologues in France. Elsewhere I have argued at length that between 1797 and 1800 Wordsworth was himself an empiricist, a follower of Locke, and a sensationalist of the most committed and uncompromising sort;[39] and in this paper I shall only add to that argument the observation that Wordsworth became an empiricist, not as a philosopher might, making an academic decision among competing truth-claims, but rather because empiricism provided that explanation of man's relation to the world most suited to Wordsworth's announced project of human advancement. Unsurprisingly then, the version of British empiricism most congenial to Wordsworth, Hartley's associationism as it appears in the abridgement of the *Observations* by Joseph Priestley, is scarcely conservative but in spirit and in principles displays deep affinities with the forms of empiricism promulgated and practiced in revolutionary France. Thoroughly sensationalist in their basic explanations of the origins of human knowledge, implicitly egalitarian in their descriptions of mind, positing a common tabula rasa, so that similarity of environmental circumstances must, of necessity, produce similar intellectual and moral consequences, these philosophers are the epistemologists of revolution par excellence, social engineers confident that by reordering human institutions one can, in effect, remold humanity itself. For these philosophers any morally accomplished individual is potentially what Wordsworth knew himself to be, a forerunner, a harbinger of betterment; since "associationism tends to make us all ultimately similar," David Hartley writes, "if one be happy, all must."[40]

So mixing receptivity of the senses, the informing and determining power of external objects, and necessity, Wordsworth produces a similar recipe for progress: "thus deeply drinking in the soul of things, / We shall be wise perforce, and we shall move / From strict necessity along the path of order and of good."[41] For Wordsworth then, looking to consciousness is a way of measuring personal progress and identifying those constituent simples that enter into the formation of his moral nature and his not unrelated sense of inner well-being. It is by inference an implicitly social activity and inherently predictive, because the goodness and happiness attainable by one readily is extrapolated into a goodness and happiness not merely possible but eventually inevitable for all. Accounting for the politics of *Tintern Abbey* does not at all depend on solving the mystery of the missing abbey. Rather it is through a discourse of virtue that Wordsworth once more signals his continuing revolutionary allegiance, his more than Roman confidence in the better time to come. Those who hear the "still sad music of humanity" do so, despite all the critical grumbling at the abstractness of that phrase, because they belong to humanity's party. Recognizing "In nature and the language of the sense" (line 108) the "soul / Of all my moral being" (lines 110–111), Wordsworth is able to produce the crucial underlying formula for an environmentally conditioned exemplary life that, as the preliminary instance of his sister shows, stands ready for general replication.

One final word. At the beginning of *The Romantic Ideology*, Jerome McGann tells us that in pursuing his new view of romanticism, he will "retrace many of the lines of inquiry which were first taken up in critical traditions we now associate with Marx."[42] But from the earliest writings of Marx himself, these same traditions have presented a similarly critical view of the French Revolution itself; they have construed its meaning as the ascendancy of the bourgeoisie in the name of society as a whole, and its use of an ethical instead of a political language as a mere "masking" that so understood serves as proof positive of the essentially bourgeois orientation of Jacobinism. Thus, the grounds on which McGann finds Wordsworth wanting are, in effect, the very same grounds on which Marxist historiography has always found the Revolution wanting, and yet the Revolution would seem to provide the only fair and legitimate standard by which to judge the politics of Wordsworth's poetry. In a series of letters to William Mathews in 1794, Wordsworth pronounced himself opposed to every species of violence and deplored the "miserable situation of the French," but he insisted on his unqualified rejection of "monarchical and aristocratical government" and "hereditary distinctions and privileged orders of every kind"[43] and declared himself a member of that "odious class of men called democrats," adding, "and of that class I shall ever continue."[44] Fidelity to the spirit of that promise during the years under discussion is, I submit, the only valid basis to decide whether Wordsworth during the period of his greatest poetry is entitled to be numbered among the "Friends of Liberty." To invoke some other criterion in the name of history, and especially one in which condemnation is almost certainly entailed by its premises, sounds like nothing so much—if I may borrow a phrase from Wordsworth himself—as "sneers on visionary minds."

Notes

1. "Mr. Wordsworth," *The Spirit of the Age*, in *Complete Works of William Hazlitt*, 21 vols., ed. P. P. Howe (London and Toronto: J. M. Dent & Sons, 1932), XI: 86–95. M. H. Abrams, "English Romanticism: The Spirit of the Age," in *Romanticism Reconsidered*, ed. Northrop Frye (New York: Columbia University Press, 1963), 26–53.

2. *The Prelude*, ed. Ernest de Selincourt, 2nd ed. rev. by Helen Darbishire (Oxford: Clarendon Press, 1959).

3. Marjorie Levinson, *Wordsworth's Great Period Poems* (Cambridge, England: Cambridge University Press, 1986), 11.

4. Jerome J. McGann, *The Romantic Ideology: A Critical Investigation* (Chicago: University of Chicago Press, 1984), 8.

5. E. P. Thompson, "Disenchantment or Default? A Lay Sermon," in *Power and Consciousness*, eds. Conor Cruise O'Brien and W. Vanech (New York: New York University Press, 1967), 152.

6. McGann, *Romantic Ideology*, 109.

7. James K. Chandler, *Wordsworth's Second Nature: A Study of the Poetry and the Politics* (Chicago: University of Chicago Press, 1984).

8. Levinson, *Wordsworth's Great Period Poems*, 57.

9. McGann, *Romantic Ideology*, 91.

10. *The Poetical Works of William Wordsworth*, 5 vols., eds. Earnest de Selincourt and Helen Darbishire (Oxford: Clarendon Press, 1947).

11. Quoted in Thompson, "Disenchantment or Default?" 158.

12. R. R. Palmer, *Twelve Who Ruled: The Year of the Terror in the French Revolution* (Princeton, N. J.: Princeton University Press, 1970), 19.

13. "A Letter to the Bishop of Llandaff," in *The Prose Works of William Wordsworth*, eds. W. J. B. Owen and Jane Worthington Smyser, 3 vols. (Oxford: Clarendon Press, 1974), I:46.

14. Ibid., I:45.

15. Quoted in Nicholas Roe, *Wordsworth and Coleridge: The Radical Years* (Oxford: Clarendon Press, 1988), 270, an extremely valuable study of Wordsworth's politics and friendships in the years leading up to the major poetry.

16. Michael J. Friedman, *The Making of a Tory Humanist: William Wordsworth and the Idea of Community* (New York: Columbia University Press, 1979), 191.

17. "Wordsworth's Model of Man in 'The Prelude,'" in *Romanticism and Ideology: Studies in English Writing, 1765–1830*, ed. David Aers, Jonathan Cook, David Punter (London: Routledge & Kegan Paul, 1981), 68.

18. "Manifesto of the Communist Party," in *The Marx-Engels Reader*, 2d ed., ed. Robert C. Tucker (New York and London: W. W. Norton & Co., 1978), 481.

19. Levinson, *Wordsworth's Great Period Poems*, 9.

20. Chandler, *Wordsworth's Second Nature*, xvii.

21. Ibid., xx.

22. Ibid., xviii.

23. Ibid., xxii.

24. Ibid.

25. Levinson, *Wordsworth's Great Period Poems*, 9.

26. *The Works of the Right Honorable Edmund Burke*, 12 vols. (London: John Nimmo, 1899) III, 346.

27. William Godwin, *Enquiry Concerning Political Justice*, 2 vols., ed. F. E. L. Priestley (Toronto: University of Toronto Press, 1946), I: 424–27.

28. Quoted in Chandler, *Wordsworth's Second Nature*, 39.

29. E. D. Hirsch, Jr., *Cultural Literacy: What Every American Needs to Know* (New York: Vintage Books, 1988), xv.

30. Ibid., xiv.

31. Jean-Jacques Rousseau, *Emile, or On Education*, trans. and ed. Allan Bloom (New York: Basic Books, 1979), 116.

32. Chandler, *Wordsworth's Second Nature*, 110–11.

33. Ibid., 219.

34. Carol Blum, *Rousseau and the Republic of Virtue* (Ithaca, N. Y.: Cornell University Press, 1986), 178–81.

35. Charles Hunter Van Duzer, *Contribution of the Ideologues to French Revolutionary Thought*, in Johns Hopkins University Studies in History and Political Science, Series LIII, no. 4 (Baltimore: Johns Hopkins University Press, 1935), 110.

36. Ibid., 91.

37. Ibid.

38. Chandler, *Wordsworth's Second Nature*, 199, n. 36.

39. *The Philosophic Mind: A Study of Wordsworth's Poetry and Thought, 1797–1805*, (Columbus: Ohio State University Press, 1973).

40. David Hartley, *Observations on Man, His Frame, His Duty, and His Expectations*, 2 vols. (Gainesville: University of Florida Press, 1966), I: 84.

41. *The Ruined Cottage* (Addendum to Ms. B), *Poetical Works*, 5:402–3.

42. McGann, *Romantic Ideology*, 1.

43. *The Letters of William and Dorothy Wordsworth: The Early Years, 1787–1805*, ed. Ernest de Selincourt, 2d ed., rev. Chester L. Shaver (Oxford: Clarendon Press, 1967), 123–24.

44. Ibid., 119.

INDEX